One Hundred Years of Winchester Cartridge Boxes

To my grandfather, William F. Harmening, who introduced me to the shooting sports when I was seven years old, and to all the other grandfathers and "grand fathers" out there who may have done the same for you. – Ray Giles, 2006.

To my grandfather, Oscar Smith, whose forty acres of woods and water held so many memorable weekends for me, toting my .22 rifle and revolver, during those wonderful years between growing up and grown up. – Dan Shuey, 2006.

One Hundred Years of Winchester Cartridge Boxes

1856-1956

Ray T. Giles & Daniel L. Shuey

Schiffer Military History
Atglen, PA

WINCHESTER is a trademark of Olin Corporation and is used with permission. Neither the authors nor the publisher are sponsored by, or associated with, Olin Corp.

All cartridge loading data regarding primers, grains and types of powder, bullet weights and types, and case lengths and types were taken directly from original Winchester catalogs, drawings, memos or other correspondence and are referred to in this book strictly for their historical interest. This data should not be considered as a guideline for the loading of ammunition nor is any responsibility assumed or implied by the authors or publisher for the use of such information in the loading of ammunition

Excerpted from the *Standard Catalog of Winchester* and used by permission of Krause Publications Books, 700 E. State St., Iola, WI, 54990.

Cartridge and firearm illustrations used from page 26 through 278 were taken from original Winchester catalogs or advertisements and are used with permission of Olin Corp.

Book Design by Ian Robertson.

Library of Congress Control Number: 2006924838

Printed in China.
ISBN: 0-7643-2541-8

We are interested in hearing from authors with book ideas on related topics.

Published by Schiffer Publishing Ltd.
4880 Lower Valley Road
Atglen, PA 19310
Phone: (610) 593-1777
FAX: (610) 593-2002
E-mail: Info@schifferbooks.com.
Visit our web site at: www.schifferbooks.com
Please write for a free catalog.
This book may be purchased from the publisher.
Please include $3.95 postage.
Try your bookstore first.

In Europe, Schiffer books are distributed by:
Bushwood Books
6 Marksbury Avenue
Kew Gardens
Surrey TW9 4JF, England
Phone: 44 (0) 20 8392-8585
FAX: 44 (0) 20 8392-9876
E-mail: Info@bushwoodbooks.co.uk.
Visit our website at: www.bushwoodbooks.co.uk
Free postage in the UK. Europe: air mail at cost.
Try your bookstore first.

Contents

Acknowledgments

There have been so many people who, over the years, have provided the sort of encouragement necessary to begin, much less complete, a book like this. The following, however, are among those who have not only been helpful and supportive along the way but have contributed vastly to our knowledge. Some actually contributed their part and passed on long before this book was even contemplated. It is here that we wish to express our most sincere thanks to all who helped, whether listed here or not.

Philip Bailey
Lou Behling
Doug Beneck
Robert Buttweiler
Doug Culver
Brook Davis
Pete deCoux
Vic Engel
Hal Ferguson
Dick Fraser
Walt Hallstein
Tom Henshaw
Tom Hollis
Howard Hoovestal
George Kass
John Kuntz
Ed Lewis
Mick McLaughlin
Mike Methe
Larry Neitzel
B.A. Oldfield
J.K. Olson
Paul Parsons*
Richard Raines
Bob Reichenbach
Denny Rinka *
Duane Robertson*
Cliff Schafer
Dave Saks
Don Sandefer
John Scott
Keith Shepard*
Bob Solomon
Ron Stadt
Sam Stilwell*
Bob Strauss*
Lew Yearout
Zachary Weighman
Ron Willoughby,

and

Our wives, Carolyn Giles and Judy Shuey, who have worked on, put up with, and suffered through, so much for so long. To them: THANKS! Beyond all that words can express!

*Deceased

Caution! Important!

THIS BOOK IS A DEFINITIVE WORK WHICH ALSO HAPPENS TO BE A PRICE GUIDE. FOR THOSE READERS WHO MAY BE TEMPTED TO SKIP THE INTRODUCTION IN ORDER TO GET TO THE PRICES, WE STRONGLY RECOMMEND YOU RECONSIDER AND READ CAREFULLY. THERE ARE MANY POTENTIAL PITFALLS IN USING THIS BOOK SIMPLY AS A PRICE OR RARITY GUIDE WITHOUT HAVING READ THE SECTIONS PERTAINING TO HOW THOSE VALUES HAVE BEEN DERIVED. IT WOULD BE TANTAMOUNT TO MAKING JUDGMENTS "OUT OF CONTEXT" AND COULD LEAD YOU ASTRAY RATHER THAN TOWARD AN ACCURATE ASSESSMENT OF VALUE OR RARITY.

FURTHER, IF YOU ARE INTERESTED ONLY IN DATING A WINCHESTER CARTRIDGE BOX AND FIND OUR COVERAGE OF YOUR PARTICULAR CALIBER OF INTEREST TO BE SOMEWHAT SPARSE, PLEASE UNDERSTAND THAT IN THE INTEREST OF AVOIDING REDUNDANCY WE HAVE COVERED SOME CALIBERS FAR MORE THOROUGHLY THAN OTHERS. IT MAY HELP YOU TO KNOW, THEREFORE, THAT AMONG 20-ROUND BOXES THE 30-30 (30 WCF) CHAPTER SHOULD BE ENLIGHTENING AND AMONG 50-ROUND BOXES THE 44-40 (44 WCF) CHAPTER SHOULD BE OF SIGNIFICANT HELP. BOTH OF THOSE CHAPTERS COME CLOSER TO BEING COMPLETE OVER A LONG TIME SPAN THAN OTHERS.

Introduction

Like a pen with no ink or a car with an empty gas tank, a firearm is a useless mechanical contrivance without ammunition. Until the mid-1980s cartridges and their boxes were largely ignored as collectibles in spite of the obvious and essential relationship with their respective guns. But times change and most gun collectors now seek contemporary boxes of ammunition to display with their collectible guns, and virtually every award-winning gun display will have one or more original cartridge boxes, as well as other accoutrements, enhancing their exhibit. In some cases, usually unbeknownst to those viewing these elaborate displays, the antique ammo is actually much rarer than the gun! The growing recognition of the rarity of many of these boxes, as well as their aesthetic and historic appeal, has led to a tremendous increase in interest in antique cartridge boxes. Unfortunately, research has not kept pace and reliable, authoritative information has been hard to come by. Even Company catalogs offered little help as cartridge boxes were seldom pictured, though individual cartridge "cuts" were prominently featured.

Shotshell boxes and .22 boxes, neither of which are covered here in any detail, have long had their respective, and very active, collecting fraternities. However, by far the majority of this book will be devoted to boxes for the centerfire metallic cartridges, so many of which, along with the legendary .44 Henry rimfire, were developed by Winchester and made famous throughout the 50 years that encompassed the Civil War, the Indian Wars, the building of the transcontinental railroads, the decimation of the buffalo herds, the great shooting matches of the Creedmoor and What Cheer ranges, the Wild West shows and, eventually, Teddy Roosevelt's African Safaris. It is hoped that the publication of this work and its revelations of the many great graphics, the multitude of calibers, the innumerable variations, and, for the first time, rarity assessments, will generate even more interest in cartridge boxes as collectibles in their own right. It should also tend to solidify their well-deserved prominent niche within the vast field of collectibles created for over 100 years by The Big Red W, the WINCHESTER REPEATING ARMS CO, NEW HAVEN, CONN. USA.

Scope and Organization of this Work

While it would be great to be able to identify, categorize, date and picture every cartridge box ever catalogued and produced by Winchester, such an encyclopedic undertaking is neither practical nor possible. The main reason is simply that there are insufficient records with which to research such a task. Much is simply unknown and with too many years having now elapsed, interviews and even word-of-mouth reminiscences are rendered nearly impossible. So we are left with a few fairly superficial books and articles, some incomplete and often undecipherable factory records, and many years of personal hands-on experience by the authors and their contacts, contributors and fellow collectors from around the world.

Still, much is known and even more can be deduced, interpolated and extrapolated from the information at hand. While we have done our utmost to remain factual, much must be inferred from the data and empirical evidence we have accumulated while handling over 25,000 cartridge boxes during the past 40 years. And while a great many types and varieties of Winchester cartridge boxes have been assembled for this work, it, for all its aspirations, by no mean purports to be complete. In fact, for most calibers, only a few examples suffice to establish a time-line sufficient to date a cartridge box within two or three years its design and manufacture.

On the other hand we have selected a few calibers, most notably 30-30, where we feel our lineage does come close to being complete. In order to make the data contained within the 30-30 section more accessible, however, we have structured that portion of the text in outline form (see Chapter 9). This should enable the reader to more readily adapt the details of the series of 30-30 boxes to the lineage of most other calibers including 50-round boxes. If further detail is needed in analyzing 50-round boxes, however, we refer you to the 44-40 (44 W.C.F.) section of Chapter 4.

There are many boxes with variations of which we are aware but have deemed too minor to be of interest here and we have no illusions about the number of undiscovered, or just plain unnoticed, types and varieties which remain out there. Undoubtedly we will have been found to have missed some things and made some mistakes. We hope you, the reader, will not only forgive them but become a fellow researcher and help us to correct them as well as informing us of any notable discoveries you may make.

But by the time we've reached the end it is expected that both gun and cartridge collectors will be able to identify and date, within narrow limits, any and every commercial Winchester cartridge box from 1861 New Haven Arms Henry boxes to those boxes produced during 1956, the last year of production at Winchester's plant in New Haven. And, as each chapter is devoted to specific Winchester gun models, matching the chronology of the cartridge boxes with their respective guns should fall easily into place. On the other hand, it has not been our intention to expound upon the various gun models which comprise most of our chapter headings. Should the reader desire to learn more about Winchester rifles there are many excellent works already out there and to which our bibliography will direct you.

It is our belief that every reader will finish this book with a much greater understanding of the significance of, and differences between, the many Winchester cartridge boxes and their labels, their construction, their colors and their content. It is also our hope that every person with an interest in either Winchester collectibles generally, or antique ammunition particularly, will not only in many ways be newly enlightened, but will enjoy our trip down this relatively unexplored part of the Winchester trail.

Factors Affecting Collectibility

In the interests of consistency and conformity and in hopes of avoiding any confusion which might occur by re-writing topics on which we have already expressed ourselves in print, we have, in the following paragraphs, excerpted portions of the explanatory and definitional topics we authored for *The Standard Catalog of Winchester* in 2000. (Used by permission of Krause Publications Books, 700 E. State St., Iola, WI, 54990.)

As with any collectible, several factors contribute to the desirability and value of cartridge boxes. Condition and rarity rank at the top as they do with most collectibles, so these will be dealt with first. *All references to cartridge box collectibility and pricing assumes boxes full of their original cartridges, not empty, partial or varying in any other particular from the way they were shipped from the factory.*

The Condition Factor

Since the labels are the focal point of any ammo box, label condition is paramount. Starting with a perfect label with all its original color, detractions can be seen as scratches, tears and other missing paper; blotches, stains, fading or discoloration; price stickers or other non-factory labels or handwritten notations; tape residue; and of course, dirt and grime.

The box itself should be solid, retaining its original integrity without internal or external reinforcement or other obvious "help." The worst "help" (unfortunately, the most often seen) is tape, any kind of tape. We've seen 'em all — transparent, cellophane, masking, white, surgical, black, paper, even duct tape — and they *all* detract significantly. Sometimes tape can be removed with heat or solvents but the risk of losing label and/or ink in the process is high and some residue or staining is a virtual certainty. If we do nothing more in this chapter than underscore the fact that one should never put tape or price labels on a box, we'll feel we've added something important to the literature on the care and feeding of cartridge boxes.

Split seams or edge separations are not serious detractions and most often should be left as they are. However, if a box is obviously deteriorating under the load of its contents, we do not find it objectionable to effect a skillful repair with a clear, flexible paste but without reinforcements. If you're not skilled enough to do a first-rate job, forget this remedy. A second-rate job ends up being about as attractive as tape.

Most gun collectors tend to disdain refinished guns; however, fragile cardboard cartridge boxes that have been carrying around a load of lead, brass, copper and corrosive chemicals for 50 to 150 years may need some help just to preserve them for future generations. In many cases, it's either "fix 'em or lose 'em" and I hate to see a piece of history self-destruct. Just be careful not to destroy something in the process of attempting to fix it.

Although our pricing in this book has been done within ranges of values and condition rather than by increments of condition, the authors felt that we should provide the reader with definitional guidelines in order to better illustrate the continuum of conditions in which boxes will generally be found.

Grading Condition

Grading, like beauty, lies in the eyes of the beholder. For instance, an "80%" condition gun may suggest a very different image in the minds of different people. So it is here. Overall box condition is the sum total of many variables, each of which will be weighted differently in accordance with the personal preferences of the individual collector or dealer. As a result, it is important to understand that assigning condition, even according to the objective criteria set forth below, remains, in the end, a very subjective exercise. Also, please bear in mind that these are *guidelines* and by no means will every box fit readily into one or the other of these categories.

Note: Sealed boxes, while worth a premium within their grade, must be judged by the same standards as other boxes. In other words, just because a box is sealed doesn't mean it is "Excellent." In *all* grades it is assumed that the box is full and correct in all respects.

Excellent—While not necessarily "as new", the box is solid and labels are clean with only negligible flaws or light scuffing. Colors will be bright and original. If it's a two-piece 50-round box, the side seal will be virtually all there. There will be no tape or signs of tape removal.

Very Good-Fine—Box may be a little weak or separated at the edges but is otherwise sound. The labels may have *minor* staining, scratches or scuffs but will be completely readable. Colors may show slight fading. There will be no tape, though tape removal stains may be present. If it's a 50-round two-piece box, the side seal will be more than half intact. If it's a one-piece box, end flaps will be sound. Note: Later one-piece boxes are not generally collectible in condition below V.G.-Fine.

Good—Box may have some repairs, reinforcements, splits or loose edges but no missing cardboard. Labels will have scuff marks, chips, stains and other detractions but no major pieces will be missing. On two-piece, 50-round boxes, side label may be partial or roughly opened. End flaps will be present on one-piece boxes, but may have folds.

The Rarity Factor

Unfortunately, even after years of grass-roots research, we have yet to discover how many boxes were made or shipped in any given caliber or box style. And even that data would be but a crude beginning in our quest to gain an estimate of how many boxes of a certain caliber, type or variety still exist. About all we have to go on are beginning and ending appearances in catalog listings coupled with what experience tells us may have survived. Relative to the number of loose rounds in existence, the boxes are obviously quite scarce with cartridges commonly outnumbering their boxes by 20 or 50 to one. Over time, as the boxes deteriorated, they were thrown away or used to start the next campfire while their contents survived in coffee cans or other containers. If the rounds got shot up the boxes were generally discarded and disappeared along with the shell casings. So sometimes rarity is simply a function of age, of how long a particular box has been around.

Some collectors assume that the quantity of guns produced in a given caliber is an indication of the rarity of the attendant ammo. We don't find this to be true. For instance, in the Winchester Model 86, 38-70 is a rare gun (under 1000 having been manufactured) but the ammo is not much scarcer than 40-82 or 40-65, calibers in which many more guns were made. On the other hand, a full box of 50-100-450 is even less likely to be encountered than the Model 1886 that is chambered for it, rare though it is. Or try finding a nice Winchester two-piece box of 303 British for the Model 1895 or a nice box of 236 U.S. Navy!

As no survey or census as yet exists in this fledgling field much remains to be discovered. However, the collective experience of a great many collectors and dealers, as well as that of the authors, has led to the rarity estimates as they appear to us at this time and which are shown in the following pages. Intrepid chaps that we are, then, we share with you these rarity assessments in the expectation that, with your help, we will be able to fine-tune this section in future editions.

Our Rarity Scale

The more common categories (Rarity 1, Rarity 2 and Rarity 3) are expressed in relative terms while the rarest categories (Rarity 4 and Rarity 5) are estimated in numerical terms. Please understand, however, that the Rarity 4 and Rarity 5 categories are speculative on our part based as they are on our personal observations (and memories), and, as such samplings go, probably have little statistical validity. Still, like so much in this book, we had to start somewhere!

Rarity 1 – Frequently or rather easily found
Rarity 2 – Occasionally found but not always readily available
Rarity 3 – Seldom encountered, hard to find
Rarity 4 – Rarely seen, fewer than 25 assumed to exist
Rarity 5 – Very Rare, probably less than 10 in existence

When combined with our Valuation Codes (See "**Valuation and Pricing**" section below), Rarity Codes will be abbreviated as follows: Rarity 1 = R1, Rarity = R2, etc. Also, plus (+) signs or minus (-) signs have occasionally been added to indicate, respectively, the upper or lower ends of a range

Other Value Factors

The correlation between Rarity and Price, while high, only speaks to the Supply side of the "Supply & Demand" pricing equation. Let's explore some of the Demand factors, things that, taken together, affect pricing every bit as much as rarity.

Assuming that even the least rare calibers are those for which a large number of guns exist, demand will always be high simply because of the number of collectors who will want to have an original box of cartridges for display with those very popular guns. And collectors who compete for prize money by exhibiting at gun shows have found that judges of the displays are liable to detract from the exhibits' merits in the absence of appropriate and contemporary cartridge boxes.

Another reason that these larger metallic caliber boxes have become the fastest growing segment of collectible cartridge boxes is the simple fact that, as alluded to in the Introduction, they are imbued with so much of the romance and drama of American history from the latter half of the 19th Century. To the extent that any caliber, label or box has the added element of historical relevance, its value will be enhanced. The "Winning of the West" and all that was a part of it, for better or worse, remains our heritage. And Political Correctness* be damned!

Graphics and color are also very important in determining cartridge box popularity. The Grizzly Bear design of the early 1940s Silvertip box is an extremely popular collectible, bringing higher prices than most other one-piece boxes, before or since. The colorful (non-Silvertip) yellow, blue and red boxes of the 1935-1945 period are also highly sought after, often more so than the earlier, though duller, blue and white ("1928" or "1932") Staynless box, even though these represent Winchester's first one-piece box and are much scarcer in nice condition.

Of the still earlier two-piece boxes, among those most highly prized are the "picture" boxes. True picture boxes, contrary to the belief of many, are those boxes (and *only* those boxes) that picture a gun for which the cartridge is intended. A cartridge picture, or "cut" (as in wood-cut or engraving) is commonly found on early boxes of all types and is usually nothing remarkable. Picture boxes feature the gun on one of the primary labels (usually the top label of a 50-round box or the front label of a 20-round box). A cut of the Winchester Model 1873 carbine on the side label of a 44-40 box, however, would be considered a picture box since the side label constitutes a primary label on 50-round boxes.

*See Glossary

1

Cartridge Boxes
An Overview

Box and Construction Types

Some of the earliest boxes were formed metal, and it is in this type that some of the earliest Volcanic rounds are found. The labels on these pre-1860 "tin" Volcanic boxes, which contained 200 cartridges, were under the lid. Metallic boxes generally did not gain significant acceptance in this country, though they were common in Europe, especially Great Britain.

By the early 1860s most American manufacturers had adopted a cardboard (or paper-fiberboard) box which had both lid and bottom sections, the lower section having an inner liner that extended upward to accommodate the lid which fit over it, the top and bottom halves meeting in the middle to form what has become known as the "two-piece, half-split" box (pictures of box types are shown at the end of this section). This style was used for most small caliber boxes in both rimfire and centerfire until about 1920. Side-seal labels were used beginning in the mid-1870s, but prior to that period boxes were never factory sealed.

While most half-split boxes were 50-round, there were also 100-round (rimfire; e.g., 22 caliber from Short to Extra Long and 25 Bacon & Bliss) as well as 25-round boxes, both rimfire and centerfire. Most of the latter sizes are found in the Spencer calibers and in an unusual red-labeled box containing .45-70 cartridges of folded-head case construction with 500 grain cast bullets. Also in 25-round boxes are "new primed empties" (NPE), .45-70 and .50-70 blanks, and a rare early blackpowder .50-110 shot offering. This type of box generally came with a single label on the top of the lid, though some will be found with a paper tape seal around the entire side joint. Wrap-around style labels for this type of box appeared circa 1910, the label acting as the seal. Many of these square boxes would be used for special orders and new primed empties into the 1930's and will be found with simple hand-written descriptions rather than printed labels.

Those rifle cartridges packaged and sold in clips came in boxes of an up-right, rectangular shaped, two-piece half-split design. Both 15- and 20-round sizes have been noted; the 15-round size seems to be found only in a 7m/m Mauser export box containing three clips of five, two facing up and the middle facing down, and using a label that covers the top and side of the lid only. The 20-round size is more commonly found in the 6m/m USN (U.S. Navy) caliber. The clips were stored two up and two down, alternating. This size box was also used for export of 30-06 and 7.65 Mauser but is seldom encountered.

Perhaps the most unusual type of box relating to clip or magazine-fed weapons is the "book" style as shown in E. Mysrakowski's book on the 6m/m Lee-Navy rifle. A standard rifle size, two-row, 20-round box lid is used, but the lower part of the box has two rows of ten cartridges separated down the center line and hinged at the bottom like a book spine, so with the top removed, the two 10-round divided compartments open like a book. This type of box was no doubt designed as a result of the Marine Corps' complaints over the difficulties involved with loading the 5-round clips for this rifle by hand. With this style box, a clip could easily be slid over 5 cartridges at a time and the spring holder fastened. The narrow 10-round tray kept the cartridges from moving side to side. A strikingly similar box was made to fill the dual magazines of the experimental .345 Machine Rifle designed and built by Frank Burton at Winchester in 1916-17. (See Shuey, Vol. I, pg 247 for illustration of loading device.)

Also in the early years there are a couple of notable two-piece boxes which had a lid on a much taller bottom section so that it could hardly be called "half"-split. The most notable of these was the famous New Haven Arms "black 100-box", one of which sold at auction (Butterfield & Butterfield, July 1994) for $19,800. This gold lettering on black (actually dark purple) box is one of the most highly recognizable and sought-after of all cartridge boxes. Another early 1870s tall box with a lid is the very scarce Spencer 42-pack, which contains six packets of seven rounds each, corresponding to the magazine capacity of the Spencer rifle. These were somewhat of an anachronism as the 42-round packaging was a Civil War item and these short-lived early-1870's boxes were soon discontinued and replaced with the 25-round square boxes which had already become the norm for Spencer cartridges among most other major manufacturers.

The other separate and distinct form of the two-piece box is the "full cover" type in which the top piece fits fully over the bottom, covering all sides. The top usually has half-moon thumb-cuts to facilitate opening and, beginning around 1920, the box was sealed with a label that covered the top and both ends and lapped over onto the bottom. Also in this category were the "flat" boxes used for many of the long-case single-shot cartridges such as Sharps, Ballard, and the proprietary "Express" numbers developed for Winchester's Model 1885 HighWall: the 38-90, 40-110, 45-125 and 50-140.

One other term used in distinguishing (mostly 20-round) box construction types is "taped" versus "folded". In the older taped method, the box parts (top, ends, sides and bottom) were literally taped together to form the box. This construction is also referred to as the "pre-1915" style. Post-1915 boxes — as always, with exceptions — were folded construction: one piece of cardboard being used for the top and another for the bottom then being folded and glued. The photo below shows the difference as seen from the bottom, the best angle from which to discern the difference.

The top and middle boxes have taped bottoms, showing the seams. The bottom box is of folded construction and is seamless.

The two-piece, half-split box traces its origins to the 1860s in Winchester boxes. They continued in use by the Company until around 1920.

This is the two-piece 20-round box which was the early style used for the longer Winchester rifle cartridges beginning in the 1870s and continuing in some calibers through WWII.

The full-cover two-piece box was brought into general use around 1920. It's duration in the marketplace was limited, however, as the two-piece boxes were to be replaced by the one-piece box beginning in the late 1920s.

A one-piece, large caliber 20-round box with tray.

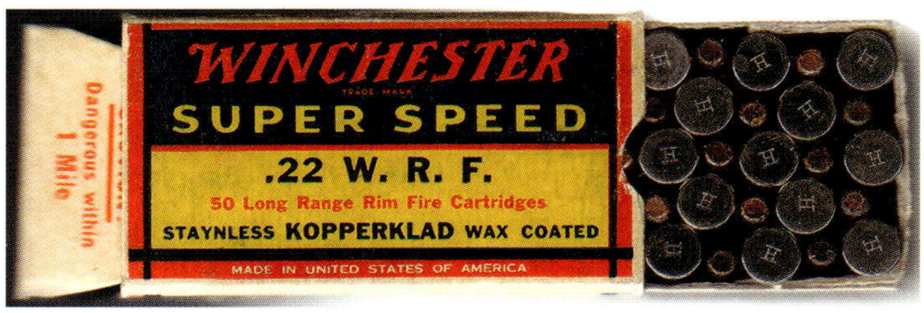

A one-piece, 50-round small caliber box.

Labels and Their Meanings

Label Colors

Some few years ago, in one of the gun collector magazines (now forgotten), there was an attempt made to categorize the various Winchester cartridge box labels by color and loading. Being incomplete and only partially accurate, if you remember it, please forget what you read and let's begin afresh. This topic is much more complex than normally assumed.

Before about 1900 there was little or no attempt by Winchester to standardize label colors in accordance with the cartridge loadings in the boxes. Indeed, 22 boxes from the 1870s are to be found in green, yellow, blue, and purple. Red was used for some export boxes in both the rimfire and centerfire lines, the 45-70 with folded head case construction and cast bullets housed in a square two-piece box of 25 being the one most commonly found. Though scarce, the 32 Short is the red box most often seen in the rimfire line. Some centerfire 20-round and 50-round Black Powder boxes which normally have green labels are found in blue label boxes and are usually accorded a premium (see further discussion below).

Of course prior to 1895 virtually everything was loaded with black powder and lead bullets. Except for export boxes colors were not intended as a coding or identification device. Loading exceptions were noted with add-on stickers or rubber-stamped callouts. Some, notably Sharps calibers, were altered with the original callout over-struck and the correct callout added in pen and ink. With the development of new powders and different types of jacketed bullets, however, things became much more complicated. Hence, shortly after 1900, the Company adopted a system of box label colors that corresponded with the loadings contained therein. Notwithstanding this fact and as discussed below, add-on labels and rubber-stamped or over-printed alterations continued throughout the entire period of our study.

It should be noted that, to our knowledge, no records exist that formally state the observations and conclusions we have set forth here. The table below, however, expresses what our studies suggest Winchester's intent was with regard to the standardization of label colors and contents, post-1900. But, in spite of their occasional value to us as dating benchmarks, color shadings or gradations from light to dark are seldom considered to have been of significance in the Company's attempt to co-ordinate the label colors of cartridge boxes with the loadings contained therein.

A word of caution: One must be careful in attempting to distinguish between original ink colorations and their subsequent fading or darkening due to age and exposure to the elements. Since relatively major color changes are possible over time, making such an assessment can be a risky task in view of the degree of subjectivity involved.

20-Round Boxes

Label Color	Powder Type	Bullet Type	Comments
Green	Black	Lead	
Orange	Smokeless	Soft Point	
Red / Purple	Smokeless	Full Patch	
Yellow	Smokeless	Soft Point	High Velocity (WHV)
Lavender / Pink	Smokeless	Full Patch	High Velocity (WHV)
"Electric" Blue	Black	Soft Point	38-55 and 32-40 only
Tan, red print	Smokeless	Short Range, Blank or Proof loadings	
Tan, black print	Black (Also New Primed Empties)	Blank, Military, Special order loadings	

50-Round Boxes

Label Color	Powder Type	Bullet Type	Comments
Green	Black	Lead	
Red	Smokeless	Lead or Soft Point	
Orange	Smokeless	Full Patch	
Yellow	Smokeless	Soft Point	High Velocity (WHV)
Lavender / Pink	Smokeless	Full Patch	High Velocity (WHV)
Gray / Gray-Green	Lesmok	Any	
Tan, red print	Smokeless	Any Blank or Proof loadings	
Tan, black print	Black (Also New Primed Empties)	Blank, Military, Special order loadings	

Exceptions

As with everything Winchester, exceptions abound. And while there is no end to these, we will do our best to cover those most likely to be encountered.

Pre-1900: As mentioned earlier, color coding was not yet formally in use except for red export labels. The most commonly found exception is the "blue" box, which according to our best estimate was a phenomenon of the mid-1890s (probably 1896) for those calibers in which this blue labeling is found. There are, however, several blue boxes that pre-date this period, chief among them in terms of collector interest is the 44 Henry box from either the late-1870s or 1880s. However the desirability of the vast majority of blue boxes is largely due to aesthetics and scarcity, not because they pre-date the green labels. Another cautionary note: Blue-green labels are more common (than pure blue) and such boxes are considered green for purposes of this discussion.

Interestingly, a few pre-1900 calibers are more often found in blue than not, most notably the Black Powder 50-110 Express and the 45-60. Surely the number of blue boxes in these two calibers broadens the time frame in which blue boxes are to be found but we can find no explanation as to why only a couple of calibers exhibit this trait.

Orange label boxes are to be found in a most unusual variety of boxes dating back to the 1880s. An early box of 32 S&W Shot has been noted as have Black Powder, Lead boxes of 32 S&W Long and 38 S&W Special, the latter likely representing the first such Winchester box in that caliber. The first 44 WCF (44-40) box, picturing a rare Milbank-primed cartridge (described and pictured in Chapter 4) was yellow.

Short Range Smokeless loadings from the late 1890s in Model 1894 calibers were given deep red labels, a practice which apparently lasted until approximately 1905. Smokeless Short Range loadings in larger calibers (30-40, 45-70 and others) during the same period, however, were generally dark orange, in some cases approaching reddish-orange. Other red label Black Powder, Lead boxes are found in 32-44 and 38-44 S&W Target (and Gallery) loadings as well as other target loadings, including 32 S&W. Another caliber in this Black Powder, Lead red label group is the interesting and very scarce 32 Protector for the Minneapolis Palm Pistol.

An unusual gray 45-20 Armory Practice square box of 20 is shown in Chapter 8 in the 45-70 section. And a real oddity, an early (probably the first) Smokeless 38 S&W box picturing a Smith & Wesson revolver, circa late-1890s, unlike any other of its type or period, is bright blue!

Post-1900: The first notable exception that we find in this period is the Smokeless box of 455 Eley, circa 1902, which has an orange label in spite of its lead bullet loading. Also unusual is its prominent callout of the use of Rifleite Powder: Winchester almost never featured the brand names of component manufacturers on their primary labeling.

A 32-20 (32 W.C.F.) Smokeless Soft Point box with an orange top label has been found (ca 1903) in spite of the existence of a predecessor box with a normal red label. Orange labels by this date would be expected to contain Full Patch (FMJ) cartridges. (See Chapter 4).

The very early and rare 32 Colt Automatic and 38 Colt Automatic boxes, before being renamed 32 and 38 "Automatic Colt", had red labels whether Soft Point or Full Patch.

An early (ca 1905) box of 35 WCF which has a red label on a Soft Point box is pictured in that section of Chapter 10. The only such anomaly known to the authors, though not really rare, is a very interesting (and affordable) variety.

The 1911-1915 period exhibits a label color curiosity among 25-20 and 32-20 W.H.V. Soft Point boxes. These labels should be yellow. However, for that time frame only, they are pink, the color normally denoting W.H.V. Full Patch loadings.

Winchester's first Superspeed offerings were introduced in 1925 and used smokeless powder behind light, jacketed hollow point bullets. The label chosen to introduce this new and very modern loading (still in the two-piece box) was, incredibly, good old-fashioned green, the color that represented Black Powder for 70 years!

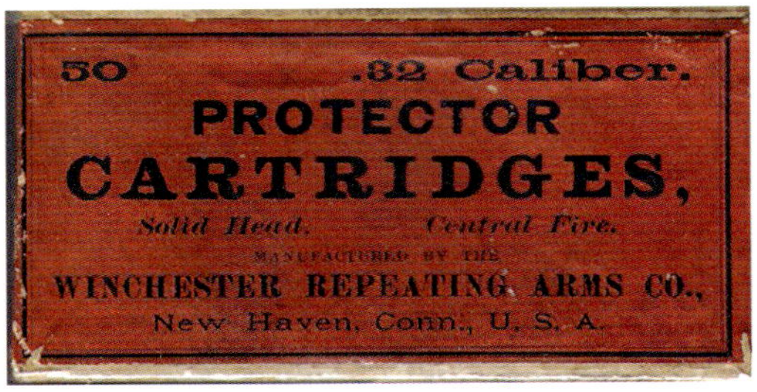

A pre-1900 Black Powder, Lead, box of the elusive 32 Protector, an extra short centerfire round made exclusively for the Minneapolis Palm Pistol, a gun manufactured for only a couple of years in the early-1890s. This box is unusual in that red label Black Powder centerfire boxes during this period were usually limited to Target, Gallery, Armory or Short Range offerings. R3+/500-1000

This bright blue 38 S&W box is a late-1890s Smokeless, Lead offering. No other boxes of the period are known to have been labeled in such a color. Oddly, the only other time this color was used, some 15 years later, it was to denote Black Powder, Jacketed loadings (in 32-40 and 38-55)! R3/100-200

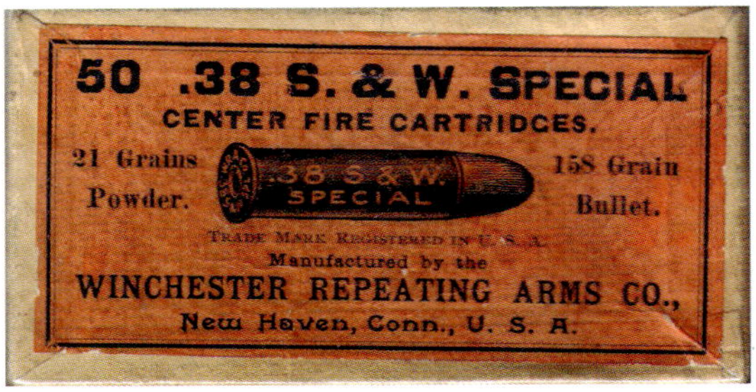

Thought to be the first 38 S&W Special box, ca 1900-1902, this orange label is on a Black Powder, Lead loading. Such a combination would typically be found in a green label box. R3+/150-300

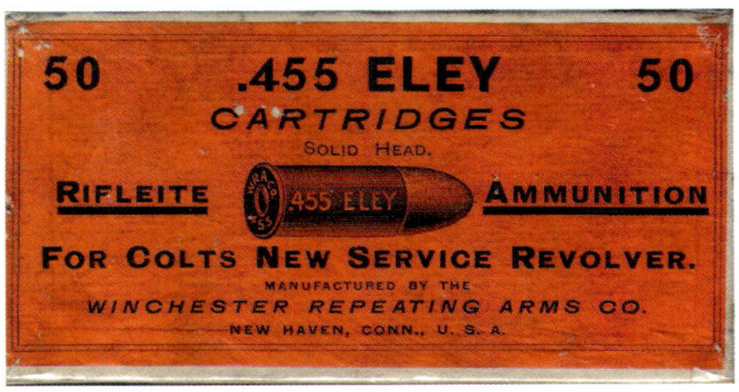

Another unusual orange label is found on this 455 Eley box, ca 1902, a year before Winchester decided to make it a proprietary cartridge by re-naming it 455 Colt. This loading is Smokeless, Lead , and normally would be found in a red label box. R4-/400-750

This "Smokeless, Full Patch" label would be expected to be orange, not red, in keeping with the Company's labeling protocol of the period. Interestingly, you can see the edges of an orange label underneath the red one. These early boxes of cartridges for Colt's 32 Caliber Pocket Model 1903 were titled "32 Colt Automatic" and bore the headstamp "WRACo 32 C.A.". Such rounds are very rare, selling for over $750 apiece in the cartridge collectors' market. R5/?

Codes, Add-On Labels and Other Markings

Codes

Beginning in 1906, two years after Winchester began making most of their own boxes and labels, the most obvious and seemingly understandable of all codes came into use: the Date Code, a hyphenated month-year expression in small numerals generally found at the right side of the label. What is not obvious, however, is what the date actually refers to. It is not, for instance, a production date as often assumed. Rather, it is a date referring to any of a number of possible changes in the specifications or labeling of that caliber and load as designated by the "other code" introduced in 1906, the one which is usually found on the left side of the same label, the File Code. The File Codes began with number one and continued into the thousands. Each number represents the Company's file regarding a specific label covering a specific loading in a specific caliber. Twenty-round boxes had two Primary labels, lid-top and front, each with its own File Code. Fifty-round boxes also had two Primary labels, the top label and the side-seal label. A File Code number never changed; but, as specifications regarding the loading or the label itself changed, the Date Codes reflected those alterations with a change in the date. Many secondary labels also exist, labels which do not explicitly denote a caliber or loading, but which call out other pertinent information applicable to several different calibers or loadings. These secondary labels can be useful in dating boxes simply because any such label might be dated well after the primary labels, thereby superseding the Primaries in their relevance as a dating criterion.

Many of you will remember having seen a series of perforations on old labels (of all kinds, not just cartridge box labels) and have probably wondered what they meant. Created by a Cummins Cryptographic machine, those little "Dot Codes" coded Winchester labels with day, month, year of manufacture and, for mostly rimfire offerings, the machine on which the ammo was loaded. These Cummins machines were put in use between1908 and 1910 and dot-codes can be found on some labels as late as the 1950s.

In 1927, upon acquiring U.S. Cartridge Company's ability to manufacture one-piece boxes, Winchester began to shift its largest-selling loadings to that style. Since the graphics on these new boxes were printed directly onto the cardboard there was no label to run through the Cummins machine. As an alternative, a new set of codes began to be stamped on the inside flap. On the loadings that remained in two-piece boxes, the codes can often be found on the box bottom. The old File and Date Codes never appeared on the one-piece boxes and disappeared from virtually all two-piece box labels designed after about 1931. They surfaced again briefly on a 1941-dated 45-90 box label, then disappeared entirely.

Labels and other Markings

Both before and after color coding was used on Winchester boxes, other means were used to label or mark boxes for special loadings, warnings, guarantees, instructions, patent data and even advertisements. The earliest and most primitive method of all was to simply overstrike a label with pen and ink and hand-write the new or correct loading. This is most commonly seen on early large single-shot caliber (mainly Sharps) labels and was a practice accepted by UMC and other cartridge makers as well. By the late-1870s rubber-stamped callouts were occasionally added to boxes and labels. And, most common of all, small add-on or "stick-on" labels were pasted on boxes throughout virtually the entire period of our study.

Significant examples of all these methods are shown throughout the book; however, we felt it would be instructive at this point to illustrate a number of them in order to provide the reader with a familiarity with some of those which are often referred to in the text though not always pictured. In addition we show here some of those which may not be found on boxes covered by this work but which are, nonetheless, found among the arcana of other Winchester cartridge boxes.

One thing that must be kept firmly in mind when dating Winchester items is that transitions in *anything* this company produced were likely to have been gradual, with old stocks of boxes, labels or parts being used up before, during or after introduction of the new stocks. As a result, and as records are also incomplete, *all dates and time periods must be considered approximate.*

Early boxes usually had primer callouts for reloading purposes. This one is from a 50-95 Express box, ca. 1879-1880.

In 1881 Winchester became a marketing agent for Anson Mills. So for the next 20 years labels may be found with an "ad" line for Anson Mills' cartridge belts included with the primer callout.

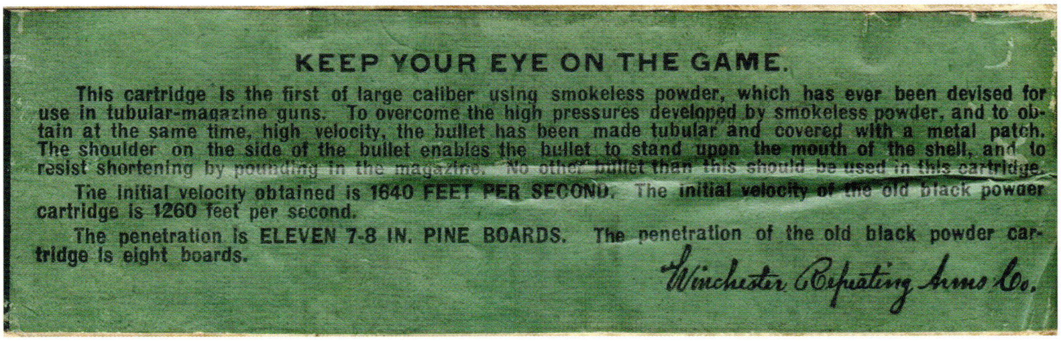

This side-seal label from an early Smokeless box of 38-40s describes and touts Winchester's new Smokeless, Patched "tubular bullet" loading. Circa 1896, both cartridge and box are very rare. (See this caliber, Chapter 4, for more pictures.)

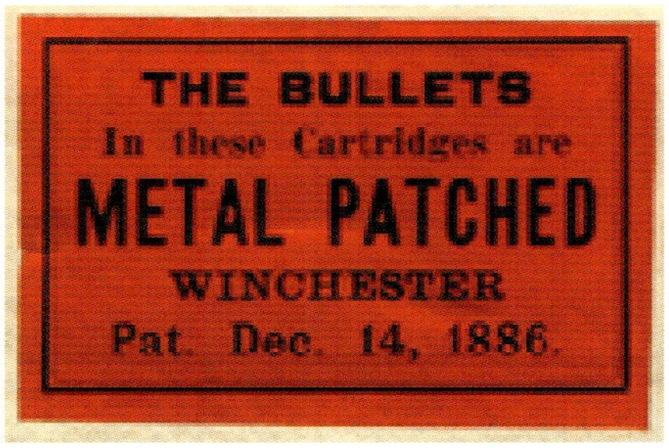

These seldom seen bright red labels were used in the early 1890s on Black Powder 20-round boxes loaded with Winchester's new [Full] Metal Patched bullets.

The "Fancy WRACo" logo was only used for a few years, from the late 1890s until approximately 1906. To the best of our knowledge it is found only on 50-round boxes.

The oft-referred to "Sunburst" labels found on so many boxes in the 1895-1902 period, before box label color coding was instituted. While still in use on some calibers after 1902, they were gradually phased out.

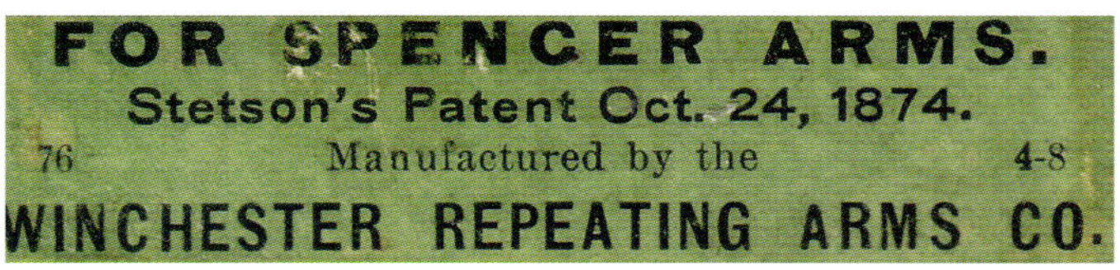

Collectors of Rimfire boxes will likely have noticed a Stetson Patent date on Winchester labels. The correct date was Oct. 31, 1871; however, Oct. 24 was erroneously used for a number of years before it was corrected. This is the latest "Oct. 24" box we have seen. The label also illustrates the File Code (76) and Date Code (4-8).

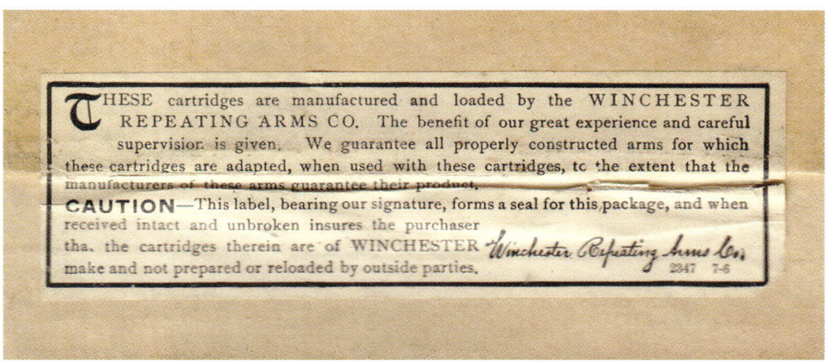

The "Guarantee" sealing label found on so many two-piece 20-round boxes in the late 1890s and early 1900s. The File Code (2347) and Date Code (7-6) can also be seen, lower right.

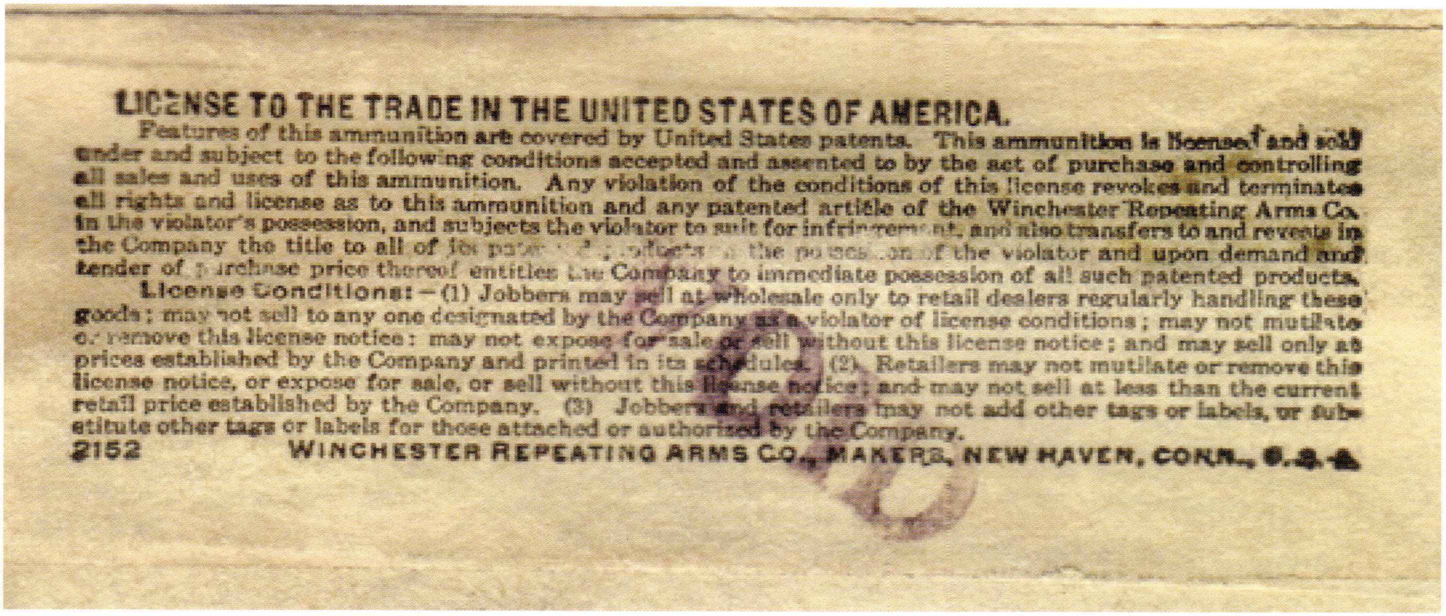

LICENSE TO THE TRADE IN THE UNITED STATES OF AMERICA.

Features of this ammunition are covered by United States patents. This ammunition is licensed and sold under and subject to the following conditions accepted and assented to by the act of purchase and controlling all sales and uses of this ammunition. Any violation of the conditions of this license revokes and terminates all rights and license as to this ammunition and any patented article of the Winchester Repeating Arms Co. in the violator's possession, and subjects the violator to suit for infringement, and also transfers to and revests in the Company the title to all of [illegible] the possession of the violator and upon demand and tender of purchase price thereof entitles the Company to immediate possession of all such patented products.

License Conditions: — (1) Jobbers may sell at wholesale only to retail dealers regularly handling these goods; may not sell to any one designated by the Company as a violator of license conditions; may not mutilate or remove this license notice: may not expose for sale or sell without this license notice; and may sell only at prices established by the Company and printed in its schedules. (2) Retailers may not mutilate or remove this license notice, or expose for sale, or sell without this license notice; and may not sell at less than the current retail price established by the Company. (3) Jobbers and retailers may not add other tags or labels, or substitute other tags or labels for those attached or authorized by the Company.

2152 WINCHESTER REPEATING ARMS CO., MAKERS, NEW HAVEN, CONN., U. S. A.

License to the Trade" labels are generally seen in the 1910-13 period with the "Void" overstamp prevailing in the latter two years.

"Rifle Cartridges"

Beginning in the1880s some 50-round boxes will be found with the words "Rifle Cartridges" prominently printed on their primary labels. The reason such an otherwise innocuous call-out deserves our attention is that the calibers so labeled are most often obviously and exclusively handgun calibers. Examples include a long list of such loadings including 45 Colt, 45 ACP, 32 S&W, 38 S&W, 44 Colt, 41 Colt, 25 Auto, 32 Auto and many others. Nor was this phenomenon limited to Winchester as the labeling of several other companies also exhibit this wording.

The earliest clue as to the significance of the "Rifle Cartridges" call-out surfaces in a requisition for separate box labels by a Winchester employee in 1891. A certain number of "Rifle Cartridges" labels in handgun calibers were ordered and destined for distribution in certain southeastern states in which pistol ammunition was either heavily taxed or regulated. It seems that by simply labeling the offending calibers as "Rifle Cartridges" in those states the ammunition makers were able to contravene the onerous governmental taxes and controls. State and local governments were somewhat slow on the uptake, it appears, as the practice continued successfully into the early 1920s. One can't help but wonder what it would have been like dealing with local government employees in those days.

A very early ad for Winchester's "Patent Metal Patched" bullets from *American Field*, August 29, 1891.

2

Volcanic Arms

The Beginnings

That our chronology of the Winchester story begins exactly 100 years before their ammunition production shut down in New Haven in 1956 is no more than a fortunate coincidence, as it was in December 1856, that Oliver F. Winchester became president of the Volcanic Repeating Arms Company. Only two and a half years earlier, two more of the best known names in the gun business, Horace Smith and Daniel Wesson, joined with a third partner, Courtland Palmer, to form the partnership which in July, 1855, would become incorporated as that very same Volcanic Repeating Arms Company.

While Volcanic produced decent toggle-link repeaters, both pistols and rifles, the poor design and performance of the Volcanic ammunition rendered the gun a failure in the marketplace. By late 1856 inadequate sales in combination with other internal problems had pushed Volcanic toward bankruptcy and Winchester and N.B. Gaston, the Company's president until his death in December of that year, made the Company a loan against a pledge of assets that was sufficient only to take the venture into early 1857, when, on February 18, it was declared insolvent. Within a month Winchester had been assigned the remaining assets of Volcanic and, in turn, on May 1, 1857, sold those assets, not the least of which were important patents, to the recently formed New Haven Arms Company. As founder of New Haven Arms, Winchester owned 40% of the new Company's stock and served as both president and treasurer. Of perhaps equal significance, however, though it could certainly not have been known at the time, was the appointment of Benjamin Tyler Henry as plant superintendent.

The closing years of the 1850s were, most importantly, spent on what would today be considered R&D. While the Company continued marketing the Volcanic line, to which Henry contributed minor improvements in both the Volcanic guns and cartridges, it had become obvious that, in order to take advantage of the gun's further development and the Company's ability to market it, a major improvement was needed in the ammunition. That story is recounted later in our discussion of the 44 Henry cartridge; however, it doesn't give away the ending to tell you that they succeeded. And the rest, as they say, is history.

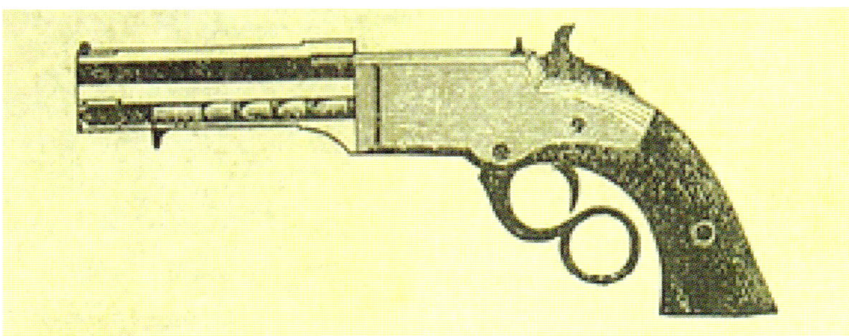

The Volcanic Guns

When Oliver Winchester took over the Volcanic Repeating Arms Co., by far the preponderance of their production was, and had been, pistols of 6" and 8" barrel lengths. Longer-barreled carbines had been listed in their earlier advertising material but only a limited number of 16" barreled pistol-carbines with detachable stocks were apparently produced. All were 41 caliber or, as stated at the time, "No.2" size. As mentioned above, the absorption of Volcanic into Winchester's newly formed New Haven Arms Company was accomplished by the spring of 1857. Throughout the balance of the decade the Volcanic line was expanded to include full length rifles and a 4" barreled pistol. Also a new 31 caliber, or "No.1" size cartridge for pistols was added to the line.

On the opposite page is the broadside announcing New Haven Arms' 1857 takeover of Volcanic Arms Co. The close-up at the bottom of the page highlights the pricing of the guns and "balls".

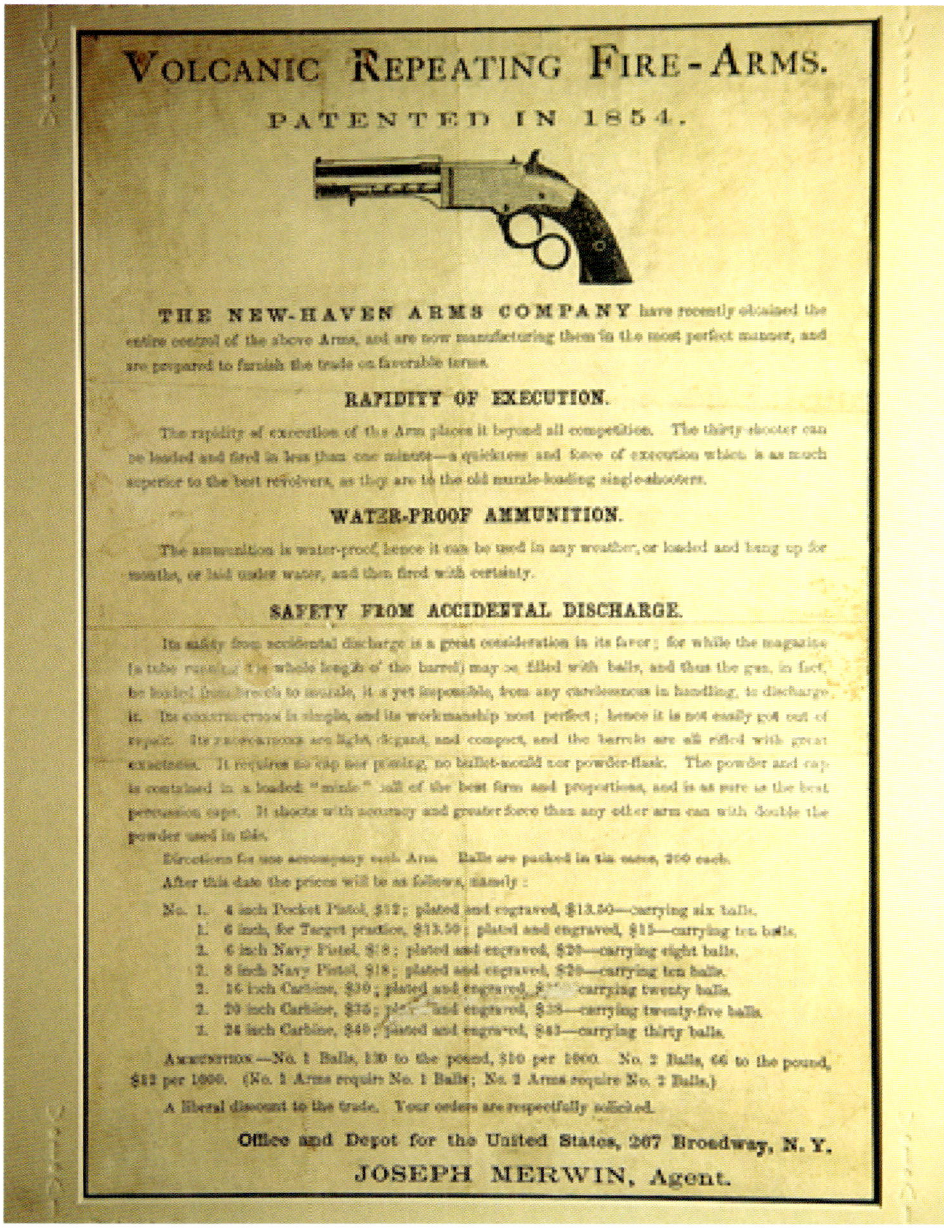

VOLCANIC REPEATING FIRE-ARMS.

PATENTED IN 1854.

THE NEW-HAVEN ARMS COMPANY have recently obtained the entire control of the above Arms, and are now manufacturing them in the most perfect manner, and are prepared to furnish the trade on favorable terms.

RAPIDITY OF EXECUTION.

The rapidity of execution of this Arm places it beyond all competition. The thirty-shooter can be loaded and fired in less than one minute—a quickness and force of execution which is as much superior to the best revolvers, as they are to the old muzzle-loading single-shooters.

WATER-PROOF AMMUNITION.

The ammunition is water-proof, hence it can be used in any weather, or loaded and hung up for months, or laid under water, and then fired with certainty.

SAFETY FROM ACCIDENTAL DISCHARGE.

Its safety from accidental discharge is a great consideration in its favor; for while the magazine (a tube running the whole length of the barrel) may be filled with balls, and thus the gun, in fact, be loaded from breech to muzzle, it is yet impossible, from any carelessness in handling, to discharge it. Its CONSTRUCTION is simple, and its workmanship most perfect; hence it is not easily got out of repair. Its PROPORTIONS are light, elegant, and compact, and the barrels are all rifled with great exactness. It requires no cap nor priming, no bullet-mould nor powder-flask. The powder and cap is contained in a loaded "minie" ball of the best form and proportions, and is as sure as the best percussion caps. It shoots with accuracy and greater force than any other arm can with double the powder used in this.

Directions for use accompany each Arm. Balls are packed in tin cases, 200 each.

After this date the prices will be as follows, namely:

No. 1. 4 inch Pocket Pistol, $12; plated and engraved, $13.50—carrying six balls.
1. 6 inch, for Target practice, $13.50; plated and engraved, $15—carrying ten balls.
2. 6 inch Navy Pistol, $18; plated and engraved, $20—carrying eight balls.
2. 8 inch Navy Pistol, $18; plated and engraved, $20—carrying ten balls.
2. 16 inch Carbine, $30; plated and engraved, $[illegible]—carrying twenty balls.
2. 20 inch Carbine, $35; pl[illegible] and engraved, $38—carrying twenty-five balls.
2. 24 inch Carbine, $40; plated and engraved, $43—carrying thirty balls.

AMMUNITION.—No. 1 Balls, 130 to the pound, $10 per 1000. No. 2 Balls, 66 to the pound, $12 per 1000. (No. 1 Arms require No. 1 Balls; No. 2 Arms require No. 2 Balls.)

A liberal discount to the trade. Your orders are respectfully solicited.

Office and Depot for the United States, 267 Broadway, N. Y.

JOSEPH MERWIN, Agent.

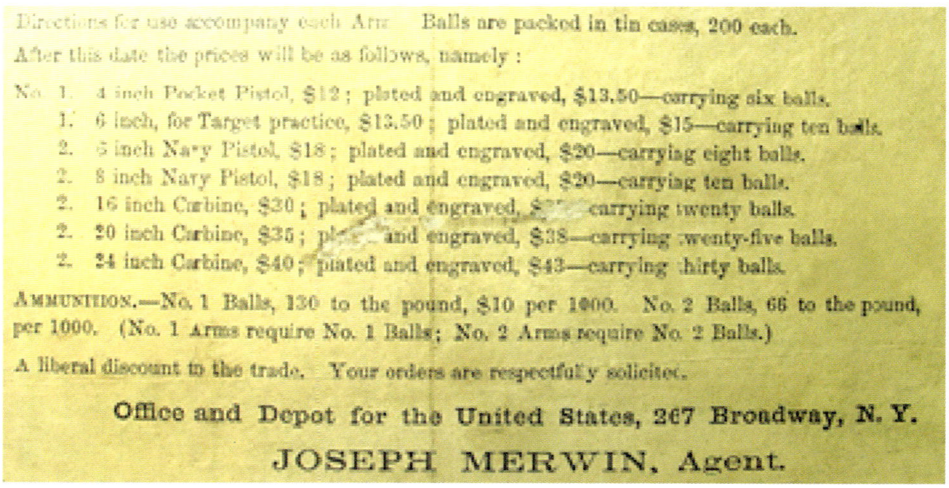

Directions for use accompany each Arm. Balls are packed in tin cases, 200 each.

After this date the prices will be as follows, namely:

No. 1. 4 inch Pocket Pistol, $12; plated and engraved, $13.50—carrying six balls.
1. 6 inch, for Target practice, $13.50; plated and engraved, $15—carrying ten balls.
2. 6 inch Navy Pistol, $18; plated and engraved, $20—carrying eight balls.
2. 8 inch Navy Pistol, $18; plated and engraved, $20—carrying ten balls.
2. 16 inch Carbine, $30; plated and engraved, $[illegible]—carrying twenty balls.
2. 20 inch Carbine, $35; pl[illegible] and engraved, $38—carrying twenty-five balls.
2. 24 inch Carbine, $40; plated and engraved, $43—carrying thirty balls.

AMMUNITION.—No. 1 Balls, 130 to the pound, $10 per 1000. No. 2 Balls, 66 to the pound, per 1000. (No. 1 Arms require No. 1 Balls; No. 2 Arms require No. 2 Balls.)

A liberal discount to the trade. Your orders are respectfully solicited.

Office and Depot for the United States, 267 Broadway, N. Y.

JOSEPH MERWIN, Agent.

Photos courtesy Ed Lewis, M.D.

The Volcanics
No. 1 Volcanic, 31 Caliber Volcanic
No. 2 Volcanic, 41 Caliber Volcanic
Catalog Listings: 1856-1865(?)*

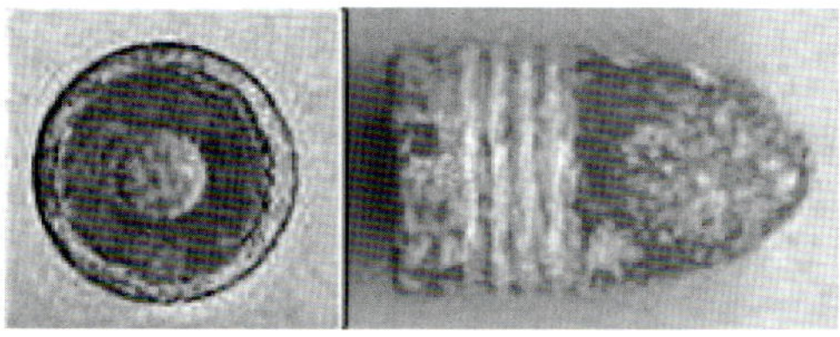

.41 Volcanic (Enlarged)

Models:
31 Caliber - Pistol, Carbine
41 Caliber - Pistol, Carbine, Rifle
Bullet types: Ld

Powder type: BP

Headstamp: NHS

With roots going back to the Hunt and Jennings "Rocket Ball" patents of the late 1840s, the Volcanic "ball", patented in 1856, contained primer and propellant within the projectile itself and was, in fact, an early self-contained cartridge. Unfortunately this design lent itself to a myriad of problems including misfires and the inherent inability of the caseless "rocket ball" configuration to prevent significant gas leakage from the breech. Further, the priming disc at the base of the cartridge, which remained in the chamber after ignition, added to the debris in the breech causing frequent action-jams.

By the time Oliver Winchester became the driving force in the Company in late 1856 and early 1857, the first Volcanic caliber, the 41 or "No.2" size, had already been on the market for some time. While we are not certain exactly when the 31 caliber "No.1" size was first offered, we know it made its appearance sometime during the 1857-59 period.

It is well-known that Volcanic Repeating Arms Co. contracted for most, if not all, of its cartridge requirements with outside ammunition manufacturers. Crittenden and Tibbals is the most commonly mentioned name but others may have been involved as well. Later, under the New Haven Arms Co. banner, Volcanic ammunition was produced in-house, but whether or not outside contractors remained in the picture is unclear.

As noted in the prior chapter, the early Volcanic boxes, holding 200 cartridges, were formed metal rectangular "tins" with the label under the lid. Even earlier round tins are rumored to have been found in a cased Volcanic set but the authors have been unable to confirm this. Later New Haven Arms Co. boxes were of more conventional pasteboard or cardboard construction with the label on the lid top.

Single rounds of Volcanic are scarce, 31 caliber being somewhat more difficult to find than 41. It should be noted that at least two other sizes (both larger than .41) have been found and are considered to be experimental or prototype rounds with no boxes known to exist. Boxes of either 31 or 41 caliber, even empty, are virtually non-existent. You may consider yourself fortunate, as we do, to be able to view the picture of the under-lid label below.

We regret that we were unable to obtain a picture of a pasteboard Volcanic cartridge box with top label; however, such a box with green labeling may be viewed as part of a cased set in the Winchester Collection in the Cody Firearms Museum at the Buffalo Bill Historical Center, Cody, WY. R5/17,500-27,500.

*There are no known dates or catalog listings regarding Volcanic ammunition; it is known, however, that stocks of Volcanic arms and ammunition existed at New Haven until at least 1865.

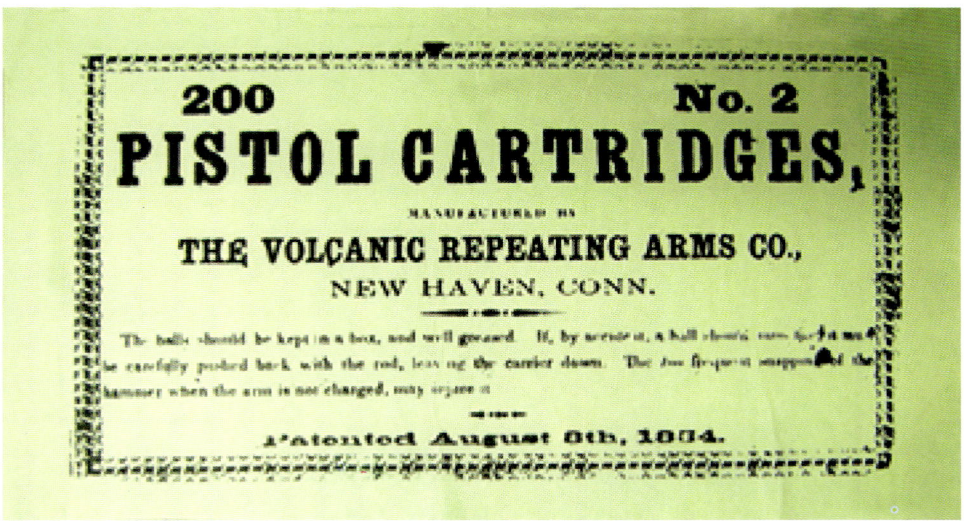

The earliest boxes of Volcanic cartridges were of formed metal and were labeled under the lid. This is an enlarged photograph of the label from the underside of a "No. 2" size (.41) Volcanic Repeating Arms Co. box, ca 1856. The first line of the instructions reads: "The balls should be kept in a box, and well greased."+ R5/17,500-27,500 *Courtesy of Ed Lewis, M.D.*

+For further pictures of Volcanic labels, see Malloy, Thomas and White; *Percussion Ammunition Packets*, pp. 61-62. (Listed in Bibliography)

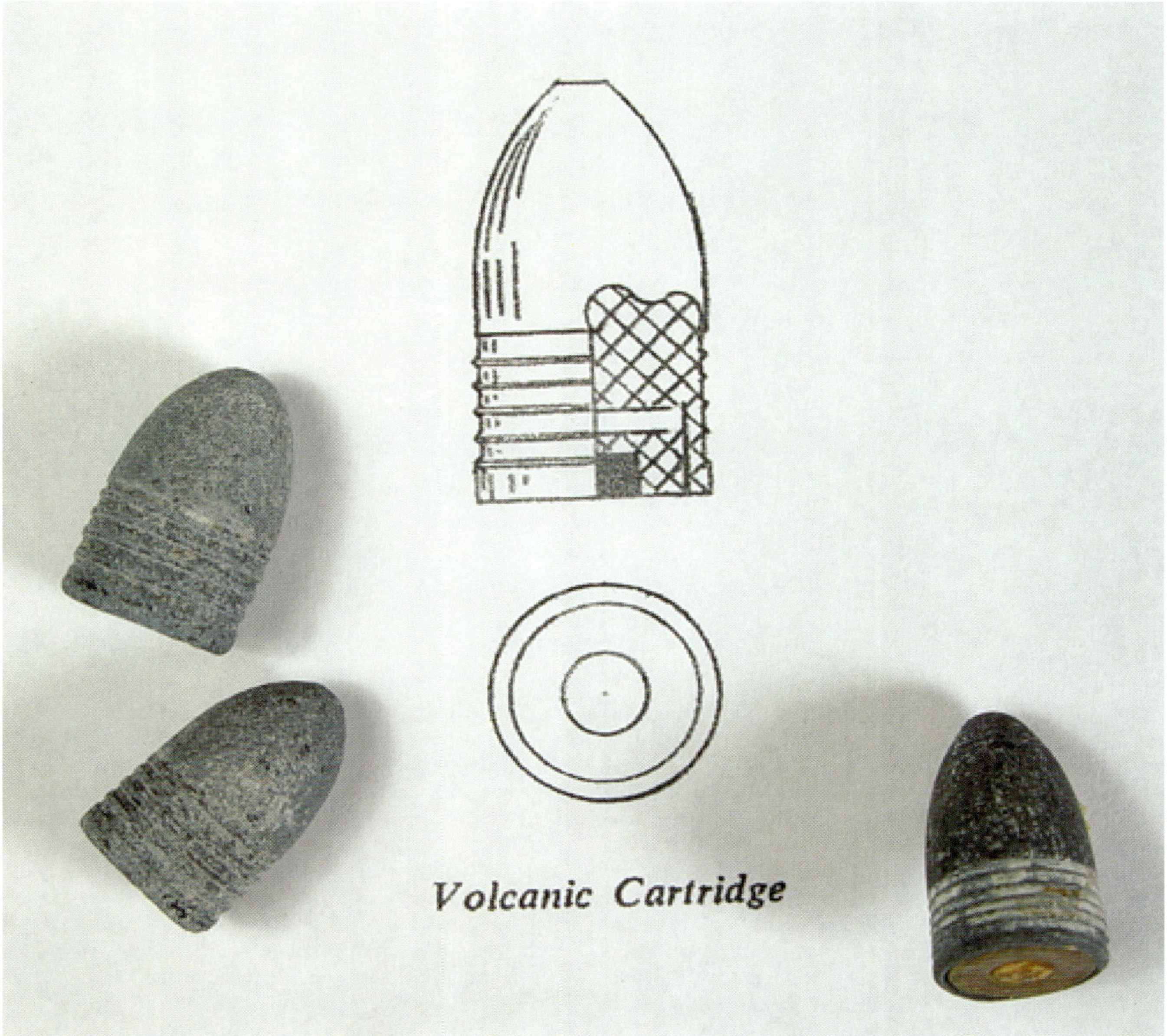

Courtesy of Ed Lewis, M.D.

3

The Henry Rifle and Model 1866
Caliber: 44 Henry (Rim Fire)

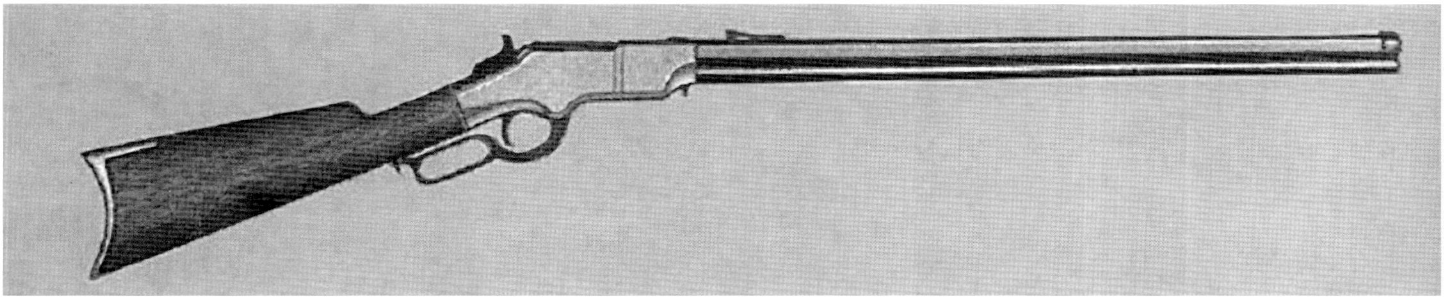

The Henry Rifle

By 1860 the 44 Rim Fire metallic cartridge had been developed and all that remained was to modify the Volcanic to handle it as a repeating rifle. The redesign of the bolt to include an extractor and a double-pointed firing pin were patented in October, 1860, and the Henry Rifle was born. Its origins in the Volcanic were instantly recognizable in its lever-operated toggle-link action and brass frame, but the new 44 Henry Rim Fire cartridge (henceforth simply the "44 Henry") set it apart.

And none too soon. By late 1860 the New Haven Arms Company was itself nearing insolvency, the result of having gone three years with a slow-selling, limited and ineffective product line while concentrating on the new cartridge and modified rifle. But 1861 is remembered for an event far more significant than anything B. Tyler Henry, Oliver F. Winchester or the New Haven Arms Company could have invented: the beginning of the Civil War in April of that year produced a cataclysm that changed the course of the United States forever and, with it, the arms business.

By October 1862, New Haven had put out 900 Henry rifles and was producing them at the rate of over 250 per month. Still, with the Spencer having won the Government contract, War Department sales were elusive and remained so throughout the War, totaling only 1731 rifles of the approximately 10,000 manufactured by the end of 1865. That low figure significantly understates the number of Henrys that saw service in that conflict, however, as a large number of guns were bought privately by Union soldiers as well as several state militias, who valued their 16-round cartridge capacity. Not surprisingly, the War Department willingly supplied them with ammunition.

By 1864 Winchester had determined that Henry's performance, given the terms of the New Haven Arms contract under which he was employed, was not being executed at a level sufficient to fulfill the conditions and demands required by the war-time economy. As a result, Winchester would not renew Henry's contract and their relationship abruptly deteriorated. According to the unpublished writings of an old-time employee, D. H. Veader, who joined Winchester in 1869, Henry left New Haven Arms in May 1864, though he was paid the remaining month of his five-year contract which expired June 11. During the summer of 1865, with Winchester on a business trip in Switzerland, Henry, who remained a stockholder, and the Company's secretary, C.W. Nott, used a power of attorney Winchester had left in his absence and engineered a choice bit of politico-corporate intrigue by changing the name from New Haven Arms Company to Henry Repeating Rifle Company. Less than a year later, through exertion of financial leverage, Winchester was able to re-incorporate under the now-famous name of the Winchester Repeating Arms Company thereby leaving Henry as a man without portfolio. Thus came to an end a relatively short but historically significant association between two key factors in the then-fledgling repeating arms industry. No guns or cartridge boxes are known to exist which bear the Henry Repeating Rifle Company name.

With the end of the War of Northern Aggression, Winchester began thinking ahead to the inevitable post-war consolidation about to take place in the arms industry. Although several important improvements were needed in the Henry rifle, Winchester also needed patent and design protection to preclude any claim Henry may have made

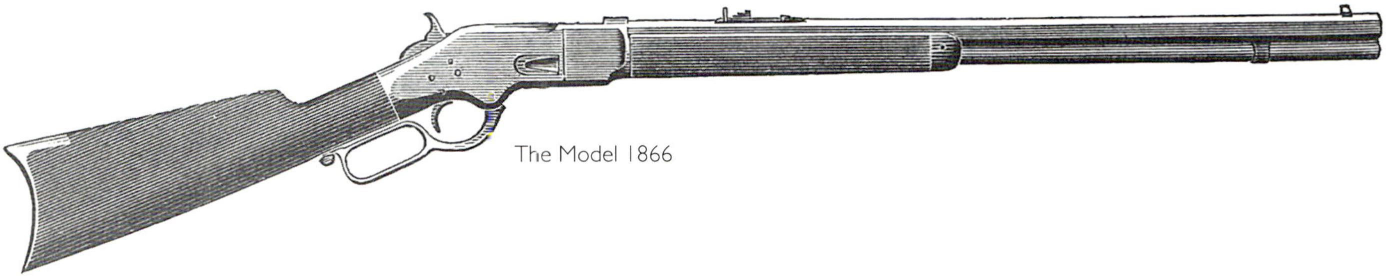
The Model 1866

with regard to any new products offered by the new company. So, by the end of 1866, with Henry already gone, the gun that bore his name also became a part of history.*

Model 1866

The year 1866 was one of great significance to Winchester. Elected Lieutenant Governor of Connecticut for the 1866-67 term, "Governor Winchester" as he was frequently called, filed for the incorporation of a new company, as mentioned earlier, to be named the Winchester Repeating Arms Company. Such charter was duly granted and operation of the new corporate entity commenced in May of that year utilizing the assets and employees of the Henry Rifle Co. as well as Winchester's personally owned Bridgeport facility. The Bridgeport factory had been opened in September of 1864, after Henry's departure, in an immediate effort to expand production. Also, with Winchester and Henry having parted ways, a new shop superintendent, Nelson King, was hired. As had been the case with Henry, King was called upon to aid in the design and engineering of improvements in the Company's firearms. Two of the main objections to the Henry rifle had been its fragile, slotted magazine and muzzle-end method of loading. Under patents acquired by both King and Winchester, systems were derived which vastly improved both features. Out of those developments would evolve the "Improved Henry Rifle". Originally referred to as simply the Winchester Repeating Rifle, this first Winchester would eventually become known as the Model of 1866.

While the brass frame of the Henry rifle was continued, a wooden fore-end was added and the now-famous profile of the Winchester Repeating Rifle was set to be emblazoned upon the psyche of a nation if not the world. It has been argued by many, in fact, that the M66, given the time period of its popularity, was the gun that truly "won the West". At the very least, it is certainly a worthy candidate.

Production of the M66 continued, albeit sporadically, through 1898 by which time approximately 170,000 had been shipped. Many of these were sent off-shore, 50,000 on military contract to Turkey alone. Also of note is the existence of a 44 Henry Center Fire chambering; approximately 1000 carbines in that caliber, found near the end of the M66 serial number range, were sent to Brazil in 1891. It was a different and much earlier .44 Winchester Center Fire, however, that eventually stole the spotlight from Winchester's landmark achievements of the 1860s: the "44-40" and the Winchester '73. But that's a chapter yet to come.

44 Henry R.F.

Catalog Listings: 1862[+]-1937

Models: Henry, 1866
Bullet types: Ld, Shot, Blank
Powder types: BP, Lsmk
Headstamps: Plain, Raised "H", Impressed "H"

New Haven, Connecticut, May 1, 1856. One hundred years before it would be shut down in that city, the ammunition-making facility of what would become the Winchester Repeating Arms Company was opened with a staff of five, foreman M. L. Babcock and four girls. In those early years, as we have already seen, the Volcanic Repeating Arms Company was the corporate entity then in operation. It would be absorbed by, and followed in turn by, the New Haven Arms Company (1857), the Henry Repeating Rifle Company (1865), and finally the Winchester Repeating Arms Company (1866), with Oliver F. Winchester remaining the financial and managerial guiding force through the turbulent first decade.

But as with the Henry rifle itself, it was B. Tyler Henry's improvements upon the original Smith and Wesson patent rights acquired out of the Volcanic insolvency that formed the basis for success in the ammunition department of New Haven Arms. Beginning in 1858 with Smith and Wesson's new 22 caliber copper-cased rimfire cartridge as a starting point, Henry abandoned the Volcanic "rocket ball" approach and experimented with an enlarged self-contained rimfire cartridge in

* Needless to say, anecdotes abound with regard to the exploits of men armed with Henry rifles. But, entertaining as they are, with so much writing already having been done on the Henry and its history as well as the many details regarding its collectibility, it is not within the purview of this work to recount them here. The reader is therefore referred to the many fine works contained in our bibliography.

[+]Price list card dated Oct. 15, 1862; the existence of earlier such cards is possible but not known to the authors.

44 caliber. By 1860 his work had come to fruition, culminating in a copper-cased, rimfire-primed cartridge containing 26 grains of black powder behind a 216 grain ("32 to the pound", as the ads stated) conical bullet. While the rifle had been redesigned to handle the new cartridge in 1860, it wasn't until 1862 that proper and expanded facilities for making both the gun and ammunition were in place. By then, however, both civilian and military markets had begun to open to them and prosperity reigned for the New Haven Arms Company through the end of the War Between the States.

While the year 1866 signaled the end of production for the Henry rifle, it was also the year in which Oliver Winchester ensured his name of a prominent place in history. Not only was the name of the Company now Winchester Repeating Arms Company, but the new Model 1866 rifle, as well as its boxes of ammunition, became "Winchester" products. Since both the Henry and Winchester rifles (as well as some later revolvers) were chambered for the 44 Henry, production of that cartridge continued unabated for 77 years beginning with its origin in 1860. It is here, then, that the earliest cartridge boxes of Winchester and its predecessor, New Haven Arms Co., are to be found.

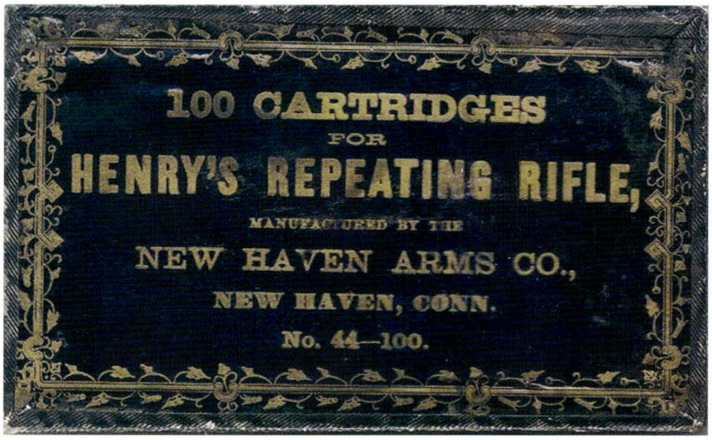

Often referred to as the "New Haven Black Box" this 100-round style is really a dark purple. While it is not known exactly when this box was introduced, it has always been the conventional wisdom that it ranks among the earliest examples, found as it is with the gilt printing and borders typical of cartridge boxes from the early 1860s. Also, it is assumed that the 100-round box would have soon been found to have been unwieldy, its size and weight prompting an early move to 50-round packaging.

The raised "H" headstamp rounds found in these boxes, however, may tempt some to question this box's position at the front of the Henry box time-line especially since unheadstamped rounds of the same case and bullet type are to be found in 50-round boxes covered below. There are at least three possible explanations for this; first, it may be that their early two-die headstamping process was not only expensive but painstakingly slow in a period when the ammunition department was trying to ramp up production in the face of escalating demand. This argument has the advantage of simplicity, a compelling factor in the test of any theory. Second, it is known that, as sales increased, New Haven bought empty cases from an outside vendor and it is quite possible that they were never headstamped, thereby eliminating a time-consuming and costly process in the production line. Another theory has it that the earliest headstamps left metal proud to the plane of the head to the extent that the cartridges, when placed on their base (head), were "wobbly". While probably not much cause for concern among shooters, one can imagine that handlers and packers in the factory might have considered it a real annoyance. Upon questioning several collectors of Henry cartridges, however, as well as through our own research, we have been unable to validate that theory. Whatever the explanation, the authors are comfortable with the conclusion that the "New Haven Black Box" does, indeed, represent the first cartridge box offering of New Haven Arms. R5/15,000-25,000

The raised "H" headstamp in a softly defined circular depression, pictured Left, is found on these "Pointed" rounds. The later raised "H" in a sharply defined circle, as found on the "Flats" (discussed further below), is pictured at Right.

Looking down upon an open 100-box shows two rows of ten cartridges each; this 20-round arrangement was then repeated in five layers. The cartridge at top left exhibits the crude crinkling just below the case mouth so often seen on these early examples. Bullets in these boxes are always of the Pointed type.

Careful examination of the inner border "leaf & vine" mot f (see also close-ups below) demonstrates the existence of at least two varieties of this box lid graphic. Until the time of this study, it had long been assumed that there was only one such variety. And as if this weren't enough, there's now (see next entry) a third "New Haven Black Box"! R5/15,000-25,000

Also a 100-box, this one has not personally been seen by the authors; however, this photo was passed along to us by a collector and researcher of the highest reputation. The lid appears to be of the same dimensions as that on a 50-round box, implying that the cartridges would have been standing up/down in two layers rather than flat in five layers as above. We welcome any first-hand information our readers may be able to contribute regarding this box. R5/17,500-27,500

Shown in the same order as the three preceding boxes, these left edge border graphics (presented here horizontally) show the left half of the first (top) two to be distinctly different. The bottom border is of exactly the same pattern as the middle one though slightly compressed as would be expected on this box of slightly narrower dimensions.

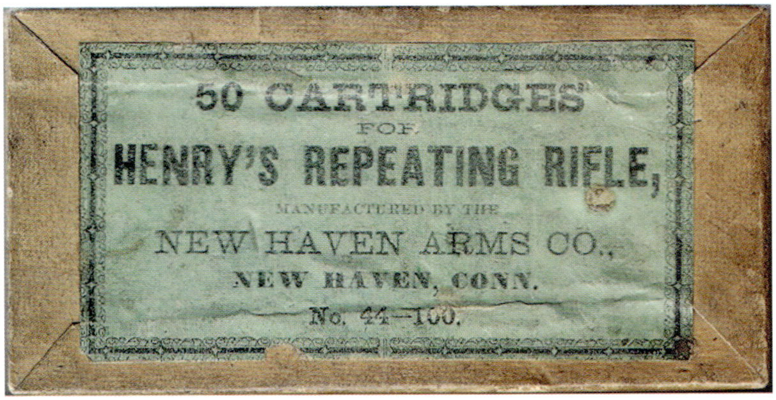

"Straight Border" labels such as this actually are to be found in three sizes, this being the Small Label variety. Cartridges found therein are generally unheadstamped and have pointed bullets though this observation should not be thought of as "etched in stone". Assumed to be circa 1862-63, there is no call-out of the bullet type. R4/9,000-13,000

A look inside of the typical "Straight Border" box containing unheadstamped cartridges with Pointed Bullets as found in the Small Label box above as well as the Standard Label box below. Unfortunately, there is no "hard" recorded evidence regarding the timing of changes in, or introductions of, headstamps or box and label styles.

Standard Label boxes such as this, like the other "Straight Border" boxes lacking a bullet type call-out, are most often found with Pointed Bullet, unheadstamped rounds. This labeling is also thought to be ca. 1862-63. R4-/8,000-12,000

Examples of 44 Henry "Pointed" and "Flat" cartridges by New Haven Arms.

The rare "44 Flat" label as seen on the left end of the "Straight Border" box lid below (at right).

While the top label is identical to the label above, the contents now consist of Flat Bullet cartridges with "raised H" headstamps in a dished circle. Believed to be circa late-1863 or early-1864, the call-out of "44 Flat" is on a separate label on the left end of the lid. By 1864 most, if not all, bullets were of the flat type. Also during this period the bullet weight was dropped to 200 grains from 212 grains. This, by the way, is the only such box known to the authors. R5/12,000-18,000

Henry boxes with this distinctive scroll border are often referred to as the "Military" style, apparently because of their similarity to later Frankford Arsenal graphics. While this and the next two boxes, all of which are "Flats" with a raised "H" headstamp in a dished circle, appear at first glance to be identical, closer examination reveals definite variations among them. This box finds "New Haven, Conn" and the "No." line below it to be of a different font from the two boxes following (see below for close-ups) and has been dubbed the "Tall 4s" box by the authors. Also note the break in the top of the scroll work on the left border not exhibited by either of the other boxes. R4/8,000-12,500

Like the boxes both above and below, this box of 44 Flats has no bullet type call-out. This variation differs from the next box only in the caliber line, most obviously in the numerals of the "44". We refer to this variant as the "Wide 4s" box and it is the one most often encountered. None of these "Military" boxes came with side labels. R3+/7000-11,000

This, the "Bold 4s" box, represents the third variation in the caliber line of these otherwise similar labels. Though we doubt that the "Tall 4s" box, with its more significant differences, would come between the other two, we have no reason to place these boxes in any particular chronological sequence. All, however, date from the 1863-65 period. R4-/7,500-12,000

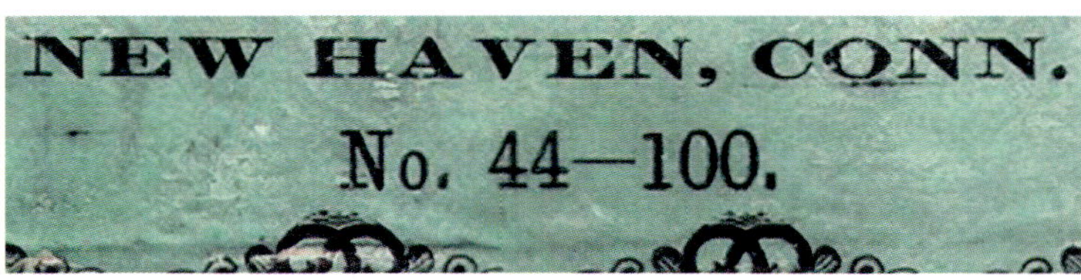

Left: The "Tall 4s" box with the "New Haven" line in a font different from that on the other two labels.

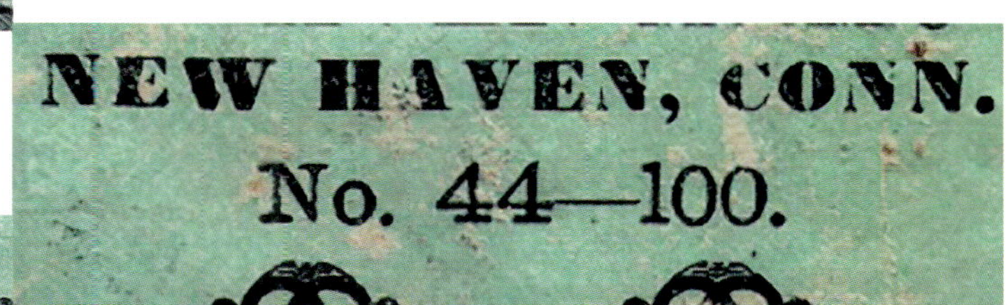

Right: A close-up of the "Wide 4s" on a "Military" box label. Note that the "New Haven" line differs from that on the "Tall 4s" box but is identical to the next, "Bold 4s", box.

Left: This "Bold 4s" label represents the other of the three variations found (so far!) on "Military" box labels. Besides the "4s", there are also discernible differences in the "N" and "1" in the caliber line.

Here is Variety 2 of the Compact Label box. Note that the "flat" bullet in the cartridge cut has now lost its rounded appearance. Further differences, however, are unique to this label and are illustrated below. That this label more fully covers the box lid is merely the result of trim outside the label borders. R5/7,500-12,500

Both Compact Label varieties are readily recognizable by the nearly imperceptible spacing between the "R" in "Winchester" and the "R" in "Repeating" (right) as compared to the Standard Label (left).

Unique to this Variety 2 Compact Label are the un-outlined numbers in the "44/100" call-out (left).

Close-ups of the cartridge cut of the Variety 2 Compact label (left) compared to Standard label (right). The cross-hatched pattern of the Variety 2 cut is also unique to that Compact Label box.

These close-ups show the relative spacing between the bullet and the text on the Compact Standard label varieties. The Compact Label is on the left.

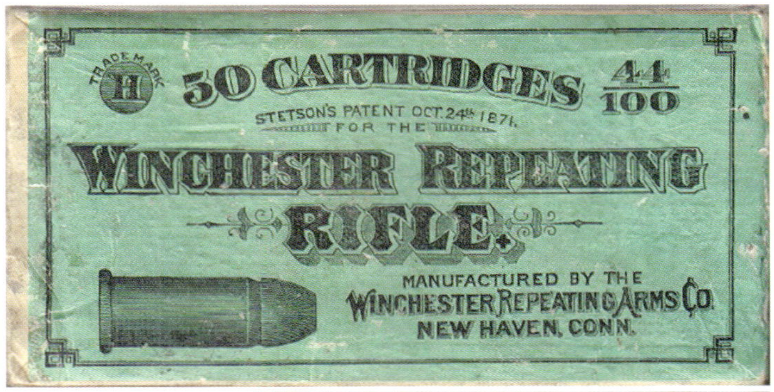

Another early Stetson's Patent box, on this variety the standard size top label wraps over the right end and is printed with the "44 Flat" call-out. While very similar to the New Haven "Straight Border" box seen earlier with a "44 Flat" call-out, this is the only Winchester box of which we are aware that exhibits either this over-end labeling or call-out. The rounds in this box also retain the "Raised H" headstamp noted in the preceding examples. At some point, probably in the late 1870s, the headstamps became impressed rather than raised. At about the same time, side-seal labels begin to be seen. R4+/7,500-12,500 [Without "44 FLAT" on end: R2+/2,500-5,000]

As mentioned above, the top label wraps over the end of the lid and calls out the "44 Flat" loading. The later boxes, with otherwise identical labels, do not exhibit this feature and from this point forward the bullet types can be discerned only from the cartridge cuts. Catalogs of the period also list a "44 Flat, W&C" (Winchester & Colt) with a lighter, 23 grain powder charge; however, no Winchester boxes are known to be so marked.

From the late 1870s, this "Pointed Ball" box shows a cartridge cut labeled as such. New Haven Arms boxes containing Pointed rounds, while rare, are found more often than Winchester "Pointed Ball" boxes. The rounds now have the impressed "H" headstamp and the box has a side-seal label. R4+/7,500-12,500

Note that the "Pointed Ball" cartridge cut has a small but distinct flat nose. Except for the very earliest New Haven rounds, this was typical of 44 Henry Pointed cartridges.

This box with the arched graphics at the top features the only Winchester labeling of 44 Henry Rim Fire known to the authors which boldly emphasizes the Model 1866. Also, ".44 Flat" is now called out on the cartridge cut and the Stetson's date has been corrected to "Oct. 31". With "Registered in U.S.A." under the trade mark, it is thought to date within the 1898-1905 period. R3/2,000-3,000

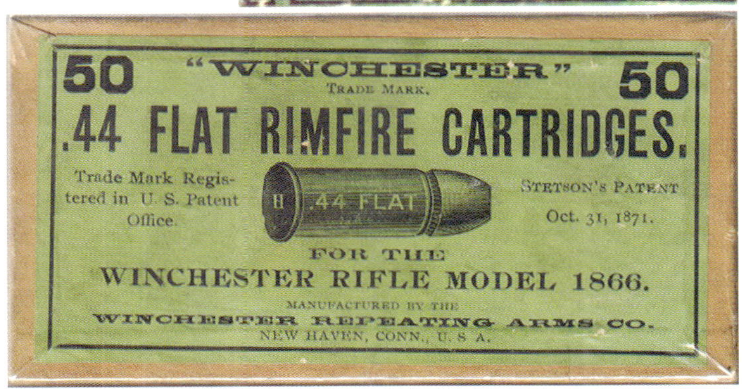

"44 FLAT" is, for the first time, part of the cartridge title. It would remain so through the end of its run as a catalog item. With the Winchester logo in block letters as well as quotation marks and with the trade mark line expanded to "...U.S. Patent Office", this labeling is readily dated within the 1906-11 period. Boxes very similar to this also exist in the 1911-13 labeling which has the Winchester logo in quotes but italicized. R3-/1,750-2,750

The same label as on the previous box is here found with an add-on label denoting its loading with the then-new Lesmok powder, ca. 1911. Winchester records show only one such loading! R3+/2,000-2,750

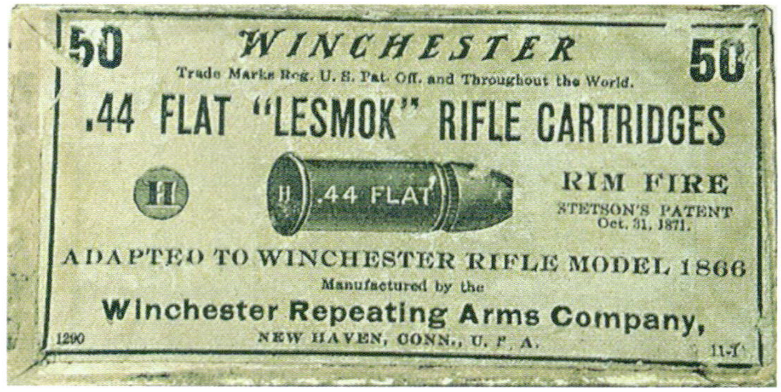

In the labeling of the 1912-19 period, with quotes removed from the Winchester logo and the extended trade mark line now appearing under it, this rare Lesmok box is dated 11-14 and is no doubt a re-box or over-labeling of the Company's one-time loading of these rare Lesmok cartridges. R4/2500-3500

Circa early-1920s, these two-piece boxes were of the full-cover type. This version, pre-K-code, still calls out the Model 1866 and "44 Flat" on the cartridge cut. R2+/1,400-2,200

The last of the Winchester boxes, this full-cover two-piece box exhibits a K-code but omits any mention of the Model 1866. Ca. mid/late-1920s to mid/late-'30s. R2+/1250-2,000

A 44 Henry Shot Box

As with the earliest Lesmok box above, this offering of 44 "Rimfire Shot Cartridges" shows a small white sticker printed in red on a primary label of the 1906-11 period. Boxes of 44 Henry Shot (as well as Blanks) are scarce but not rare. Both are more often found as loaded by UMC. R3+/1500-2500

A theory...

In the late 1860s roughly 1.5 million rounds of surplus Civil War era 44 Henry cartridges were repurchased by Winchester from the Government. By the look of the two cartridges in the comparative photo below one might reasonably conclude that war-time New Haven unheadstamped Pointed bullets have been cut off to make Flat bullets. It is our opinion that these were indeed so cut by the factory and marketed as "44 Flat" in pre-Stetson label boxes, of which, by the way, there are two known minor varieties. While three labels are revealed at the lower right box corner (see close-up), the top two appear to be the same given the graphics and positioning of the labels. The third and bottom-most label, however, bears no resemblance to any Henry box we have seen and we won't even speculate here as to its origins.* R5/10,000-15,000

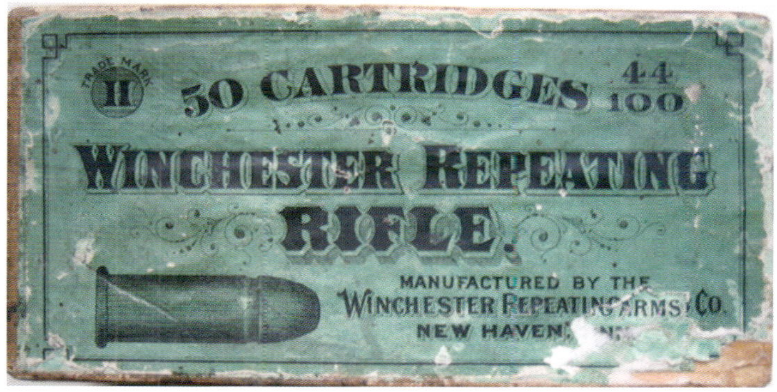

*The authors wish to thank Phil Bailey of Auckland, New Zealand, for his special contributions to this chapter.

And an Enigma...

Sometime in the early/mid-1860s, probably 1863-65, this gold-on-black box appeared. As there is no callout of the manufacturer, it is often referred to as the "Generic Black Box". Of the three that the authors have examined, one was empty and two were found with New Haven Arms 44 Pointed cartridges with raised "H" headstamps. The temptation, to which we ourselves in earlier years had succumbed, is to attribute the box to New Haven Arms. Several points argue against that conclusion, however. First, Oliver Winchester seldom, if ever, passed up the opportunity to put his (or his company's) name on products. Second, the loose-pack box style (as opposed to the usual "heads & tails" cartridge arrangement) was unlike any other New Haven or Winchester 44 Henry box. Third, the box construction itself differs from New Haven / Winchester. Fourth, side-seal labels were not used on Winchester boxes until the 1870s. And, last, the callout "No. 44" was never used on Henry labels by either New Haven or Winchester (see foregoing examples in this section).

The fact that "H" headstamped were found in two of these boxes is irrelevant. There is no way of knowing whether they were original to the box or just replacements by later owners who assumed (or wished) them to be of New Haven or Winchester production. Complicating the picture is the fact that it is known that New Haven contracted for outside production of 44 Henry cartridges. So it's possible that the rounds that have been found in those boxes known to us were, indeed, native to the box; but, it is just as possible that they came from an outside contractor.

Crittenden & Tibbals, interestingly, had the manufacturing wherewithal to produce the larger Rimfire calibers during the 1863-65 period. They are also known to have advertised (and presumably sold) the 44 Henry cartridge during that same period. And yet not a single 44 Henry box or label by C&T has ever been found with their name on it. Hmmm... R4+/9,000-13,000.

4

Models 1873, 1892, 53, 65, 43
Calibers*: 218 Bee, .22 Hornet, 22 RF, 22 W.C.F.**, 25-20 W.C.F., 32-20, 38-40, 44-40

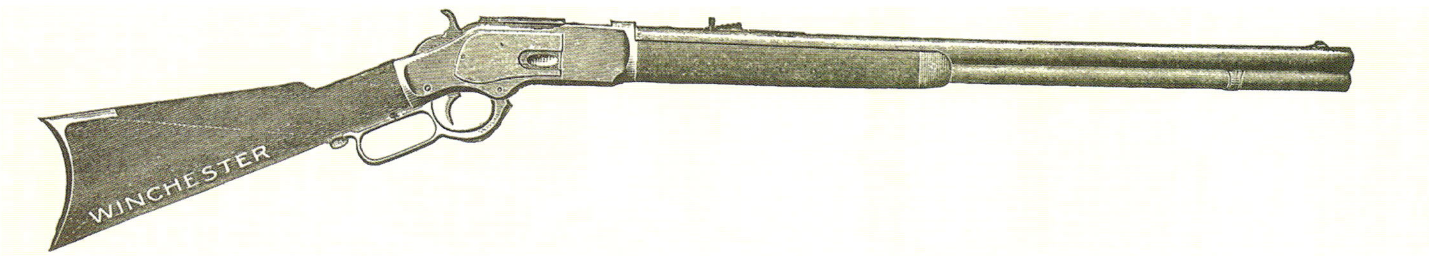

Model 1873
(22 RF, 22 W.C.F., 32-20, 38-40, 44-40)
Realistically speaking, there was no single "Gun that Won the West". The competitors for that glamorous title were both numerous and worthy: Colt's revolvers, the Henry rifle, Winchester's Model 66, Sharps, Springfield, and many more. But in the minds of those judging from afar, over 100 years later in Twentieth Century America, the winner clearly would have been the Winchester '73. True, a couple of movies by that name had popularized the cause by then, but the more than 720,000 guns that left the factory during the 50 years beginning in late 1873 tell a story of their own. The gun was obsolete by the early 1890s, yet over 300,000 were yet to be sold, both at home and abroad, by the time production ceased in 1923.

The New Model of 1873, as it was called at its introduction, was a continued refinement of the toggle-link system of its predecessors. In a major departure from its antecedents, however, the M73 used iron in place of brass in the frame, greatly adding strength while slightly reducing weight. Most important, however, was the new chambering in 44 W.C.F., destined to become famous as the "44-40", Winchester's first proprietary Center Fire offering. While a few guns were made and shipped in 1873, manufacturing problems with the gun itself and even greater problems with the ammunition held up production. The catalog of 1875, then, became the first to showcase the new Winchester M1873.

It has been often stated, if not generally conceded, that the Winchester 73 "44-40", put more meat on the table of more families than any other rifle. Well, maybe any rifle of its time anyway. Who are we, after all, to take issue with a legend?

Model 1892
(25-20 W.C.F., 32-20, 38-40, 44-40)
The excellent design of the Company's eminently successful M1886, which had rendered the M1876 almost instantly obsolete, was downscaled to handle the short M1873 calibers in the hopes that it, too, would obsolete the older model. While, as we have already pointed out, the M73 continued to find a market, the new and lighter M92 sold

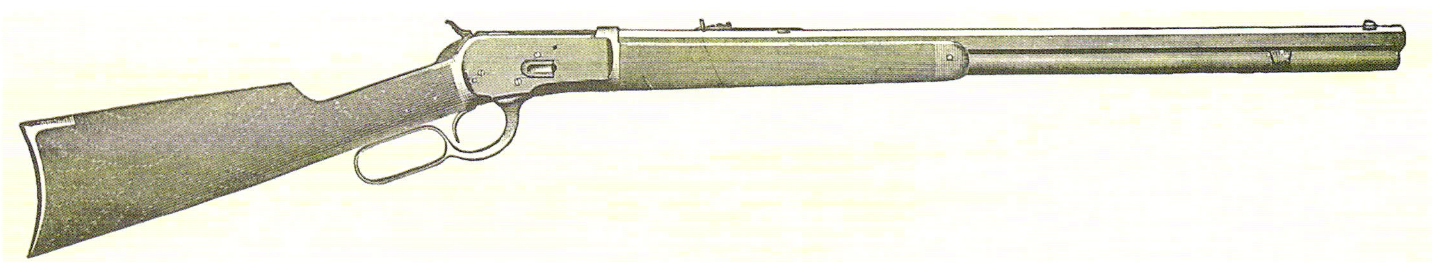

*For coverage of .22 Hornet, please see Chapter 14. For coverage of 22 RF, please see Chapter 7.

**It should be noted that the November 1885 catalog listed the 22 W.C.F. as being available in the M73. However, none have been found and factory records show none as having been produced.

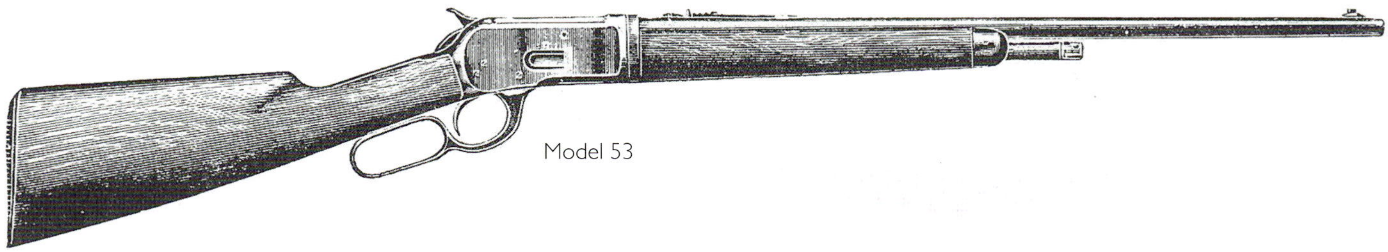

Model 53

extremely well, finally ending its run in 1941 with over 1,000,000 having been sold. It should be noted that some M92s are found in 218 Bee, a caliber for which this model was, however, not cataloged.

Model 53
(25-20 W.C.F., 32-20, 44-40)
With a semi-beavertail fore-end, shotgun butt, and a ramp front sight on a 22-inch barrel, the M53 was intended to be a modernized replacement for the M92 rifle. Introduced in 1924, it met with but moderate success over its eight-year production life. Including guns assembled from parts, sales continued in small numbers past 1940. While some 218 Bee M53s are to be found, they, like the M92 in this same calber, were not a catalog item. A total of less than 25,000 of this model were made including some which were numbered in the M92 range.

Model 65
(218 Bee, 25-20 W.C.F., 32-20)
A further refinement of the M92 and M53, the M65 was first offered in 1933 and is the rarest of all Winchester lever action rifles. With a bolt-mounted peep sight, beavertail fore-end, and pistol grip stock it was, in their new (1939) 218 Bee caliber, as modern a lever-action gun as Winchester was capable of producing. Yet, over its eight-year production period (the same as the M53), only 5717 of these were turned out, including parts guns assembled after 1941. All were numbered in the M92 range.

Model 43
(218 Bee, 22 Hornet*, 25-20 W.C.F., 32-20)
The 1949 introduction of the M43 represented Winchester's last attempt to prolong the life of its smaller proprietary calibers as well to take advantage of the popularity of the non-proprietary 22 Hornet in an affordable bolt action rifle. Often referred to, at least in print, as the "poor man's Model 70", the M43 was nothing of the kind: the M70 was a long-action, high caliber big game and target rifle that only coincidentally happened to chamber the 22 Hornet, the only caliber they had in common (or even CLOSE to being in common). The M43 was a short-action rifle of mid-range quality with attractive lines, to be sure, but it was strictly a small caliber varmint and small game rifle. Perhaps a "boy's M70" if such a comparison must be made.

*As the .22 Hornet was chambered in the Winchester M54 and M70 long before being offered in the M43, please refer to Chapter 14 for coverage of this caliber.

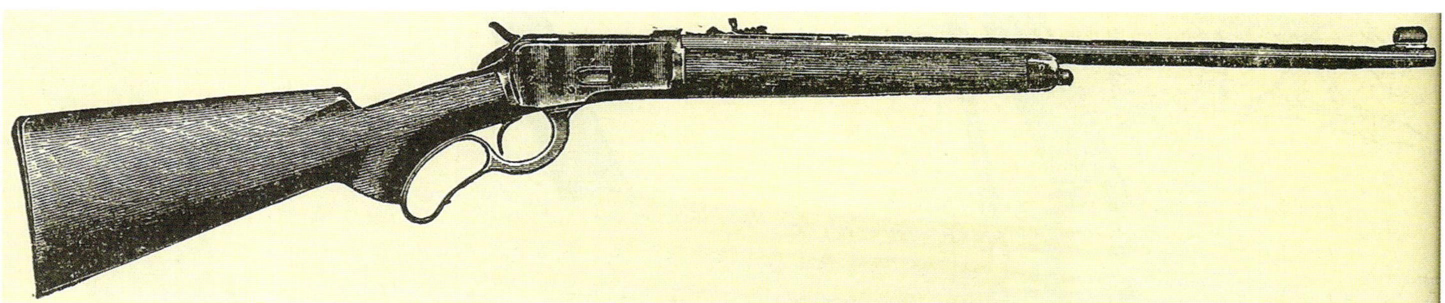

Model 65

Model 43

The production of 25-20 W.C.F. and 32 W.C.F. rifles was discontinued in 1951; however, parts guns in those calibers again appeared in 1955-56. By 1957 the gun had been discontinued and the "eight-year hex", which had also attended the brief lives of the M53 and M65, wrote the final chapter on three of Winchester's classic small-bore cartridges.

218 Bee
Catalog Listings: 1939-

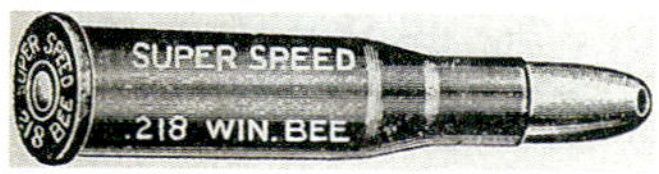

Models: 65, 43
Bullet types: SP, MCHP, FMJ
Powder types: Smkls
Headstamps: SS

In an effort to "juice up" their state-of-the-art M65, which had been saddled with the old 25-20 W.C.F. and 32-20 calibers and hadn't sold very well, Winchester necked down the old casing of those calibers even further and inserted their successful 22 Hornet bullet to form the 218 Bee. The result was a ballistically attractive little varmint cartridge that the trade felt needed a scoped bolt action rifle to handle properly. That would come later in the M43, but, as we have seen, the Bee wasn't enough to save the M65.

The fact that the 218 Bee was first loaded in 1936, three years before being cataloged, is of interest. The reason was that, like the 219 Zipper and 348 W.C.F., the 218 Bee's development fell into a time-frame when Winchester was struggling with the compatibility of their Staynless priming and Smokeless powders of the period, especially in the higher velocity ranges. By the late 1930s the chemistry problems had been solved and the Bee took flight.

The 218 Bee, in spite of its fairly recent appearance on the scene, has produced several interesting and scarce to rare boxes. The 45 grain Soft Point loading was produced in 1939-40 only and is very hard to come across. And, though uncataloged, factory records show one lot of a 46 grain Full Patch loading in 1949 as well as one lot of 50 grain Pointed Soft Points in 1951. While the authors have yet to encounter only the latter, both should be considered rare.

The earliest Bee box is this "1935" style with its call-out for the M65 rifle and the "Winchester Repeating Arms Co." line across the bottom. These graphics exhibit little or no change throughout the 1936-38 period of their issuance. Bear in mind, however, that this caliber was not cataloged until 1939, making this "1935" style box quite scarce. R3/125-225

The patent number refers to the July 30, 1935 patent granted Winchester chemist J.D. McNutt. This is the third of his four patents regarding the Company's new Staynless priming mixture and the one most commonly found on boxes in the mid- to late-1930s.

In the "1939" style box we find no changes except those that typically distinguish it from its predecessor; that is, the absence of the "Winchester..." call-out on top and the addition of the "Western..." call-out on the side. R2-/65-125

With the W-code now having replaced the K-code and the M43 having replaced the M65 call-out, this early-1950s box represents the last of the "1946" style. The authors are not aware of this caliber in a "1954" box. R1/30-60

In April 1949, one run of a Full Patch loading was produced. The earlier version had a white wrap-around label with the Full Patch call-out and K-code. As can be seen here and in the picture below, this add-on label encircled all sides of the box. R3+/125-225

A call-out for the Model 65 remains on this "1946" style box at a time, only eight years after its introduction, when no guns were being produced chambered for this round. The add-on label shows a "C" suffix (denoting rifle calibers) and was switched from a "T" suffix in 1948.

The later version of the rare Full Patch box, ca. late-1949 or early-1950, shows black-outs and a re-printing of the appropriate bullet, bullet weight and K-code on the ends and one side of the box. The M65 call-out, however, remains in spite of the 1949 introduction of the M43 which chambered this cartridge. R3+/125-225

25 W.C.F., 25-20 W.C.F., 25-20 Winchester

Catalog Listings: 1895-

Models: 1885, 1892, 53, 65, 43

Bullet types: Ld, SP, MCHP, FMJ

Powder types: BP, Smkls, Lsmk

Headstamps: WRACo, WRA, SS

The Company was busy experimenting with necking down several Black Powder calibers during the mid-1890s, the early years of Smokeless Powder, and the 25-20 W.C.F. was one of their earliest successes. Based on the necked-down 32 W.C.F. (32-20) case, this was the only caliber created by Winchester especially for the M92. The same combination of bullet and powder charge was available in the 25-20 Winchester Single Shot cartridge (which actually used 19 grains of powder, 2 more than the 25-20 W.C.F.) but the action of the M92 was too short to handle it.

The earliest box showed a cartridge cut with a "25 W.C.F." headstamp, leading to the belief that such a round actually exists; however, none are known to the authors. Interestingly, a couple of the rarest offerings in this caliber are products of the 1940s: the 86 grain Pointed Soft Point loading of 1940 and the Lead Smokeless loading of 1947. Factory records show one lot of each having been produced. The early Winchester High Velocity (W.H.V.) boxes, especially in FMJ, are, as always, very scarce and collectible. Later "W.H.V." loadings in a 60 grain jacketed Hollow Point, while still very collectible, are fairly common.

Black Powder Boxes

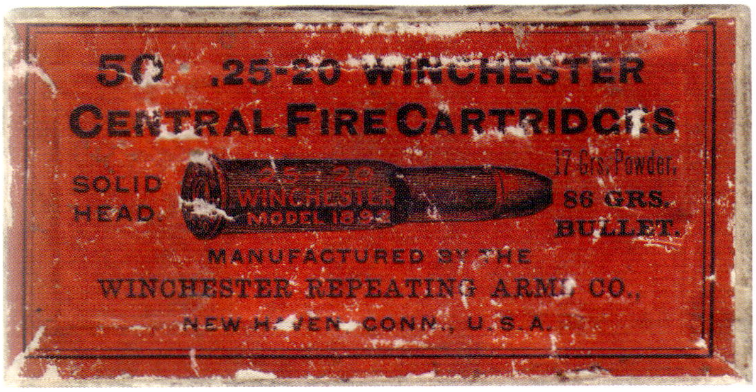

This red Black Powder, Lead labeling is representative of the earliest 25-20 boxes, ca 1890s. They are all very scarce. R4-/200-400

This undated box, ca. 1903-05, set the pattern for Black Powder boxes from that period through 1920. With the changes in logo and trade mark call-outs that were typical of the period, the graphics changed but little during those years. For details highlighting those changes, the reader is referred to the Smokeless section of this discussion below. R3/150-250

Left: The orange side-seal specifically calling out the "25-20 Winchester Repeating Rifle, Model 1892" (from box at upper left) is unusual among Winchester side labels.

The 10-6 dated label with "Winchester" in quotes and an expansion of the trade mark line. Those changes and the addition of the "red W" logo on the side-seal represent the only changes from the prior box. R3/150-250

A K-coded full-cover two-piece box of the mid-1920s. The blacked-out label remains a mystery. Has anybody out there got a box like this without the black-out? If so, please let us know. R3/125-225

A Lesmok Box

Introduced in the 1911 catalog, Lesmok offerings in this caliber are very difficult to find. This one has a label date of 4-11 and, except for the "Lesmok" call-outs on the top and sides, is typical of other boxes of the 1911-13 period. R3+/250-450

Smokeless Boxes

As with the Black Powder boxes in this caliber we have no examples prior to 1900 to show the reader, a fact which attests to the scarcity of early boxes in both loadings. This undated box is ca. 1903-05. Interestingly, the headstamp on the cartridge cut is "25 W.C.F.", a headstamp that was, to our knowledge, never actually used on cartridges. Also this Lead bullet loading has no label call-out for bullet type. R3/150-300

As we have seen previously, this 1906-1910 style box (dated 1-7) displays "Winchester" in quotes and a revised trade mark line. Otherwise it very closely resembles the earlier labeling, including the lack of a Lead bullet call-out. R3/150-300

A 7-8 dated label, the graphics have changed to include "Model 1892" in the title line. The Lead bullet call-out has now been added as well, but the headstamp on the cartridge cut remains "25 W.C.F." R3/150-300

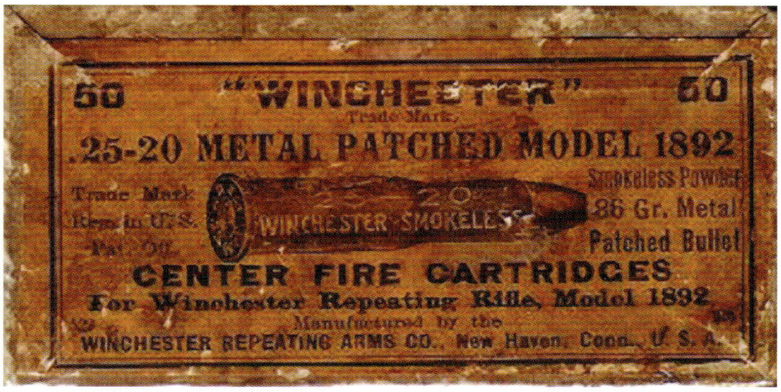

Though not in the greatest of shape, the orange label Metal Patched (FMJ) label is nonetheless worth showing as it exhibits graphics all its own. It's dated 9-9, but the headstamp on the cartridge cut is still "25 W.C.F." R3/150-300

The italicized 1911-13 style logo along with the expanded trade mark line, are found on this 6-11 Soft Point box. Other changes are relatively insignificant, however the headstamp on the cartridge cut has finally become "25-20 W.C.F." R3+/200-350

Then comes an 8-11 label which not only adds the "June 28, 1910" patent callout underneath the cartridge cut but changes the "Manufactured by Winchester Repeating Arms Co" lines from all capital letters to upper and lower case. Likewise, the "New Haven" line has gone to all caps from upper and lower case. Other type size and font changes are apparent as well. Why two months had such an effect upon the boys in the design room will remain forever a mystery! R3/150-300

On the other hand, this 1913-20 style label, which drops quotation marks and repositions the trade mark line under the logo, shows "Smokeless Soft Point" on the title line for the first (and only) time in this caliber. This box is dated 5-14. R3-/150-275

The full-cover two-piece box with its wrap-over 7-20 dated label (as are all), was in the line from 1920 until the new Staynless offering in one-piece boxes, ca. 1928. This one is pre-K-code, ca. 1920-22. R2+/125-200

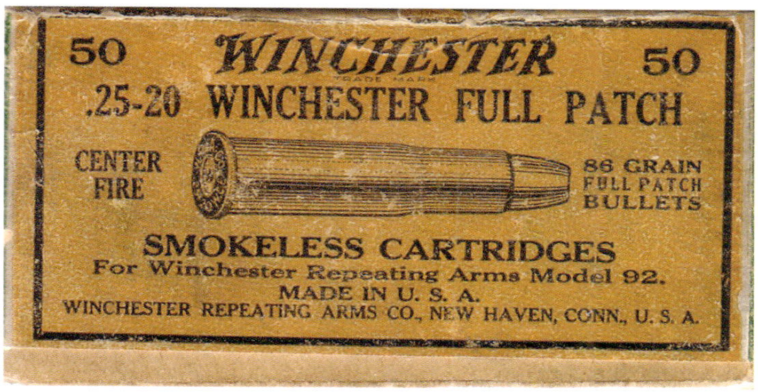

Here is an example of the same two-piece, full-cover box in "Full Patch" with an orange label denoting that loading. It also is K-coded, ca. 1923-28. R3-/150-275

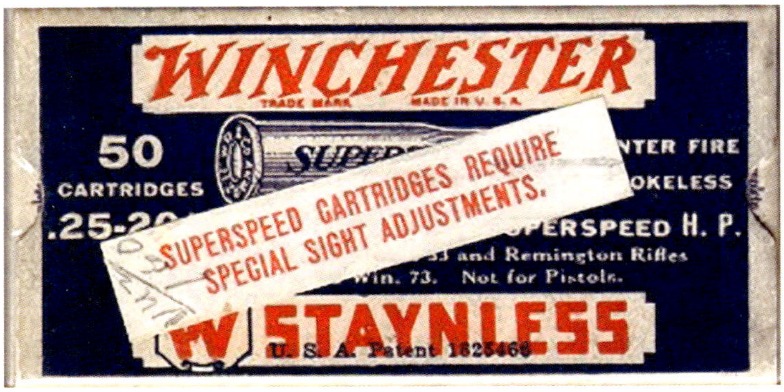

Super Speed loadings with their lightweight JHP bullets frequently have add-on "Sight Adjustment" labels like the one shown here. While called the "1928" box, the patent number over-printed on Staynless is from 1931. R3/125-225

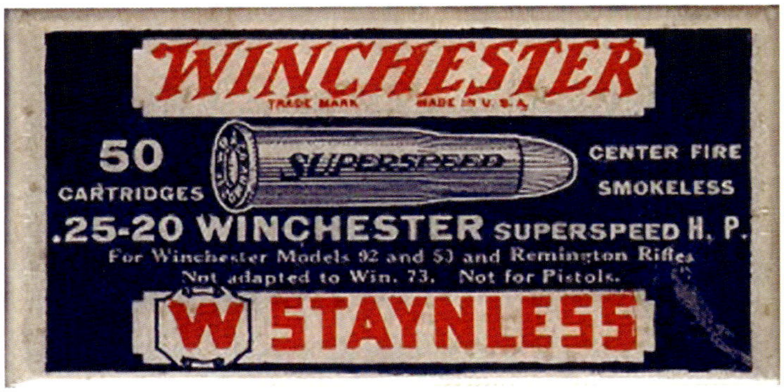

This picture is from the bottom of the above box and is shown simply to give the reader a better idea of the graphics without the Sight Adjustment sticker. Note that the patent information is on the top only.

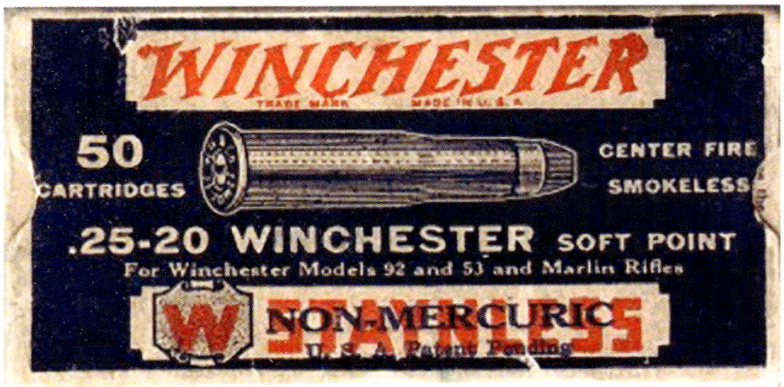

When the Company's Non-Mercuric priming compound was introduced in late 1931, over-stamped boxes like this provided the transition from the "1928" box to the "1932" box. This is the Soft Point loading. No reason is known for the difference between the shaded and unshaded shield graphic that surrounds the red "W". R2/75-150

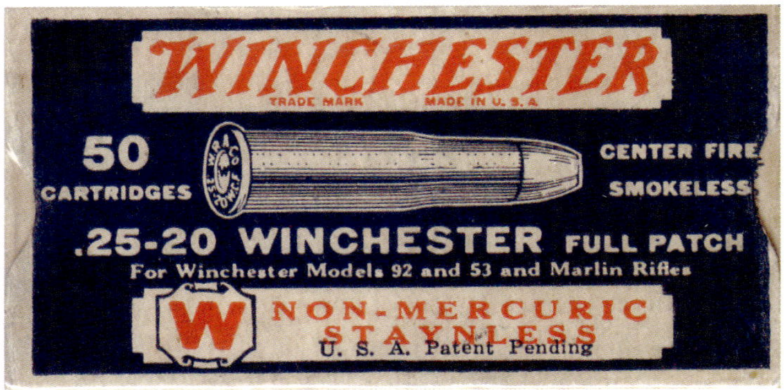

Full Patch is always a scarcer loading than either Lead or Soft Point. Except for the bullet type call-out and the type and color of the bullet in the cartridge cut, these "1932" boxes show a high degree of standardization. R3-/125-200

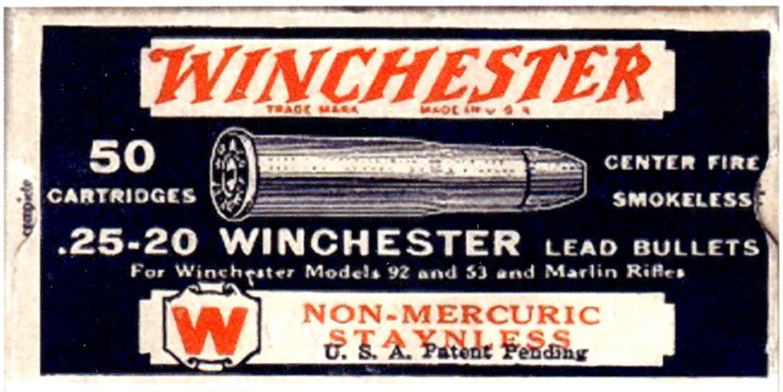

The Lead bullet version of the "1932" box. Note that the bullet in the cartridge cut is darker so as to better portray a lead bullet rather than the FMJ bullet on the previous box. R2/75-150

The Lead loading in this "1945" box lacks the model call-out line that can be seen on the Soft Point box below. Other than a couple of minor differences in type face and size, the only differences are the color and appearance of the bullet in the cartridge cut and the bullet type call-out. Of more significance is the absence of both a "1935" box and a "1939" box in these standard loadings, the "1932" box having been utilized until the debut of the "1945" box. R3/100-175

This Soft Point "1945" box, as mentioned above, has the model call-out: "For Winchester Models 92 and 53 and Marlin Rifles." R3-/85-150

The Olin Industries call-out which distinguishes the "1945" box from the "1939" box.

The "Unfinished Symphony" of cartridge boxes: the bottom of the "1946" boxes generally exhibit the same caliber callout as the top of the box, the graphics being essentially the same on both sides. In the case of this 25-20 Soft Point box, however, the title line is missing! R?/100-150

This is what the bottom of the "1946" box normally looks like although this box contains the Full Patch loading, an offering seldom seen in this style box. While these boxes used "K-codes" into the early 1950s, the suffix was changed from "T" to "C" in 1948. R2/50-80

High Velocity (WHV) Boxes - Soft Point

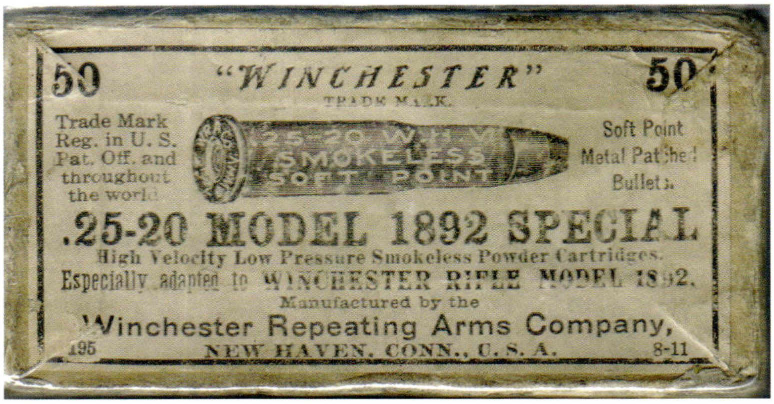

While not the earliest label (see "Metal Patched" below), this somewhat cluttered label showing the cartridge cut near the top is similar to all 25-20 WHV labels from 1905 to ca. 1913. However, with the slight "pinkish" tinge expected on W.H.V. Full Patch labels, this 8-11 Soft Point box initially makes one wonder if there was an error in the print shop. Then we find the following 1-15 box. R3+/250-450

With the title line now above the cartridge, this 1913-1920 style displays a significant difference from the earlier styles. Of greater interest, though, is the fact that this label is more obviously pink than the preceding box and makes it clear that significant label color anomalies do indeed exist during this period. The presence of a similar "pinkish" label on a 1915-dated 32-20 W.H.V. Soft Point box (see 32-20 section below) further exemplifies this fact. R3+/250-450

A half-split two-piece box with a top label dated 11-22 is surprising in itself. But with a 2-23 dated side-seal without a K-code this box is an anachronism. A box this late would be expected to be full-cover and have a K-code. Only the trade mark line under the logo is typical of post-1920 labeling. At least the label color has returned to "normal" yellow! R3+/225-425

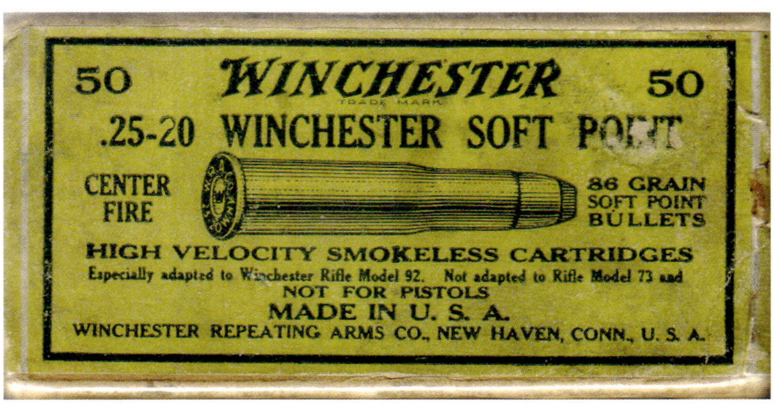

Here is the box that one would expect to find from the early 1920s: full-cover two-piece construction with a 7-20, K-coded wrap-over label. R3/150-250

As opposed to the 60 grain JHP Super Speed offering covered earlier, this is a true W.H.V. loading. The full weight 80 grain Soft Point and W.H.V. headstamp as well as the title line attest to this fact. Note also the call-out for "Winchester Models 92, 53 and 65 Rifles" and the warning against use in M73s and pistols. Pistols? Who made 25-20 pistols? R3-/100-200

The last of the K-coded 25-20 "W.H.V." boxes, this "1946" box of 60 grain JHP rounds, in spite of their "WHV" headstamps, is not really a W.H.V. loading. It is shown here because it has been so-titled by the Company. R2+/40-80

High Velocity (WHV) Boxes - Full Patch

Undated, this lavender label would be expected to represent the earliest Full Patch box in this rare loading introduced in 1905. However, the logo in block letters and quotes is in the 1906-1910 style (which is normally dated) and, incredibly, it has a 4-18 side label! This was obviously not a fast selling item and its rarity should not be a surprise. R4-/250-500

Like the previous box, this one uses a 4-18 side label. The top label, however, is 8-11 dated and the box is of the full-cover construction typically found in the 1920s. Catalogs show this loading as having been listed through 1937. It is hard to imagine this labeling being used until that date, especially after the introduction of Staynless/Non-Mercuric priming, but no later such boxes are known to the authors. R3+/200-400

A Rare "Definitive Proof" Box

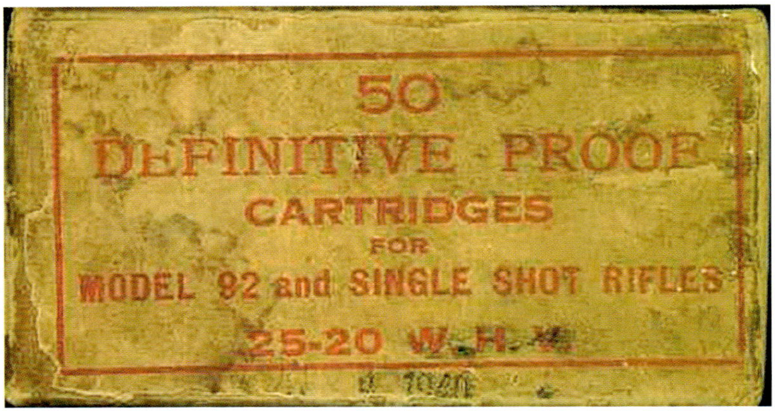

Before leaving the factory, all Center Fire rifles would be "proofed" by firing at least one test shot with this type of cartridge. Rarely encountered by the collector, especially in their original box, these cartridges were loaded 30+% above standard chamber pressures and were made for in-house use only. Date-stamped by hand "1940", the label date is 3-19! R4/200-400

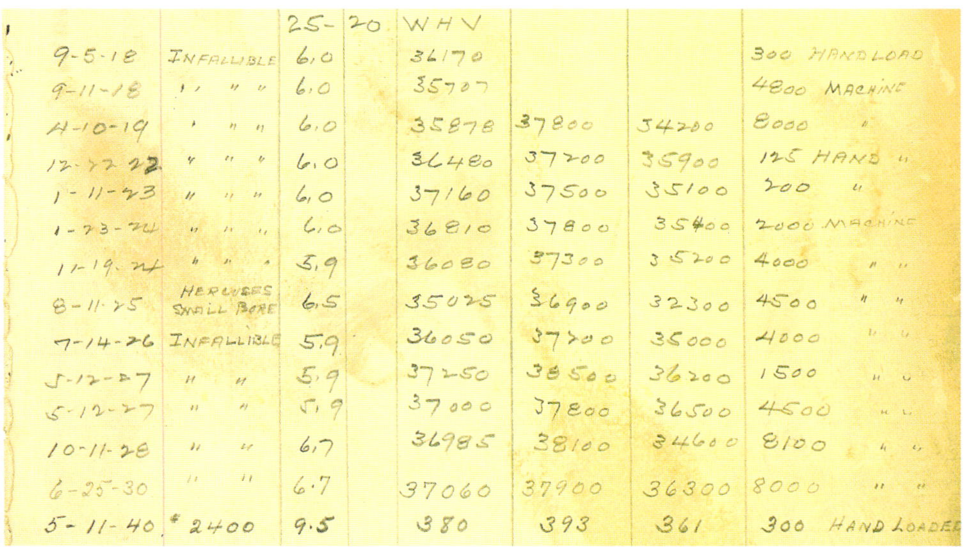

		25-	20	WHV			
9-5-18	INFALLIBLE	6.0		36170			300 HANDLOAD
9-11-18	" " "	6.0		35707			4800 MACHINE
4-10-19	" " "	6.0		35878	37800	34200	8000 "
12-22-22	" " "	6.0		36480	37200	35900	125 HAND "
1-11-23	" " "	6.0		37160	37500	35100	200 "
1-23-24	" " "	6.0		36810	37800	35400	2000 MACHINE
11-19-24	" " "	5.9		36080	37300	35200	4000 " "
8-11-25	HERCULES SMALL BORE	6.5		35025	36900	32300	4500 " "
7-14-26	INFALLIBLE	5.9		36050	37200	35000	4000 " "
5-12-27	" "	5.9		37250	38500	36200	1500 " "
5-12-27	" "	5.9		37000	37800	36500	4500 " "
10-11-28	" "	6.7		36985	38100	34600	8100 " "
6-25-30	" "	6.7		37060	37900	36300	8000 " "
5-11-40	#2400	9.5		380	393	361	300 HAND LOADED

The Ballistics Lab kept ledger books for all Proof Cartridge loadings. The last entry relates to the box seen above. Proof cartridges invariably used tinned cartridge cases for easy identification.

32 W.C.F., 32 Winchester, 32-20, 32-20 Winchester
Catalog Listings: 1882-

Models: 1873, 1885, 1892, 53, 65, 43
Bullet types: Ld, Ld HP, SP, MCHP, WRA, FMJ, Shot, Blank
Powder types: BP, Smkls, Lsmk
Headstamps: Plain, WRACo, SS

Developed by Winchester as a small-game load, for which it was not badly suited, the 20th Century sporting press eventually bad-mouthed it into virtual oblivion. Its recent resurrection with Cowboy Action shooters has been almost as miraculous as the earlier Resurrection.

The original M73 Black Powder loading used a 115 grain Lead bullet. In 1929 the standard weight of the Lead bullet Black Powder rounds was reduced to 100 grains although the jacketed bullet remained 115 grains until after WWII when it, too, went to 100 grains. Scarce and desirable Black Powder loadings include Lead Hollow Points as well as any jacketed-bullet offering. Lesmok-marked boxes are also very scarce.

Among Smokeless listings which, for purposes of discussion here, are considered to be M92 loadings, the Winchester High Velocity (WHV) boxes are most desirable, especially the rare FMJ lavender boxes. These WHV loadings actually had "M-92" in their headstamps as well as on the box labels so as to preclude their use in M73s or pistols. The Super Speed 80 grain Metal Cased Hollow Point was introduced in 1925 and was loaded sporadically until 1968. The post-War cartridges no longer call out the M92 on the headstamp; however, the boxes retain their warnings against use in M73s and revolvers. The earlier W.H.V. boxes, through the "1946" style, are quite collectible and not yet terribly expensive. In dating the "1946" boxes it should be noted that the K-code suffix was switched from a "T" suffix (denoting pistol calibers) to a "C" suffix (denoting rifle calibers) in 1948.

Black Powder Boxes

Though the M1873 is called out on the side-seal, the top label of the earliest 32 W.C.F. box mentions only the "Winchester .32 Cal. Rifle". This labeling, most commonly found in green, was apparently in use from the early 1880s until about 1898. There may—indeed should—be a label showing an unheadstamped cartridge cut, but such has not been seen by the authors. R3+/250-500 [Green: R2+/175-350]

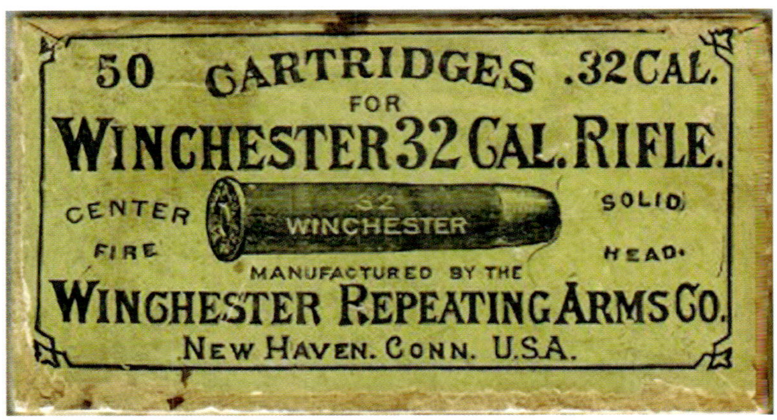

In 1898 the Company officially changed the "Central Fire" denotation to "Center Fire". That change represents the only difference between the previous box and this one on either the top label or the side-seal label, which still stubbornly refuses to call out the M1892. R2+/175-350

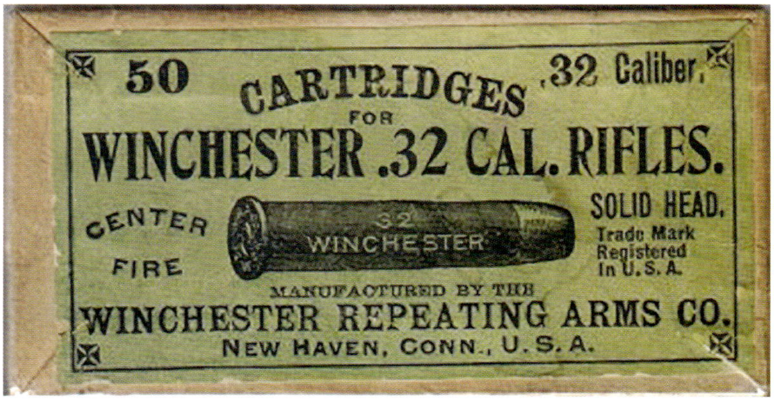

"Caliber" is now spelled out in the upper right corner and "Trade Mark Registered in U.S.A." appears for the first time under a new "Solid Head" line. The most important difference, however, is the new primary callout: "Winchester .32 Cal. Rifles" (plural). For the first time, the M92 is called out on the side label. All labels remain undated with Maltese crosses in the corners. R2+/165-275

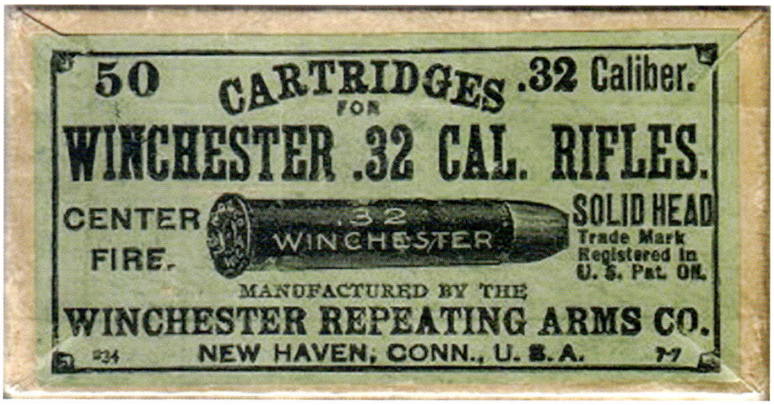

"Center Fire", like "Solid Head" in the previous example, is now printed in straight lines. The 7-7 label date represents the only other change from the earlier label. Note the absence of the Maltese crosses. R2/150-250

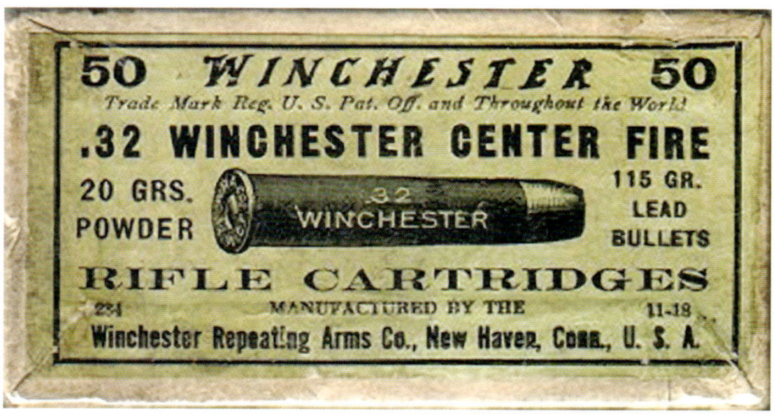

Dated 11-18, this design typifies the labels in use throughout the 1913-1920 period. Of particular interest is the fact that the side label on this box is dated 10-9 while another box in the authors' collection, with an 11-18 top label identical to this one, has a side label dated 1-20. This simply attests to the fact that one never knows what mix of labels might be found on any Winchester box! R2/135-225

With a K-coded end label, this full-cover two-piece box is from the period 1923-28. This represents the last of the two-piece box styles and was in use in Black Powder loadings until 1940. R2-/100-175

Smokeless Powder Boxes

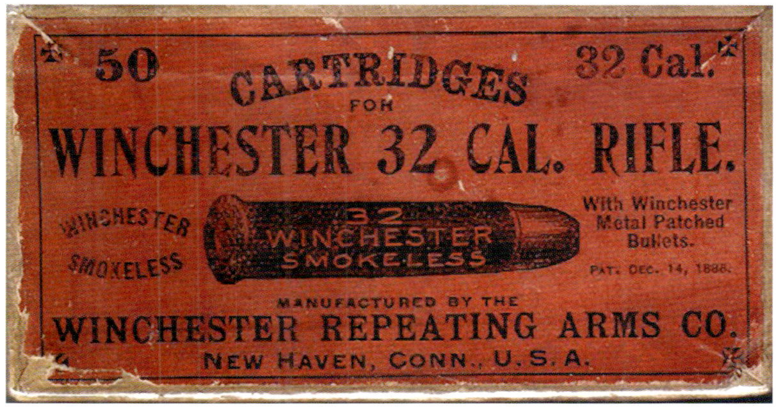

Here is the first Smokeless Soft Point labeling, ca. mid-1890s. The green side-seal label displays both the Smokeless and Soft Point "Sunburst" stickers (see below). Unlike the early Black Powder offerings, these gave the M1892 equal prominence in the model call-out on the side-seal. It is interesting to note, however, that "Rifle" remains singular on the top label, a holdover from the pre-M1892 days. R3+/ 250-500

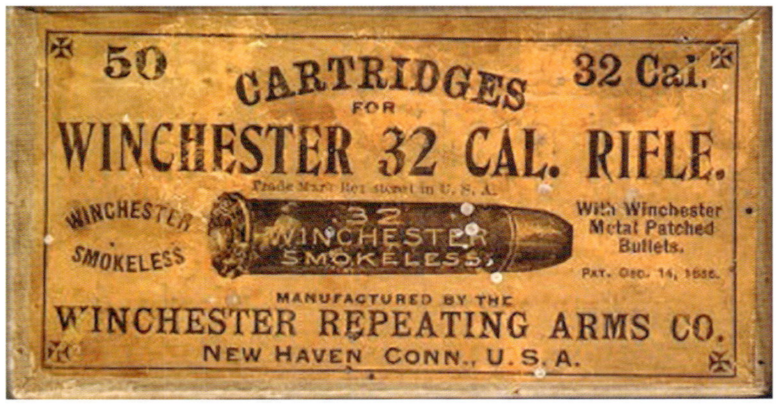

With label colors standardized post-1900, this orange label Soft Point box is an anomaly. By the time the "Trade Mark Registered in U.S.A." line began appearing shortly after the turn of the 20th Century, Soft Point Smokeless labels had been standardized as red. Except for color and the Trade Mark line (just above the cartridge cut), the labeling on this box is identical in all respects to the previous box including side labels and both "Sunburst" labels. The orange label would be expected to denote the Full Patch (FMJ) loading by this date, a fact rendered even more mysterious in that a "proper" red soft point version preceded it (see above)! R4-/300-550

Side label with model designations and the "Sunburst" Smokeless sticker.

The end labels of the early Smokeless boxes clearly call out the Company's two biggest introductions in cartridge technology during the early- to mid-1890s: Metal Patched Soft Point bullets and Smokeless Powder.

With "Winchester" in quotes and italics, this 10-11 label is common to the 1911-13 period. Compare the title line graphics with the box below. Here "Soft Point" is boldly called out in the title line with "Smokeless" in small letters to the right of the cartridge cut. R3-/150-250

The next style, ca. 1913-20, has the quotation marks removed and the full trade mark statement under the logo. Note that the "Soft Point" and "Smokeless" call-outs on this box and the preceding one have swapped positions in their label location with "Smokeless" now in the title line. This example is dated 12-13. R2+/100-200

Other than label color and bullet call-out, this orange Full Patch Smokeless top label has essentially the same graphics as the previous Soft Point box. It is, however, a much scarcer box. R2+/125-225

Model call-outs have now become simply "Models 73 and 92", dropping the "18" from each, a revision that occurred on most Winchester model call-outs ca. 1919. Otherwise, the only noticeable difference in graphics is that the Winchester logo is more compact. This box is label-dated 4-19. R2+/125-200

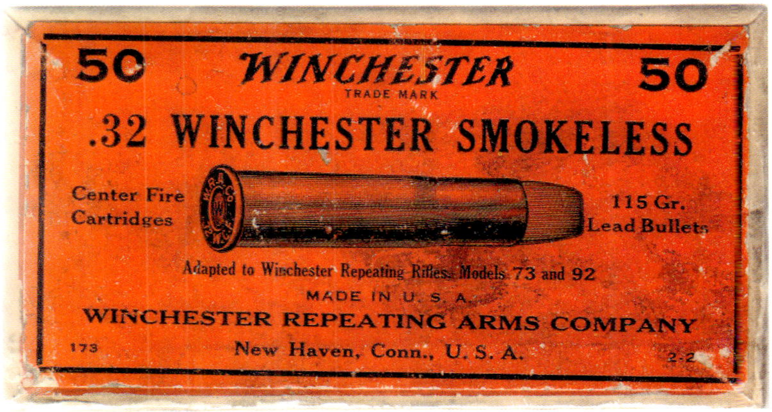

With a top label dated 2-21, a side label dated 5-21 and no K-code, this half-split two-piece box is quite scarce, being an uncommon loading in a combination of box and label styles that were likely in use for under two years. The existence of the following box (see below) further reaffirms the rarity of this one. Smokeless Lead offerings from this period are actually scarcer than the same loading from later periods. R3/175-275

Unlike the previous 1921-dated Smokeless Lead offering with its distinctive side-seal label, this one utilizes the wrap-over label designed for the much more common full-cover two-piece boxes of the 1920s, all of which were dated 7-20. What makes it unusual is the fact that this is a half-split, not a full-cover, box. It is also pre-K-code. Since such codes began to appear on most Winchester boxes shortly after their adoption in 1922, this box, like the one above, should be considered very scarce. R3-/150-250

This full-cover two-piece Soft Point box with its K-coded wrap-over 7-20 label is the one that most typifies the 1920-1928 period. R2-/100-200

Winchester's first Super Speed loading was introduced in this full-cover two-piece box in 1925. While scarce (though not rare), these boxes are highly collectible not only as the first Super Speed, but as the only Super Speed style utilizing a two-piece box. Like the W.H.V. loadings, the label cautions against use in the M73 and pistols. R3/175-300

The first Staynless box, ca.1928-31, this is an example of the scarcer Full Patch loading. These Staynless boxes also represented the Company's first use of the one-piece type of box construction. R2+/125-200

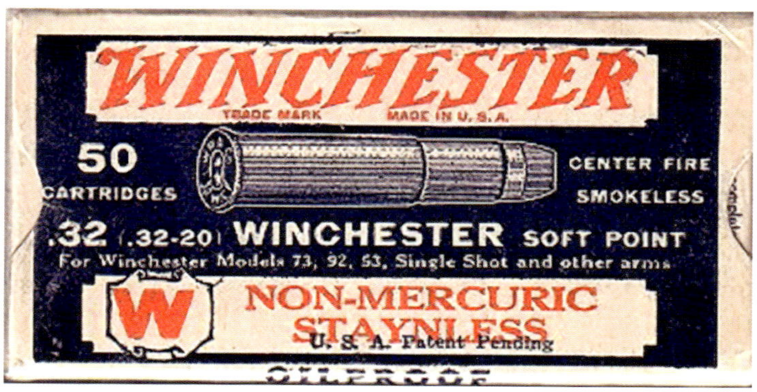

With the addition of "Non-Mercuric" and "Oilproof" (on bottom edge), this represents the "1932" box style. As with many of the older calibers with Black Powder origins, this box was apparently used in the standard velocity loading until the later "1939" or even "1945" styles. R2-/80-150

The original Super Speed 80 grain Hollow Point offering is here seen in the "1939" box. Note addition of the M65 call-out as well as a caution against use in pistols. In order to help prevent use in handguns the headstamps on the cartridges in these boxes were "32 WHV M-92". R2+/100-200

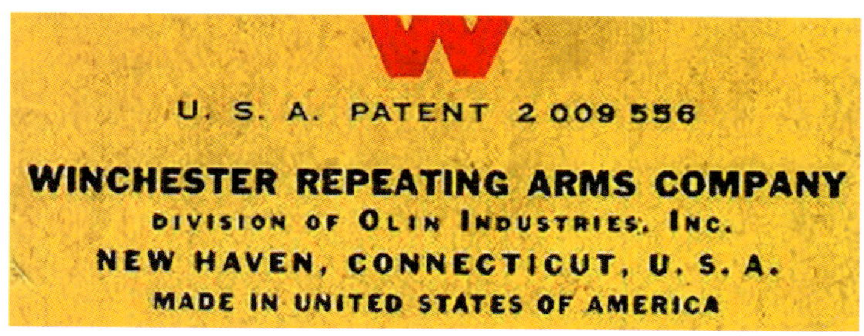

Olin Industries is called out on the side of this "1945" Soft Point box. This 115 grain loading lasted only until 1947 when the standard loading became 100 grains in both Soft Point and Lead. These loadings will be found in the "1946" style box, an example of which can be found in the High Velocity section following. R2-/60-120

High Velocity (WHV) Boxes

A lavender box like this should attract every collector's attention. Not only is it rarely seen, it represents one of the most collectible series in the realm of Winchester cartridge boxes: the "Full Patch W.H.V." loading, here referred to as the "Model 1892 Special". This undated earliest top label shows pre-1906 graphics but the side-seal is dated 10-13. We can only guess how far beyond 1913 this first label was used, but it is clear that it took a number of years from its 1905 introduction to use up the initial stock of labels (if, indeed, they ever were used up). R4-/300-600

This is a "label only" from the Winchester archives. Except for the Soft Point bullet call-out, the wording on this label is identical to the Full Patch WHV loading above. Note, however, that it is orange rather than yellow as finally adopted for the Soft Point WHV loading..

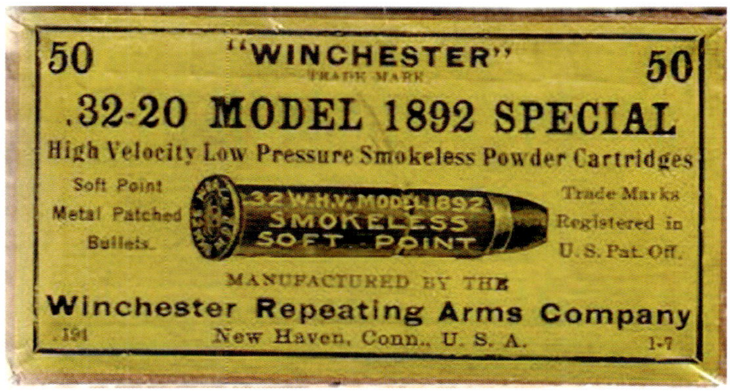

Yellow labels denote the Soft Point W.H.V. offering. Also introduced in 1905, this 1-7 labeling would represent the second box in the W.H.V. series. The ".32-20" call-out is unusual for this period when all other loadings in this caliber had been, and continued to be, titled ".32 Winchester". R3+/200-400

Here for the first time in this loading "Winchester High Velocity" is spelled out. Also ".32-20" has been dropped. The logo and other graphics are typical of the 1913-20 period. What is not typical is the "Full Patch" pinkish label color, similar to those found on 1911 and 1915-dated 25-20 High Velocity Soft Point boxes in the prior section. These boxes remain an enigma. R3+/200-400

The 1920's label on the full-cover two-piece box, for some reason, down-played the High Velocity aspect of this special catalog item. K-coded, this box is post-1922. R3/150-250

Here are the end labels from two 7/20 dated wrap-over labels, both with top portions identical to those on the previous box. Note, however, that the one on the left covers a half-split box and lacks the K-code, making it ca. 1920-22. The other is from the K-coded box above.

A 115 grain Soft Point bullet in the Super Speed W.H.V. loading is believed to be the only 32-20 offering to be found in the "1935" box. This was a true high velocity load as the bullet was full weight and velocity was 400 fps above the standard loading. R3/150-250

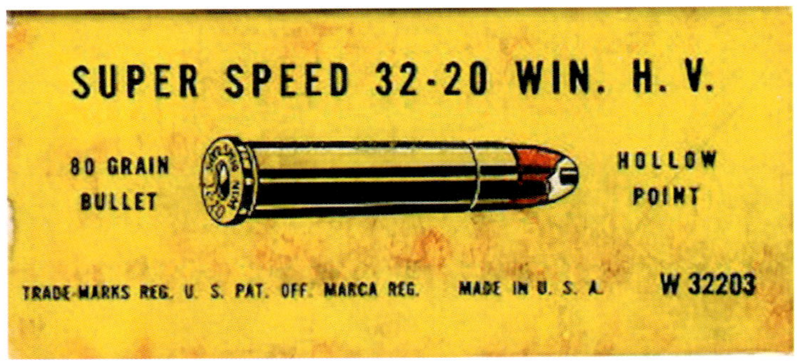

The "1946" W.H.V. box with the 80 grain JHP bullet. "W.H.V. M-92" has been dropped from the headstamp. Now using a W-code instead of the old K-code, this box can be dated to the post-1952 period. R2/50-100

A Shot Box

Only the side label calls out the Shot charge on this M1873 box. At the bottom of the side label the call-out "No. 10 Shot" may be seen with the "10" having been weakly stamped in ink. The top label is standard for the 1880s Black Powder Lead loading. R3/175-350

38 W.C.F., 38-40 Winchester

Catalog Listings: 1880-

Models: 1873, 1885, 1892

Bullet types: Ld, Ld HP, SP, MCHP, FMJ, Shot, Pistol Blank, Rifle Blank

Powder types: BP, Smkls, Lsmk

Headstamps: Plain, WRACo, WRA

Never as popular as its sister cartridge the 44 W.C.F., of which it is a necked-down version, the success of the 38 W.C.F. was, ironically, assured by Colt. As with the other M73 calibers, Colt began offering the 38-40 in their Single Action Army revolver, in this case it was an 1886 introduction. Having lain dormant for many years, the caliber has a gained new-found respect among modern day Cowboy Action shooters.

Though actually a 40 caliber, it was probably called a .38 because Company executives couldn't bear the thought of hearing everyone around the shop referring to their two best-selling M73 calibers together as the "forty-forty and forty-four forty".

The uncataloged jacketed Tubular bullet loading of 1896 is one of the great Winchester cartridge box rarities (see below, p 62).

Any Hollow Point box is scarce with both the 150 grain Lead and the 165 grain MCHP loadings especially so, the latter not being a catalog item. As with most calibers, Black Powder boxes with jacketed bullets are very difficult to find as are Smokeless, Lead bullet loads. Lesmok loadings are worth a substantial premium and the Pistol Blanks, so labeled, are rare.

Winchester High Velocity (WHV) boxes are always desirable, especially in FMJ. However, one of the great rarities in Winchester box collecting is waiting to be found here among the 38 WHVs. The first such offering in this caliber was headstamped simply ".38-40 W.H.V.", rather than the later ".38 W.H.V. M-92". The redesigned headstamp resulted from the realization that the M73 and some revolvers could not handle the increased chamber pressures of this round. Thus, "M-92" was added to the headstamp as well as to the box and catalog titles. The authors are not aware of the existence of any of these first "38-40 W.H.V." boxes.

In dating the "1946" boxes it should be noted that the K-code suffix was switched from a "T" suffix (denoting pistol calibers) to a "C" suffix (denoting rifle calibers) in 1948.

Black Powder Boxes

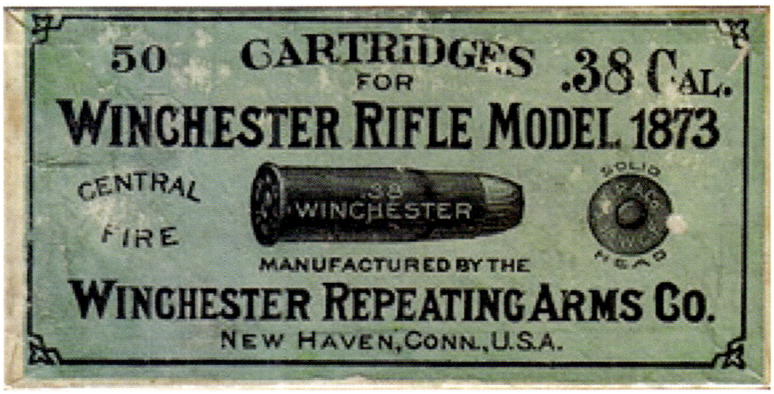

A "Central Fire" call-out and a cut of the cartridge head highlight these boxes apparently introduced in the mid-1880s. As some of these boxes are found with a "Center Fire" call-out on the side label we may conclude that this box was in use until 1900-1902. An earlier label, ca.1880-1885, exhibiting an unheadstamped round most probably exists, but we have not yet located an example. R2+/400-650

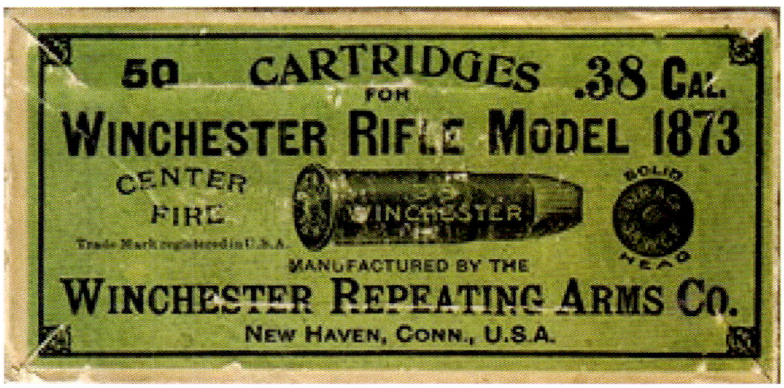

With the Center Fire call-out along with trade mark line now in place, we can date this box in the 1902-1905 period. The end label has the "fancy WRACo" logo also typical of that time frame. Unlike the side labels on Black Powder 44-40 boxes, there is no picture of the M73 on *any* 38-40 box. R3-/400-600

More in line with label graphics for Shot and Blank loadings, this 10-7 Black Powder "Metal Patched, Soft Point" box is most unusual and rare in this uncommon loading. Incredibly, the side label is dated 12-19, meaning these labels could not have shared this box until 1920! R4-/500-1000

Dated 12-8, this top label, unlike the previous one, has been "modernized" with the graphics and call-outs typical of the post-1906 period. Note, however, that the M1892 has now been prominently added to the model call-out, some 16 years after its introduction! R2+/350-650

While a nice example of the next style "Winchester" logo, this 5-12 dated box is especially significant as it contains one of the rarer 38-40 loadings: the 165 grain Hollow Point. R4-/600-1000

Now showing the call-outs for "Models 73 and 92", rather than the earlier "1873 and 1892", this full-cover box is label-dated 12-19. Normal period graphics such as the removal of quote marks from Winchester and the addition of the elongated Trade Mark line began ca. 1912 on these labels. Interestingly, there also exists a 1-20 dated label (not shown) with no textual differences and only very minor graphic variations from this box, making this 12-19 labeling quite rare. R3+/450-750. [1-20 labeling with or without K-coded side label: R2+/350-600]

As has been seen is other calibers, Winchester boxes began to display a much higher degree of standardization by the very early 1920s. This full-cover box represents the last type of two-piece box construction common throughout most of the Company's line of calibers having black powder origins. The end labels during this period are K-coded. R2+/200-350

While an available option in law enforcement loadings as early as the late 1920s, the "Oilproof" call-out came into the commercial line in selected calibers in the mid-to-late-1930s. This labeling, then, represents the last style of the Black Powder offerings in this caliber. It remained in the line until 1940. R3-/200-350

Lesmok Powder Boxes

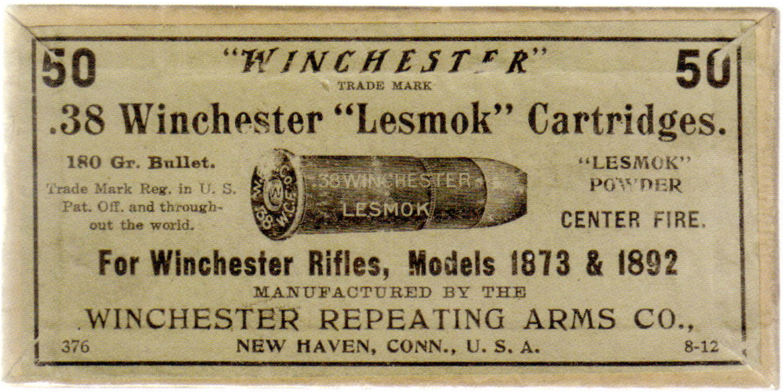

Left: This 8-12 label represents an early box as it was first cataloged in 1911. The only thing remarkable about it is the Lesmok loading, which, as mentioned earlier, is a "premium" find. While a number of Rim Fire calibers may be found in Lesmok, very few Center Fire offerings were cataloged and they are seldom seen. Right: The cartridge cut from the side-seal label, like the one on the lid label, clearly calls out its Lesmok loading. R3+/400-800

Shot loadings were never cataloged in Lesmok; however, here is one such box, obviously an extreme rarity. Note the "red "Lesmok" sticker. The labels are undated. R4-/400-700

Smokeless Powder Boxes

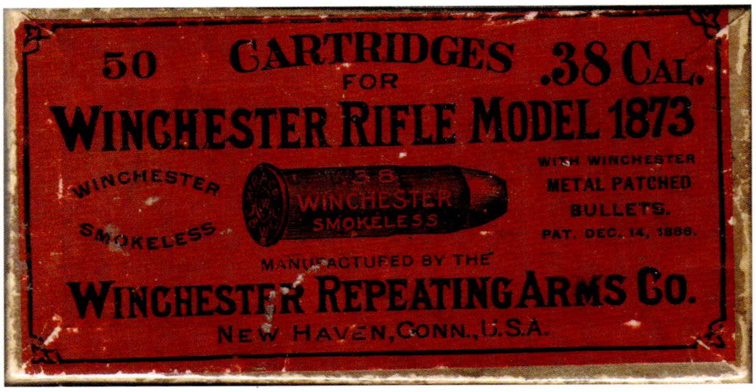

In 1896 Winchester began offering 38-40 in Smokeless Powder with the jacketed "tubular" bullets. We have no way of knowing when this loading was discontinued as it was never mentioned in the catalogs. There is no question, however, as to its extreme rarity. The complete absence of a M1892 call-out on this box is inexplicable. R5/2500-5000

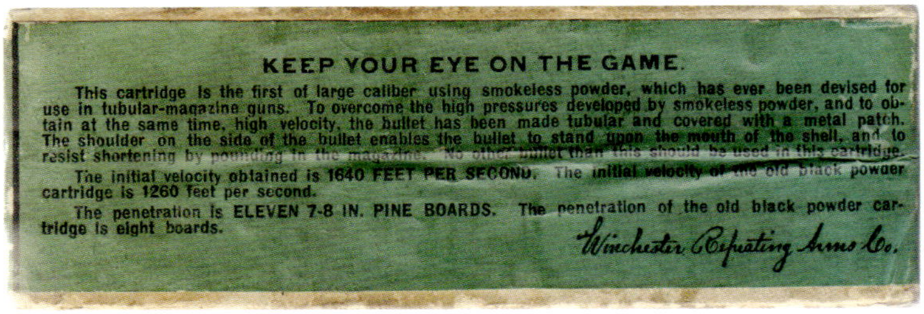

Left: The text of this lengthy but very interesting "Keep Your Eye On The Game" label also extols the new "patched tubular" bullet design, individual examples of which are rare and avidly sought by collectors today. This label is shown more readably in Chapter 1, page 20. Right: End label showing the "Patched Bullets" call-out and related patent date.

This earliest Smokeless Soft Point label differs from the above box only in the additional "Sunburst" sticker and the redesign of the side seal so that both sides are the same, eliminating the "Keep Your Eye on the Game" verbiage.

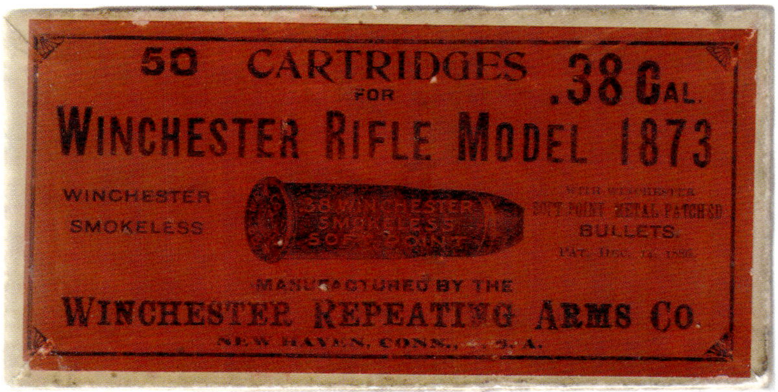

Lacking trade mark data but displaying the "Fancy WRACo" logo on the left end, this box can be dated to the period 1899-1902. The side label calls out the M1892 as well as the M1873, but the M1892 is conspicuous by its absence on this top. R3+/400-700

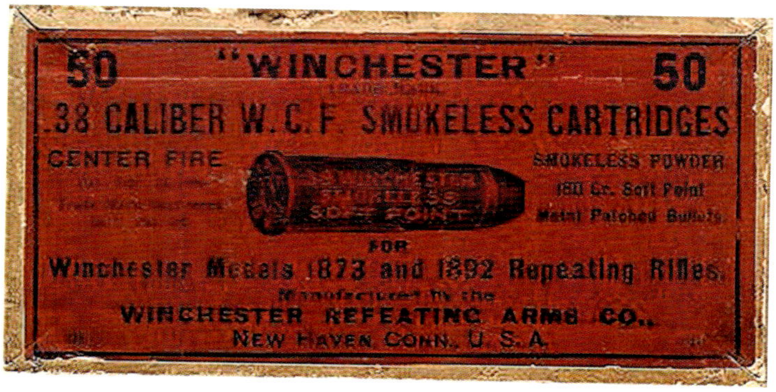

Now calling out the M1892 as well as the M1873 on this 1-8 dated top label, the post-1906 format is here exemplified. Note that "Winchester" is in block letters as opposed to the italicized logo in the following example. R3+/450-700

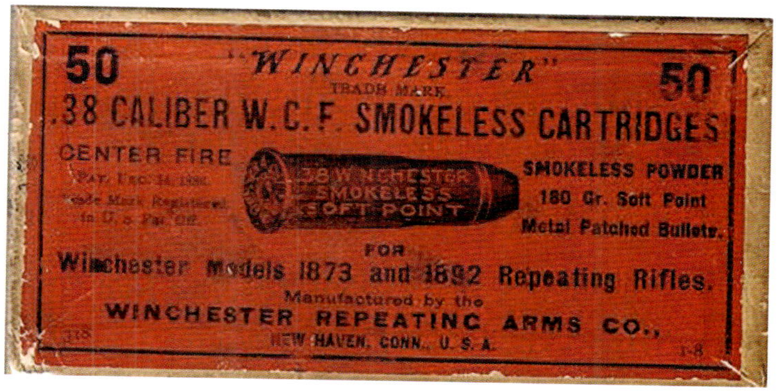

Also dated 1-8, the "W nchester" logo on this top label is in italics and from a different font. No other changes are to be found. The side label is dated 6-10, however, demonstrating that this is the logo that was used on top labels subsequent to 1-8. It may be assumed, therefore, that the earlier 1-8 box is a scarce, if not rare, variety. R3-/400-650

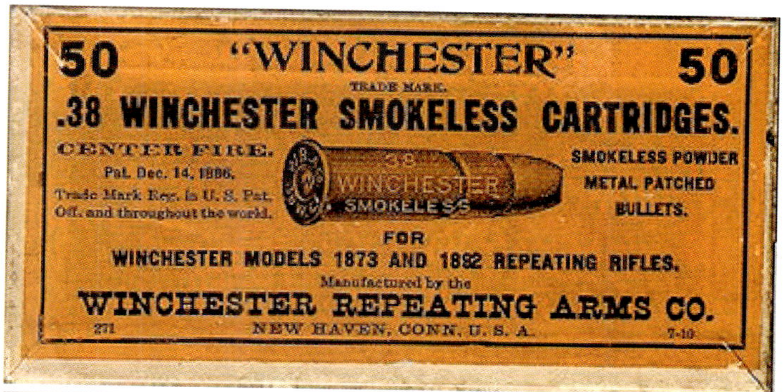

With a 7-10 label date this Metal Patched (FMJ) box contrasts in both color and graphics with the Soft Point boxes of the period. After ca. 1902, the orange label was standard for FMJ loadings in Winchester's 50-round boxes. Given that the logo was designed in block letters as shown here on this 1910 label, one wonders why the change was made in the 1-8 labels above. The "Colt Revolvers" call-out is not seen on standard Black Powder or Smokeless Soft Point labels in this caliber, only on this side label of the Smokeless FMJ loading. It is, therefore, assumed to be very uncommon. R3+/450-700

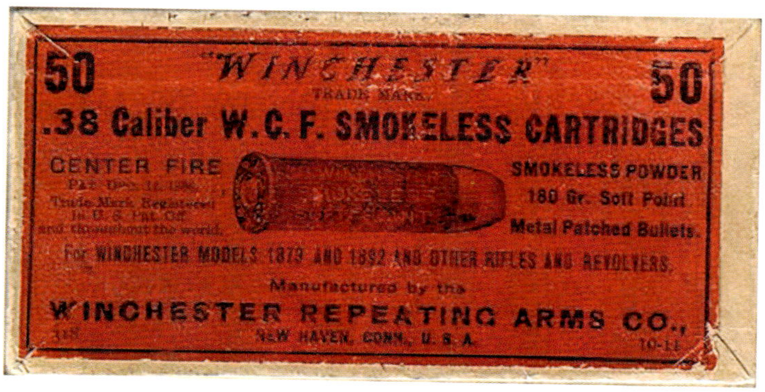

Some subtle changes become apparent on this 10-11 box relative to earlier Soft Point labels. The model call-outs are here expanded to include "Other Rifles and Revolvers". Also, the trade mark line has the extension "...and throughout the world" and the cartridge cut displays a bullet jacket that covers about twice as much of the bullet as formerly. R3-/400-650

Though not as rare as the Black Powder loading, this Smokeless Lead Hollow Point is still very scarce and highly collectible. Dated 5-12, the top label prominently illustrates the hollow point bullet in cutaway. The 2-11 dated side label also displays that cartridge cut. R3+/550-900

44 Model '73, 44 W.C.F., 44-40, 44-40 Winchester
Catalog Listings: 1875-

Models: 1873, 1885, 1892, 53

Bullet types: Ld, Ld HP, SP, MCHP, FMJ, Shot, Pistol Blank, Rifle Blank

Powder types: BP, Smkls, Lsmk

Headstamps: Plain, WRACo, WRA

Winchester's first commercial center fire cartridge also became one of its biggest-selling and most famous. Developed by the Company, it utilized a 200 grain bullet, the same weight as the 44 Henry it was destined to replace. The 44 Henry, however, in deference to its weaker, thin-walled copper rim fire case was limited to 28 grains of Black Powder. The new 44-40, as it was commonly referred to and as denoted in its nomenclature, packed 40 grains of Black Powder into its stronger brass shell. Upon Colt's 1877 offering of this caliber in their Single Action Army revolver, the Winchester '73 and the Colt Frontier Six Shooter, as the Colt came to be called, became the most popular companion pieces of the Old West.

The earliest variation of the 44 W.C.F., though not successful, had a short paper patch on the bullet and utilized the seldom-seen Milbank primer. Even without the rare first box which pictures a Milbank-primed cartridge, these rounds are a great find for any collector. Lead Hollow Points were produced in both Black Powder and Smokeless, first with 166 grain bullets (1910-12) and later with 180 grain bullets (1912-23). The former are rare, the latter very scarce. Other hard-to-find loadings include jacketed Black Powder and, Lead bullet Smokeless rounds as well as Pistol Blanks (and labeled as such).

While all Winchester High Velocity (W.H.V.) boxes are highly collectible, the early 44 W.H.V. boxes are especially desirable. Even more so are any and all FMJ W.H.V. loadings.

Black Powder Boxes

While the primer on this cartridge cut appears to have been struck, this earliest M73 44 W.C.F. box actually displays a Milbank primer. As mentioned above, Milbank-primed rounds, though rarely seen, do exist. Of the three boxes known to the authors, however, two full ones were found to have contained Boxer-type primed cartridges which were patented in 1874 by John Gardner, a Winchester employee. The other is said to have contained "eight to ten un-headstamped rounds", though not Milbank primed. Also note the early 44/100 ("44 over 100") caliber call-out. R5/7500-12,500

Early top labels such as this wrapped over the right end of the lid.

The top label of this second box shows an un-headstamped round with a Boxer primer and a grease groove. On the earlier version (ca.1874-76), the top label, in the fashion of the New Haven "44 Flat" box discussed in the previous chapter, wraps over the right end of the box lid. The other, later, version (ca.1876-77) simply covers the lid top but has a side-wrap label. R3+/1250-1750

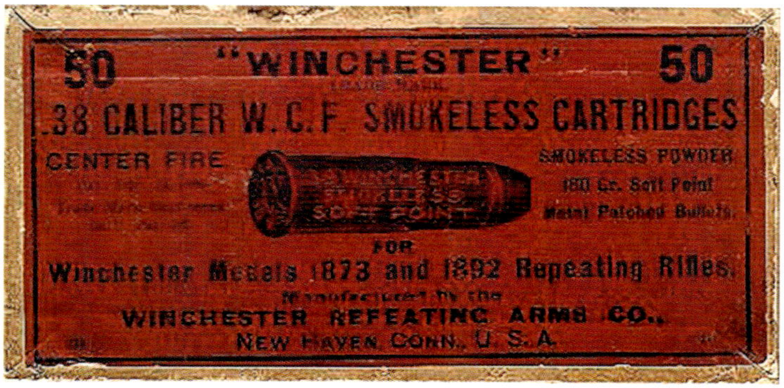

Now calling out the M1892 as well as the M1873 on this 1-8 dated top label, the post-1906 format is here exemplified. Note that "Winchester" is in block letters as opposed to the italicized logo in the following example. R3+/450-700

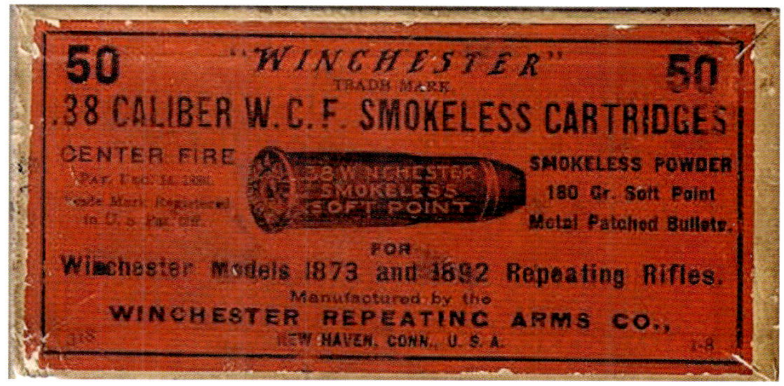

Also dated 1-8, the "W nchester" logo on this top label is in italics and from a different font. No other changes are to be found. The side label is dated 6-10, however, demonstrating that this is the logo that was used on top labels subsequent to 1-8. It may be assumed, therefore, that the earlier 1-8 box is a scarce, if not rare, variety. R3-/400-650

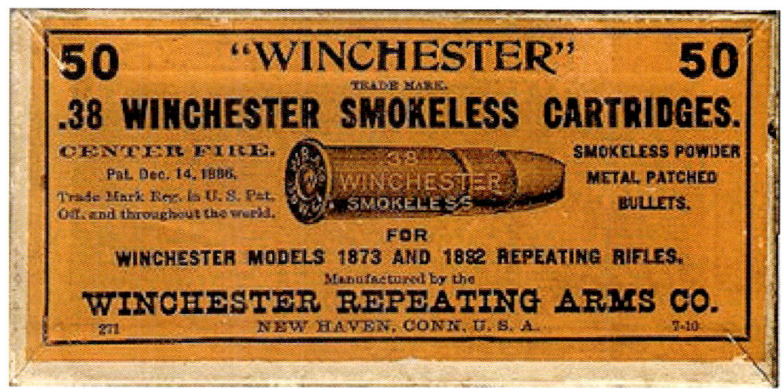

With a 7-10 label date this Metal Patched (FMJ) box contrasts in both color and graphics with the Soft Point boxes of the period. After ca. 1902, the orange label was standard for FMJ loadings in Winchester's 50-round boxes. Given that the logo was designed in block letters as shown here on this 1910 label, one wonders why the change was made in the 1-8 labels above. The "Colt Revolvers" call-out is not seen on standard Black Powder or Smokeless Soft Point labels in this caliber, only on this side label of the Smokeless FMJ loading. It is, therefore, assumed to be very uncommon. R3+/450-700

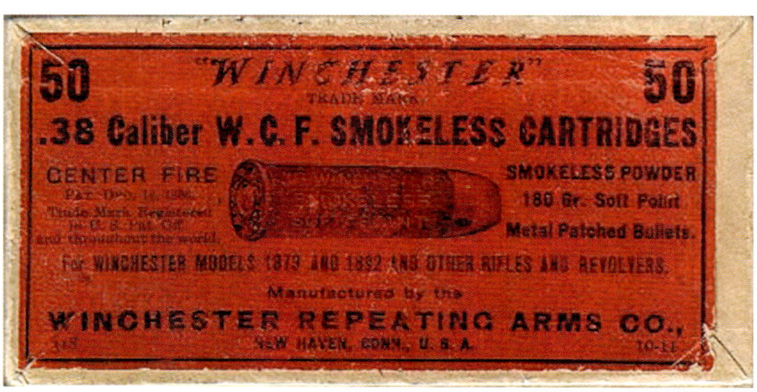

Some subtle changes become apparent on this 10-11 box relative to earlier Soft Point labels. The model call-outs are here expanded to include "Other Rifles and Revolvers". Also, the trade mark line has the extension "...and throughout the world" and the cartridge cut displays a bullet jacket that covers about twice as much of the bullet as formerly. R3-/400-650

Though not as rare as the Black Powder loading, this Smokeless Lead Hollow Point is still very scarce and highly collectible. Dated 5-12, the top label prominently illustrates the hollow point bullet in cutaway. The 2-11 dated side label also displays that cartr dge cut. R3+/550-900

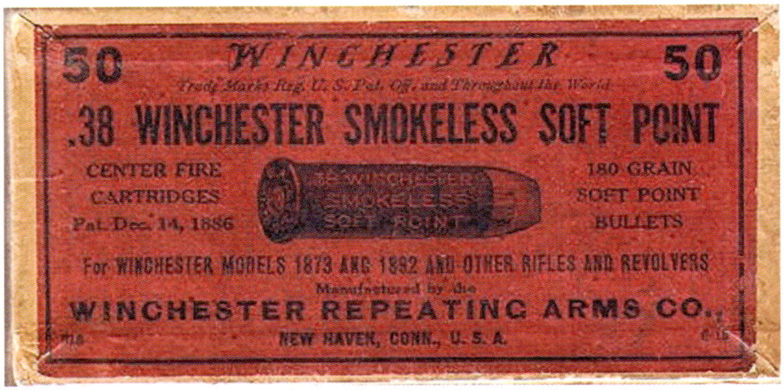

Without quote marks around *Winchester* and with the long trade mark line now under the logo, this 6-15 Soft Point box is typical of the period ca. 1913-1919. R3/400-650

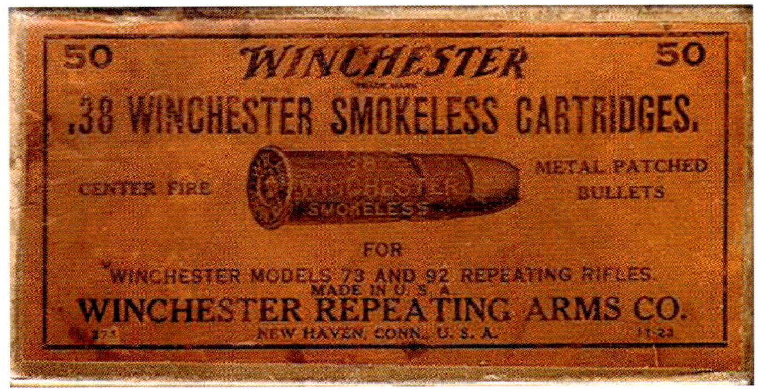

With its prominent orange label this box is quickly identified as a "Metal Patched" (FMJ) offering. The model call-outs on this 11-23 label refer only to "Models 73 and 92 Repeating Rifles. The "Trade Mark" line under the logo has gone "retro", reverting to the way it was first used in the then-new 1906 graphics. R3+/450-750

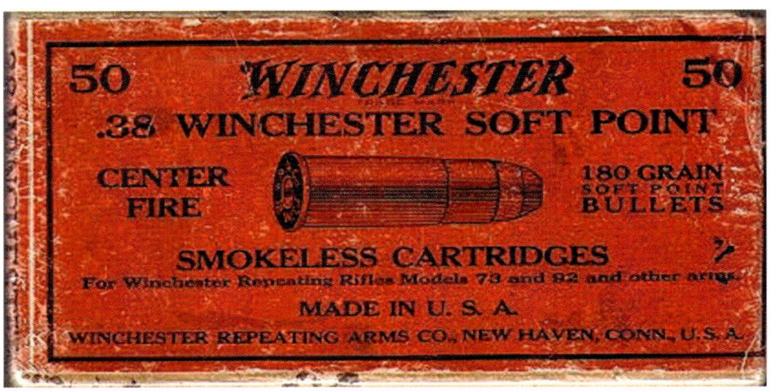

The full-cover two-piece box most commonly found in the early 1920s was the last design before the Company went to the one-piece box construction in 1927-28. This one, while bearing a 7-20 label date (as nearly all this style of box did), is post-1922 as evidenced by the K-code on the ends. R2+/200-400

All Full Patch loadings are scarce in this caliber. This is an example of the "1928" box. The "1932" box (not pictured) closely resembles this one but adds the Non-Mercuric call-out on the top and the bullet weight call-out on the end flaps. R3/150-250

The "1939" box is thought to have succeeded the "1932" box described above, skipping the "1935" box. (See 44-40 section for further details and comments). R2+/80-150

An example of the "1946" box with the later W-code, ca. 1952-54. Earlier examples used the K-code; otherwise, there are no important differences between the two varieties. R1+/50-80

High Velocity (WHV) Boxes

Above: This "label only" from the Winchester archives likely represents those found on the first WHV boxes in this caliber. It is the Soft Point loading and is yellow according to label color protocols of the period. Right: While not the earliest box in the WHV loading introduced in 1903, this 10-9 example exhibits all the traits of the 1906-1912 period. Its primary interest, however, lies in the "Model 1892 Special" call-out, a designation that was dropped ca. 1919. The headstamp, "38 W.H.V. M-92" (which continued until the discontinuance of the WHV loading) was intended to keep these high velocity loads out of Model '73s. Interestingly, it is the only series among the two-piece boxes that refers to the caliber as ".38-40" rather than the usual ".38 W.C.F." R3+/450-750

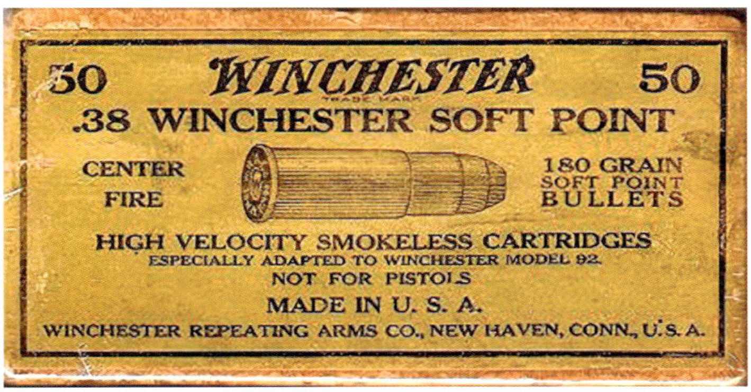

The 7-20 dated full-cover two-piece box of the early- to mid-1920s, this one K-coded. Gone is the prominent "Model 1892 Special" call-out and the format has become very much like the standard loadings. R3/375-650

This Stayrless box, with its bold red over-stamp, "Non-Mercuric" call-out and sight adjustment sticker, s likely ca. 1932-35. R3/350-600

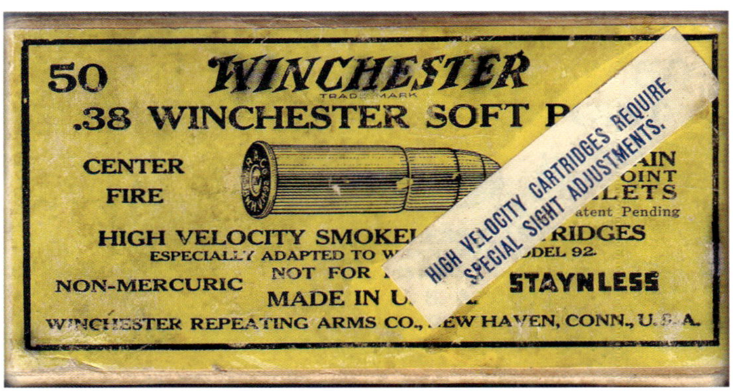

Thought to be the last in the 38 W.H.V. line, ca. 1935-41, "Stayn ess" is now printed on the lower right while "Non-Mercuric" has moved to the lower left. R3/350-600

44 Model '73, 44 W.C.F., 44-40, 44-40 Winchester

Catalog Listings: 1875-

Models: 1873, 1885, 1892, 53

Bullet types: Ld, Ld HP, SP, MCHP, FMJ, Shot, Pistol Blank, Rifle Blank

Powder types: BP, Smkls, Lsmk

Headstamps: Plain, WRACo, WRA

Winchester's first commercial center fire cartridge also became one of its biggest-selling and most famous. Developed by the Company, it utilized a 200 grain bullet, the same weight as the 44 Henry it was destined to replace. The 44 Henry, however, in deference to its weaker, thin-walled copper rim fire case was limited to 28 grains of Black Powder. The new 44-40, as it was commonly referred to and as denoted in its nomenclature, packed 40 grains of Black Powder into its stronger brass shell. Upon Colt's 1877 offering of this caliber in their Single Action Army revolver, the Winchester '73 and the Colt Frontier Six Shooter, as the Colt came to be called, became the most popular companion pieces of the Old West.

The earliest variation of the 44 W.C.F., though not successful, had a short paper patch on the bullet and utilized the seldom-seen Milbank primer. Even without the rare first box which pictures a Milbank-primed cartridge, these rounds are a great find for any collector. Lead Hollow Points were produced in both Black Powder and Smokeless, first with 166 grain bullets (1910-12) and later with 180 grain bullets (1912-23). The former are rare, the latter very scarce. Other hard-to-find loadings include jacketed Black Powder and, Lead bullet Smokeless rounds as well as Pistol Blanks (and labeled as such).

While all Winchester High Velocity (W.H.V.) boxes are highly collectible, the early 44 W.H.V. boxes are especially desirable. Even more so are any and all FMJ W.H.V. loadings.

Black Powder Boxes

While the primer on this cartridge cut appears to have been struck, this earliest M73 44 W.C.F. box actually displays a Milbank primer. As mentioned above, Milbank-primed rounds, though rarely seen, do exist. Of the three boxes known to the authors, however, two full ones were found to have contained Boxer-type primed cartridges which were patented in 1874 by John Gardner, a Winchester employee. The other is said to have contained "eight to ten un-headstamped rounds", though not Milbank primed. Also note the early 44/100 ("44 over 100") caliber call-out. R5/7500-12,500

Early top labels such as this wrapped over the right end of the lid.

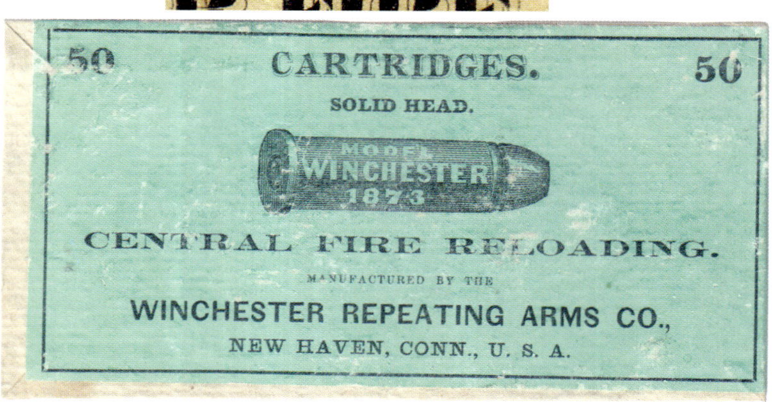

The top label of this second box shows an un-headstamped round with a Boxer primer and a grease groove. On the earlier version (ca.1874-76), the top label, in the fashion of the New Haven "44 Flat" box discussed in the previous chapter, wraps over the right end of the box lid. The other, later, version (ca.1876-77) simply covers the lid top but has a side-wrap label. R3+/1250-1750

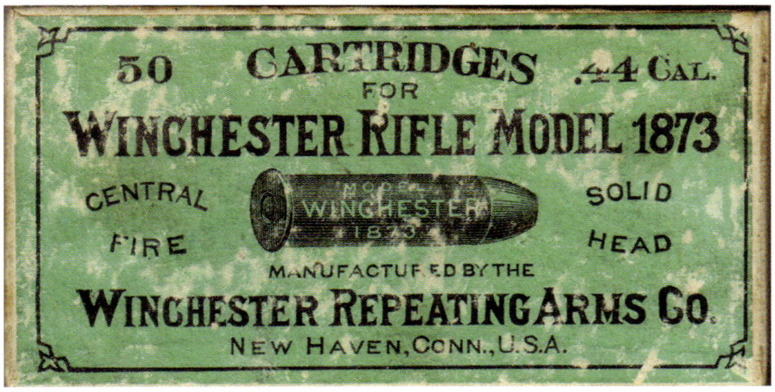

Though only the third style, this box is always in great demand because of the "old-time" graphics coupled with the fact that Black Powder 44-40 boxes from this and later periods picture a M73 carbine on the side label. Note that, unlike the previous style label, the cartridge cut no longer has a grease groove. However the most significant and obvious feature differentiating this box from the vast majority found in this and future styles is the lack of a headstamp on the cartridge cut. Other than that, the top label appeared much the same until the late 1890s. R3+/1100-1600

The un-headstamped cartridge cut is all-important in determining the age, rarity and value of this most uncommon variation of an otherwise common labeling.

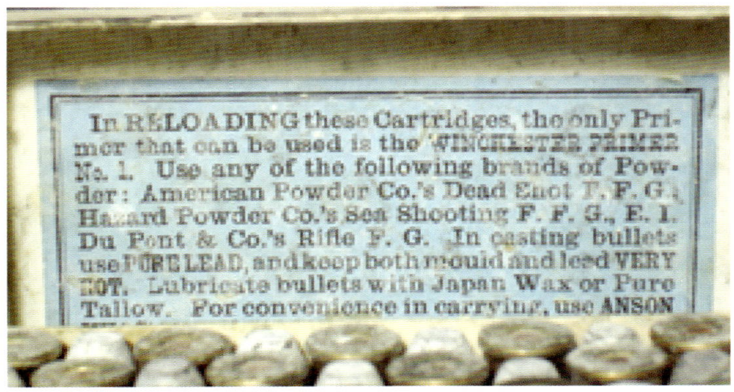

Another, and certainly less obvious, way of dating this box is by the reloading label found under the lid top. The particular powder callouts on this label help date this to the early 1880s. The label also mentions Anson Mills (though the last line is not seen here), a fact which prevents us from speculating that this box might date as far back as the late-1870s.

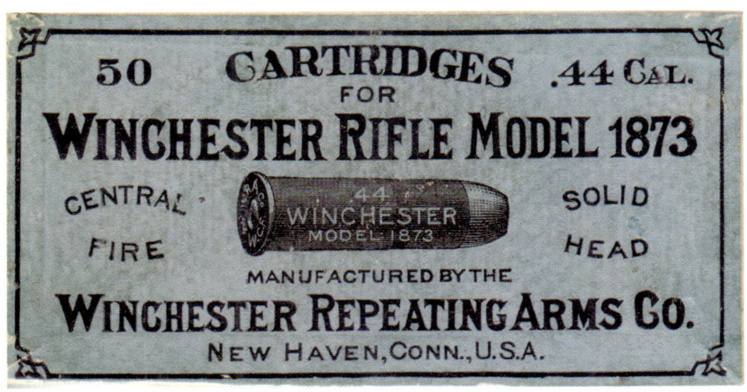

This second variation of the third style box, is the one most commonly found and is always in great demand for the reasons mentioned earlier. Blue label boxes in this caliber, such as the one pictured, always command a premium. R3/800-1250 [Green label: R1+/450-800]

Three different M73 side-label cuts are to be found over the years: the most conspicuous differentiating features on this one are the presence of a forward barrel band and a rifle style rear sight.

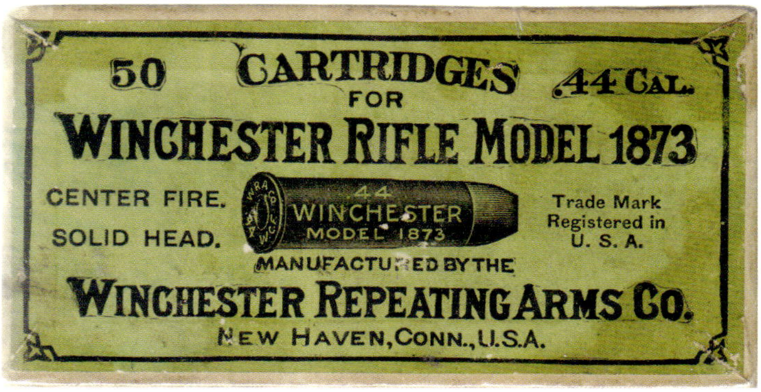

Shortly before the turn of the 20th Century, "Central Fire" gives way to "Center Fire" and just a few years later "Trade Mark Registered in U.S.A." begins to be seen on all Winchester labels. This box is ca 1902-05. R2+/400-800

Note that the barrel on this side label cut no longer has a forward band. Also, the rear sight is now a carbine sight rather than a rifle sight.

Interestingly, this fancy "WRACo" end-label logo is most often seen in the 1898-1905 period, but the trade mark line underneath it as well as the other end label showing "Winchester" in block letters and quotes, is normally found 1906-1910. Dated 4-6, this would have to be among the very last side-seal labels before introduction of the "Red W" logo that same year.

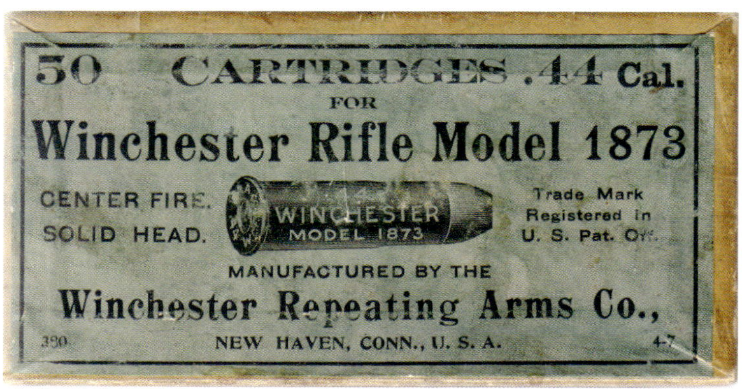

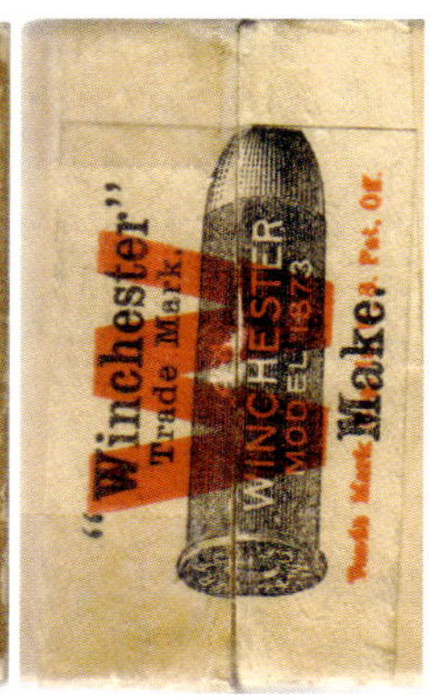

This 4-7 dated top label as well as the overprinted end label showing "Winchester" in quotes, the "Red W" logo, and the trade mark data, all clearly identify this as a 1906-1910 style box. Unusual among Winchester labels of this period, however, is the lack of the "Winchester" logo on the top line. R3+/400-800

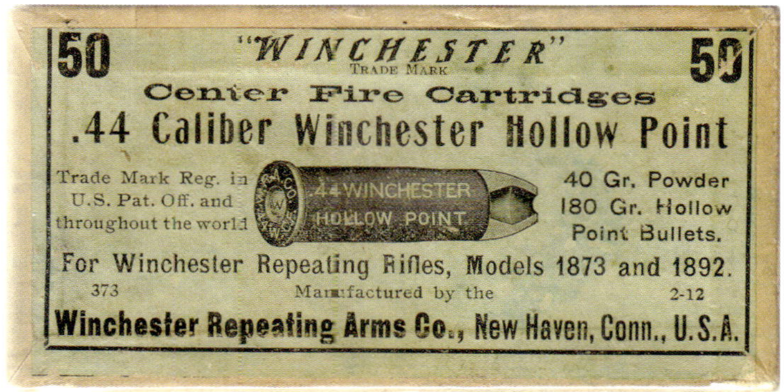

A Black Powder Hollow Point box is always a rare find. This one is label-dated 2-12 and has the italicized "Winchester" in quotation marks, graphics typical of the 1910-12 period. R4-/850-1500

By the time this 11-15 label came out the Winchester line had become italicized and lost its quotation marks; also, the trade mark line had been expanded to include "throughout the world". These logo and call-out changes are among those generally found in the period 1912-1920. R3-/350-600

Other than a couple of changes in type size and spacing, the wording of this 1-19 label is much the same as on the previous label. The main change concerns the call-out for the "Models '73 and '92" which replaced the earlier "Models 1873 and 1892" call-out. R3-/350-600

Again, few changes are to be found on this 4-20 label. We can see that the apostrophes have been taken away from "Models '73 and '92" to create simply "Models 73 and 92". Also, the "50" in each upper corner is now smaller. R3-/350-600

With neither a label date nor a K-code to help us date this box we can only observe that "Oilproof" was a 1927 announcement. Our best guess is that it is an export box from the 1930s, during which period label dates, with few exceptions, were phased out. R3/375-625

The third style cut of the M73 carbine on the side label shows a return to the front barrel band, the retention of the Carbine rear sight and the word "Winchester" added to the lower stock. Not all of these side labels call out "Oilproof", however.

Now displaying the "Division of Western Cartridge Company" callout, this yellow box is clearly from the 1939-45 period and likely an export box. "Made in United States of America" is now spelled out in full. Note, too, the presence of the K-code in the lower right corner. The box has no side-seal label. R3-/300-500

"Olin Industries" is called out on this late-1940s Black Powder box made for export. Like the previous box, the K-code is present and the side label is absent. Why the label colors should be so different remains a mystery. R3/350-600

Lesmok Powder Boxes

All Lesmok boxes are scarce or even rare in center fire calibers. This loading, begun in 1911, is shown here in a 4-11 dated box. R3+/800-1400

The 2-12 label shown here is virtually identical to the previous box; however, the cartridge cut now shows a "w" on the primer and the word "Lesmok" on the case under "44 Winchester". R3+/750-1250

Smokeless Powder Boxes

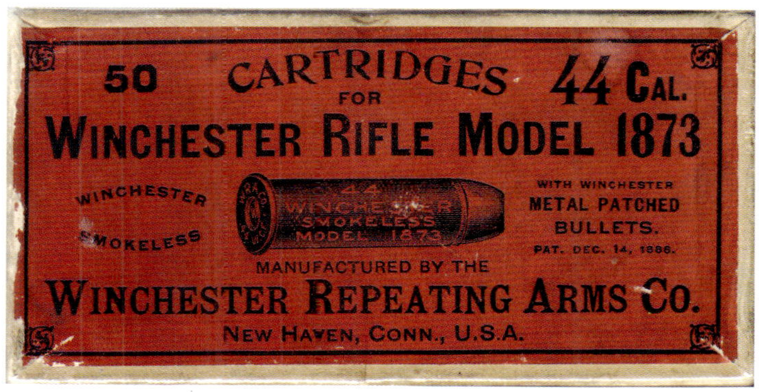

The first Smokeless loading in this caliber was listed in 1895. It is not known whether this box, with its arched "Cartridges" at the top and green side-seal, represents the first 44-40 Smokeless Soft Point offering, but it is certainly very early. Note that the top label calls out only the M73 while the side labels (both sides are identical) add the M92 almost as an afterthought. R3+/650-1100

The end labels ignore the M92 also, referring only to the M73.

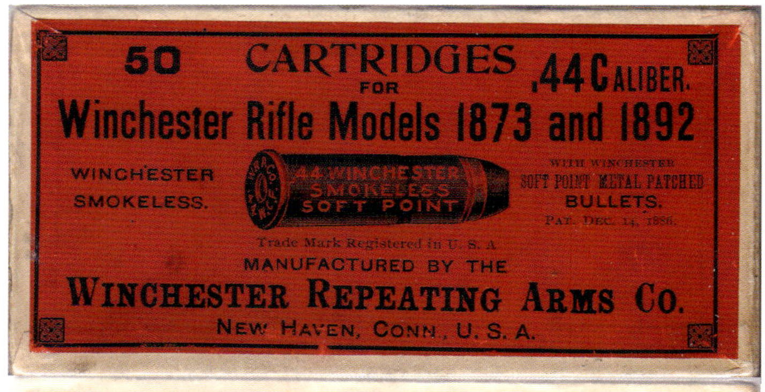

The M1892 is now given equal billing with the M1873 on the top label of this Soft Point box, thought to be ca. 1900-1903. However, the side label, which now states "Not for Pistols", still seems to feel the M92 deserves no more than second billing... R3+/750-1250

...and the end labels still ignore it altogether.

Unlike the previous example, the side labels are no longer the same on this box. As can be seen here the "fine print" concerning the Company's guarantee has now been added.

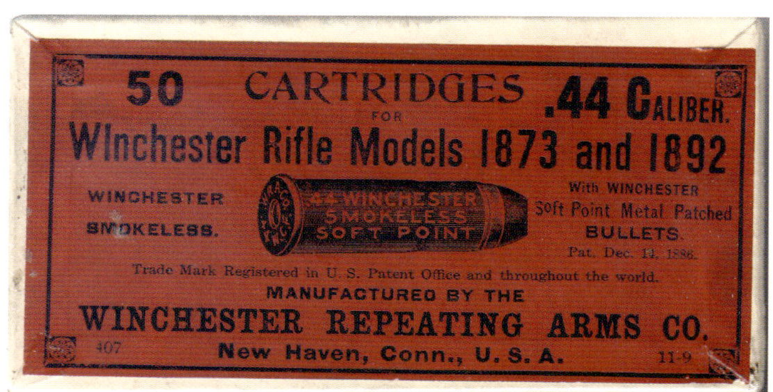

An 11-9 dated label showing minor changes in graphics. The expansion of the trade mark line to include "and throughout the world" is typical of this period and lasted until 1920; however, it is seldom found prior to 1910. The side label is the same as the previous except "Soft Point" has replaced "Not for Pistols". R3-/500-900

The silver "W" logo shows up nicely on these red boxes in the period 1907-1912, this one dated 11-9. Except when used on red boxes or labels, the "W" logo is printed in red directly onto the boxes or on tan labels attached thereto.

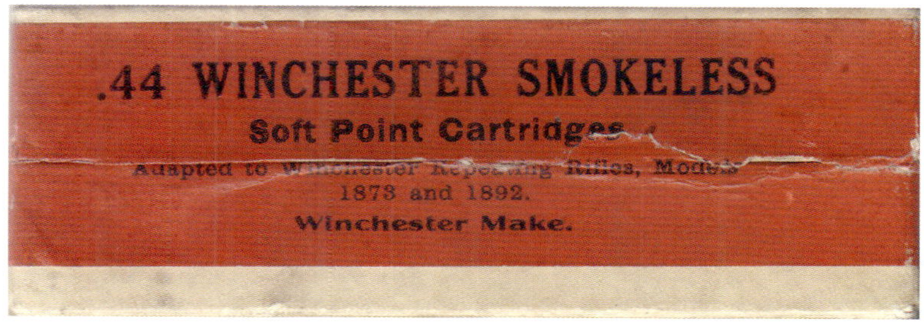

While the top label of this box is the same as the preceding, the side label is dated 4-14 and differs substantially from the earlier versions. Of greater import is the presence of a 1914 side label on a box with a 1909 top label. It is obvious that, even in popular calibers, many labels went unchanged for years while others show multiple varieties in one month! R3/500-900

The Silver "W" was replaced by this white-outlined version of the end label. This is part of the 4-14 side label above.

You may not have paid much attention to, or even been able to see, the decorative graphics in the corners of the three preceding lid labels: Here they are up close.

The "Full Patch" Smokeless offering was offered in an orange-labeled box like as this 10-15 example. Such loadings are scarce in .44 W.C.F. Note that the familiar "Winchester" logo line is now at the top. R3/600-1000

The last of the 44-40 half-split two-piece (see Chapter 1, pp 14-15) Soft Point boxes displayed this 9-19 label. The "Model 1873 and 1892" call-out is now "Model 73 and 92" on both top and side labels. R3/500-900

You can see in this close-up of the side label that the 4-14 side label (discussed earlier) has been altered to simply delete the "18s" from in front of the 73 and 92. This side label from the above box is dated 2-21.

Often referred to as the "1920" box because of its 7-20 label-dating in all calibers in which it is found, this labeling is usually found on full-cover two-piece boxes (see Chapter 1, pp 14-15) such as these. The presence of these 1920-dated boxes makes the existence of the 2-21 side label on the previous example even more interesting, even problematic. R2/250-450

The graphics on these "1920" boxes tended to be more uniform among the various loadings than on previous boxes. Except for color and the Soft Point versus Full Patch call-outs, they are identical. There is also a Black Powder box in this series with green labeling, though Full Patch is the scarcest. R2+/300-500

The "1920" end labels are the same except, of course, for their distinguishing colors and, in this case, the presence of a K-code on the Smokeless box. This makes the Full Patch box ca. 1920-1923 and the Smokeless box, 1923-28.

In March 1928 the Company began loading this caliber with their new Staynless priming which had been announced a year earlier. This was their new one-piece box in which it was introduced and first marketed and which is termed the "1928" box style. R2+/100-175

With the advent of their improved "Non-Mercuric" Staynless priming, the changes which can be seen here created what we refer to as the "1932" box style. This one is in the scarce Full Patch loading. R3-/125-200

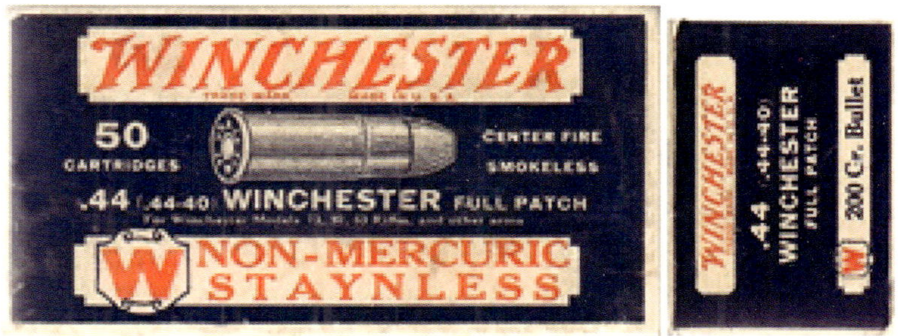

What's a Model 93? This erroneous call-out (it should be Model 92) is on both the "1939" and "1945" boxes. The latter is essentially identical to the "1939" box except for the Olin Industries call-out.

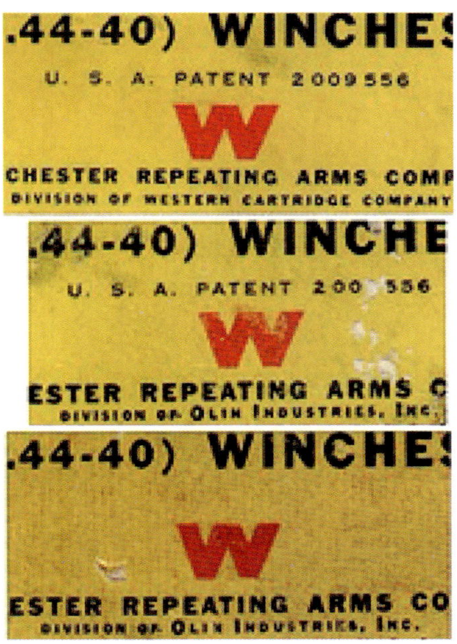

As the authors are aware of the "1932" box being utilized in .44-40 as late as 1938, it is thought that this "1939" style box with the Western Cartridge Co. call-out is next in the lineage. The "1935" style, in the opinion of the authors, does not exist. If someone out there finds one, please share it with us! R2-/80-150 ["1945" Olin box: R2/100-175]

This Soft Point Olin Industries "1946" box has been identified as having been made in April, 1955. With the exception of the Olin Mathieson call-out, the "1954" style box displays the same graphics as this "1946" box. In dating the "1946" boxes, however, it should be noted that the K-code suffix was switched from a 'T' suffix (denoting pistol calibers) to a "C" suffix (denoting rifle calibers) in 1948. R1/40-80

High Velocity (WHV) Boxes

Dated 10-9, this faded Winchester High Velocity box is not the earliest WHV box but it does exhibit the call-outs that tended to be common among all such boxes from 1903 until its discontinuance in 1938. As opposed to the standard loadings, these WHV labels not only gave the M92 call-out top billing, but insisted that the M92 was the ONLY lever-action rifle for which this loading was appropriate. Note that the box is a full-cover, rather than half-split, box type yet uses the side-seal from the earlier type. In addition, it is dated 8-20, further validation that the top labels on 44-40 boxes from this period (1909-1920, also see above) underwent little or no change. R3+/500-1000

The fine print on the side-seal label on the above box states that "These cartridges should never be used in Winchester Model 73 rifles". The caution against use in pistols is less subtle.

Highlighted by the trade-marked "Red W", the end labels remained less "busy". All the rounds in these High Velocity boxes had "W.H.V. M92" headstamps in this caliber.

Among the later versions of the WHV box, perhaps even the last, this Staynless Non-Mercuric label also exhibits the "Special Sight Adjustment" sticker common to WHV offerings in the 1930s. R3-/400-700

Except for the word "Special" having been dropped from the M92 designation and the addition of a K-code, the end label call-outs show much the same wording as the early boxes.

Shot Boxes

A 6-15 dated "half-split" box with an add-on "Chilled Shot" label, this box is typical of the 1910-20 period. As in this case, Shot box labels from earlier periods also closely resembled those of the standard loadings. R3-/250-500

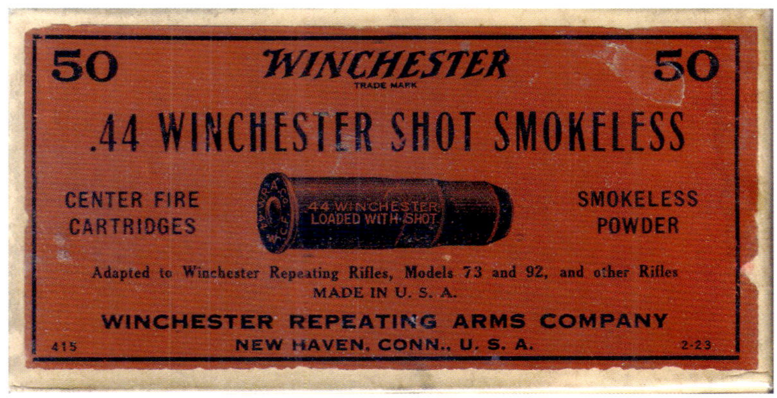

Full-cover two-piece boxes with the simplified trade mark call-out epitomize the 1920-27 period. R3-/250-500

An Interesting Rarity

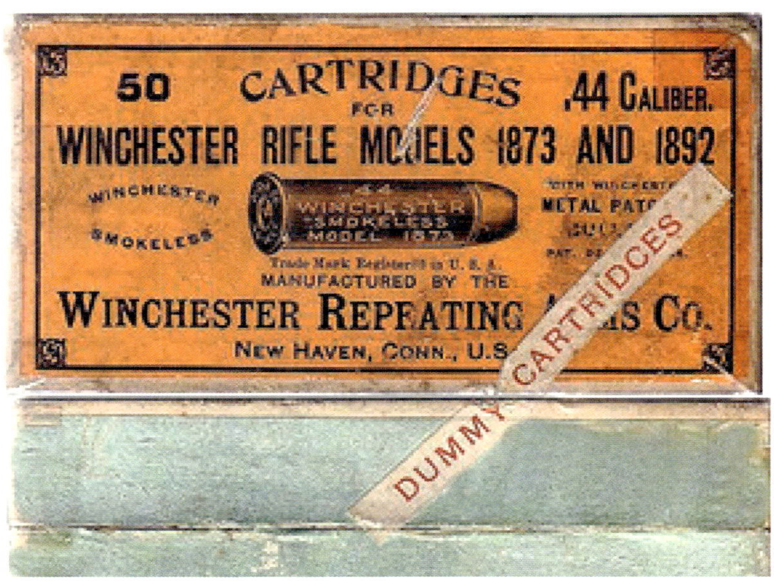

From immediately after the turn of the Twentieth Century, this box of Full Patch dummies is the only one of its type of which the authors are aware. Never a catalog item, it is nevertheless known that dummies were produced in very small quantities. These are action-proving dummies rather than the somewhat more commonly seen (though still scarce) cartridge board dummies. R4/400-800

And a Rarity of the Highest Order

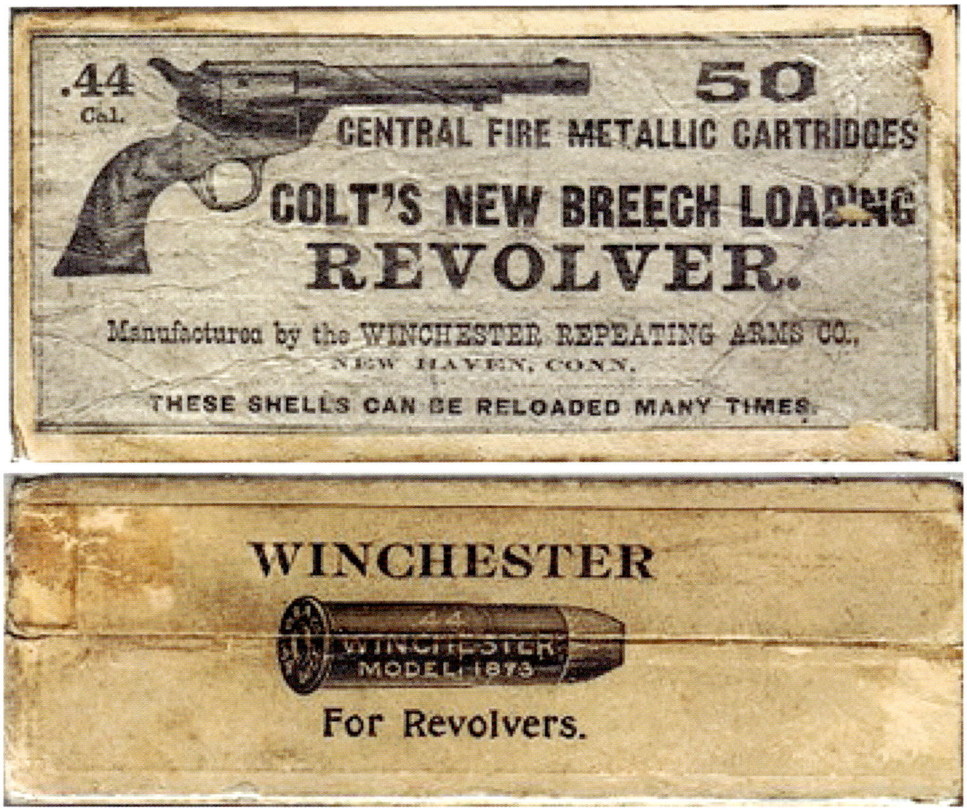

Two "special" (uncataloged) loadings "For Revolvers" are mentioned in Company records. This one is thought to be an example of the earlier one, ca. 1891-92. The existence of any Revolver box of either loading in this caliber, with the exception of the one shown here, is unknown to the authors. Whatever the caliber, any Winchester box picturing the Colt Single Action Army is of the highest rarity and desirability. R5/10,000-15,000

As Well as a Shameless Imitation

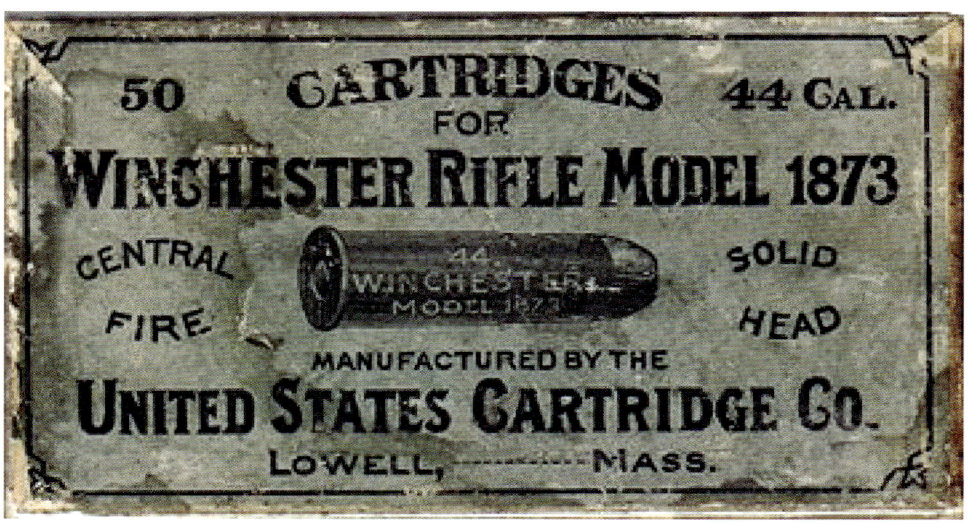

To anyone not paying attention, this box by United States Cartridge Co. is a dead-ringer for the third type Winchester Black Powder box. R3+/400-600

5

Model 1876
Calibers: 40-60, 45-60, 45-75, 50-95

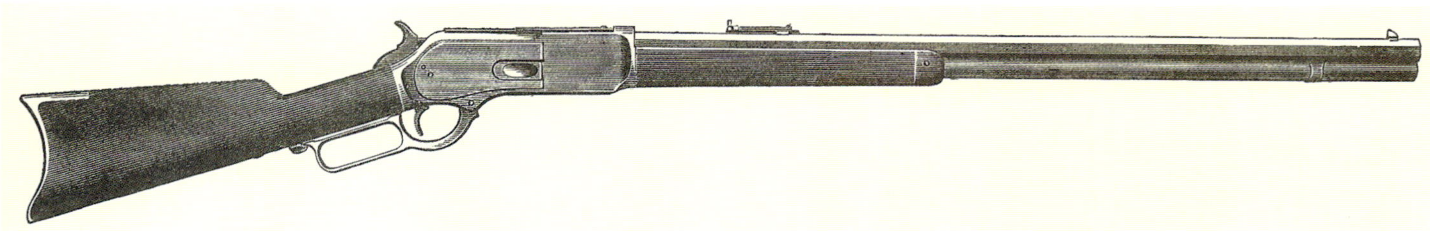

First show-cased at the 1876 Philadelphia Centennial Exposition in Philadelphia, where Winchester won the award for "The Best Magazine Rifle For Sporting Purposes Yet Produced", the new Model '76 was yet another iteration of the Company's by-then famous and successful toggle-link system. Dubbed the Centennial Model, it was simply an enlarged and strengthened Model '73. Still, it represented the Company's first attempt to chamber a repeating rifle in calibers large enough to compete with single-shot rifles of the period. Winchester then designed a series of cartridges within the limited dimensions allowed by the M76's action.

The Model '76 was well received by the public with over 60,000 having been produced by the end of 1886. The introduction of the Model 1885 single-shot and the Model 1886 repeating rifle, along with a flurry of new cartridge offerings, sharply curtailed sales of the M76 and only about 3500 more of the guns were sold by 1898, the year it was discontinued.

40-60 W.C.F.
Catalog Listings: 1884-1938

Models: 1876, 1885
Bullet types: Ld, Shot, Blank
Powder types: BP
Headstamps: Plain, WRACo

Not to be confused with the longer (2.1" case) .40-60 Marlin/Colt, the 40-60 W.C.F. was the "varmint" cartridge of the M76 line. It was never terribly popular as it was introduced only two years before the gun's production went into sharp decline. While Blanks are rare, the normal Black Powder Lead bullet loading is not all that uncommon, especially in light of what must have been the small number of guns chambered for the caliber. Interestingly, the early loadings contained 62 grains of black powder, unusual in that the Company normally loaded their ammunition either in line with, or with slightly less than, the cartridge nomenclature, in this case 60 grains of powder. In the early 1900s, this was reduced to 57 grains.

As can be seen above, Winchester's only bulleted loading was Black Powder, Lead. In an interesting footnote, Remington-UMC, Winchester's major competitor in ammunition in the early 1900s offered a jacketed bullet, Smokeless loading in 40-60. It was most unusual for any competitor to offer an up-graded loading in a proprietary Winchester caliber when Winchester itself failed to do so.

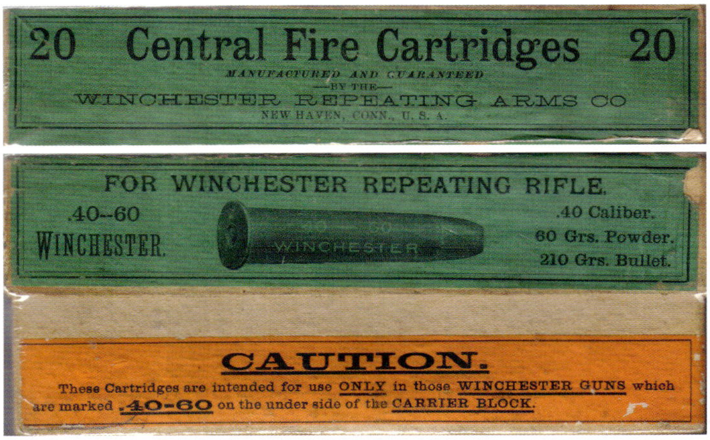

Characterized by an unheadstamped cartridge cut, this is thought to be the earliest 40-60 W.C.F. box, ca. mid-1880s. Many (if not most) of these boxes, however, are found to contain headstamped rounds, a not uncommon occurrence with regard to these early box lables relative to their contents. R3+/400-750

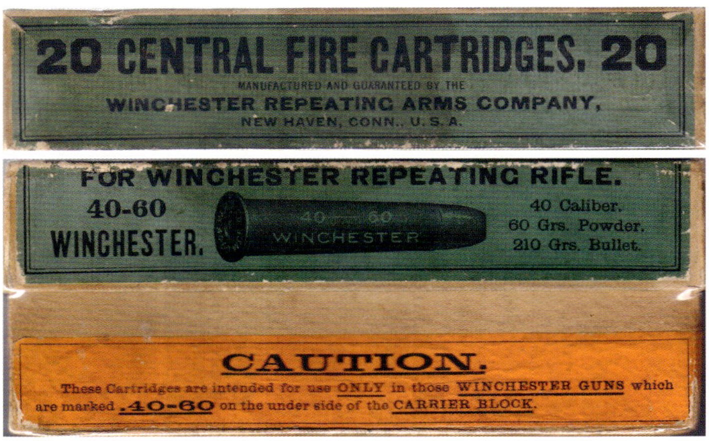

Still displaying "Central Fire Cartridges" (now in caps) and "Manufactured and Guaranteed..." on the lid top, the wording on all the labels of this box is exactly the same as on the previous one. The font, however, is now a bolder "modern" block, sans-serif type. Ca. late 1890s. R3/250-450

This is the post-1915 square-cornered box common to the late two-piece Black Powder box period. While the K-coded primary labels are dated 3-23, the orange "Caution" label on the back is 1-28. It is likely that these are the box graphics that ended this caliber's run. R3-/225-400

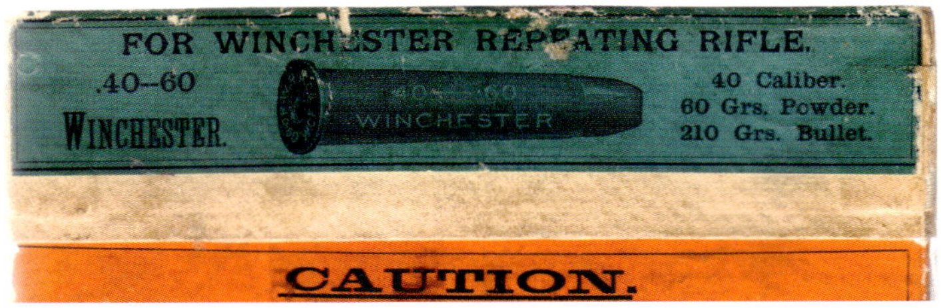

Other than the fact that the cartridge cut now shows a headstamp, the graphics on this label are identical to those on the earlier box. Probably ca. early-1890s. R3/300-500

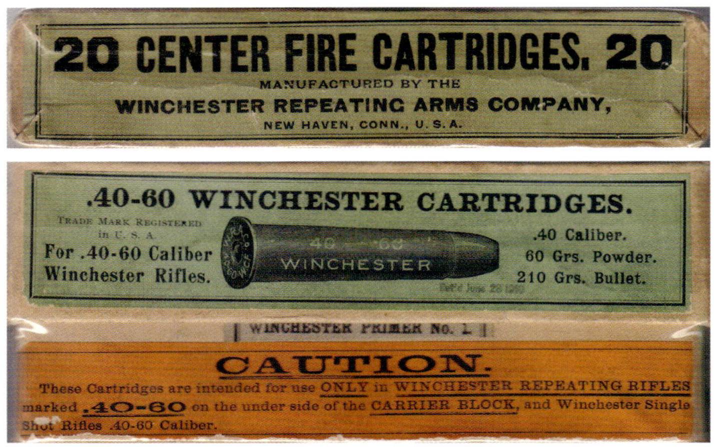

Of the style that covers the period ca. 1900 through 1914-15, this round-cornered box wins the Most Labels Award. In addition to the four labels visible in the photos there are four end labels, a "Guarantee" label on the back and a "License to the Trade" label on the bottom, a total of nine! A close-up of the "June 28 1910" patent date over-stamp represents an improved design in primer construction. R3/250-450

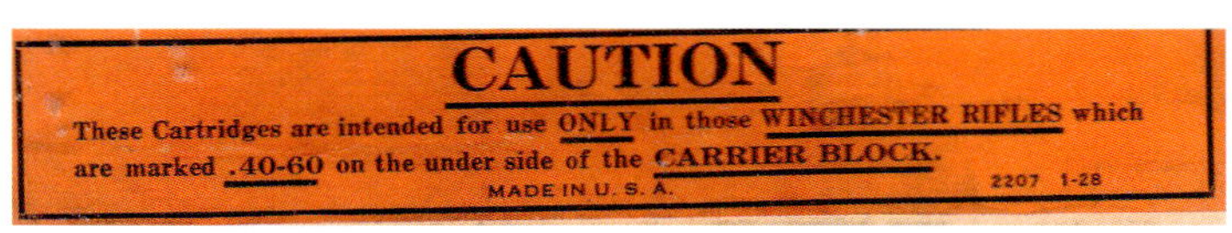

Caution label and close-up of date.

45-60 W.C.F.

Catalog Listings: 1880-1938

Models: 1876, 1885
Bullet types: Ld, Shot, Blank

Powder types: BP
Headstamps: Plain, WRACo

A popular caliber for the Model '76, the 45-60 is reputed to have been an early favorite of the famous bounty hunter, Tom Horn. Early loadings contained 63 grains of black powder which was unusual in view of the caliber's nomenclature (see preceding 40-60 W.C.F. Section). The later loadings, including the last in 1938, used 56 grains. This is one of the few calibers where blue box labels are seen about as often as green in the early Black Powder offerings. Shot loads are scarce; Blanks are rare.

As there is a very interesting and traceable trail of label varieties in this caliber, we have included more examples here than usual, this in spite of the fact that other M76 calibers do not follow exactly the same graphics progression. Unfortunately, while we can establish a time-line sequence of these early boxes through 1898, it is impossible to date the individual variations with any degree of accuracy.

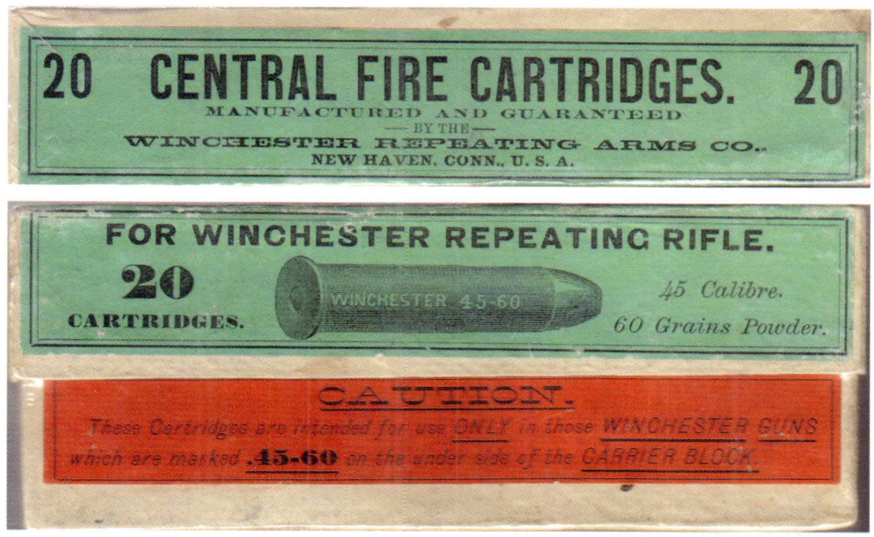

The earliest box, ca 1880, displayed an unheadstamped cartridge cut containing the words "Winchester 45-60". The call-outs for ".45 Calibre" (note spelling) and "60 Grains Powder" are in italics. R3+/400-800

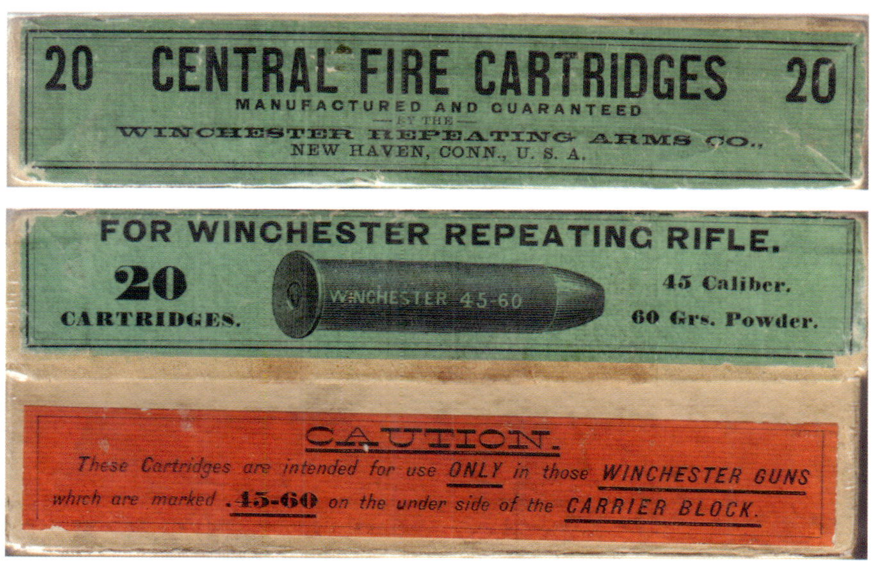

While the cartridge cut remains the same, the caliber and powder call-outs are now in block letters. Note also that the "Manufactured and Guaranteed" line on the lid-top is less spread out than on the preceding box. R3/350-700

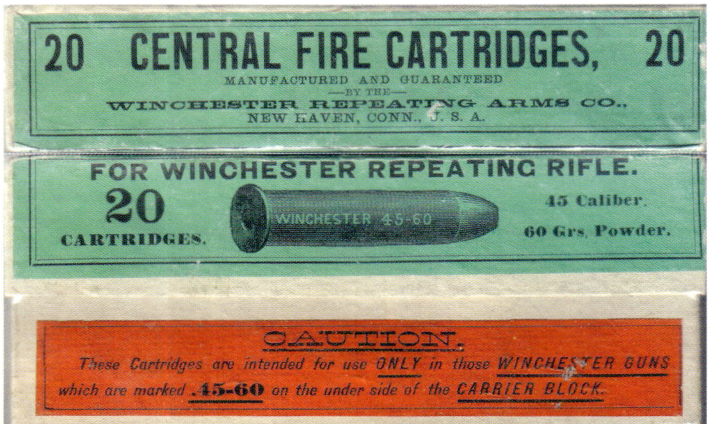

This third box retains the cartridge cut and the call-out graphics of the second box but the "20" on the lid-front is in a very different type face. Also, the "Manufactured and Guaranteed" line has narrowed even further. R3+/375-750

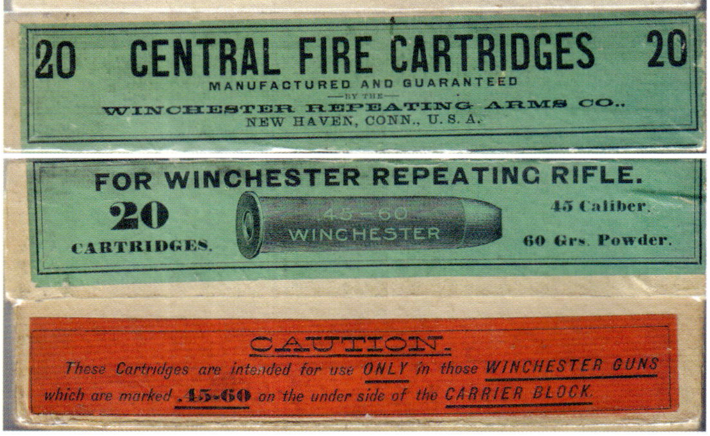

On this, the fourth box, the cartridge cut remains unheadstamped but the head is viewed at a sharper angle. Also the wording on the body of the cartridge cut is now on two lines and states ".45-60 Winchester." Oddly, the "20" on the front has reverted to the font of the first and second boxes and remains in that style until after 1900. Notice, however, that "20" at the left end of the lid-top is of a different type from the traditional one on the right end. R3/350-700

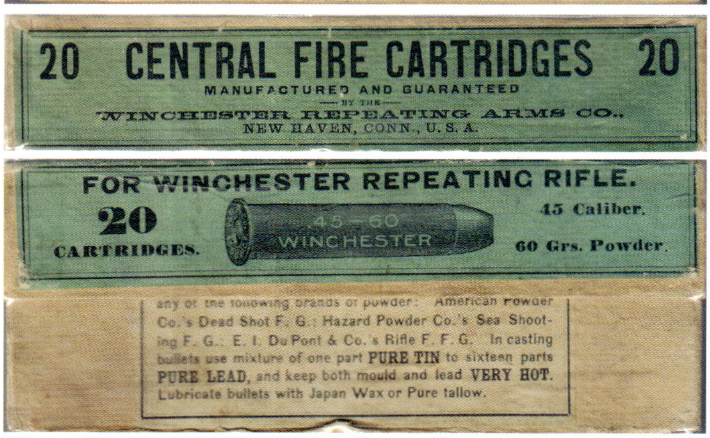

At this fifth point in our sequence the cartridge cut now displays a headstamp. Both lid-top numbers are again in the traditional type face. The red "Caution" label remains but is unseen on the back of this box. Such label placement was inconsistent throughout the period. R3-/300-600

A blue label sixth box, also with the red "Caution" label on the back, is much the same as the previous box except for the lid-top numbers which now are both in the style of the left lid-top number on the fourth box (above). R3/350-700

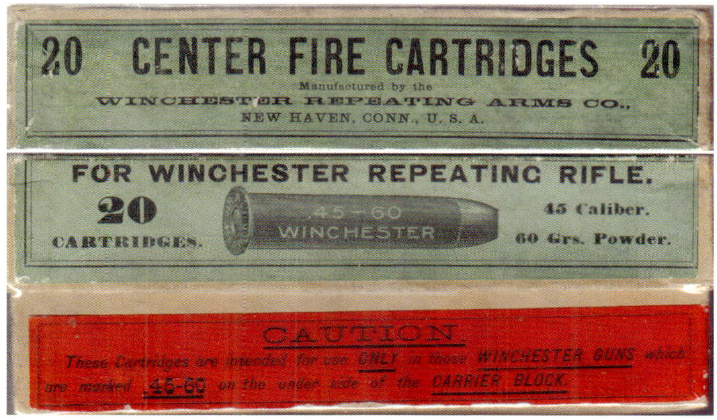

In 1898 "Central Fire" became "Center Fire" and the "Manufactured and Guaranteed by..." line on the lid top became simply "Manufactured by..." The front remained as before. R3/300-600

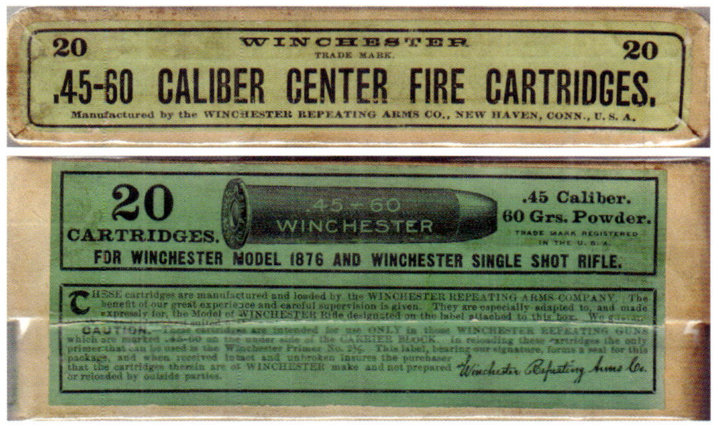

In line with other calibers, around 1900 the boxes became round-cornered and front labels provided a full front seal. Patent registration also began to be called out. R3/275-550

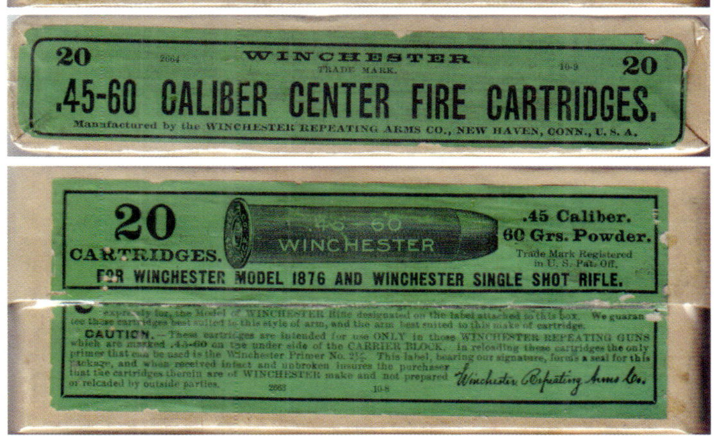

With a 10-9 top label date, one would expect this box to show "Winchester" in quotes reflecting the 1906 logo change. Except for the trade mark references and label dates and codes, both labels are identical to those of the previous box. End labels are dated 7-12 and 5-14, demonstrating the fact that these label graphics changed but little from the very early 1900's until 1915-16. R3/275-550

The typical box of the post-1914 period: the cartridge cut is moved to the lower part of a re-designed front-sealing label on a square-cornered box. The top label has also been re-designed in line with many other cartridge boxes of the period in the Winchester rifle caliber line. It is probable that this box, possibly with minor variations, was the last basic design for the 45-60 W.C.F. cartridge. R3/275-550

The cartridge cut, which has hitherto had no headstamp, now displays the standard "WRACo 45-75 W.C.F." This would point to a late-1880s dating. End labels also begin to appear on these boxes. R3/500-1000

The words are the same but the graphics are different. Note the numerous changes in type face and spacing in both lettering and numbers. Also, for the first time, it's "Caliber" rather than "Calibre". This is thought to be the labeling used from the early-1890s until ca. 1898. R3/500-1000

"Center Fire" replaced the "Central Fire" call-out circa 1898. Also at about that time "...and Guaranteed" was eliminated from the lid top. This is last of the desirable "Model Centennial 1876" boxes. R3/500-1000

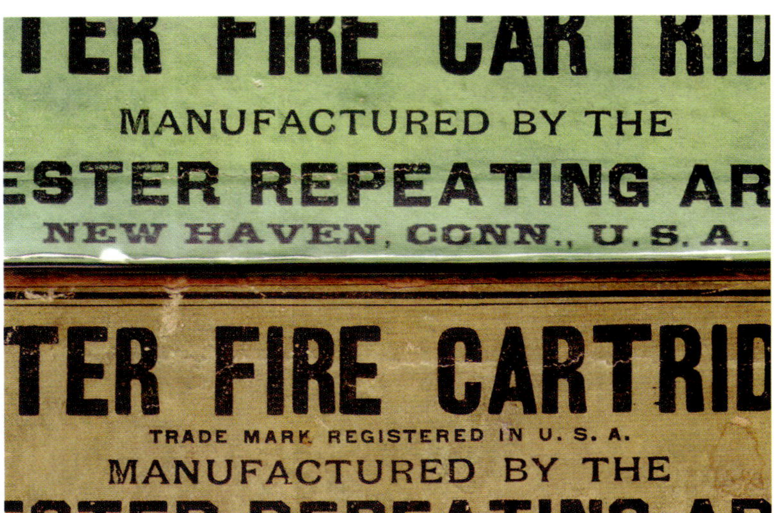

Neither of these round-cornered boxes of the very early 1900s exhibit label dates or "Red W" end labels. The only difference is the "Trade Mark Registered in the U.S.A." line. In the authors' opinion, the top box is ca. 1900-1902 and the lower one 1903-1905.

This box also has undated primary labels and lacks quote marks around "Winchester" but the 1-7 "Red W" label places this box in the post-1907 period in any event. It is likely that this variety dominated 45-75 boxes through 1914. R3-/400-750

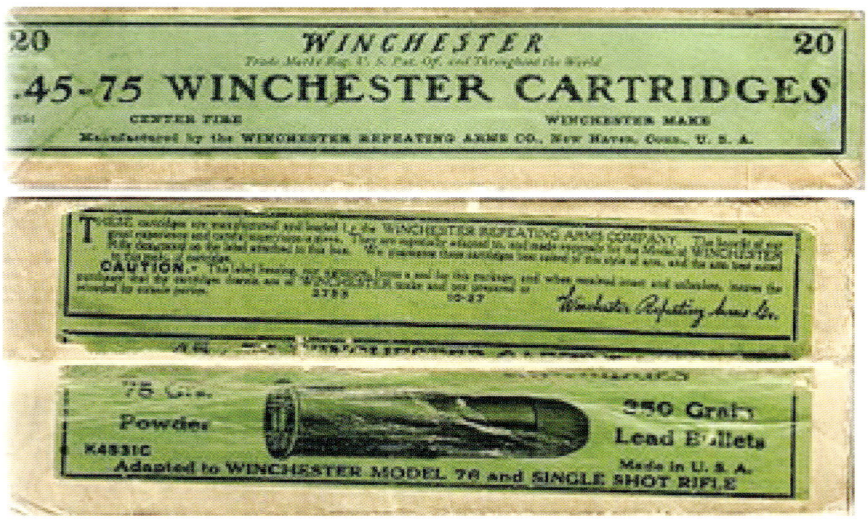

By the 1920s, a box of 45-75 would have been a slow-moving inventory item. The square-cornered 1915-style box with the cartridge cut on the lower front carried into that period and, while the lid-top label is dated 5-16, the K-coded front-seal label is dated 10-27. R3/400-750

What is likely the last style labeling in this caliber is represented by these undated top and front labels. This lid-top label is of the post-1920 style and both the front and end labels are K-coded. Label dating of two-piece box labels for the vast majority of calibers was phased out in the 1929-32 period leading us to believe that this is a 1930s box. R3/400-750

50 WINCHESTER EXPRESS, 50 EXPRESS

50-95 W.C.F., 50-95 EX.

Catalog Listings: 1879-1921

Models: 1876, 1885
Bullet types: Ld, Ld Ex, SPHP Shot, Ld "Keene"
Powder types: BP, Smkls
Headstamps: Plain, WRACo

This great M76 cartridge, the first commercial 50 caliber cartridge developed by Winchester, was introduced in the catalog of May 1, 1879. It was listed simply as the "50 Express" but using bullets "...having a hollow point that is filled with a copper cup and modeled after the famous English bullets." By August, 1880, it had been relabeled the "50 Winchester Express" and cartridges were cataloged with "...all forms of hollow, pointed and expanding bullets...including the celebrated split pointed bullet invented by Lord Keene." The "Keene" boxes, marked with an over-stamp on the lid front, are very rare and desirable. They are also very interesting in that their cross-split expansive lead bullets were partitioned into quadrants with tissue paper and are scarcely discernable as such without magnification. One might even view these rounds as the first factory-made "dum-dums"!

Other unusual finds in 50-95 would include the full case Shot variant (see 45-75, preceding) and the Smokeless Jacketed Hollow Point offering. The latter appeared only in the Company's 1896-97 catalogs and boxes are very rare. A run of the FMJ loading appears in the factory records but was not a catalog item.

Two calibers are found on headstamps in this caliber: "50-95 W.C.F." and "50 EX". Logically, the "50 EX" would be expected on the 300 grain Express or Hollow Point loadings with the "50 W.C.F." being found on the 312 grain Solid bullet loads. That is not the case, however, and no information has been found to explain the two headstamps.

This earliest 50-95 "EXPRESS" box is also an example of the very rare "Keene" over-stamped label. One clue which leads us to believe that this is the first box is the absence of the Anson Mills Belt mention on the primer label (on the back of the box in this case). A more subtle distinction can also be made in comparing the 2's in the 20's on the front labels of this box and the ones following. The "2" on the right is still seen on later boxes though the one on the left disappears by the time the cartridge cut makes its debut on the front labels (see below). R4-/1500-2500

A comparison of the "2s" in the "20" call-outs as mentioned above.

Primer call-out without mention of Anson Mills Belt, 1879-1880.

Note the much bolder "EXPRESS" call-out on this second box. Also the primer label now shows the Anson Mills Belt advertisement line. These cartridge belts were first advertised in Winchester's 1881 catalog. It's again interesting to note the difference between the 2's on the lid-top. Such an occurrence was also pointed out in our discussion of the 45-60. R3+/1400-2250

Primer call-out label including mention of Anson Mills Belt. Winchester was the sole distributor for these patented Anson Mills woven cartridge belts until the early 1900's. (See end of this section for picture)

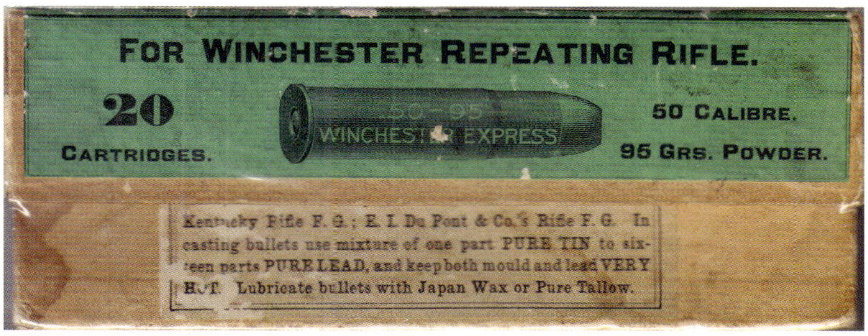

The first of the boxes to picture the cartridge, these labels depict an unheadstamped round. R3/1400-2200

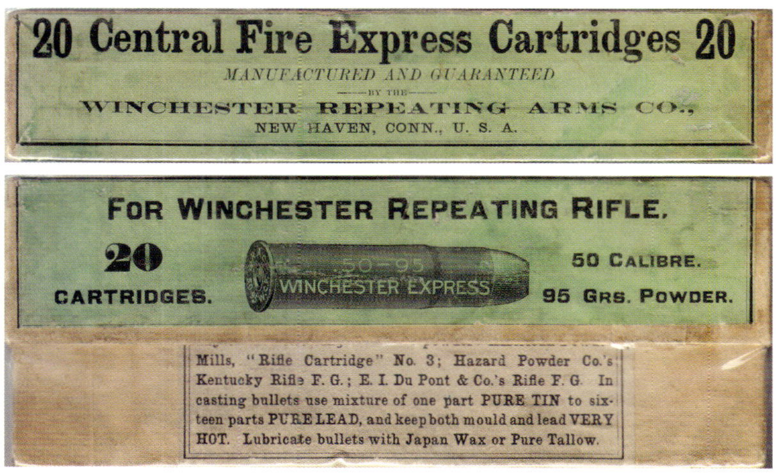

A headstamped cartridge appears here for the first time on a 50-95 box. Curiously it is stamped "50-95 W.C.F." rather than the much more commonly seen "50 EX" which never shows up on these cuts (see discussion at the beginning of this section). R3/1200-2000

Dating from the period during which Winchester purchased the Hotchkiss patents, this November 1876 U.S. military contract Black Powder box is the earliest 45-70 box issued by the Company. R4-/400-750

Showing an unheadstamped 405 grain cartridge cut and italicized caliber and bullet call-outs, this Black Powder box would appear to have been issued during the early 1880s. Though titled simply "For U.S. Government Rifle" and having all the look of a common label, it is actually quite rare. R3++/300-500

The cartridge cut is now headstamped but the italicized call-outs suggest pre-1890 labeling. The "Government Standard for Target Use" call-out was used into the 1920s and is quite common, especially in the 500 grain bullet loading. This is the scarcer 405 grain. R3/175-350

Black Powder top label from the box below but identical to the one above.

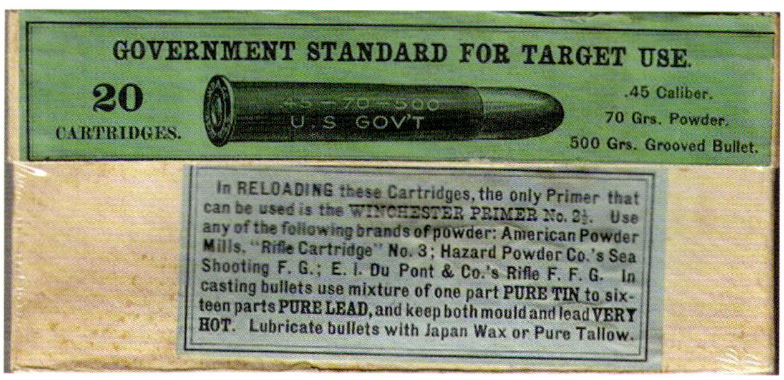

This 500 grain offering with block letter call-outs and with "Central Fire" as well as "...and Guaranteed" on the top label, we would date this box in the mid-1890s. R3-150-300

The left end of the above string-pull box.

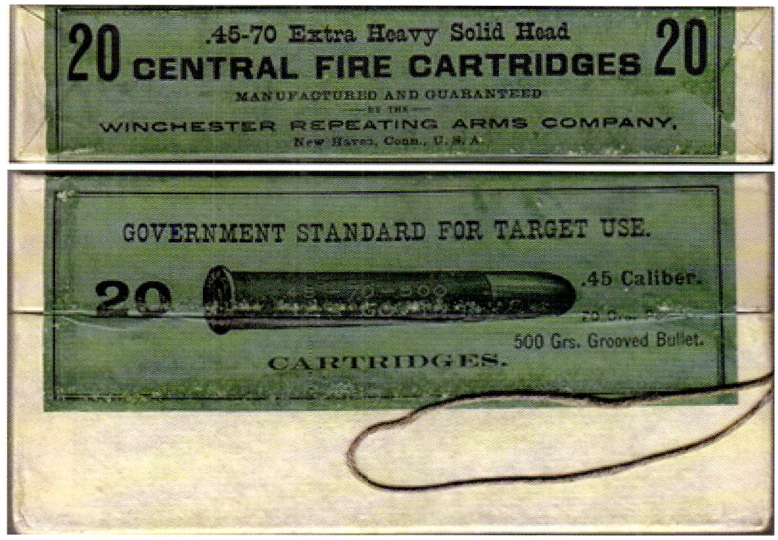

The military contract heavy-duty double-walled box has a distinctive label which wraps over the top from one side to the other exhibiting identical graphics on both sides. The box is opened with a string which is pulled (in this case) from the right end around the middle seam breaking the seal formed by the label. These Black Powder, 500 grain Lead bullet boxes, found with either green or tan labels, are quite common. R1/75-150

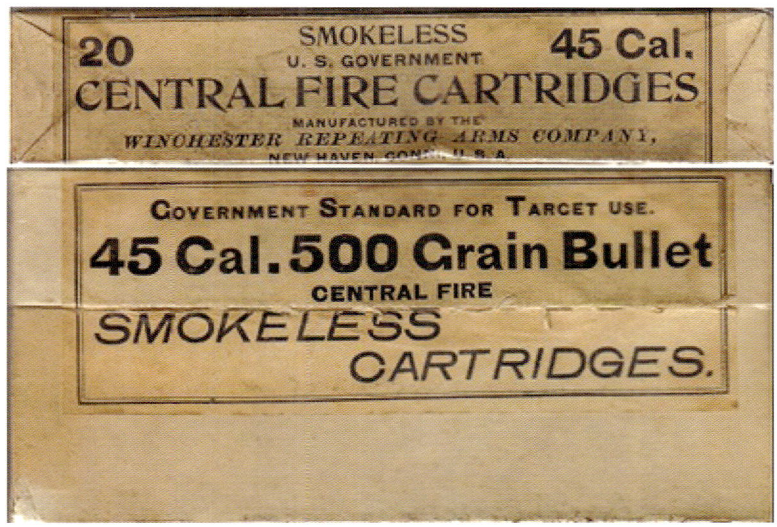

As opposed to the previous Black Powder box, Government contract Smokeless boxes such as this are very scarce. Ca. 1895-98. R4-/450-750

The Unusual Red "Folded Head" Box of 25

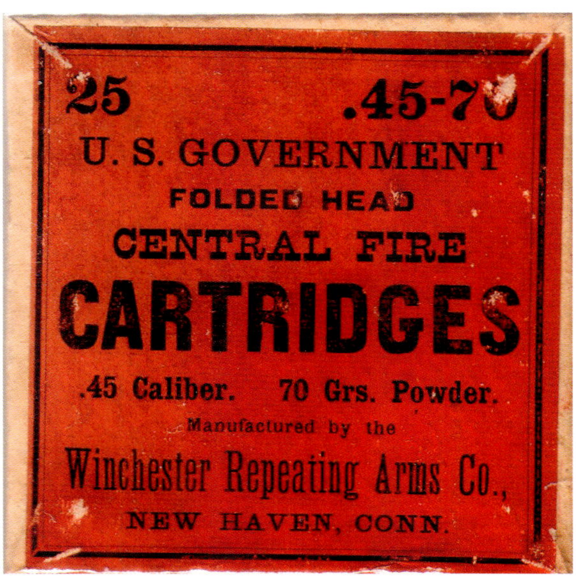

While not really rare, this mid-1880s Black Powder box is most unusual. First, it contains 25 rounds rather than the normal 20. Second, the callout is for "Folded Head" cases rather than "Solid Head". Third, the contents exhibit cast lead (500 grain) bullets rather than swaged bullets. And fourth, the red label, indicative of an export box, is a color seldom seen on Black Powder boxes. Referred to in Company records as the "Mexican label" boxes, they were, indeed, largely used for export to Central and South America. R3/175-350

7

Model 1885 Single Shot Calibers: See Below

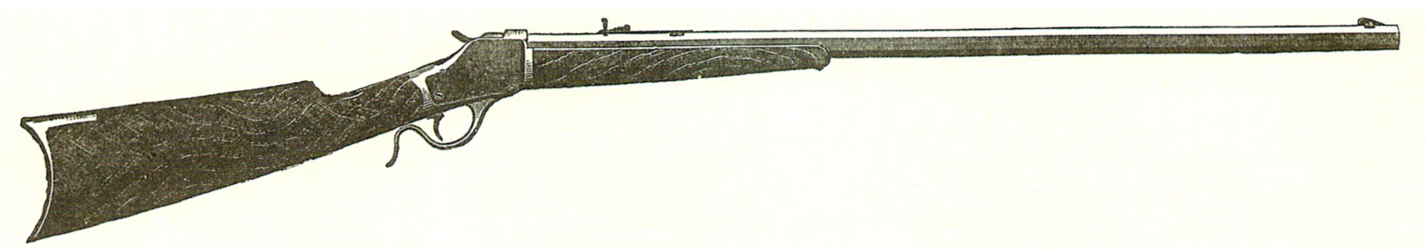

This is the firearm that, arguably, brought together the most significant combination of talents in the evolving firearms industry of the 19th Century: the genius of John Browning's inventive talents and the engineering, manufacturing and marketing capabilities of Winchester. Beginning with Winchester's 1883 purchase of Browning's Model 1879 single shot rifle patents, the Browning-Winchester relationship lasted until after the turn of the Century. During that period Browning sold his inventions exclusively to Winchester. The Company bought the patents for over forty rifle-related designs and improvements from Browning including, as will be seen in future chapters, those upon which Winchester's most famous and important gun models of the late 1880s and 1890s were derived.

Originally titled the "Winchester Single Shot" these guns have become even better known as the "High Wall" and "Low Wall" rifles. The latter type, with a shorter receiver profile, was generally used for the rim fire and smaller center fire cartridges though it is known in the 32-40 and 38-55 case length. The exceptionally strong design of the M85 elevated Winchester to the level of, and in some cases beyond, Sharps (though by then defunct), Ballard, Bullard, Remington, Rigby and a host of others in the single shot field.

While the April 1886 catalog lists the standard calibers available in this model, the November 1885 catalog which introduced the M85 listed no specific calibers at all, simply stating "...with barrels of all ordinary lengths and weights, and for all standard cartridges." Also, "...these guns will be adapted to all the standard sizes of cartridges, both rim and center fire." It led one to believe that if you wanted a M85 in virtually any caliber on the market at the time it was yours for the asking. And that is essentially what transpired with over 100 different chamberings having been recorded in a myriad of barrel lengths and weights by the time of its discontinuance in 1919.

When it was announced in 20 gauge in 1914, the M85 became unique among Winchester firearms as the only gun to ever be offered commercially as both a shotgun and rifle. The following are contemporary shot shell boxes shown in Krause Publications' *The Standard Catalog of Winchester* (2000): pp 204 (bottom), 205 (top), 207 (both). Page 206 (right), however, is actually the most appropriate in either Rival or First Quality grade. While the boxes shown in that work may be of a different gauge, the labeling would be the same or very similar.

Based upon surviving specimens encountered by the authors, the Union Metallic Cartridge Co. (UMC), Winchester's main competitor in the ammunition field, seems to have out-sold Winchester in several M85 calibers. This would not be unexpected as many calibers selected by Winchester for their Single Shot rifle would have been those created by other companies that had already met with at least a modicum of success. Among those boxes where UMC seems to have won the marketing battle are found the Ballard, Sharps and Remington calibers as well as the 32 Ideal. As a result these boxes are relatively scarce in Winchester brand in spite of the popularity of several of the calibers.

Following the scope of this work as set forth in Chapter One, we have covered here only those calibers in which the M1885 was either listed in the gun model section of the catalogs or in the ammunition section of the catalogs in those calibers which specifically called out the M1885. To cover every caliber listed in the shipping dockets and special order books, as well as those known to have been used for special cartridge testing purposes in New Haven, would require a separate work altogether. Even so, we have found it necessary to group the forty cartridges covered here by type and, in some cases, sub-grouped them further by case length. The groups are as follows: Rim Fire Calibers, Winchester M85 Express Calibers, Sharps & Related Calibers, and Miscellaneous & Other Calibers. We hope that these efforts will enable the reader to navigate more efficiently within the virtual maze of calibers represented by the Model 1885.

The calibers in which the M1885 was cataloged or for which the M1885 was called out are listed below. Many have been covered in other chapters within this work and are so noted.

Model 1885 Calibers

CENTER FIRE

22 WCF	
236 USN (Rimless)	(See Lee)
25-20 SS	
25-20 Win SS	
25-35 WCF	(See M94)
30 WCF (30-30)	(See M94)
30 Army (30-40 Krag)	(See M95)
303 Brit	(See M95)
32 S C.F.	
32 L C.F.	
32 XL C.F.	
32 Ideal	
32 WCF (32-20)	(See M73)
32 WS	(See M94)
32-40	(See M94)
33 WCF	(See M86)
35 WCF	(See M95)
38 S C.F.	
38 L C.F.	
38 XL C.F.	
38 WCF (38-40)	(See M73)
38 Ex (38-90)	
38-55 Ballard	(See M94)
38-55	(See M94)
38-56 WCF	(See M86)
40-50 Reg (BN)	
40-50 Sharps Str, 1 7/8"	
40-70 Reg (BN)	
40-70 Sharps Str, 2.5"	
40-60 Marlin	
40-60 WCF	(See M76)
40-65 WCF	(See M86)
40-70 Ballard	
40-82 WCF	(See M86)
40-90 Sharps & Rem	
40-90 Sharps Str. 3.25"	
40-90 Ballard	(Combined with 40-70 Ballard, 40-85 Ballard)
40 Ex (40-110)	
405 WCF	(See M95)
44 WCF (44-40)	(See M73)
44-60 Sharps & Rem	
44-77 Sharps 2.25"	
44-90 Sharps 2.25"	(Combined with 44-77 Sharps)
44-90 to 105 Sharps 2 5/8"	
45-60 WCF	(See M76)
45-70 USG (45 Govt)	(See Hotchkiss and M86)
45-75 WCF	(See M76)
45-82 WCF	(See M86)
45-90 WCF	(See M86)
45 Sharps 2.1" to 3.25"	
45 Ex (45-125)	
50 Eley	
50-90 Sharps (2.5")	
50-95 WCF	(See M76)
50-110 Ex	(See M86)
20 Gauge Shot Shell	

RIM FIRE

22 Short	
22 Long	
22 Ex Long (XL)	
22 WRF	
25 L Stevens	
32 Short	
32 Long	
32 Ex Long (XL)	
38 Short	
38 Long	
38 Ex Long (XL)	
44 Flat (Henry)	(See Henry)

Model 1885 - Part I
Rimfire Calibers
(22 S, 22 L, 22 XL, 22 WRF, 25 L Stevens, 32 S, 32 L, 32 XL, 38 S, 38 L, 38 XL, 44 [Henry] Flat*)
Catalog listings: See below

Model: 1885

Bullet types: Ld, Shot, Blank

Powder types: BP, Lsmk, Smkls

Headstamps: Raised "H", Impressed "H"

Prior to 1873 Winchester's range of Rimfire production had been somewhat limited. Of the twelve calibers shown above for the M85, all but four were first listed in 1873 with the 44 Henry having been, as we have already seen, a much earlier introduction and the 22 XL appearing in 1878. Only the 25 Stevens and 22 WRF, both first listed in 1890, came after the introduction of the M85. However, of those early (pre-1885) calibers the 32 XL, 44 Flat and all three 38s were dropped from the list of M85 offerings by mid-1887. The reader will note that we have made an exception here and show contemporary examples of the various 22 calibers in which this model was offered.

*See Chapter 3 on the Henry and Model 1866 rifles where this caliber is covered in its entirety.

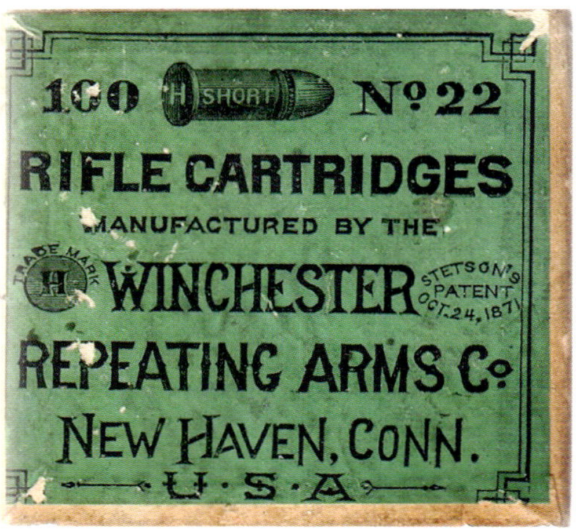

An 1880s style box of 22 Short. In the 1860s-1880s the standard size box for all 22s was 100-count such as this. The 50-round versions which began to appear around 1880 were considered half-boxes and were so marked on the side label. R3/350-650

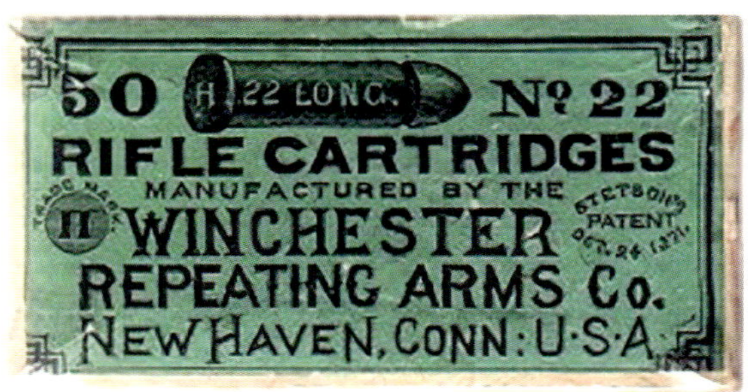

The "half-box" of 50 longs, also ca 1880s. R2/125-225

Appearing as they do in just a few calibers, these early diagonal label Winchester boxes are especially scarce and desirable. This one is in 22 Extra Long and is from the 1880s. R3-/275-550

The 22 Winchester Rim Fire, or WRF as it has come to be known, was first listed in 1890 for the M90 22 rifle. It was added to the list of M85 calibers in 1892 in a box of this style. Graphics on labels in this caliber exhibited very little change throughout the 1890s. R3-/175-250 [Green: R2+/125-200]

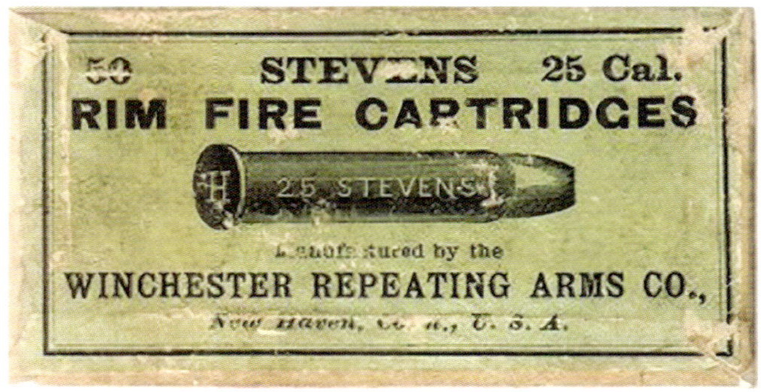

In 1890 the 25 Stevens Rim Fire was added to the line and listed as a M85 caliber. This is thought to be an example of the earliest style labeling. R3/100-150

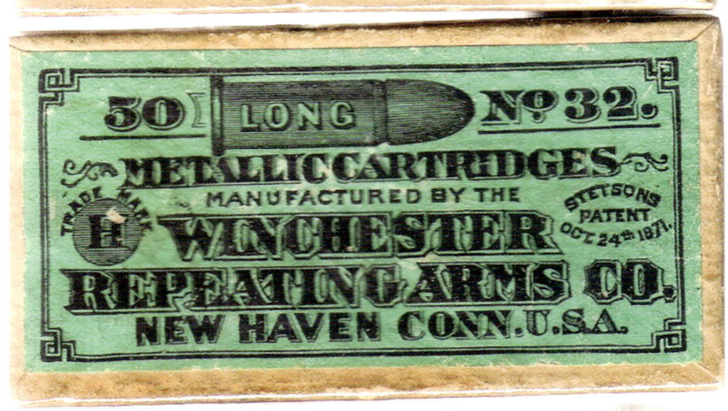

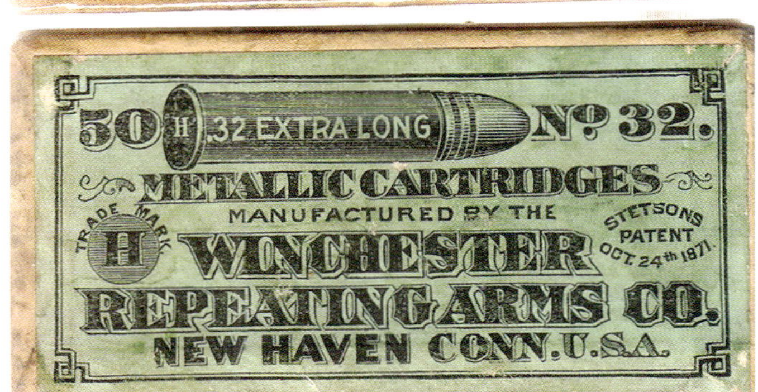

Early boxes of the three lengths of 32 Rim Fire (Short, Long and Extra Long) are virtually identical except for the "Rifle Cartridges" call-out on the Short box versus the "Metallic Cartridges" call-out on the other two. The only other notable differences relate to the cartridge cut and case length call-out. The "Metallic" call-out is the earlier, but it is not known exactly when the "Rifle Cartridges" labels were phased in. In the opinion of the authors, both styles were in use in the mid-1880s with "Metallic" stretching back to the 1870s and "Rifle" going forward to the 1890s and beyond. The Extra Long was omitted from the M85 listing in 1887. [Short, Long, or Extra Long: R3-/100-200]

Known to have been used for export, red label boxes such as this 32 Short Rim Fire are rarely encountered. R3+/150-225

The comments regarding the 32 Rim Fire boxes above apply here as well. Interestingly, however, all three of these calibers were dropped from M85 listings by June, 1887. [Short: R2+/75-150] [Long: R2-/60-120] [Extra Long: R3/125-225]

Model 1885 - Part II
The Big Three
M1885 "Express" Calibers: 38-90, 40-110, 45-125
Catalog Listings: 1886-1917 (40 Ex, 45 Ex), 1921 (38 Ex)

Actual size all cartridges is 3 3/4"

Model: 1885
Bullet types: Ld (38-90)
Ld Ex (40-110, 45-125)
Powder types: BP
Headstamps: Plain, WRACo

These long-case cartridges were created by the Company "Expressly for WINCHESTER Single Shot Rifle" as the box labels stated. "Express" in this case probably implied high velocity, though both the 40 and 45 caliber offerings were also loaded with the copper-tubed "express" bullet. The 38 was cataloged as having a plain lead bullet. (Though uncataloged, the fabled 50-140 Express is very rare and seldom encountered in any form.) The lighter-than-average bullets would have, indeed, provided velocities above standard loads in most black powder rifles of the period. Ballistics from the March, 1897, catalog show all three Express calibers posting velocities higher than the other thirty Winchester Black Powder loadings tested. Still, no other American gun-makers adopted any of these Express calibers and Smokeless Powder was soon to obsolete them all. M85 chamberings in these three classic Winchester cartridges were last offered in 1909.

38-90 (38 Express)

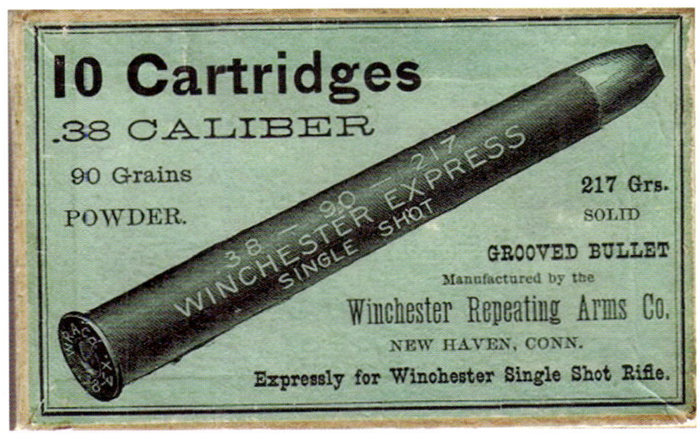

The earliest of the label versions found on these boxes has "Cartridges" in upper and lower case letters and "Powder" in smaller type than the succeeding label version. Also, the "10" is in a plain type face and the "217 Grs." callout is in a different font from the box following. R3/400-600

On what is thought to be the second iteration of this box, the "Cartridges" line is now all upper-case letters of a different font and "Powder" is in larger letters. Otherwise, the format and graphics are essentially the same as the prior box. It is possible that a labeling exists with the "Winchester Repeating Arms Co." line all in capital letters similar to the second type 45 Express box discussed below. R3-/350-550

Top labels wrap over the right end of the box to create an end-label. This graphic is identical on both of the above boxes.

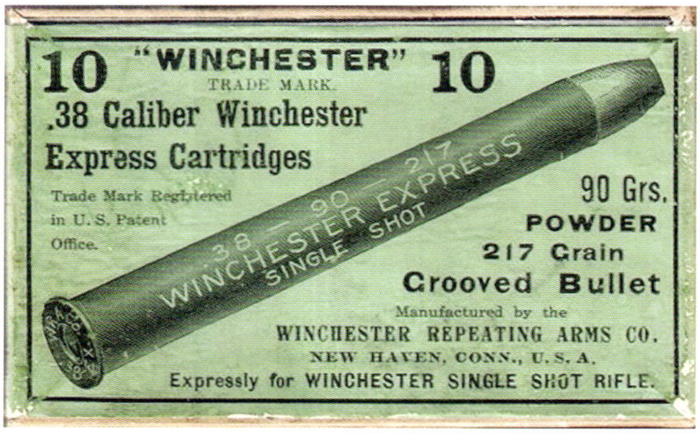

Entirely re-designed, these graphics of the post-1906 period show "Winchester" in quotes, a "...U.S. Patent Office" call-out and a "Red W" end label. This third type of box is much scarcer than the previous, older two. R3+/400-600

The top label now covers both ends and wraps over the bottom forming a seal. It is our opinion that this represents the Company's first use of a wrap-around sealing label, dated 7-9, which became common in the early 1920s. The partially obscured label is the commonly found "guarantee" label of the early 1900s.

The "Red W" logo and other call-outs are found on both ends of this wrap-over sealing label and are identical.

40-110 (40 Express)

The only label style we have to show of the 40 Express (40-110) box is this one, similar to the second type above and below. It is presumed that a first type exists, but a third type is doubtful (see also 38-90 and 45-125). Cartridges with special order solid Lead (rather than Hollow Point Express) bullets are known to have been shipped in boxes such as these but are rubber-stamped "Solid Ball" on the label. R3/500-850

Though the early type formats of the "Big Three" caliber end labels differ somewhat, they all convey essentially the same information.

45-125 (45 Express)

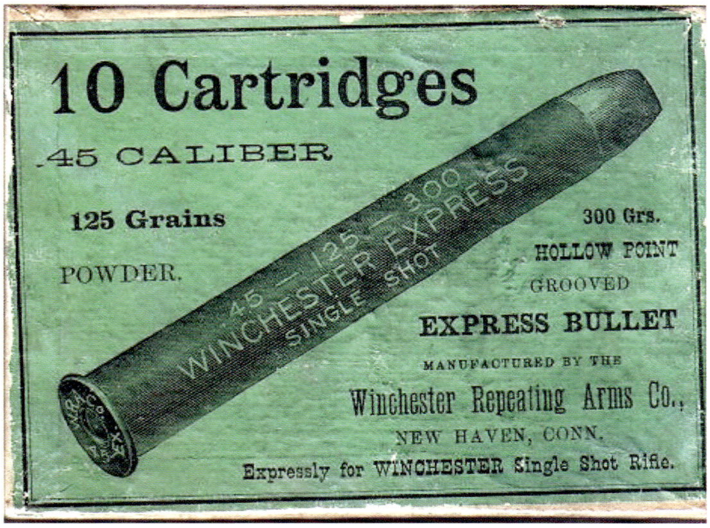

Except for the "125 Grains Powder" line, which is italicized here, the end labels are the same on both this first type as well as the second type labels.

The "Cartridges" line of the first type 45 Express (45-125) box, as was seen on the 38 Express box earlier, is in both upper and lower case letters and the "10" is different from the those on subsequent labels. Also, the "Powder" call-out is in smaller type and the "125 Grains" is further from the left margin in comparison to graphics on the box below. R3+/1000-1750

Other than the distinguishing points made relative to the first type box above, this box of the second type is identical in content and very similar in format. Note, however, that the "Winchester Repeating Arms Co." line is all in capital letters whereas the prior box is both upper and lower case. It is also possible that there exists a box similar to the second type 38 Express box above, where the "Cartridges" line is in caps but the "Winchester..." line is both upper and lower case. R3/900-1600

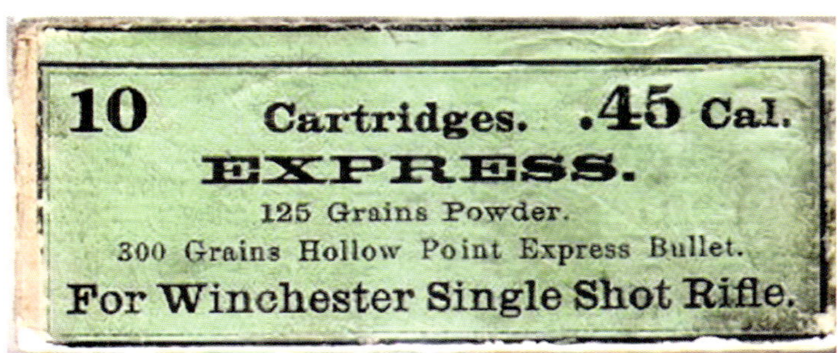

As seen earlier the end labels on both styles are very similar, the difference here being that the "Powder" call-out line is no longer italicized.

Model 1885 - Part III
Sharps and Related* Calibers

40 1-7/8 (40-50 Str.), **40 1-3/4** (40-50 BN), **40 2-1/2** (40-70 Str), **40 2-1/4** (40-70 BN), **40 2-5/8** (40-90 BN), **40 3-1/4** (40-90 Str.), **44 1-1/8"** (44-60BN), **44 2-1/4** (44-77), **44 2-5/8** (44-90), **45 2.1, 45 2.4, 45 2.6, 45 2-7/8, 45 3-1/4, 50 2-1/2, 50 3-1/4**

40 Sharps 1-3/4 BN (40-50 Sharps BN)
Catalog listings: 1875-1917

Models: 1885
Bullet types: Ld PP
Powder types: BP
Headstamps: Plain, WRACo

This smallest of the bottle-necked Sharps cartridges was also a very early entrant into the Sharps Rifle Mfg. Co. line, circa 1869. Likewise, it was an early Winchester listing appearing among their very first ammunition offerings in 1875. Unfortunately it was obsolete by the time it was called out for the M85 in the ammunition section of the November, 1885 catalog. Approximately one year later that designation was dropped.

Featuring graphics from the mid-to-late 1880s, this 40-50 Sharps BN box is another example of the 20-round two-piece boxes in which the smaller Sharps calibers were offered. Notice the apostrophe in the "Sharp's" call-out. Winchester found every possible way to get it wrong. (See the following section on the 40-70 Sharps BN for an earlier version.) R3/500-900

40-50 Sharps Straight (1-7/8)
Catalog listings: 1880-1917

Models: 1885
Bullet types: Ld PP
Powder types: BP
Headstamps: Plain, WRACo

Though most often loaded with 45 grains of powder by both Sharps and Winchester, this little number was essentially a follow-on to the 40-50 Sharps Bottleneck but with a straight 40 caliber case. Unlike most of the Sharps cartridges, the 40 Sharps 1-7/8 stayed in the catalogs with a Winchester Single Shot call-out until 1917.

The shorter-cased Sharps calibers were typically found in these 20-round two-piece boxes common to the period. The main difference is that the Sharps calibers had the "Powder" and "Bullet Grs." call-outs stamped on the front label. In this case, 45 Grs. And 265 Grs., respectively. Interestingly, the end label (not shown) called out the generic "40/50" title by which this caliber was commonly known and cataloged. R3/450-800

*These calibers were either introduced or popularized by Sharps prior to the introduction of the Winchester M1885.

40 Sharps 2-1/4 BN (40-70 Sharps & Remington BN)

Catalog listings: 1875-1917

Models: 1885
Bullet types: Ld PP

Powder types: BP
Headstamps: Plain, WRACo

One of the few Sharps cartridges that Winchester marketed before it had gained real success with Sharps itself, the 40-70 BN nevertheless only lasted as a first-year call-out for the M85.

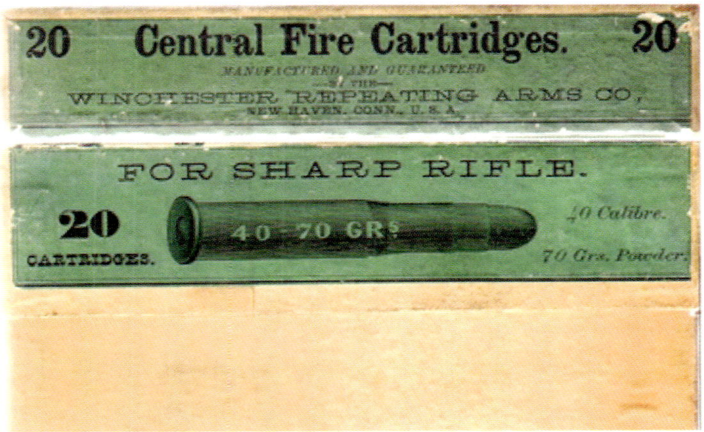

Unlike UMC which marketed this caliber in 10-round flat boxes, Winchester offered the 40-70 Sharps BN in 20-round boxes, the same two-piece style in which most of their lever-action calibers were sold. Note the lack of a final "s" in "Sharps" in the "For Sharp Rifle" call-out. This was an error Winchester labels of the period repeated in other calibers as well. The end label (not shown) gets it right, however. With the "Sharp" spelling and the lid-top label in both upper and lower case letters the graphics of this box suggest production in the early-to-mid 1880s. R3/500-1000

40-70 Sharps Straight (2 1/2)

Catalog listings: 1880-1914

Models: 1885
Bullet types: Ld, Ld PP

Powder types: BP
Headstamps: Plain, WRACo

Probably the most commonly found Sharps caliber, the "40-70 SS" was actually loaded with 65 grains of Black Powder by Sharps, Winchester and, most often, UMC (which apparently did load some with 70 grains). Contrary to common belief, however, the "SS" in the Winchester headstamp for these straight-walled Sharps calibers stood for "Straight Shell", not "Sharps Straight". While Sharps-derived cartridges typically were loaded with paper-patched bullets, a significant number of the 40-70 Straights were sold with "Grooved" bullets, meaning un-patched lead bullets with grease grooves.

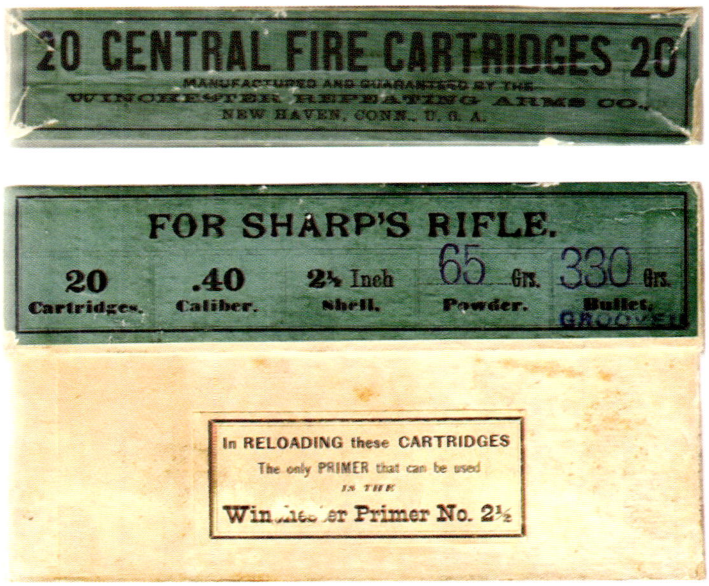

With the "Central Fire" call-out, "Manufactured and Guaranteed..." line and small Primer label this square-cornered box is late-1880s to early-1890s. This is the "Grooved" bullet offering which was listed separately from the patched bullet entry in the catalogs. This was most unusual in that bullet options, and there were often many, were generally to be found in the fine print within the listing for each caliber. R3-/450-750

Close-up of the hand-stamped call-outs for Powder and Bullet. Note also the hand-stamped "Grooved" under the word "Bullet".

The end label always used the catalog nomenclature, in this case "40-70", no matter what the actual loading stamped on the front happened to be. As can be seen both here and on the front lid label above as well as on the labels of later boxes (see below), "Sharp's", with an apostrophe, is an error that was perpetuated for years.

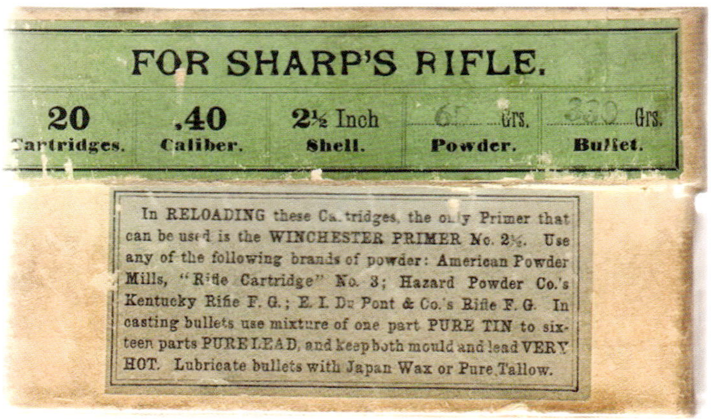

The call-outs on the lid-top label of this round-cornered box , as well as a "Red W" end confirms its dating as post-1906. While Winchester boxes in this caliber are not altogether uncommon, UMC flat boxes of ten 40-65 and 40-70 Sharps Straight are by far the most often seen of all Sharps boxes by any maker. R3-/400-700

Here is a close-up of the hard-to-read hand-stamped "Powder" and "Bullet" loadings. In the absence of the "Grooved" call-out as seen on the previous box, this would be the standard paper-patched bullet offering.

40 Sharps 2-5/8 BN (40-90 Sharps & Remington BN)

Catalog listings: 1878-1917

Models: 1885
Bullet types: Ld PP

Powder types: BP
Headstamps: Plain, WRACo

Along with the 44 Sharps 2-5/8 BN (44-90), this caliber was introduced by Sharps in 1873 and, again like the 44-90, became quite popular. Winchester added it to the list of calibers calling out the M85 upon that gun's introduction in November, 1885. And like so many of the Sharps calibers it was dropped in mid-1886. As with most other paper-patched Single Shot calibers, the Company packaged these only in ten-round boxes.

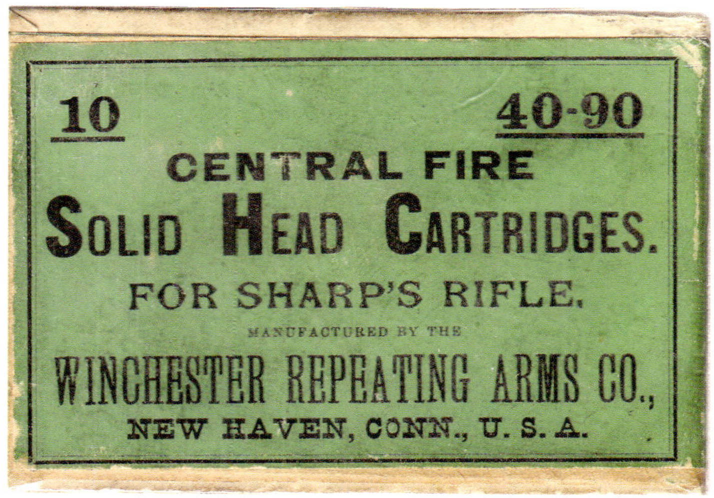

The 40-90 Sharps BN is most commonly found in this 10-round box. Note that there is no call-out of the case length or type in spite of the fact that the company also marketed a 40-90 Sharps Straight offering. R3-/400-800

40-90 Sharps Straight (3")

Catalog listings: 1884-1917

Models: 1885
Bullet types: Ld PP

Powder types: BP
Headstamps: WRACo

Such was the image of Sharps that even cartridges born after that company's demise in 1882 were accorded the Sharps designation. This is true of all the 3-inch length so-called "Sharps" calibers of the 1880s. The 40-90 Sharps Straight which was an 1884 introduction, first in the Remington-Hepburn then in the Winchester M1885, is but one example (the 45 3" and 50 3" are the other two). This caliber, however, like the 40-70 Straight previously discussed, were chambered in a fairly large number of Model 1885 High Walls and the cartridge remains listed in the catalogs with that call-out until 1917. Interestingly, the labels of most of these "Sharps" calibers were printed in the 1890s and, while they were cataloged and loaded until 1909-1917, boxes continued to display the older labels.

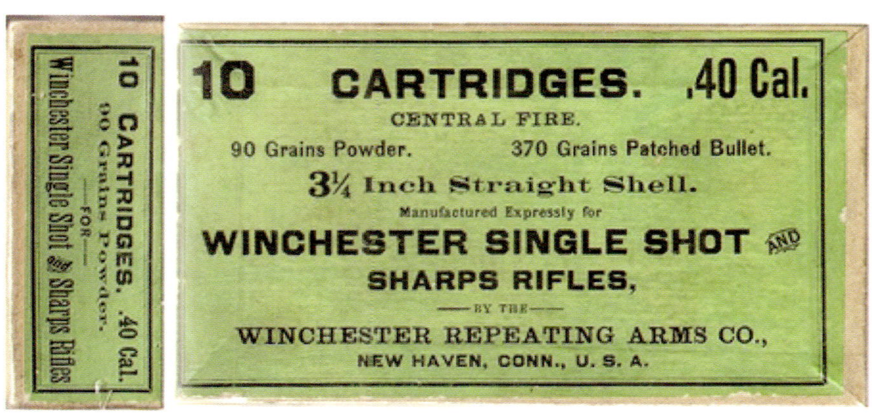

These flat 10-round boxes with the label over-lapping the left end are the ones most often found in this caliber. In fact, with regard to Winchester boxes of all "Sharps" calibers, this is one of the most frequently encountered although a white label exists which is somewhat scarcer. Other than on the labels of the three "Express" calibers, the bold call-out of the "Winchester Single Shot Rifle" as seen here is most unusual. R3-/400-800

44 Sharps 1-7/8 BN (44-60 Sharps & Remington)

Catalog listings: 1875-1910

Models: 1885
Bullet types: Ld, Ld PP

Powder types: BP
Headstamps: Plain, WRACo

An early Sharps cartridge, Winchester first listed the 44-1 7/8 BN in 1875, the same year in which it was discontinued by the Sharps Rifle Co. It's actually a wonder that it was ever cataloged in the M85, being, as it was, obsolete when first listed for that model in November 1885. It was then omitted as a M85 caliber in mid-1886. A short (and obsolete) cartridge, a short M85 existence, a short paragraph describing it: the full story of the 44-60.

Several clues point to an early-to-mid 1880s dating of this 44-60 BN 1-7/8". First, note the "Central Fire Cartridges" wording as well as the type style in which it is printed. That font is not found past the 1880s and the Central Fire, as well as "Manufactured and Guaranteed" wording is pre-1898. The cartridge cut exhibits an unheadstamped round typical of the early 1880s and the italicized powder and "Calibre" call-outs are also of that early period. It was also common for cartridge makers to label these early Single Shot boxes as being for different guns even though the boxes and their contents were identical. In this case the marking is "For Remington Rifle"; however, boxes in this caliber with a "For Sharp Rifle" call-out also exist. R3/450-900

44 Sharps 2-5/8" BN (44-77, 44-90 Reg)

Catalog listings: See below

Models: 1885
Bullet types: Ld PP

Powder types: BP
Headstamps: Plain, WRACo

One of the first Center Fire sporting cartridges ever produced, the 44-77 also became one of the most popular. After its introduction by Remington in 1869, it gained its greatest recognition as a Sharps caliber in the early 1870s.

Unfortunately, there is no better example than the Sharps "2-1/4" to demonstrate why Sharps denotations need to be according to case length rather than powder loads. There are two Sharps 44 bottle-necked cartridges, the "2-1/4" and the "2-5/8". Both would hold 90 grains of Black Powder, but unlike many straight-cased shells, these were by no means interchangeable. In a most unfortunate decision by Winchester in 1878, a 44 "2-1/4" BN case loaded with 90 grains of powder was, albeit within normal Winchester cartridge-naming protocol, dubbed the 44-90 Regular. This new round utilized exactly the same case and 470 grain bullet as was used in the popular 44-77 Sharps, which had been loaded by Winchester since 1875 and of which this 44-90 was a "hopped-up" version. Unfortunately it was readily confused with the longer "2 5/8" BN loading which was already well-known as the 44-90 Sharps. So beginning in the late 1870s, two very different bottle-necked cartridge cases shared the Sharps "44-90" designation, both lasting in the catalogs until 1917. In the case of the 44-90 Regular 2 5/8", the box called out "44-90...for Sharps Rifle". On the "44-2 5/8" box it was titled "44-90 to 105" for "Sharps Creedmoor" on the end label. (The "44-2 5/8" is covered in the next section.)

This side label from the above box is really a part of the top label that laps over the right side of the lid.

Left: If it weren't for the rarity of this very early 44-77 box we might be reluctant to show it. However, this seldom encountered diagonal label box is thought to be among the earliest in this caliber, ca. late-1870s. R4-/750-1300

The lid top of this 44-77 twenty-round box, with its "Central Fire" call-out and "Manufactured and Guaranteed..." line, dates this box to the 1890-98 period. As typical in these 20-round Sharps boxes, the bullet weight, 470 in this case, has been hand-stamped into the appropriate box on the front lid label. R3+/750-1400

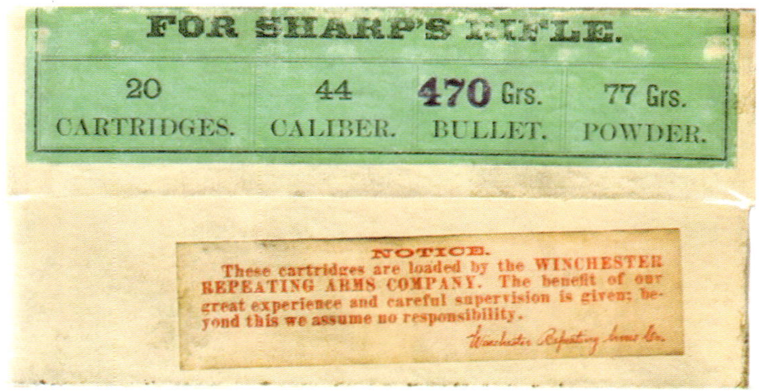

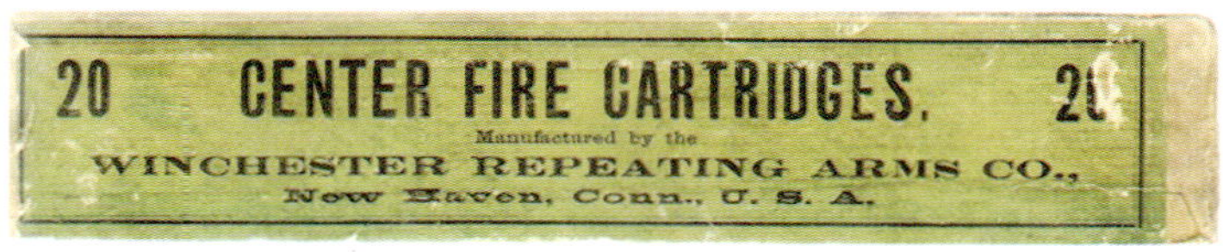

The next iteration of the foregoing square-cornered box calls out "Center Fire" and merely "Manufactured by the" Winchester Repeating Arms Co. Ca. 1900, the front graphics are identical to the preceding box, including the stamping of the bullet weight. R3/650-1250

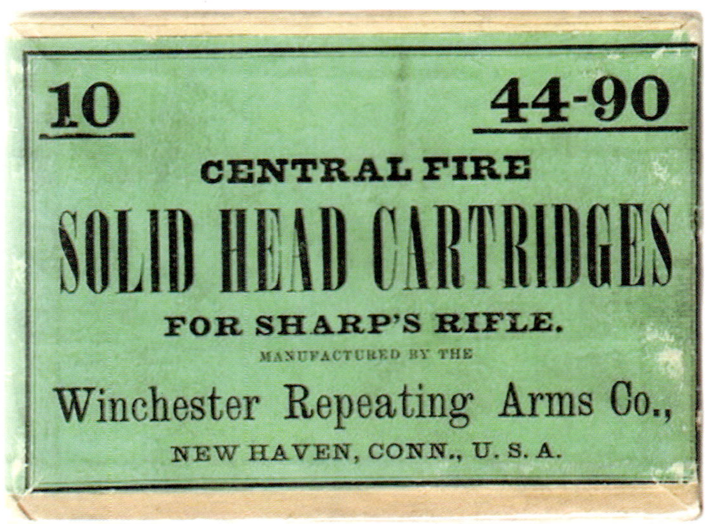

Variously referred to as the 44-90 Regular ("as adapted to Remington Special Creedmoor Rifle", according to the Winchester catalogs), the 44 2-1/4 BN (as listed by Sharps), or the 44-90 Sharps as seen here on a Winchester box label, this was a caliber that might well evoke confusion, now as then. R3/600-1200

44 Sharps 2-5/8 BN (44-90 to 105)
Sharps & Remington
Catalog listings: 1876-1917

Models: 1885
Bullet types: Ld PP
Powder types: BP
Headstamps: Plain

The 44 "2-5/8 BN" is the one most often referred to as the "44-90". While this round was introduced by Sharps in 1873 and found considerable success as a "buffalo" cartridge, it was succeeded in popularity by the newer 45 Sharps offerings before the end of 1876. Its fame as a long-range target cartridge was also substantial, most notably in the Sharps M1874 Creedmoor rifle. Far more common in boxes by UMC and E. Remington & Sons, Winchester's competitors in the ammunition business, it is a great find under a Winchester label.

Desirable and rare, this early 44-2 5/8 box is marked "44-90 to 105 Gr." on the unheadstamped cartridge cut. The end label, calling out "Sharp's Creedmoor", is just as likely to be found with a Remington call-out as both makers used this cartridge and Winchester catered to both. Interestingly, examples of later, less "sexy" boxes than this diagonal label are even rarer. So much so, in fact, that we have none to show you. R3+/600-1200

45 Sharps (2.1, 2.4, 2.6, 2 7-8, 3")
Catalog listings: See below
Shown: 45-75 Sharps 2.1"

Models: 1885
Bullet types: Ld PP
Powder types: BP
Headstamps: Plain, WRACo

Sharps typically marked their rifles and cartridges according caliber and case length as opposed to Winchester's (and others') method of caliber followed by grains of Black Powder and, sometimes, bullet weight. The reason, of course, was that the Sharps cases were frequently loaded (and reloaded) by the riflemen themselves rather than by the factory and loadings could vary greatly as to both powder charge and bullet weight. As a result, the 45 Sharps listing, as seen above, culminates in five case lengths. They were typically sold in five- or ten-round boxes and various aspects of the loading, including length, bullet weight and powder grains, were commonly crossed out with a pen stroke and re-titled according to the actual contents of the box. UMC and Sharps also followed this practice and, indeed, more of those boxes are to be found than Winchester.

Taking the cartridges individually, the 45 2.1, commonly called the 45-70 Sharps or 45-75 Sharps, was first produced in 1886 and first listed in the M85 that same year. It lasted as a M85 caliber in the ammunition section of the catalogs until 1909, but stayed in the catalogs as a Sharps listing until 1916.

The other four case lengths all were listed as M85 calibers in the ammunition section of the November 1885 catalog and all were discontinued as such in 1893. The 2.4 and 2.6 case lengths were first produced by the Company in 1884 and last cataloged in 1913. The 2.6 was only chambered by Sharps itself for about 8 months before being succeeded by the 2.4 in June, 1877. Both were loaded by that company with 100 grains of powder behind a 550 grain bullet. The 2.4 was originally a Sharps target cartridge and was (like the 2.6 before it) essentially obsolete well before 1885. One wonders why they were mentioned for the M85 at all.

The highly popular 45-2 7/8 had the longest run, beginning in 1878 and ending in 1917. The huge 45-3 1/4, which held 120 grains of powder and was available in bullet weights up to 620 grains (though never offered by Sharps), was first cataloged by Winchester in 1884 and last listed in 1917. Arguably, it was superior to the "Big Fifty" both ballistically and in stopping power. While we don't have a 45-3 1/4 box to show, it is our feeling that the graphics will very closely resemble those of the 45-2 7/8 boxes shown below and will more likely be a box of five rather than ten.

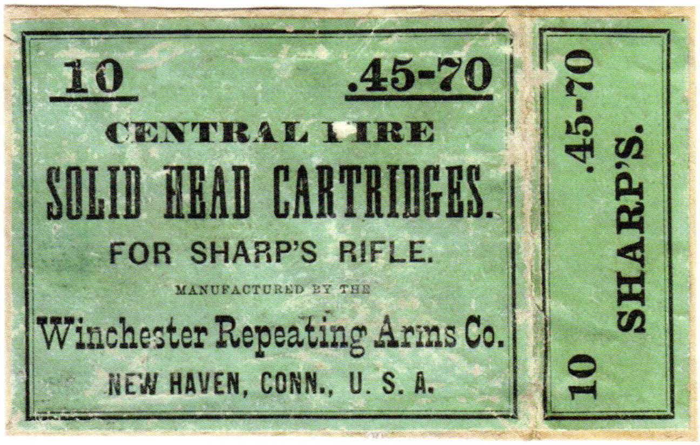

The 45-70 and 45-75 Sharps utilized the same 2.1 case as the 45-70 Government but used a 420 grain paper-patched bullet. This is an example of the 45-70 version. R3+/750-1250

With a rec "W" on the end label, this 45-75 box can be dated as post-1906 and is quite rare so marked. All Sharps 45 caliber 2.1 boxes by Winchester are very scarce in both the 70 grain and 75 grain loadings. R4-/850-1500

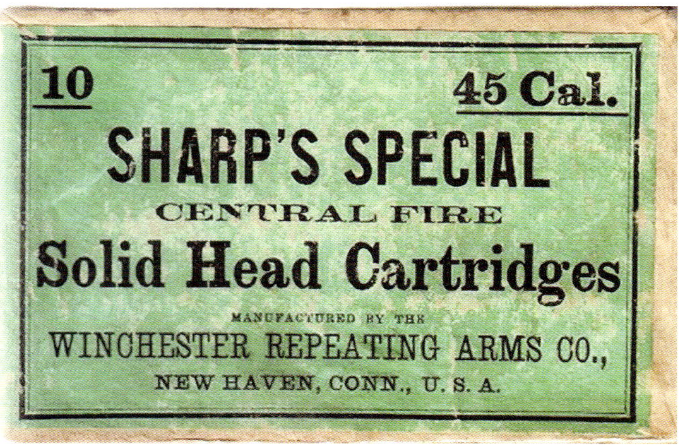

Without examining the cartridges, the lack of a case length call-out makes it impossible to distinguish the 2.4 from the 2.6 Sharps boxes. Both were listed as "Sharp's Special" in the catalogs and could have had any combination of 500 or 550 grain bullets with a powder charge of 100 or 120 grains. Either case length: R3/750-1500

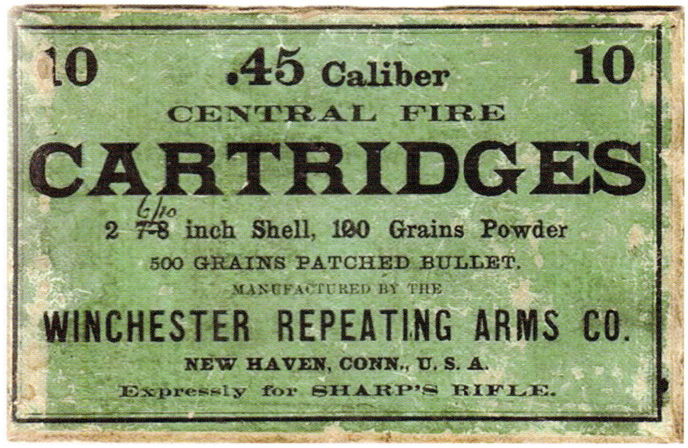

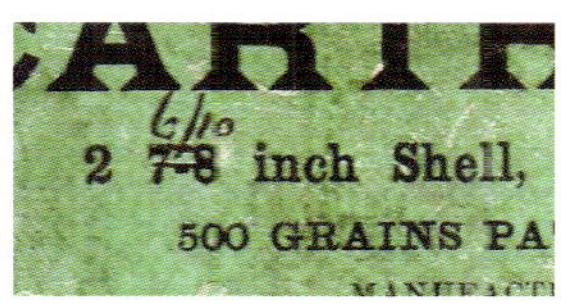

A box of 45 Sharps "2 6/10" marked in ink over the "2 7-8" call-out. This was a common way of marking the various Sharps loadings among all manufacturers. It seems that there were so many varieties of case length, bullet weight and powder charge that it wasn't practical to have labels printed in every possible combination. This one was loaded with 100 grains of powder (written over "120") and a 500 grain bullet. R3/700-1250

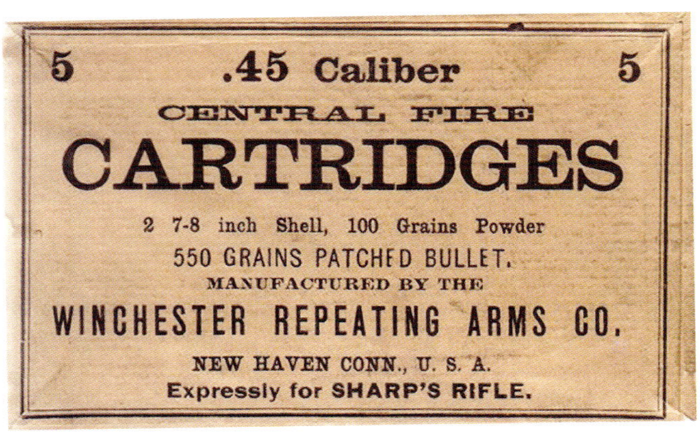

Tan labels were typical for early Sharps Rifle Co (Hartford) boxes but unusual for Winchester. This is also a scarcer five round box (ten-rounders were more common) of 2-7/8 inch rounds containing 100 grains of powder behind a 550 grain bullet. R3+/750-1300

More often found in 45 2-7/8 inch is this green 10-round box. While the call-outs on this label appear, at first glance, to be identical to the 2-6/10 box shown earlier, closer examination shows this to have the higher 120 grain powder charge. R3/700-1400

50-90 Sharps
Catalog listings: 1878-1910

Models: 1885
Bullet types: Ld PP
Powder types: BP
Headstamps: Plain

Here's one that needs no introduction even though it was not originally a Winchester caliber: the Sharps "Big Fifty". With its 473 grain bullet and 90 to 100 grains of Black Powder in a 2.5 inch case it had already gained a fearsome reputation (though whether deserved or not is open to question) before Winchester chambered the M85 for it in October, 1886. By then Sharps had declared bankruptcy and the buffalo were, unfortunately, about gone. Today, as then, the number "50" stands tall among both shooters and collectors alike. Yes, guys, size matters!

The 50-90 (2 1/2) Sharps is one of the most sought-after boxes by both Sharps and Winchester collectors. Though by no means common, this is the box most often found. All the other boxes in this style which we have examined have had labels which wrapped over the right end of the lid. As can be seen here, the 50 Sharps labels wrapped over the left end. R3+/ 1500-2500

A rare 50-100 box, in this case with the "100" overstruck in ink and "90" written in. This was a common practice with Sharps boxes, but more especially among the 44 and 45 calibers. R4-/ 1750-2750

Model 1885 - Part IV
Other Center Fire Calibers

22 WCF; 25-20 Single Shot; 32 C.F. S, L, XL ; 32 Ideal; 38 C.F. S, L, XL; 40-60 Marlin; 40-70 and 40-90 Ballard; 50 Eley

22 W.C.F.

Catalog Listings: 1885-1940

Model: 1873, 1885

Bullet types: Ld

Powder types: BP, Smkls, Lsmk

Headstamps: Plain, WRACo

The only small caliber offering of the original M1885 Winchester cartridge designs, the 22 W.C.F. eventually morphed into the 22 Hornet of the 1930s, a cartridge which retains a loyal following yet today. In Europe, where it was loaded to higher velocities, it became popular as the 22 Vierling (5.6x35R). In the November, 1885 catalog introducing this caliber for the M85, it was also touted as a new chambering in the M1873. To the best of our knowledge, however, no M73 guns are recorded as having been made in 22 W.C.F. Incredibly, the very next catalog (April, 1886) makes no mention of that caliber in either the M73 or M85 blurbs, OR among the cartridge listings!

Black Powder was last loaded in 1928 and Lesmok was used in its place though labels may not reflect this. Smokeless was last loaded in 1924 and represents one of the few instances in which the Smokeless loading of a caliber was phased out before Black Powder or Lesmok.

Black Powder Boxes

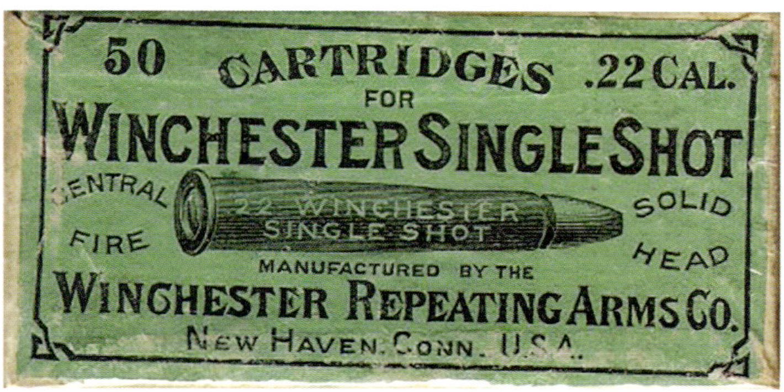

This Black Powder box is almost certainly the earliest box in this caliber first listed, as it was, in the M1885, ca mid- to late-1880s. Though the cartridge cut is unheadstamped, nearly all such boxes are found to contain the "22 W.C.F." headstamp. Note, too, that the bullet shows a grease groove. This bullet was used until 1890 when it was replaced by the internally lubed 22 WRF bullet although cartridge cuts on labels continued to show grooved bullets until around 1910. R2+/150-300

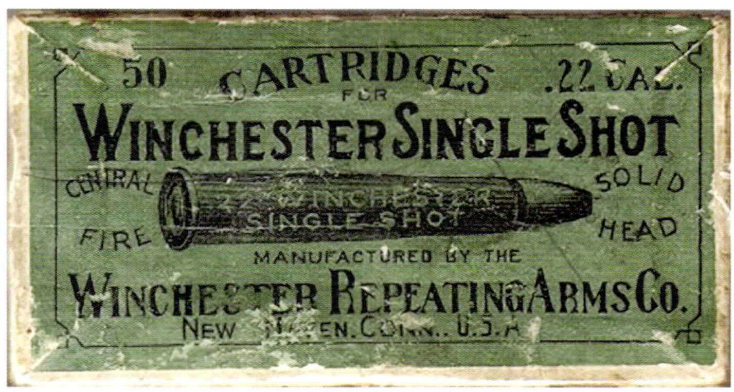

While the layout of this label design is identical to the box above, later type font differences are readly discernable. With the Central Fire call-out (but still lacking the headstamp) this box is ca. 1890-98. R2+/125-250

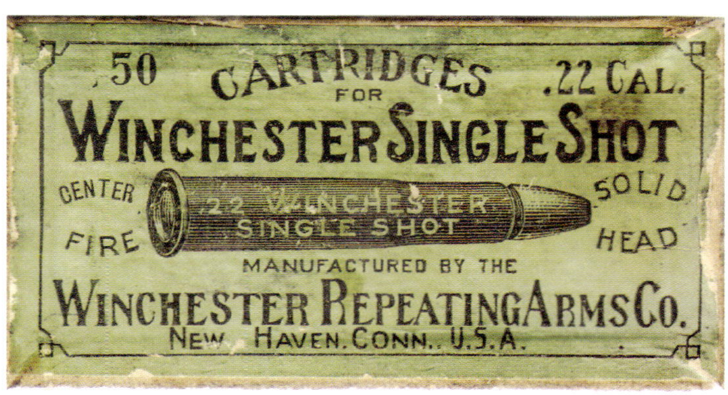

Circa 1898-1900, the only significant difference between this and the previous box is the change in call-out from "Central Fire" to Center Fire". R2+/100-200

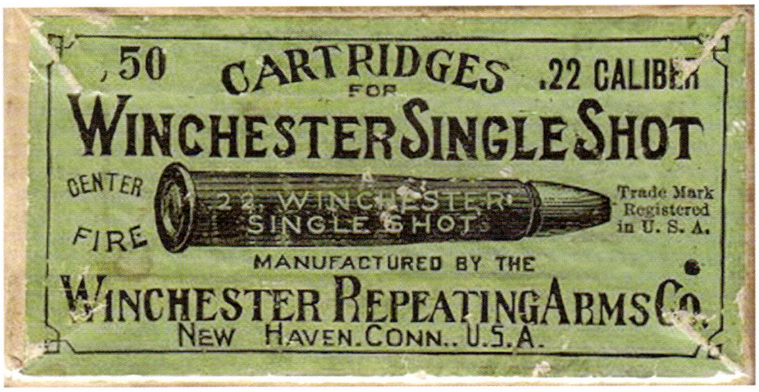

The "Center Fire" call-out and trade mark line of this Black Powder box date it circa 1900-1903. Note that the cartridge cut remains unheadstamped and has the grease groove. R2+/100-200

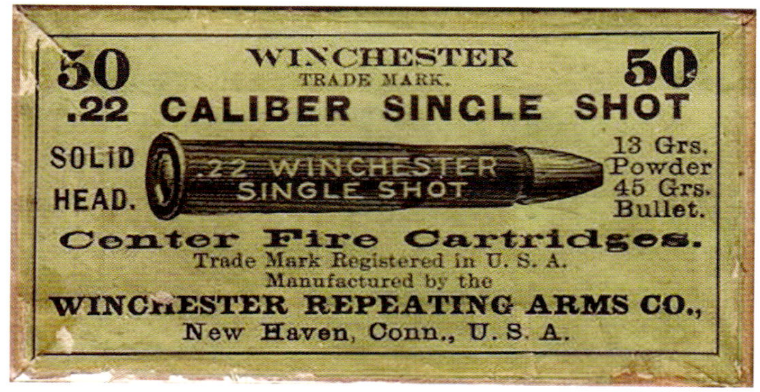

An undated label with revised graphics, including no quotes around Winchester and the early trade mark line, help us to place this box within the 1903-06 time-frame. Still, the cartridge cut has no headstamp and retains the grease groove. R2+/100-200

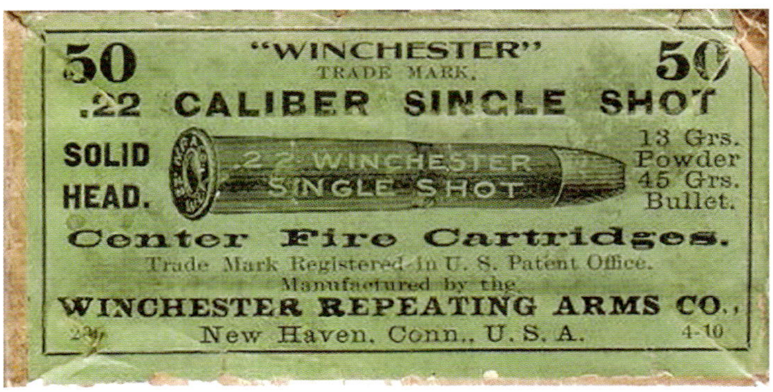

With Winchester now in quotes and with the longer trade mark line calling out "...U.S. Patent Office", both representative of 1907-1911 graphics, it is no surprise to find the label dated 4-10. And, finally, the cartridge cut exhibits the "22 W.C.F." headstamp and an internally lubed (un-grooved) bullet. R2+/100-200

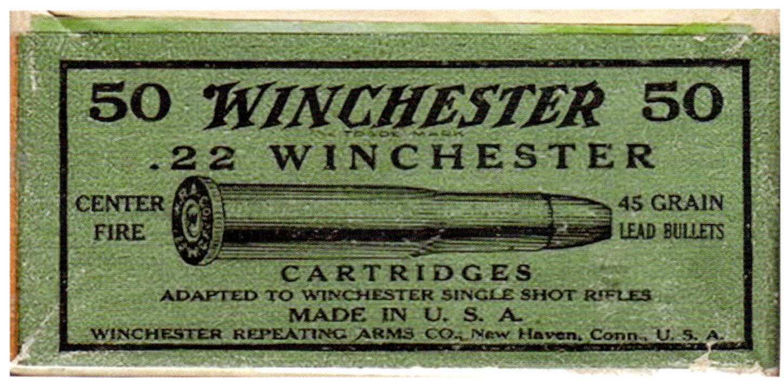

The wrap-over (top and ends) label was typical of the early 1920s on most 50-round boxes and is found well into the 1930s on the older cartridges with Black Powder origins. K-coded, this label may represent the final iteration of this Black Powder loading. R2/85-175

Smokeless Powder Boxes

The earliest smokeless 22 W.C.F. loading appeared with an overstamp on a period Black Powder box, ca. 1896. R4/400-700

The top label graphics (formatting, Winchester without quotation marks and the trade mark line) as well as the older style orange side-seal label all point to a dating no later than the 1903-06 period; however...

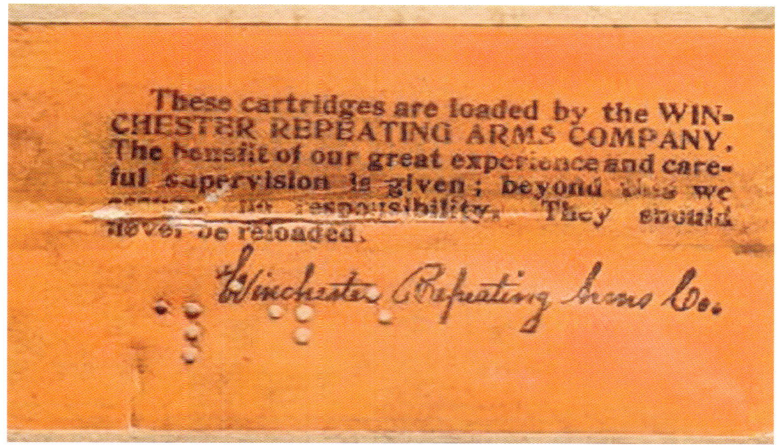

...the fact that the side label is also dot-coded dates this to 1908 at the earliest. Red label boxes after 1906 generally have red side labels. The cartridge cut on this box, like the post-1900 Black Powder boxes covered previously, still has no headstamp and shows a grease groove. R3-/150-275

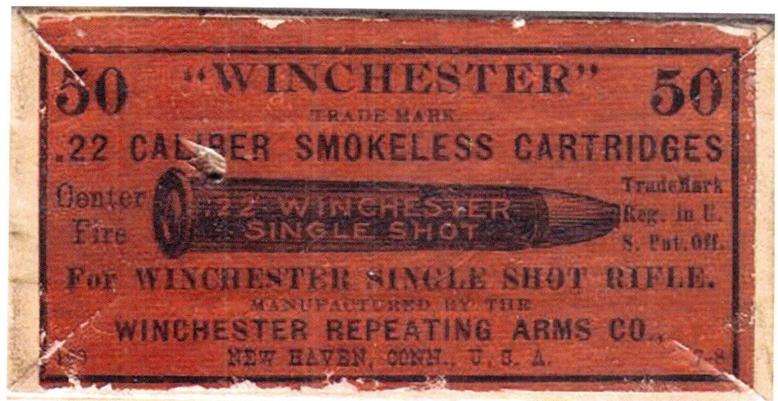

Several unusual items make these 7-8 dated graphics interesting; first, note that the cartridge cut remains unheadstamped in spite of the fact that this caliber had been headstamped since at least 1886. Second, the "U.S." in the trade mark call-out has been split between two lines, the "U" on the second line and the "S" on the third. We do not recall seeing this treatment on any other label. The low quote mark at the left of "Winchester" is also unusual but has been seen before. Finally, the bullet still is grooved although the change to an internally lubed bullet was made in 1890. R2+/125-250

Not unusual for the 'Teens, this box has purple labels: 4-19, top, and 3-19, side. The format and graphics are typical of the 1913-20 period. And, finally, we see the correct headstamp and internally lubed bullet on the cartridge cut. R2+/125-250

With Smokeless loadings in this caliber having been discontinued in 1924, this early '20s box is a scarce item. While K-codes were assigned in the early 1920s it is not known whether such codes were ever printed on 22 W.C.F. labels of the period. This wrap-over label lacks the code and is ca. 1920-23 (and maybe '24!). R2-/75-150

25-20 Single Shot (25-20 Stevens)

Catalog Listings: 1890-1946

Model: 1885

Powder types: BP, Smkls, Lsmk

Bullet types: Ld, SP, FMJ

Headstamps: Plain, WRACo

Said to have been derived from the 32 XL C.F. (Ballard) casing by the well-known sports writer and cartridge innovator, J. F. Rabbeth, the 25-20 SS was adopted by a number of gun manufacturers from the 1880s through the early-1900s. First chambered by Winchester in the M85 in 1890, it remained a catalog offering in that model until 1917. Often confused with the M92's 25-20 W.C.F. offering (especially in today's gun market for used M85s) the 25-20 SS is longer than the W.C.F. (M92) version which was based on the 32-20 case. The Company initially produced the 25-20 SS in unheadstamped cases with the small #1 primer. These are rare. By 1893 the primer had been changed to the larger #2-1/2 and the cases were headstamped, though cartridge cuts continued to show the smaller primer throughout the period of this cartridges production. In 1896, the first year in which this caliber was offered in Smokeless Powder, the title became "25-20 Winchester Single Shot" for the Smokeless loading only. That designation was dropped in 1900, but those labels using "Winchester" within the 25-20 SS call-out is also a rare box. Another very scarce box in this caliber was the FMJ (Full Patch) loading which, along with Soft Point bullets, was first cataloged in 1905.

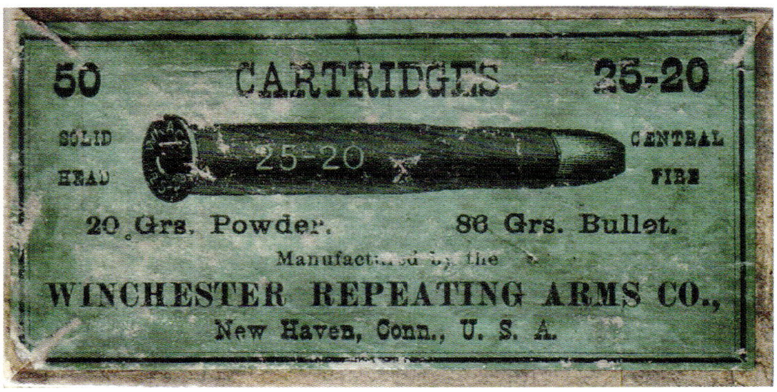

Whether or not there exists an earlier 25-20 SS box is open to question. The cartridge cut shows a headstamp whereas the very earliest rounds are known to have been UN-headstamped. On the other hand, by 1890 most Winchester cartridges were, indeed, headstamped; and, if they weren't, it is no stretch to assume that cartridge cuts on any newly designed label graphics would be, whatever the caliber. R3+/250-500

Note the erroneous(?) "20 Grs. Powder" call-out on both of these label close-ups. Catalog and factory records both show the loading as 19 grains. In the absence of contrary evidence, however, we'll assume the latter information is correct. A fair amount of label graphics are found to be either anachronistic or in error. The upper close-up is from the box above, the lower from the following.

The only difference between this and the previous box, other than the space between the Powder and Bullet call-outs referred to earlier, is the fact that there are now periods after "Solid Head" and "Central Fire". From the mid-1890s, this "Central Fire" label calls out 20 grains of Black Powder. R3/175-350

Given the styling of the trade mark line, we can date this Black Powder Center Fire box to the 1902-1905 period. The Powder call-out has been changed (corrected?) to "19 Grs." R3-/150-300

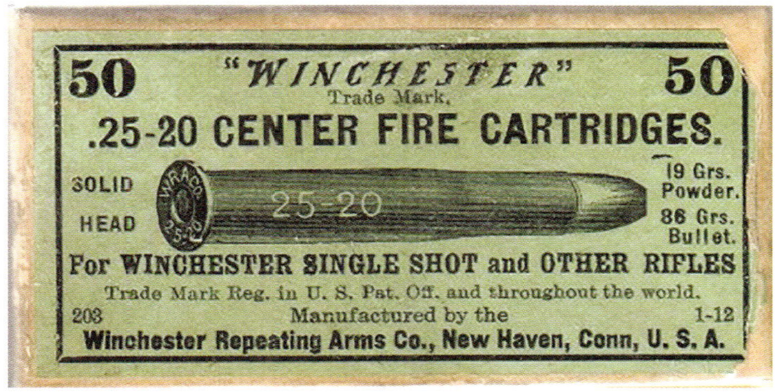

Dated 5-12, this Black Powder box is typical of the 1910-12 period and contains cartridges using the large #2 1/2 primer. The 1914 catalog shows a change in primer size back to the smaller #1. R2+/125-250

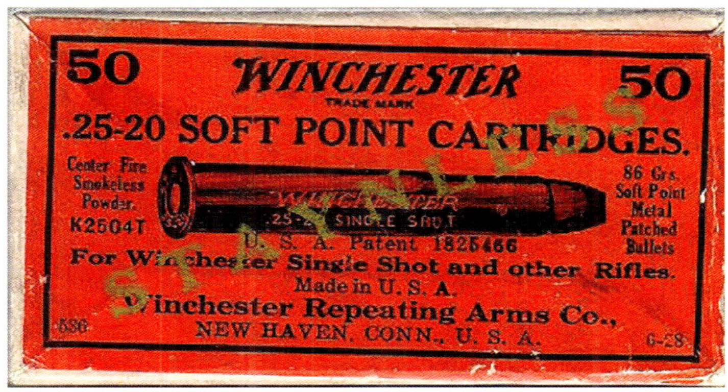

Here "Staynless" is diagonally printed in gold on a 6-28 dated top label. This label appears in many over-printed forms varying by call-outs for Staynless, Non-Mercuric, patent data, and side label graphics. Three box styles also appear with these graphics: two-piece half-split and two-piece full-cover both with and without thumb-cuts. This box has a 7-31 dated side label, early for a Non-Mercuric call-out. R2+/125-225

32 C. F. (Short, Long, Extra Long)

Catalog Listings: See below

Model: 1885

Bullet types: Ld, Shot, Blank

Powder types: BP, Lsmk, Smkls*

Headstamps: Plain, WRACo

The 32 Short and Long Center Fire offerings derived mainly from the popularity of the Colt, Webley and Tranter revolvers of the period, all of which were called out on the side labels of many of Winchester's early boxes in these two calibers. Both were first loaded in 1878 and were among the earliest listings for the M85. Success in such an arm as the Low Wall was, unfortunately, not forthcoming in these revolver calibers and they were discontinued as offerings for the M85, as were the 32 Rim Fire calibers, in mid-1887. Being essentially the same loadings as, and interchangeable with, the 32 Short and Long Colt, the 32 Short and Long C. F. offerings were merged with the Colt calibers in 1904. The 32 Short and 32 Long Center Fire boxes are, however, notably rarer than the 32 Colt calibers.

On the other hand, the 32 Extra Long C.F. was originally a rifle caliber and was often referred to as the 32 XL Ballard. It was first loaded in 1879 and while it continued in the line until 1918, it was dropped from the M85 list, along with the Short and Long, in June of 1887. As will be seen below, all three boxes exhibit much the same graphics.

*Smokeless was loaded in Long only and is a rare find.

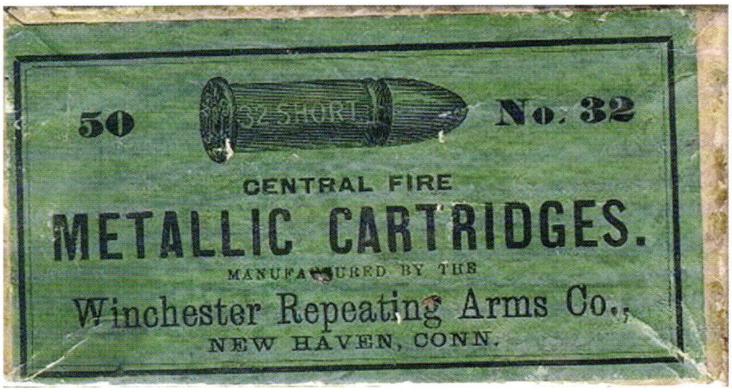

Circa mid-1880s, this box of 32 Short C.F. would have been contemporary with its early listing in the M85 caliber line-up. Note the single grease groove on the cartridge cut and "Central Fire" call-out. R3/100-200

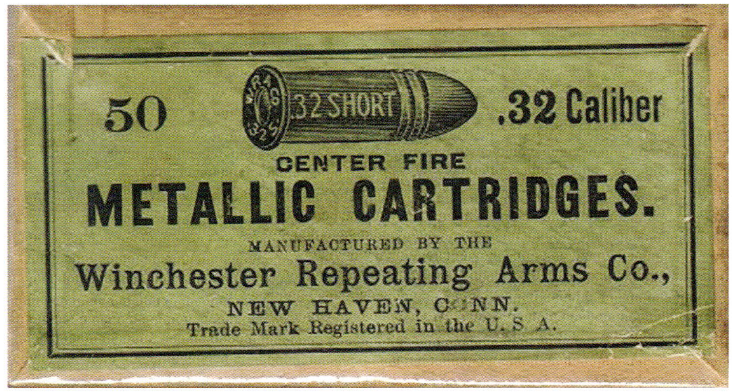

Now with 2 grooves on the cartridge cut, a "Center Fire" call-out and a full Trade Mark line, this box can be dated to the 1901-04 period. R2+/75-150

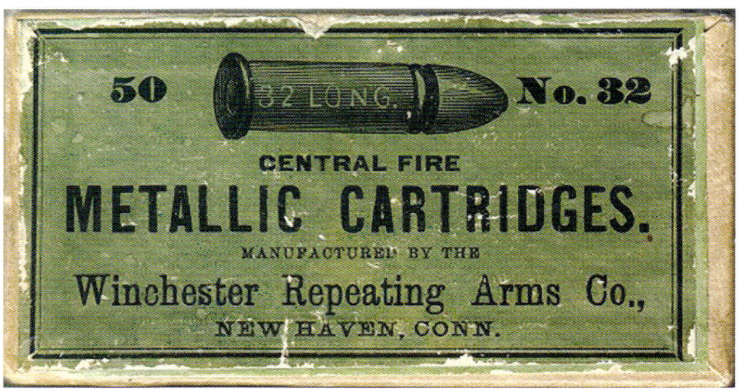

Here is an example of an early 32 Long C.F., ca. early-to-mid 1880s. This has the same graphics as the earliest Short box above except the cartridge cut here lacks a headstamp. R3/100-200

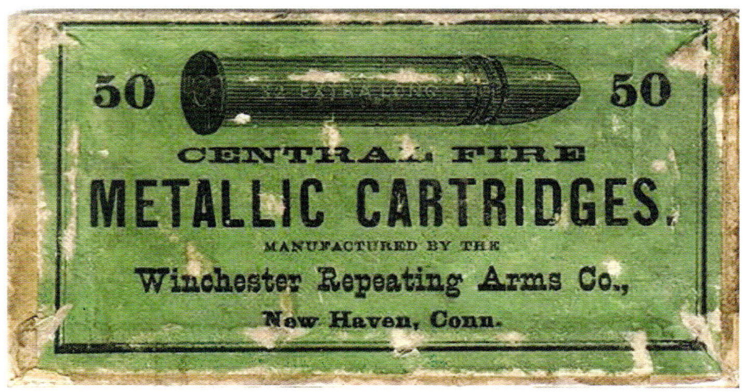

While the graphics differ slightly from the 32 XL's shorter brethren pictured above, the similarities are obvious: "Central Fire", and no headstamp, the difference being a double grease groove on the cartridge cut. Ca. early-to-mid 1880s. R2+/75-150

A Rare Shot Box

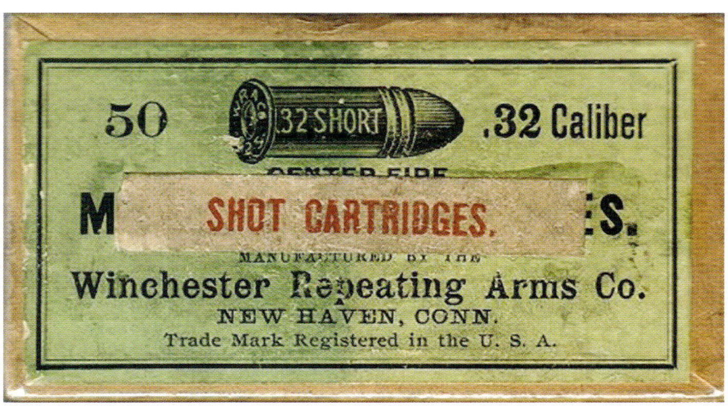

This rare box of Shot cartridges is in the uncommon 32 Short offering. Most Shot cartridges were offered in Long. R3+/100-200

32 Ideal
Catalog Listings: 1897-1921

Model: 1885
Bullet types: Ld
Powder types: BP, Lsmk*
Headstamps: WRACo

By the late 1890s there were so many shot-out and corroded single-shot rifle barrels in use that the Ideal Manufacturing Company ran ads offering to reline barrels of these old guns in the new "32 Ideal" chambering. For a mere $4.50 including postage, Ideal would have the shooter back on the firing line or in the field. Ideal was, and still is, well known for their bullet molds and loading tools. Their 32 Ideal cartridge was an improvement over the 32 XL Ballard and was chambered by Stevens in a creditable number of their single-shot rifles as well as the M85 Winchester. Boxes of primed shells are found about as often as loaded rounds, but boxes of loaded cartridges by UMC are far more common than are Winchester boxes.

*Though listed in the catalog as a powder option, no Lesmok loadings in this caliber are to be found among the New Haven records.

Exhibiting the only label design known to the authors, this "less-than-ideal" example of a Winchester 32 Ideal box is all we have to offer the reader as most of the boxes we've seen are in lousy condition. R3/125-250

38 C. F. (Short, Long, Extra Long*)
Catalog Listings: See below

Model: 1885
Bullet types: Ld, Shot, Blank
Powder types: BP, Lsmk, Smkls
Headstamps: Plain, WRACo

Having been first listed by Winchester in 1875, these calibers are among the Company's earliest Center Fire offerings. The Short and Long calibers were adapted to a wide variety of pistols and rifles and the Extra Long (XL) was a single shot rifle caliber most extensively used by Ballard and Wesson. Colt's first double-action revolver, the "Lightning", introduced in 1877, used either the Short or Long and boxes of both called out Colt prominently on the labels. The Longs actually are difficult to find in any pre-1900 box *except* those picturing the Colt Lightning revolver. In the early 1890s the Long loading changed from an outside-lubed bullet (with visible grease grooves) to an inside-lubed bullet (with no visible grease grooves). The earlier 38 Long boxes are rare. As with the 32 C. F. calibers, all three 38 C.F. calibers were omitted from M85 listings in June, 1887.

*Extra Long loaded with Lead bullets and in Black Powder only.

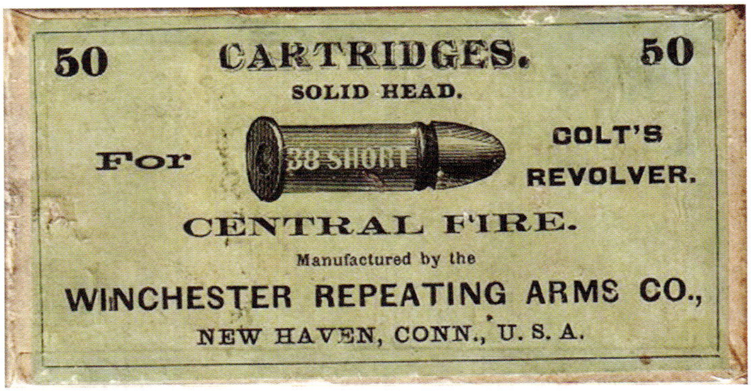

Unheadstamped and with a "Central Fire" call-out, this Black Powder labeling is clearly early to mid-1880s. Note the single grease groove on the bullet of the cartridge cut, also a typical feature of the earlier boxes. R3/100-200

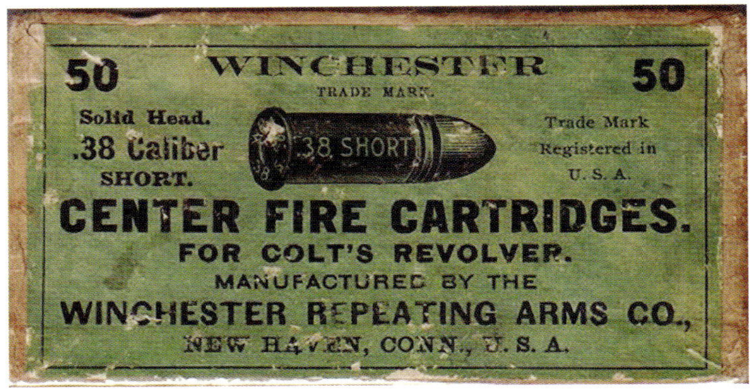

Circa 1901-05, this Black Powder 38 C.F. Short box exhibits two grease grooves and a headstamp on the cartridge cut. A full trade mark line is also present. R3-/80-160

As was typical of early 38 Long Center Fire boxes, the dominant feature of this label is a Colt Lightning revolver. These graphics, often called "picture boxes", were used into the early 20th Century and are found, with some variations, on red Smokeless label boxes as well. R3-/450-850

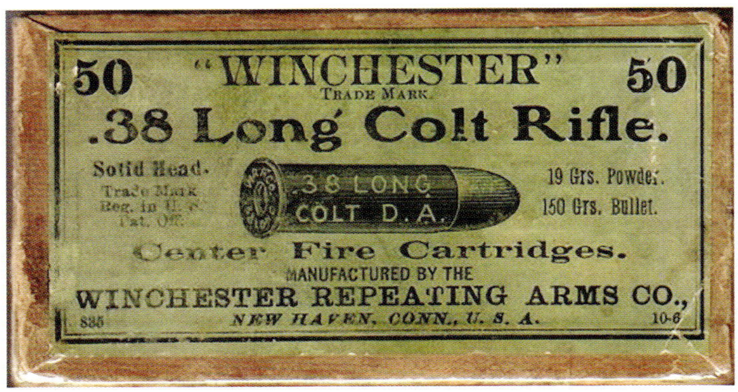

This Black Powder box label-dated 10-6, though not as valuable, is more difficult to find than the Colt Lightning picture box. R3/85-175

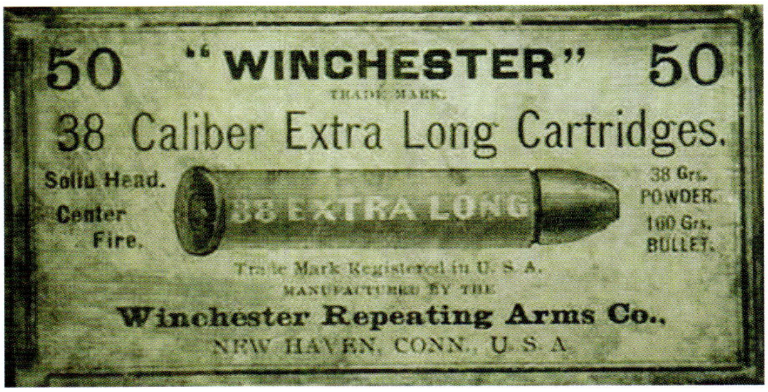

This unusual 38 Extra Long C.F. box has no headstamp and a single grease groove on the cartridge cut, graphics of the early 1880s. It also has quotes around "Winchester", a graphic of the 1906-10 period. The trade mark line is ca. 1902-06. This is the kind of thing that keeps us interested and, at the same time, drives us crazy! R3+/200-400

40-60 Marlin

Catalog Listings: 1882-1918

Model: 1885
Bullet types: Ld
Powder types: BP
Headstamps: Plain, WRACo

This one is confusing, so best pay attention.

The 40-60 Marlin was originally designed by Marlin, based on the 45-70 casing, for their M1881 rifle. Winchester then mentioned it in the ammunition section of their January 1884 catalog as a Hotchkiss caliber but dropped that reference before year-end. Then, in 1885, the Company listed it for their M1885 but dropped it again in 1886 after only one year. In 1887 Winchester announced a "new" 40-65 W.C.F. chambering for their recently introduced lever-action M1886. The 40-65 W.C.F. casing was identical to the 40-60 Marlin except for primer size (the Marlin's being smaller) and the two calibers were interchangeable, noting only that the 40-65 was loaded with five more grains of powder. For some reason, however, the 40-65 W.C.F. wasn't listed for the M85 until 1890.

Still with us? Good. Let's continue.

In 1884, right in the middle of all this, two more cartridge introductions further muddied the waters. First, Bullard Arms introduced a cartridge called the 40-70 Bullard. Using the same case as the 40-60 Marlin (and 40-65 W.C.F.), it was loaded with a lighter bullet and a heavier powder charge; however, the Bullard catalogs advertised that the 40-60 Marlin could be used in place of the 40-70 Bullard, creating still further confusion as to interchangeability. (There was a 40-75 Bullard loading that also used this case, but that's yet another story).

Secondly, also in 1884, Winchester announced a 40-60 W.C.F. chambering for their old M1876. This 40-60 W.C.F. had a shorter case than the aforementioned calibers and was not interchangeable with them. Then, to complicate matters further, in 1887, the same year Winchester introduced their 40-65 W.C.F., Colt chambered their new Lightning Magazine Rifle in 40-60 Colt, sometimes labeled by ammunition manufacturers as "40-60 Colt and Marlin". This was logical enough: the 40-60 Colt and 40-60 Marlin were exactly the same cartridge in differently labeled boxes. So, to sum up, the 40-60 Marlin, 40-60 Colt and 40-65 W.C.F. could be used interchangeably and all three could be used in place of the 40-70 Bullard. All four, then, as they shared the same case, could be used in the Single Shot M1885. The 40-60 W.C.F., though, was a different cartridge entirely.

In Winchester boxes the 40-65 W.C.F. is fairly common, the 40-60 Marlin and 40-70 Bullard are quite scarce and the 40-60 Colt is very rare. Examples of the 40-65 W.C.F boxes will be found in Chapter 8 while the Colt and Bullard boxes can be found in Chapter 15.

Thank you for your attention. Are there any questions?

This close-up of an early 40-60 Marlin blue label lid-top shows the "Central Fire" call-out and "Manufactured and Guaranteed" line typical of the square-cornered boxes of pre-1898 vintage. R3+/500-900

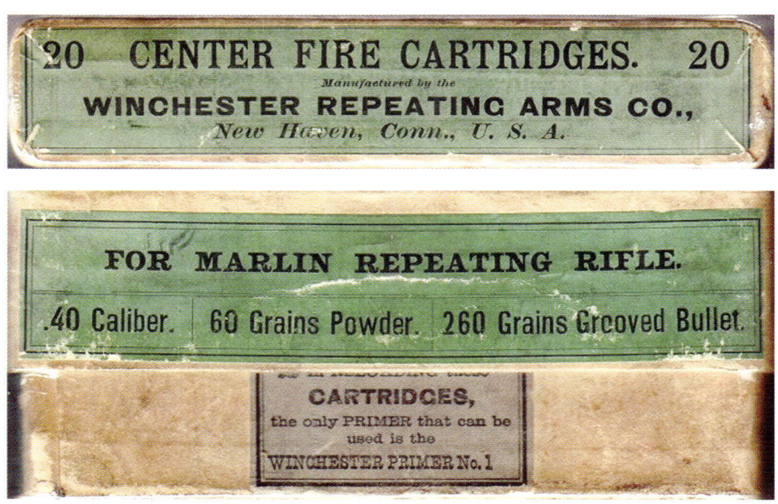

Now "Center Fire" and omitting the "...and Guaranteed..." wording, this round-cornered box may be considered post-1898, but a closer dating would be difficult as this labeling was in use for a number of years. All loadings in this caliber were Black Powder and are scarce. R3/400-800

40-70 Ballard, 40-90 Ballard

Catalog Listings: 1882-1918

Model: 1885
Bullet types: Ld PP
Powder types: BP
Headstamps: Plain*, WRACo

These two Ballard-developed single-shot calibers were already popular by the time Winchester brought out their High Wall model in November of 1885. The essential difference between the two is, of course, case length, the 40-70 being 2 3/8 inches while the 40-90 is 2 15/16 inches. Both cartridges used paper-patched bullets, the 40-90 using a slightly heavier 370 grain bullet compared to the 40-70's 330 grain. Both entered the line of M85 offerings in the gun's first year and both were dropped from the M85 call-out in 1909. Interestingly, the Winchester box most often found in Ballard calibers is the 40-85 Ballard, a five grain lighter loading in the 40-90 case, and is marked "...expressly for the Ballard Rifle". No call-outs for the M85 or for "Winchester Single Shot Rifles" is to be found, a most unusual omission when the Company chambered a gun in any caliber for which they made ammunition.

*Plain heads are frequently found on 40-70 Ballard cases but 40-90s are generally headstamped.

Shown here is the lid and lid-top label from an early 40-70 Ballard offering thought to date to the mid-1880s. Boxes which picture the gun for which they are intended are always worth a premium. Note also the uncommon "Folded Head" call-out on the lid top. R3+/750-1500 (Photo courtesy of Lou Behling)

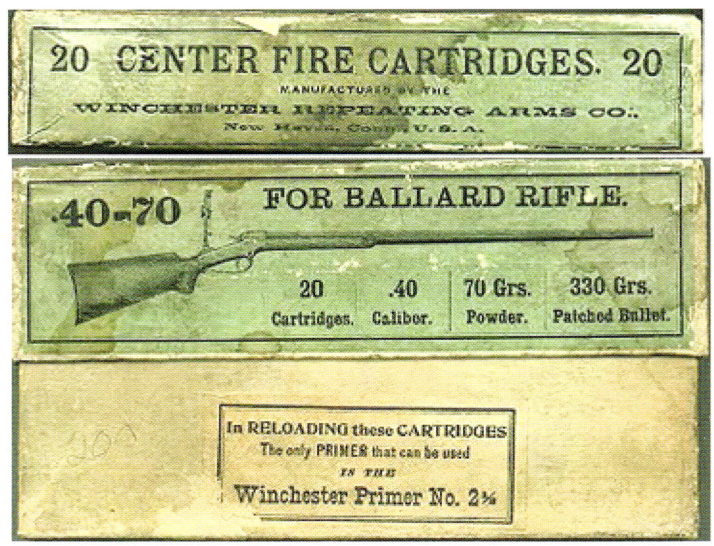

Dating from the 1898-1900 period, this 40-70 Ballard "Picture Box" now shows a different gun model facing right rather than left as in the previous graphic. While this box has the over all appearance of an 1880s labeling, the attentive reader will note that the lid top calls out "Center Fire" rather than "Central Fire" and lacks the "...and Guaranteed by" wording of the earlier labels. R3++/650-1300 (Photo courtesy of Lou Behling)

Boxes of the longer Single Shot cartridges were often found in sizes of five or ten rounds. This 40-85 Ballard offering is typical of that type as used by Winchester. UMC and Sharps appear to have pioneered this style packaging in the 1870s. R3+/350-600

50 Eley

Catalog listings: (See below)

Model: 1885
Bullet types: Ld
Powder types: BP, Smkls
Headstamps: Eley Bros. (?)

The 50 Eley is first mentioned as a M85 chambering in the 1894 English language edition of the Export catalog where it was referred to as the "English 500 Express". It wasn't until 1910 that it was listed in the Domestic catalog; however, in spite of its listing as a M85 caliber, it is believed that the Company never manufactured this cartridge. There are no known examples of a Winchester "50 Eley" nor is there any record of their having been produced. Rather, it is likely that "Eley Brothers" new primed cases were used for whatever testing occurred in this caliber: a number of casings so headstamped were found at the old New Haven factory and records there do refer to "Definitive Proof" loadings in "50 Eley S.S." on January 7, 1911 and again on October 18, 1911. A file record from the New Haven Proving Room states, however, that the 50 Eley "...will not be carried in stock," a fact which should come close to settling the issue for us within the confines of this work. Unfortunately the mystery will undoubtedly remain unsolved as a wide array of referrals to this caliber are to be found among Winchester records — from tooling to gauges to rifles actually shipped — leaving the 50 Eley as one of the great oddities in the annals of the M1885.

Given all the above, it will come as no surprise that there are no boxes to be shown here. The caliber has been included only because of its listing in Winchester catalogs as a M85 chambering.

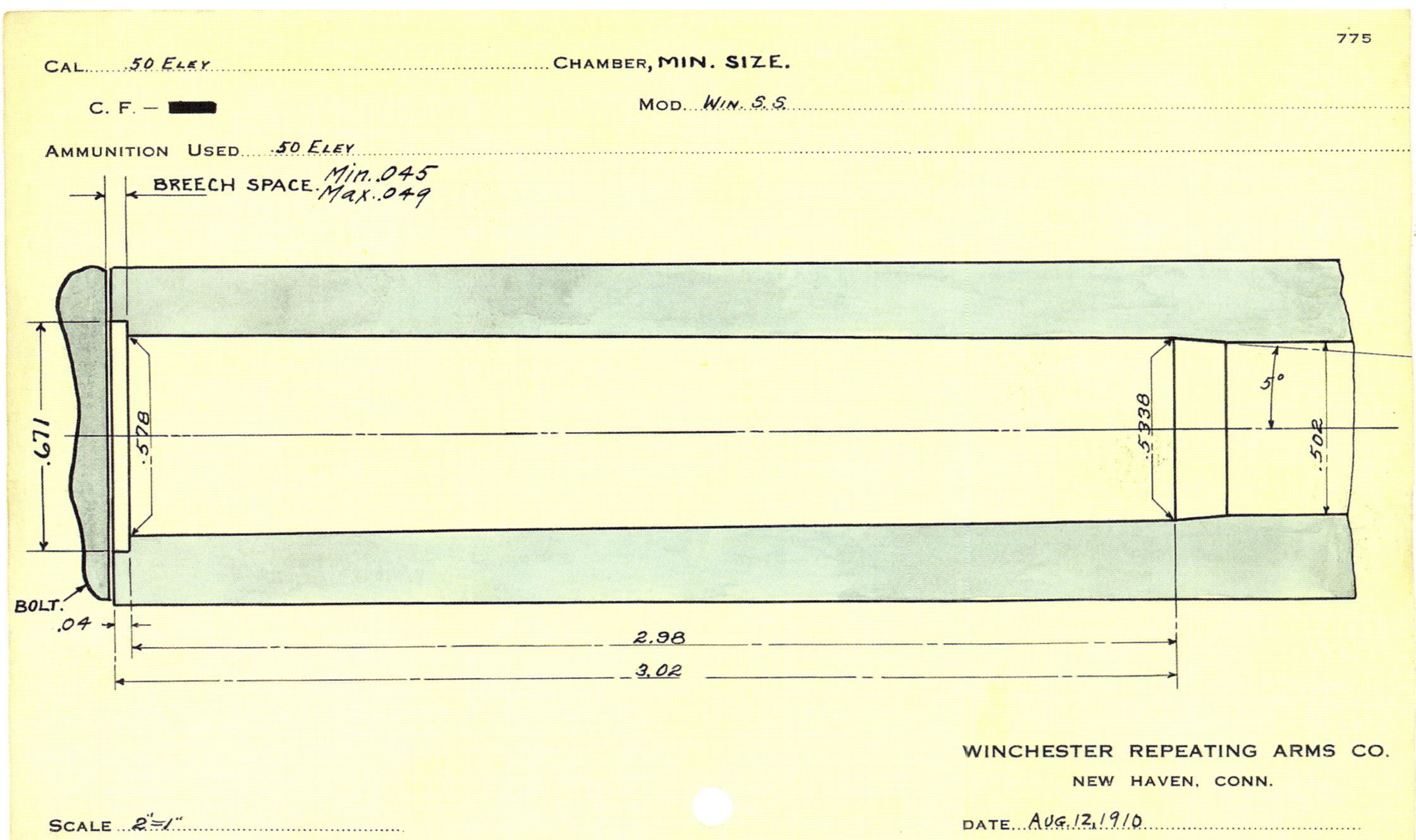

Winchester's Ballistics Laboratory kept files on dimensions for all of the Company's firearms chambers. This one such for the 50 Eley and is designated for the Winchester Single Shot rifle.

The scarce 10-9 dated front label with both the Winchester logo and "Trade Mark" call-out along with the picture of the cartridge. In keeping with the Company's typical 1906-1910 logo, note that quote marks now surround "WINCHESTER". This is probably the last label exhibiting this unusual combination of graphics. R3/200-400

Close-up of the previous 10-9 front-label. While there may be other calibers which exhibit this same combination of graphics, the authors are not aware of them. If others do exist they will almost certainly fall within the 1902-1910 time frame.

Lid-top labels dated 7-8 (on the 10-9 box above), 6-13 and 4-14 showing the three distinct "Winchester" and "Trade Mark" call-outs as represented by the 1906-1919 period.

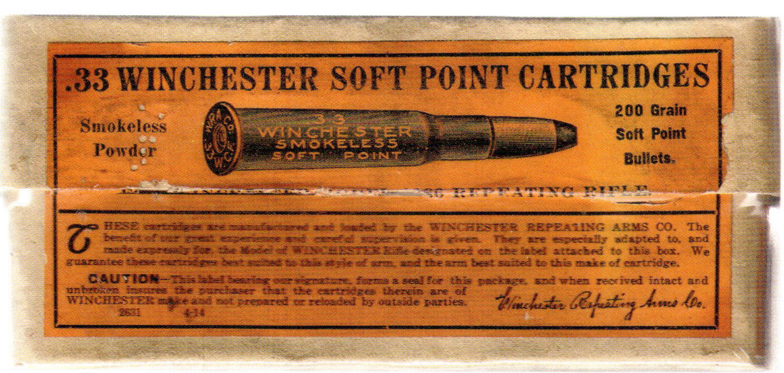

The front of this sealed 4-14 box is like all other pre-1915 boxes except the anomalistic 10-9 box above. This is also the last of the round-cornered box style. R2/200-400

Note the label differences between this 5-16 (now square-cornered box) and the 4-22 box below. The earlier box calls out the "Model 1886" on the bottom line while the later one shows "Model 86". Also, the 4-22 box has no call-outs on the cartridge cut. R2/200-400

The "Winchester" and "Trade Mark" treatment as contrasted between the pre-1919 and the post-1919 lid-top labels. As always, these dates are approximate and vary slightly by caliber.

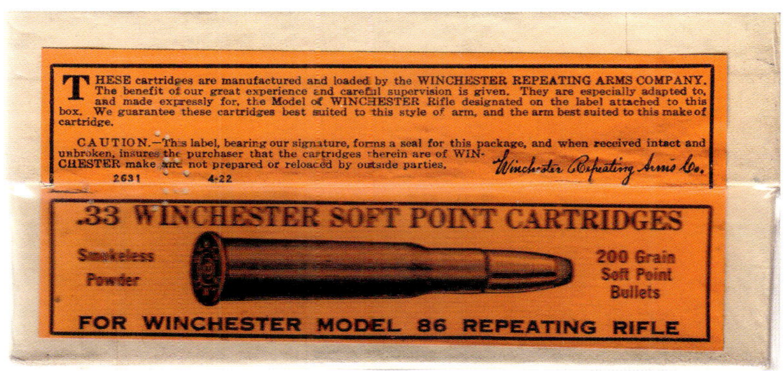

A nice sealed example of a pre-K-code box, ca 1922. R2/200-400

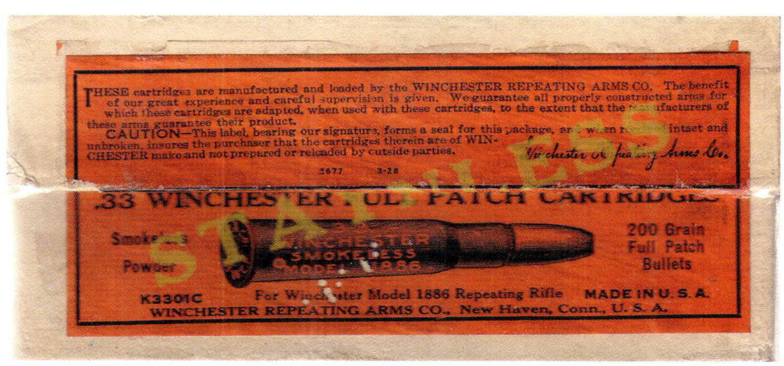

A colorful Full Patch box from the late-1927 to 1931 period, pre-"Non-Mercuric", and one of a handful of calibers exhibiting the large-letter yellow-gold "Staynless" overstamp on top and front. These were limited to slow-selling loadings, most of which were discontinued by the end of the decade. R3/200400

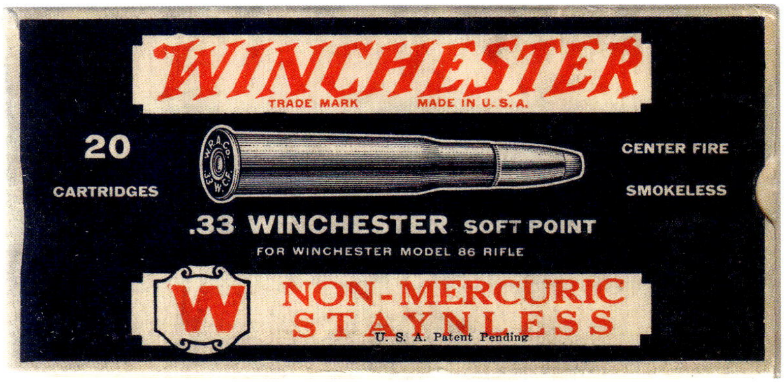

A "1932" type "Staynless, Non-Mercuric" box which appears to have been used until around 1940; therefore, no "1935" boxes will be found in this caliber, a not uncommon occurrence in non-"Super Speed" calibers. While "1928" one-piece boxes similar to this may exist it is just as likely that the two-piece box lasted into the early 1930s. R2/75-150

The "1939" box which lasted until the "1946" style pictured below. No "1945" boxes have been noted by the authors and are presumed not to exist. R2/75-150

The "1946" box, used until discontinuance of the caliber in 1955. R1/60-120

An Interesting Box: "Standard Cartridges", 1916.

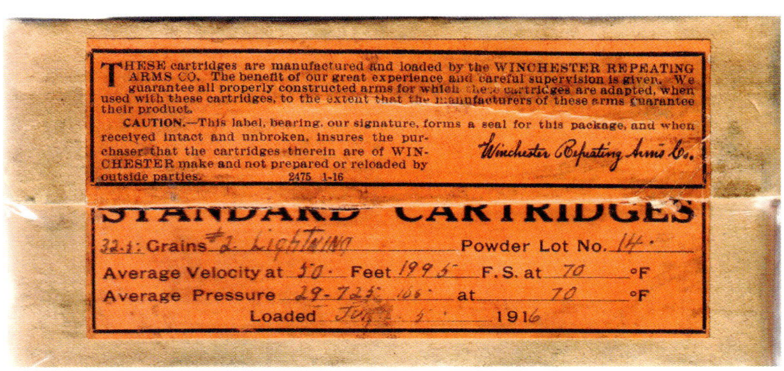

These cartridges were used to calibrate pressure and velocity in test rifles. This particular box was loaded July 5, 1916, using "#2 Lightning" Smokeless powder. R5/300-500

348 Winchester
Catalog listings: 1936-

Models: 71
Bullet types: SP, ST, FMJ
Powder types: Smkls
Headstamp: SS

The 348 was derived from necking down the big 50 caliber chamberings of the M86. It was cataloged in three bullet weights, 150, 200 and 250 grains, with the 200 grain offering gaining the most popularity. With the introduction of their new Silvertip bullet in the now-famous "Grizzly Bear" box in January 1940, one of the most popular and collectible Winchester boxes of the era came into being. In the case of the 348 only the 250 grain bullet was available with the Grizzly graphics, but the other bullet weights remained in the line as Soft Point offerings. By 1953, all three bullet weights were offered in Silvertip, the 150 grain and 200 grain continuing in Soft Point as well. A Full Patch offering was cataloged in the late '30s but is not known to have been loaded according to factory records nor has it been seen by the authors.

A 150 grain "1935" box with the Winchester Repeating Arms" line on front. All three bullet weights appeared in this box. R2/80-150 [250 grain: R3/125-250]

The "1939" box with Western Cartridge Co. call-out on side. While it is possible that a 250 grain offering exists in this box, the authors have yet to find one. R1/65-125

The Silvertip bullet was announced to the trade in January 1940. This new offering was introduced in the "Grizzly" box and, in 348, was available only in the 250 grain Silvertip. R1/100-200

The "1946" box with the 150 grain Soft Point (non-Silvertip) bullet. The M71 call-out is on a side panel only. R1/45-75

A 250 grain Silvertip "1946" box. Note the Model 71 call-out is on the front of this box while absent from the front of the Soft Point box above. The back panel describes in detail the Silvertip bullet and its potential. R2/75-100

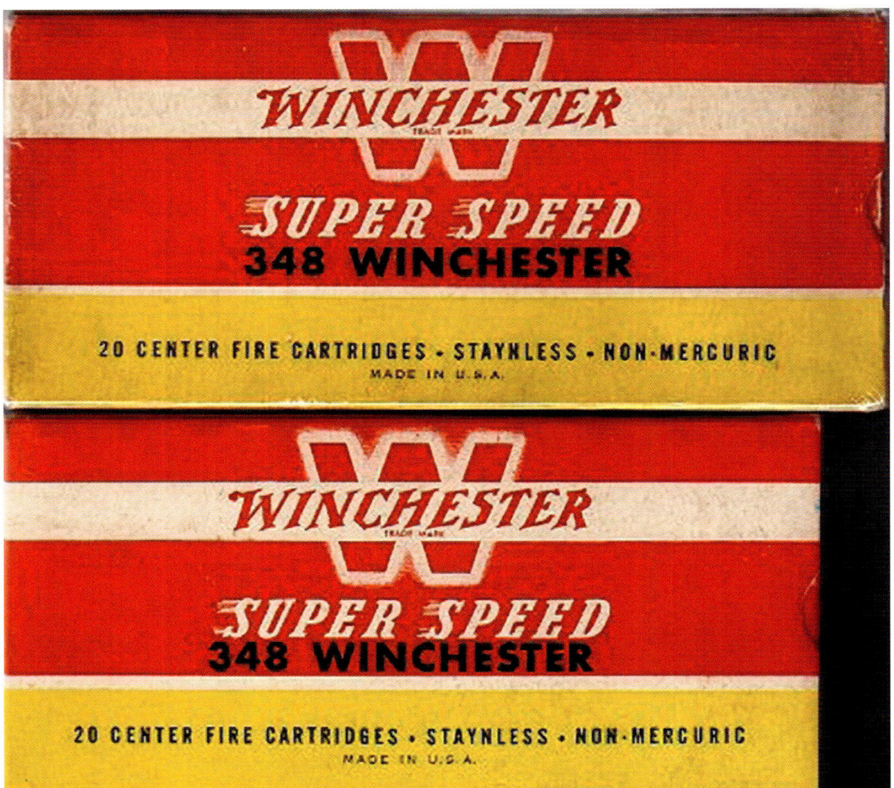

It's not uncommon to find both of these box sizes in 348 during the 1940s and early 1950s. Grizzly boxes are also subject to this anomaly. R1/40-80 [Both]

38-56 W.C.F.

Catalog listings: 1887-1940

Models: 1885, 1886
Bullet types: Ld, SP, FMJ, Shot, Blank

Powder types: BP, Smkls
Headstamps: WRACo

Though never having made it into the one-piece box, this is one of the more common Winchester Center Fire calibers of those developed before the turn of the 20th Century. The Full Patch boxes are scarce, while Black Powder jacketed bullet as well as Shot loadings can both be considered very scarce. Blanks, though otherwise considered uninteresting, are rare.

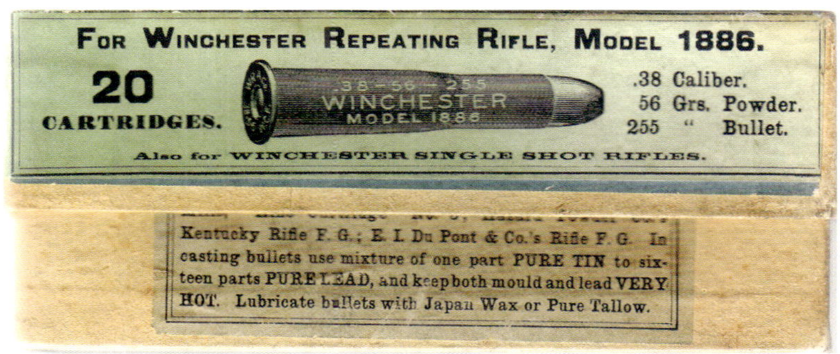

A pre-1898 Black Powder box with "Manufactured and Guaranteed..." line. R3/250-450

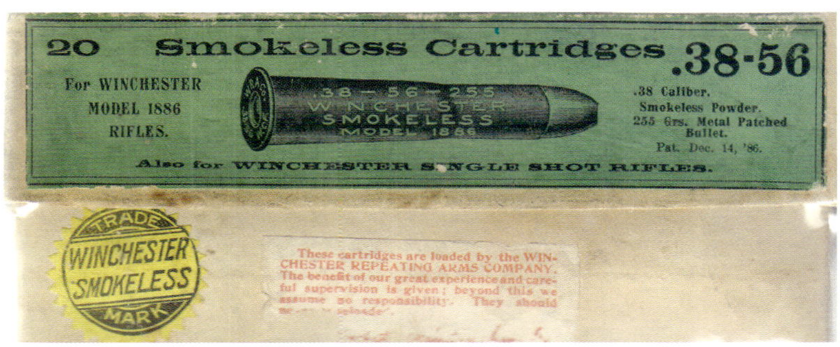

Smokeless loadings began in this caliber in 1896. This box, lacking the "...and Guaranteed" wording, is ca. 1898-1900. R3/250-450

A nice example of the round-cornered version of the Black Powder box, ca. 1901-04. R3/225-425

The (undated) full front-seal label on the Black Powder box, ca 1905. R3/200-400

This Smokeless "Metal Patched" round-cornered box lasted only until 1906. R3/300-500

With an unusual undated narrow front label and a 12-6 lid-top label, here is what is thought to be the earliest orange label Smokeless Soft Point box. R3/300-500

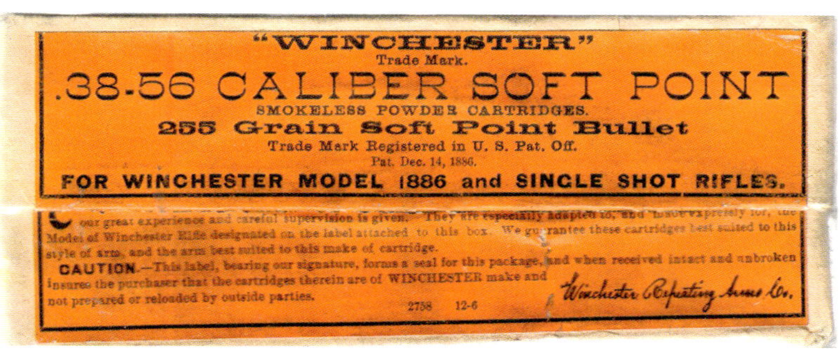

"Winchester" in quotes and a 12-6 date on the front and top characterize this 1906-10 box. R3/250-450

An 11-10 date, a different type font and a slightly different layout of the lower text are about all that distinguish this box from its predecessor. This is one of the few calibers in which a cut of the cartridge is absent on the orange Smokeless Soft Point labels. R2/250-450

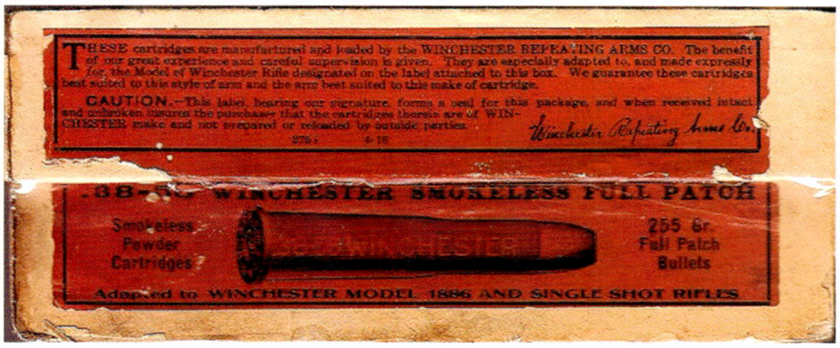

The only "Smokeless Full Patch" M86 caliber boxes to have been offered with red (and/or purple) labels are the .33 WCF, 45-70 and the 38-56. The last two are both rare and represent the only two M86 calibers with black powder origins that are found in red/purple 20-round boxes. The top and front labels are both dated 4-16, the only date the authors have found on such boxes in this caliber. R3/350-550

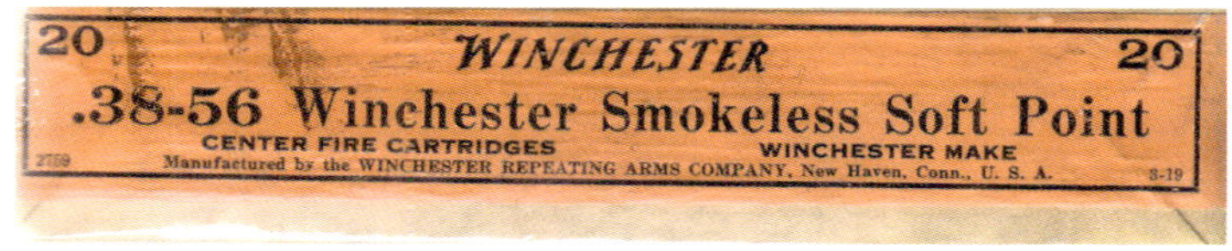

The lack of any Trade Mark call-out on the lid-top label make this 3-19 box highly unusual in any caliber, not to mention RARE! R4?/400-600

The sealed front label of the 3-19 box without the over-printed "clutter" of the subsequent Smokeless Soft Point labels (see above).

Notice that this 3-30 lid label has "Smokeless" replaced with "Staynless" and the Non-Mercuric call-out with "USA Patent Pending". Otherwise it's much the same as the preceding 3-19 label. R2/200-400

Except for numerous added-in call-outs, the front label of the above 3-30 box also closely resembles the 3-19 front label Note the very cluttered appearance of these over-printed labels. R2/200-400

By 1939, labels began to mention "Division of Western Cartridge Co." This call-out can be seen on the bottom line of this lid-top label...

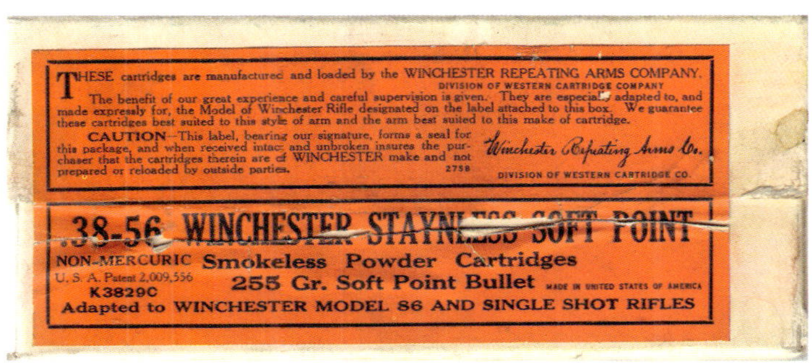

...as well as the second line of this front label. Also of note is the fact that "Patent Pending" has been replaced with "U.S.A. Patent 2,009,556" on both the front and lid-top labels. R2/200-400

38-70 W.C.F.

Catalog listings: 1894-1921

Models: 1885, 1886
Bullet types: Ld, SP, FMJ, Shot
Powder types: BP, Smkls
Headstamps: WRACo

Owing to the fact that fewer than 1000 guns were produced in 38-70, the ammunition was never a big seller and, in spite of remaining in the catalog until 1921, production of all loadings of that caliber had been discontinued by the end of WWI. Still, boxes and single rounds, especially in Black Powder Lead, are not that difficult to find. Black Powder metal patched loadings, on the other hand, are very scarce.

Also among the scarcer rounds are the earliest (1894) which were headstamped simply "WRACo .38-70", the "W.C.F." being added in 1895. This and the 40-70 WCF, which was introduced at the same time, share this unusual history. Winchester was notorious for adding "WCF" to any caliber which they thought they could pass off as proprietary. To have left it off the headstamps of two calibers which were, indeed, of their own design was totally out of character.

Typical Black Powder lid label of the mid-1890s also represents the 38-70 boxes throughout the period. These labels were one-piece, wrapping from the top over the front.

This front portion of the label shows the cartridge cut with the "WRACo 38-70 WCF" headstamp. The box, however, contains the early "WRACo 38-70" stamping. No boxes have been found with the latter headstamp on the cartridge cut. R3/300-500

Smokeless was introduced in this caliber in 1896. This lid top of an early Smokeless box is thought to be the first in this caliber, ca 1896-97.

The powder grain call-out will be found on the front portion of this lid-label from the above 1896-97 box. R3/250-450

Front of the 1897-98 box. While all the wording remains the same, note the differences in the first and last lines as compared to the 1896-97 box above. These are the graphics most commonly seen on all calibers throughout the "Green Smokeless Box" period. R3/250-450

40-65 W.C.F.

Catalog listings: 1887-1946

Models: 1885, 1886
Bullet types: Ld, SP, FMJ, Shot Blank

Powder types: BP, Smkls
Headstamps: WRACo

One of the early introductions in the M86, the 40-65 became one of its more popular calibers, one of the few that managed to survive WWII. The power, accuracy and reasonable recoil associated with this cartridge has made it popular in recent years as a Cowboy Action "Buffalo Match" caliber. As with the rest of the M86 calibers the early green Smokeless boxes as well as the jacketed bullet Black Powder boxes are scarce and worth a premium.

The early Black Powder, Lead Bullet box with top-to-front wrap-over lid label, pre-1898. R3/300-500

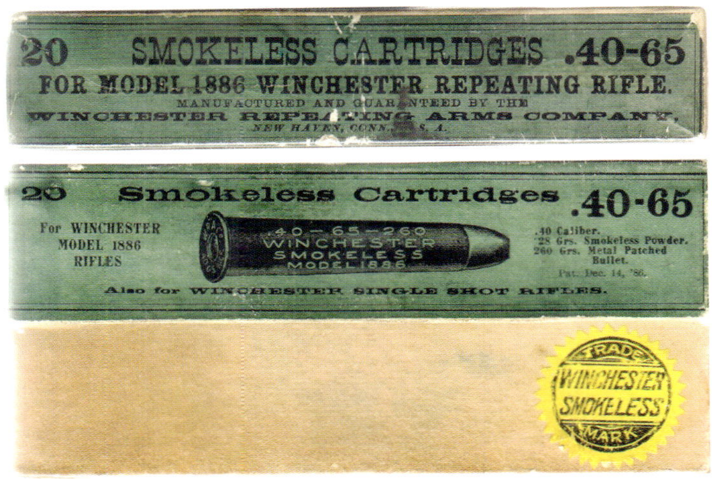

This green Smokeless box with "28 Grs. Smokeless Powder" call-out is circa 1896-97. Contrast these graphics with those of the box below. R3/300-500

Also a square-cornered green Smokeless box, but lacking the "28 Grs" call-out as well as the "...and Guaranteed" wording, this labeling is circa 1898-1900. While the remaining wording is the same on this box as on the earlier one, the differences in font and layout make for a significant variation. R3/250-450

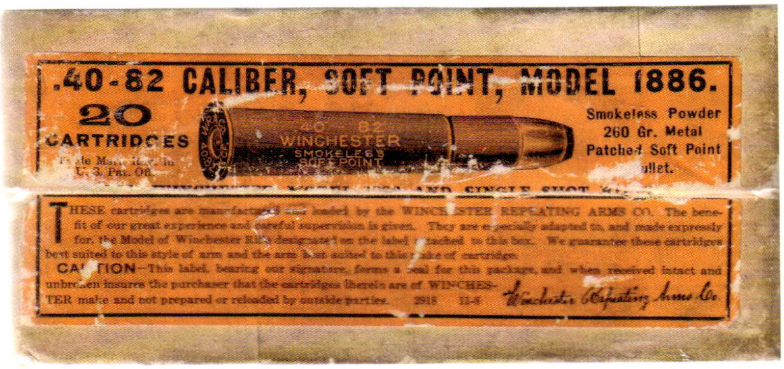

An 11-8 dated Smokeless Soft Point box, the basic style of which was around ca 1902-04 until WWI. R3/250-450

A sealed Black Powder box with cartridge cut on the lower part of front-sealing label, this one dated 4-16. R3/225-425

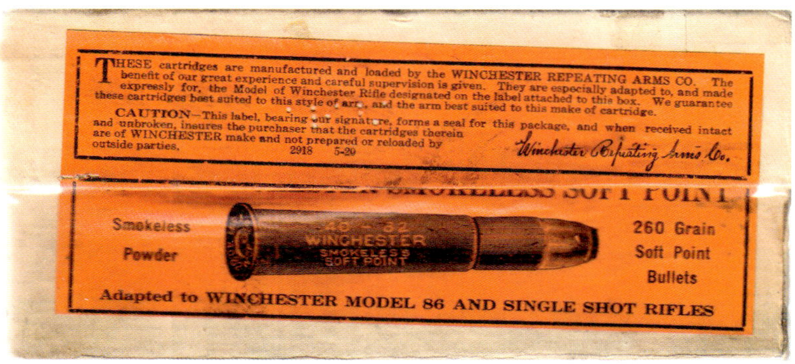

This sealed, 5-20 dated Smokeless Soft Point box is typical of the early-1920s labels preceding the Staynless era. Pre-K-code, it still exhibits the 1911-style trade mark data on the lid top (not shown). R3/225-425

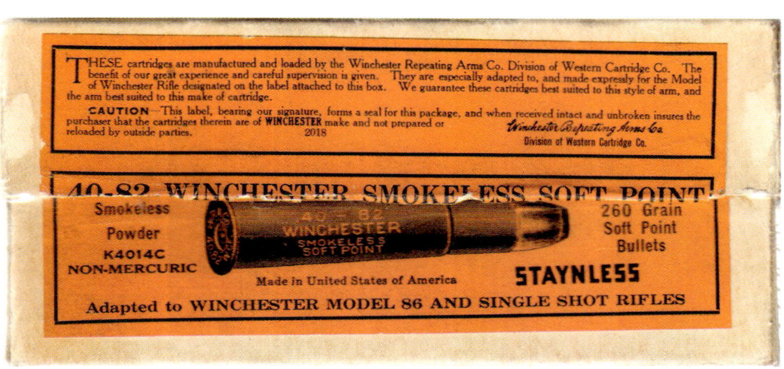

Here is what we believe to be the last box in 40-82 (right). The "Western Cartridge Co." call-out is present on both the lid-top and front labels (see close-ups below). R3/200-400

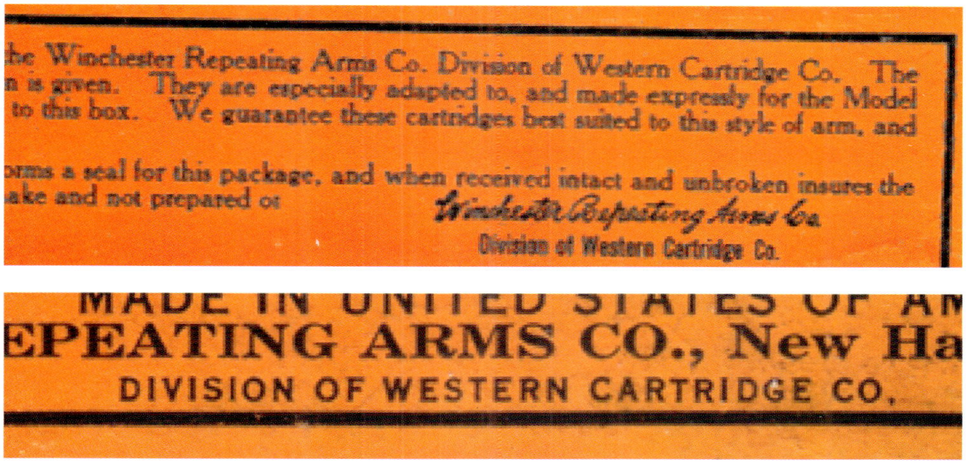

In spite of the fact that Western had owned Winchester since December 1931, it wasn't until 1939 that "Division of Western Cartridge Company" began to appear on Winchester boxes. But since the Company never threw anything away, labels of slower moving calibers (such as these older calibers with Black Powder origins) did not always reflect the Western call-out. This is one caliber that made the transition.

The Rare Black Powder Shot Box...

An example of the rare Black Powder "Shot" box with add-on label with call-out: "SHOT CARTRIDGES". This box is ca 1904-05. R4/400-750

...and a Rare "Loaded in France" Box.

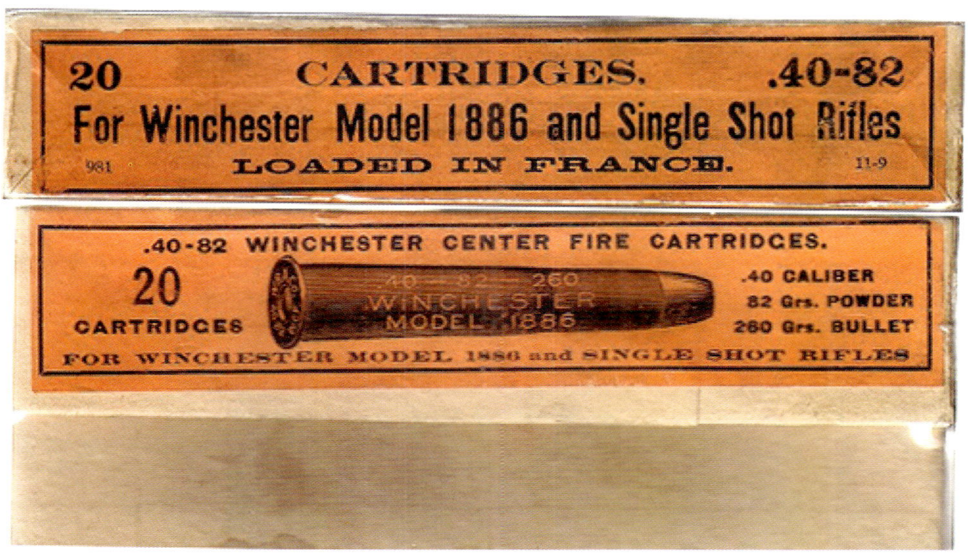

With an 11-9 lid-top date this ranks as one of the earliest "Loaded in France" boxes. It is also among the rarest calibers in this uncommon labeling. In fact, we are not aware of any others. R4?/400-750

45-70, 45-70 U.S.G., 45-70 Model '86, 45-70 W.H.V.

Catalog listings: 1876-

Models: 1883 (Hotchkiss), 1885, 1886

Powder types: BP, Smkls

Bullet types: Ld, Ld HP, Ld SR, SP FMJ, Shot, Blank

Headstamps: Plain, WRACo, WRA, Dated*

Developed by the U.S. Government for the Model 1873 Springfield rifle and carbine, the 45-70, within 15 years, gained dominance in both the military and sporting arenas of the American West as well as abroad. With the M86, Winchester was finally able to offer a gun that could handle the popular Government rounds, something the M76 couldn't do. And while a huge number of varieties exist in the combinations of powder and bullet types, we will concentrate here on those loadings for which, excepting the Short Range and Armory Practice loadings, Winchester specifically called out the Model 1886 in the catalogs or on the cartridge boxes themselves.

The early catalogs (1887-93) specified the Government 405 grain and 500 grain loadings for the M86 along with the "45-70 Marlin Flat Nose". The standard 2.1" case was loaded by the Company, like the Government, with 405 and 500 grain bullets. Unlike the Frankford Arsenal loadings, however, which reduced the powder charge behind the lighter carbine bullet, the Winchester M86 405 grain slug was propelled by the full 70 grains of black powder. Before Winchester was through, however, they had added various powder loadings and bullet types with weights of 140, 200, 230, 235, 240, 330 and 350 grains in addition to the standard 405 and 500 grain offerings. Again excepting the Short Range and Armory Practice loadings nearly all boxes with the M86 call-out will exhibit flat-nose bullets, a catalog specification that began in 1894. Ranging from scarce to rare are such loadings as the Smokeless Lead, Gould Hollow Point, Short Range, Armory Practice (especially the 140 grain Round Ball), the 500 grain FMJ and the WHV Full Patch.

* Dated rounds were from Government contracts in the late-1870s to the late-1890s and are occasionally found in commercial boxes.

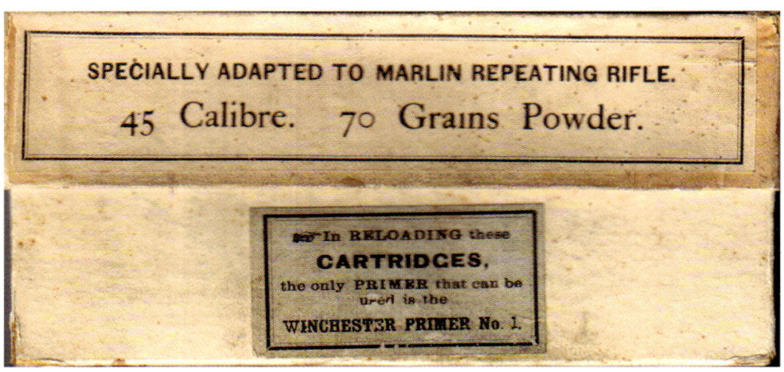

Unpalatable as it may be to Winchester purists, the earliest 45-70 listings, pre-1893, failed to call out the M86. It was the 45-70 Marlin with its flat-nose 405 grain bullet and small primer that, along with the "Gov't" loadings, that was specified in the catalogs for this model. Note the reloading label at the bottom front calling for use of the "Primer No. 1", Winchester's smallest primer and, as with the bullet profile, a Marlin specification. R3+/450-900

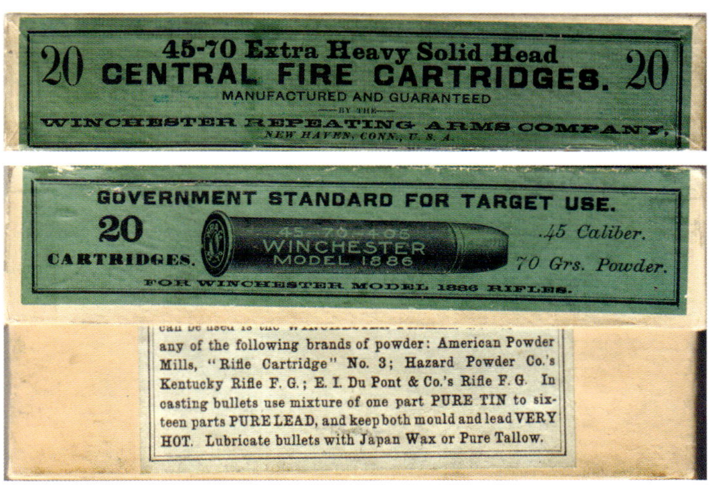

A close-up of the M86 call-outs from the box at left.

First marked for the "Model 1886" in 1894, this box with the italicized caliber and (black) powder call-outs and the "Manufactured and Guaranteed" line as formatted is thought to be from the 1894-96 period. Prior to this the "45-70 Marlin" loading was specified in the catalogs for M86s chambered in 45-70. R3/200-400

The seldom-seen Black Powder 350-grain Lead bullet box, ca 1894-95, with "Central Fire" and "...and Guaranteed" call-outs on lid-top label. R3+/400-700

Also note that the "New Haven" line on the lid-top is in block letters.

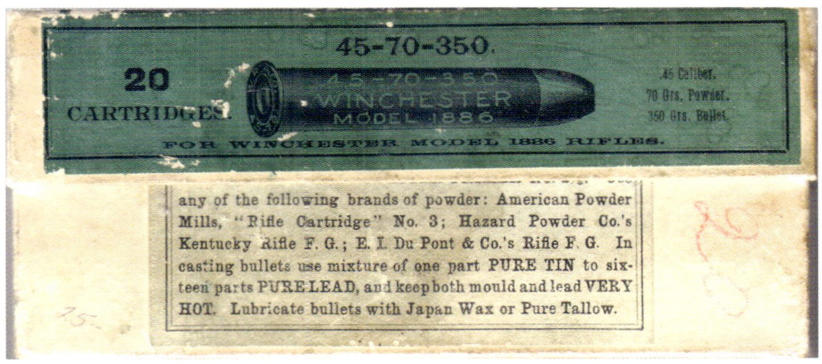

With virtually the same graphics as the preceding box, this later box, ca 1896-98, shows the "New Haven" line now in italics, a practice which continued in this caliber into the 20th Century. R3+/400-700

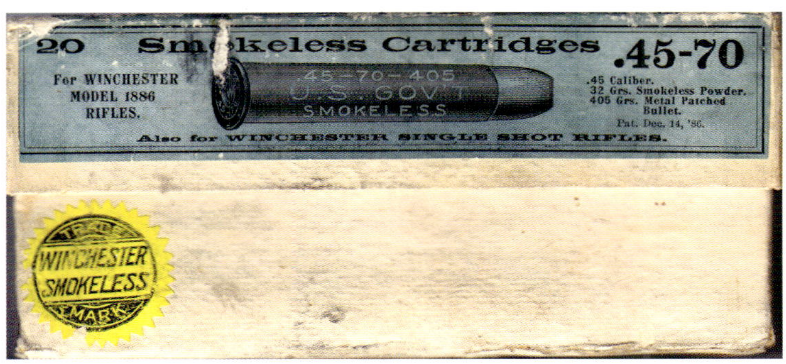

A very scarce blue label on what is thought to be the first Smokeless Soft Point box, circa 1895-96, calling out "32 Grains Smokeless Powder" and containing the earlier small ringed-head rounds. The front label now adds "Also for Winchester Single Shot Rifles", the first reference on 45-70 boxes to the M85 High Wall. Note the somewhat different label wording format, both top and front, between this box and the next. R3+/500-800

Still pre-1899, this green label retains the call-outs of the previous box with slightly different graphics. R3/250-500

Yet another square-cornered early Smokeless box but lacking the "...and Guaranteed" phrase on lid top. This box circa 1899-1901. Essentially the same graphics are found on a round-cornered box, ca 1902-05. R3/200-400

With undated top and front labels, this rare 350 grain Smokeless box with "Soft Point" stamped on the front in red also has a pre-1906 Soft Point "Sunburst" label, a 7-6 back-seal label and a 1-7 "Red W" end label. R3+/400-800

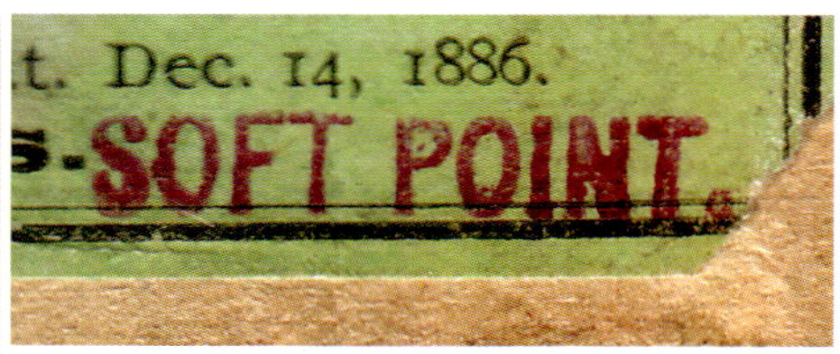

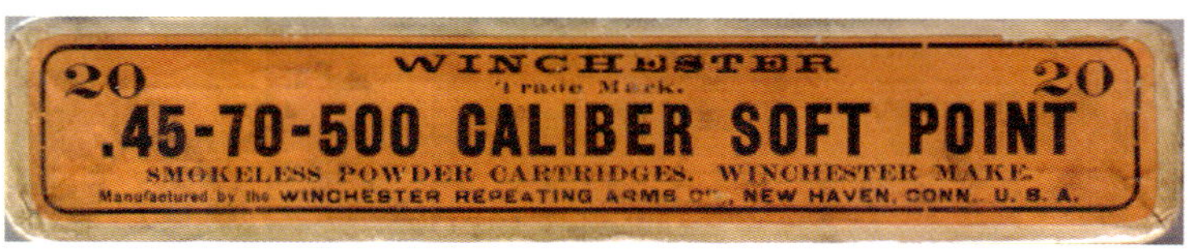

Any jacketed 500 grain bullet offering is very rare in this caliber. While the lid and front labels are undated and exhibit 1903-1905 style graphics, there is a voided "License to the Trade" on the back, circa 1913-14. Obviously these labels were not used up very quickly. Note that the cartridge cut displays a round-nose bullet along with the M86 call-out, a highly unusual combination. The cartridges in the box, by the way, ARE round-nosed. R4-/750-1000 [500 grain FMJ: R4/1000-1500

Red FMJ boxes are only known to the authors in two M86 calibers that had Black Powder origins: 45-70 and 38-56. Label-dated 12-6, these red Metal Patched (FMJ) boxes are very rare in 45-70. R4/500-800

What might appear to be a fairly common Black Powder box is actually relatively scarce due to its "Headline" call-out of the Model 1886. Label graphics point to production circa 1907-10. R3/300-500

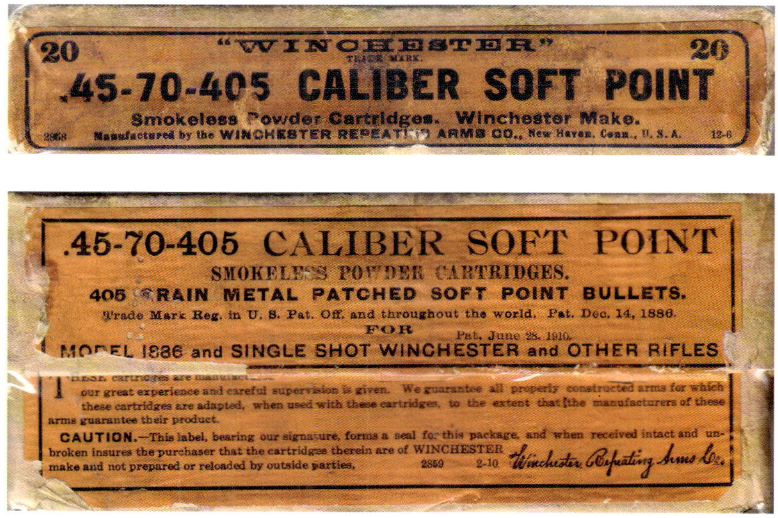

This round-cornered Smokeless Soft Point box is ca. 1910. From this time forward, cartridges are no longer displayed on the label. R3/200-400

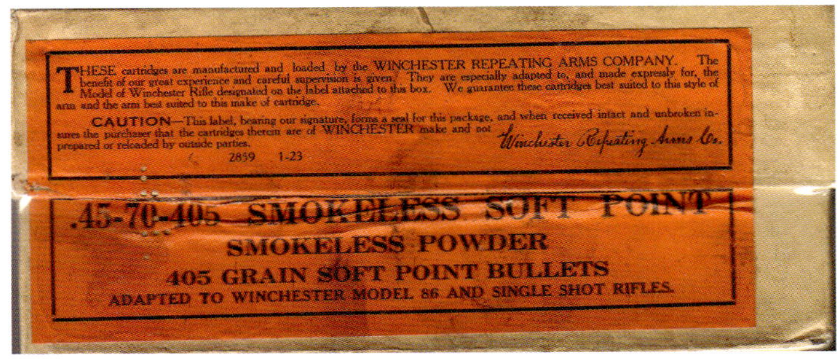

The return to the square-cornered box is ca 1915. This box is dated 4-16: note the minor differences between this and the 1-23 box below. A 3-25 box with a further, though very minor, difference in the textual layout of the lid-front also exists and is thought to be the last style before the 1928 Staynless one-piece box introduction. R2/200-300 [All]

Relative to the front labels of the above 4-16 and 1-23 boxes, the differences in the graphics are more pronounced on the lid-top labels.

The "1932" box, Staynless Non-Mercuric. While neither this nor its look-alike predessor "1928" box is rare, neither are easy to find in clean, solid condition. R2/125-200

Though somewhat more common than the preceding boxes, this "1939" box is subject to the same comments as above blue and white boxes, probably due to the weight of its contents. R2/80-150

The red and yellow graphics of the "1946" and "1954" boxes; this is an example of the earlier variation. Note the Model 86 call-out remaining in the bottom line. R1/25-60

High Velocity (WHV) Boxes

The distinctive yellow two-piece box denoting Winchester High Velocity Soft Point loadings was introduced in this caliber in 1903 and remained in the line until its discontinuance in 1940. This example with its undated primary labels and Sunburst end labels is ca. 1903-05. R3/250-500

In 1906, minor changes in text and logo resulted in this version of the WHV box which appears to have been used with very minor alteration until the post-1915 square-cornered box made its appearance. R3/200-400

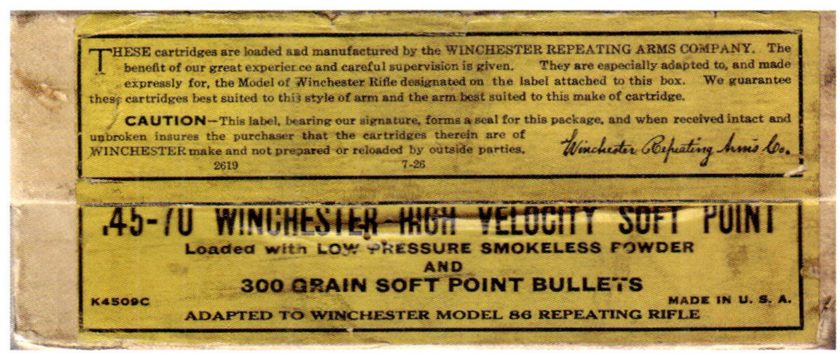

This next (and last) major variation exhibits significant label changes. The square-cornered box of this style appears to have been of the old taped construction until the mid-1929 introduction of Staynless priming in this caliber. A very high percentage of these post-1915 45-70 WHV boxes will have the 7-26 date on both top and front, the later ones with many and various over-prints of Staynless, Non-Mercuric and patent data. All will exhibit the K-code. R2/200-400

This comparison of the 7-26 lid-top labels of the box above as well as the one following shows all the added callouts of the later over-printed labels.

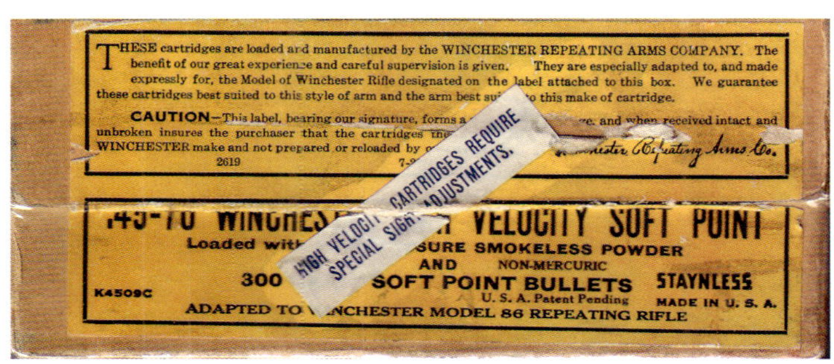

"High Velocity Cartridges Require Special Sight Adjustments" according to the over-label on this late Staynless box, which is still dated 7-26 on both top and front primary labels. R2/200-400

"Gould" Hollow Point Boxes

In 1894 the Company began loading a 330 grain Hollow Point Lead bullet in the 45-70, crediting A.C. Gould, editor of *Hunting and Fishing* magazine, who had been advocating such a loading in his early 1890s writings. The listing was discontinued in 1920. All such boxes are scarce and desirable.

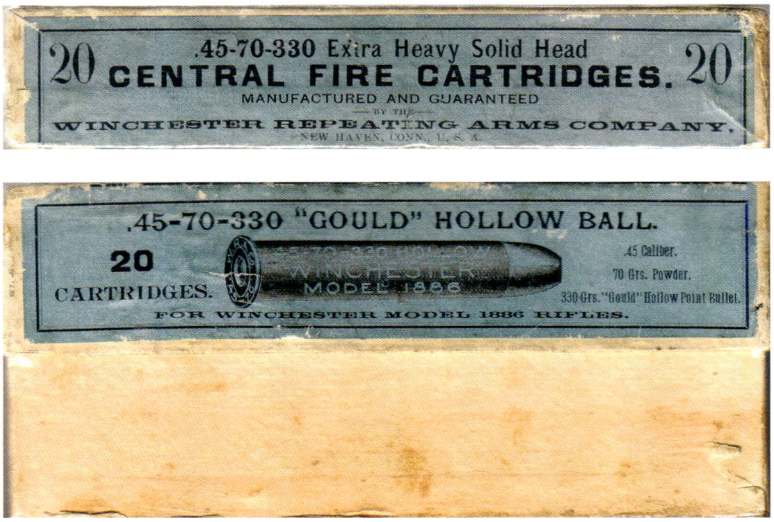

The square corner blue label Black Powder box, ca 1894-98. These same boxes are also found with green labels. After 1898 the "...and Guaranteed" phrase is dropped from the lid top and by 1902-03 the boxes have round corners. R3+/600-1000 [Same with green label: R3/400-750]

Except for color and the Sunburst label, the basic graphics on this early Smokeless box are identical to those of the preceding one. Ca 1896-98. R3+/400-750

The green Smokeless box, ca 1898-1901. While the 45-70-330 call-out has become even more prominent on the lid top, the "Gould" call-out is now in small print to the right of the bullet. These top and front labels on round corner boxes also exist ca 1902-03. It is interesting to note that many of the labels on these boxes, even early ones, are over-labeled on other loadings. The vertical black border line of the under-label is visible at the front right margin. R3/350-700

Short Range Boxes

The rare Smokeless 200 grain Short Range offering was introduced in 1897 and was only cataloged for five years. This box would appear be ca. 1899-1901. R3+/450-800

The 230 grain Smokeless Short Range loading was first offered in the January 1902 catalog. Always a slow seller, all Short Range boxes are very hard to find. R3+/400-750

Armory Practice Boxes

This rare "5 Grs. Powder, 140 Grs. Round Ball" Black Powder loading, was first listed in 1892. The "Central Fire" call-out on this box would normally point to manufacture between 1892 and 1898. However the absence of the "...and Guaranteed" wording (after "Manufactured by...") is indicative of post-1898 labeling. R3+/450-800

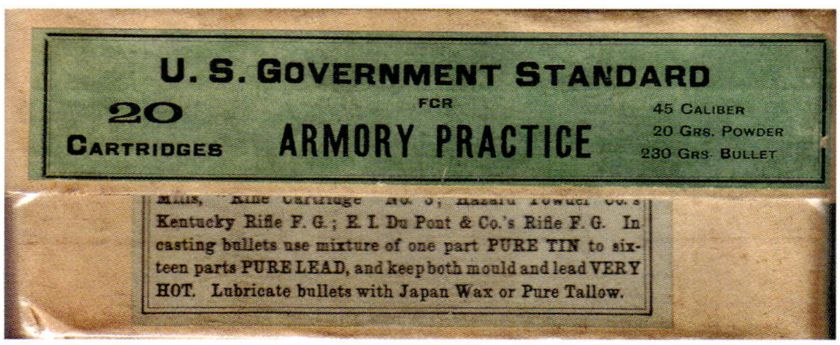

In 1897 the 45-20 Armory Practice, using the 130 grain 45 Schofield revolver bullet, was listed for the first time. This round-cornered Black Powder box is of the style of the very early 1900s. An earlier square-cornered box has identical labeling. All Armory boxes are very scarce. R3+/450-800

A Rarity

In 1893, one year before the Gould Hollow Point was listed, Winchester introduced the 330 grain Hollow Point loading but without crediting Mr. Gould. This is a great example of that rare one-year box. R4/750-1250

45-82 W.C.F.*

Catalog listings: 1887-1917**

(No catalog picture available)

Models: 1885, 1886
Bullet types: Ld
Powder types: BP
Headstamps: WRACo

Probably the least encountered of the M86 calibers and one of the rarest Winchester cataloged boxes to be found in any caliber, the 45-82 was destined to answer a question no-one had apparently asked. It is, in effect, a 45-90 case using the heavier 405 grain 45-70 bullet as opposed to the standard 300 grain 45-90 bullet. As early as 1892, Company records show that they used 45-90 headstamped cases when needed. No guns were specifically cataloged for it and it is said that the rifling twist of the 45-90 rifles would not properly stabilize the heavier bullet.

Between 1900 and 1913 two lots of uncataloged Smokeless loadings were run on special order, the earlier one having Soft Point bullets and the later one Lead. Needless to say, both are very rare.

* Also see 45-90 W.C.F.
** Cataloged by Winchester under "45-90".

Lid top from a square-cornered box dating to the 1887-97 period showing "...and Guaranteed" on the top label. Front label graphics on this box are identical to the label on the round-cornered box shown below. R3++/900-1400

The round-cornered box of the late-1890s and early-1900s on which "...and Guaranteed" is now omitted. An interesting feature concerning this particular box, as well as most others n this rare caliber, is the fact that it is over-labeled on what is thought to be a 50-110 or 50-100-450 box judging by its measurements. Over-labeling was not uncommon; any number of slower-moving items are to be found that way. R3+/750-1250

A Rarity

Here is an example of the uncataloged Smokeless Lead loading of 1913. Found empty, the rounds are nonetheless known. Note that the "82 Grains Powder" call-out has been lined out by the factory as the 82 grain call-out obviously applied to the Black Powder loading. R4/1250-1750

Unlike normal labels of this style which cover the top and wrap over the front, Winchester printed a 45-82 Smokeless version of the lid top portion and pasted it over the Black Powder label which was already in place. The overlap of the edges is evident.

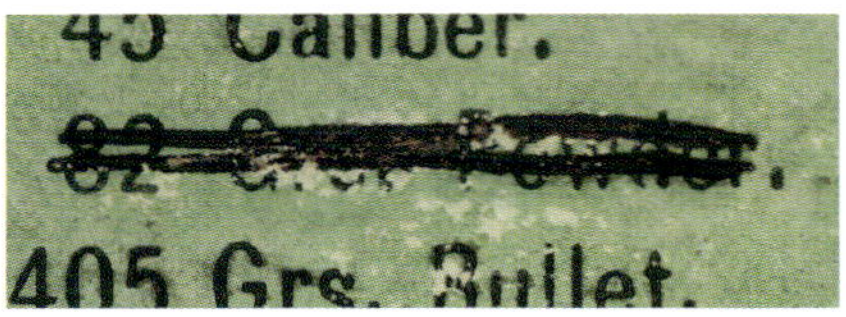

As can be seen in this close-up the "82 Grs Powder" call-out, made erroneous by the lighter 23.5 grain Smokeless loading, has been crossed out.

This back-seal shows a 4-12-12 date and an un-voided "License to the Trade" sticker is on the bottom. Both labels verify the 1912-13 time period for manufacture of the boxes, labels and cartridges.

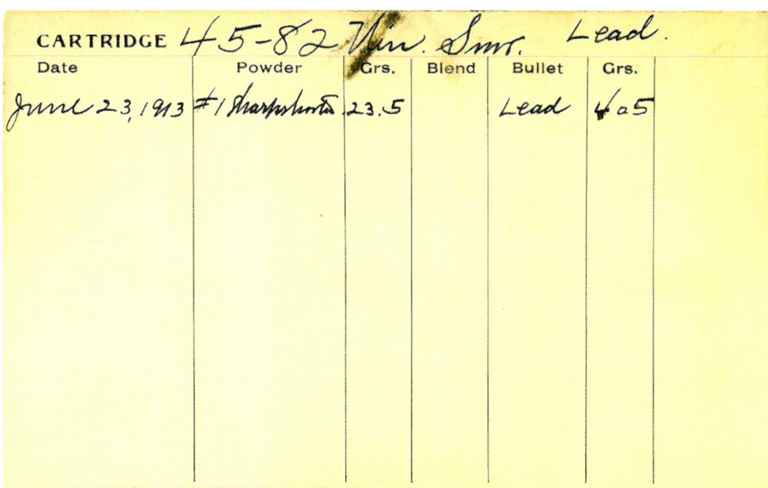

CARTRIDGE 45-82 Win. Smo. Lead.

Date	Powder	Grs.	Blend	Bullet	Grs.
June 23, 1913	#1 Sharpshooter	23.5		Lead	405

303 CENTER FIRE LOADING MEMORANDUM 200 1-13

Here is the factory "Center Fire Loading Memorandum" (bottom left, fine print, but commonly called the Loading Card within the Company) for the box shown above. Titled "45-82 Win. Smo. Lead.", it is dated June 23, 1913, and calls for 23.5 Grs of #1 Sharpshooter [smokeless powder] with a Lead bullet of 405 Grs.

45-85 W.C.F.*

Catalog listings: 1887-1917**

(No catalog picture available)

Models: 1885, 1886
Bullet types: Ld, Ex
Powder types: BP
Headstamps: WRACo

Like the 45-82, here's another 45-90 variation with its own box and headstamp but no guns specifically cataloged for it. As the box says, "...to be used in Winchester Model 1886 Rifles, chambered for the .45-90 Cartridge, and marked on barrel 45-90 W.C.F." Two very distinct variations exist under the 45-85 nomenclature: a 300 grain Express bullet loading and a 350 grain Solid Flat Point bullet loading, both utilizing the standard 45-90 case. The "Express" box is very scarce; the "Solid" box is rare. Several different uncataloged loadings in both Black Powder and Smokeless are known and are also rare. (This cartridge with its 2.4" case should not be confused with the 45-85 Marlin/Colt/Bullard which carried a 285 grain bullet in a 2.1" case).

*Also see 45-90.

**Cataloged by Winchester under "45-90".

The early version of the rare 350 grain Solid Flat Point loading. R3+/500-800

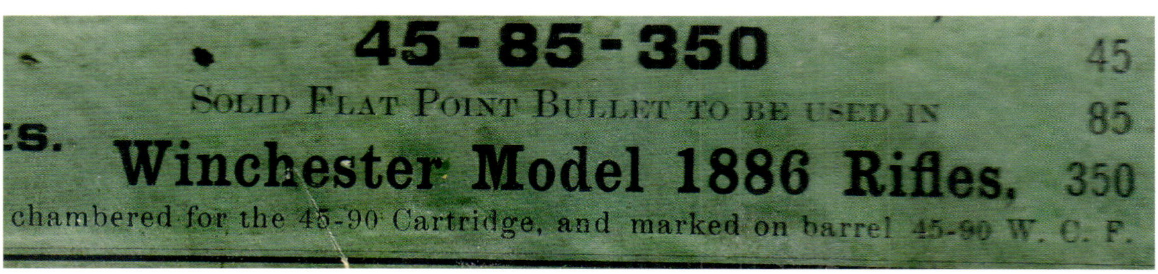

A close-up of the "350" grain and "Solid Flat Point Bullet" call-outs.

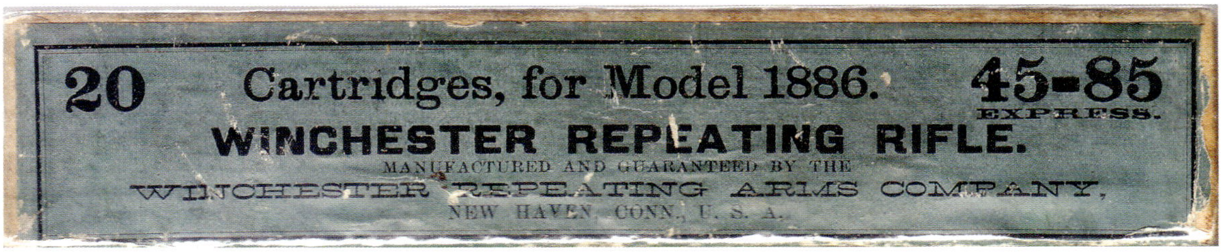

An early blue label "45-85 Express" box with "and Guaranteed" wording, pre-1898. R3+/750-1200

Here is an unusually clean example of the square-cornered box of the post-1898 variety. Round-cornered boxes with nearly identical graphics begin to be seen circa 1903-05. They are seldom encountered, however, as both loadings in this caliber, in spite of their catalog availability, seem to have virtually disappeared before 1910. R3/550-900

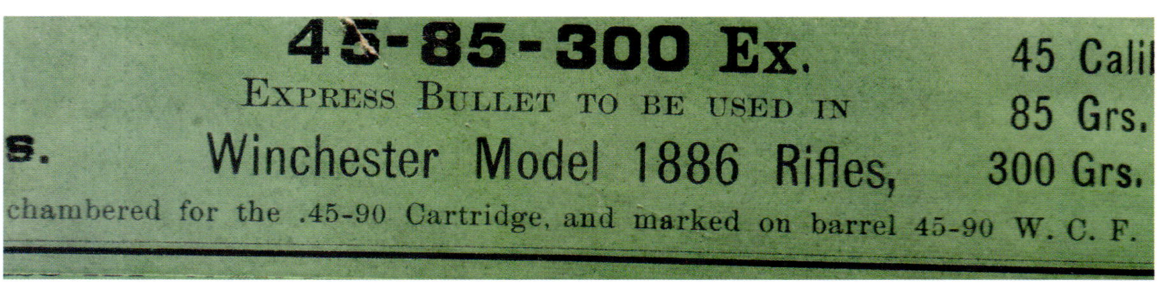

Here is a close-up of the 300 Grain Express Bullet call-outs from the lid-front label of the box pictured above. While more common than the 45-85-350, the 45-85-300 Express has always been more prized by collectors. The copper-tubed Express bullet, and even the word "Express" itself, seem to have made this the "sexier" version.

45-90 W.C.F.*, 45-90 W.H.V.

Catalog listings: 1886-1946

Models: 1885, 1886 **Powder types:** BP, Smkls
Bullet types: Ld, Ex, SP, FMJ, Shot, Blank **Headstamps:** WRACo

Sharing the spotlight with the introduction of the Model 1886 in their October 1886 catalog, was Winchester's unveiling of a brand new cartridge, the 45-90. This new caliber had a longer case length (2.4") than the 45-70 (2.1") and held sufficient black powder to render it superior to that venerable Government round. The reality of that superiority, however, was another matter. While the 300 grain 45-90 bullet left the barrel at a slightly higher velocity than did the 405 grain 45-70, mid-range trajectory at 300 yards was only 1.75" better, 27.25" versus 29". Considering the superior energy generated by the 35% heavier bullet of the 45-70, any claimed advantage by the 45-90 would appear to have been largely illusory, all things considered. Still, the caliber enjoyed considerable success throughout its long history of catalog listings.

Jacketed bullets were available beginning in 1892. The August 1895 catalog began offering such bullets in 45-90 in either Black or Smokeless Powder. Jacketed Hollow Soft Points have been encountered, though rarely, and were not a catalog item. Shot loadings and Blanks were Black Powder only, the former being uncommon and the latter rare.

Winchester High Velocity (WHV) loadings were introduced in this caliber in 1903 in Soft Point only. The Full Metal Patch (FMJ) offering was added in 1905 and such boxes are rare. Interestingly, Great Britain used the M86 with 45-90 WHV rounds to shoot down German observation balloons in WWI.

* See also 45-82 and 45-85 W.C.F.

Black Powder Boxes

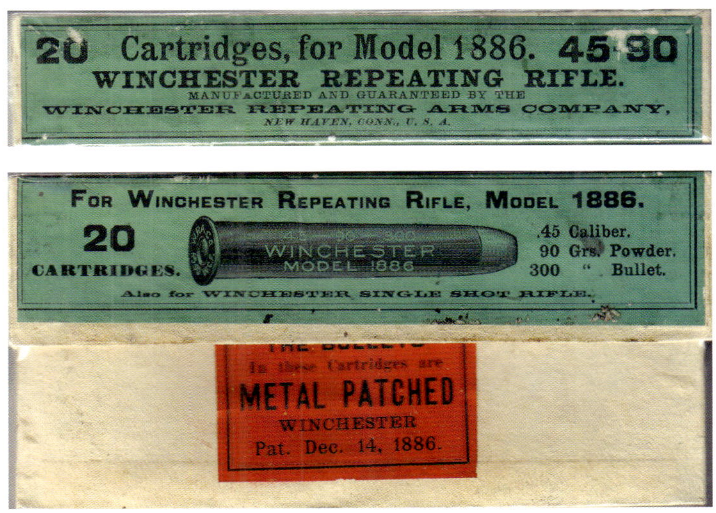

A beautiful example of a rare item: the early 1890s Full Metal Patch, Black Powder box. In spite of the normal 300 grain Lead bullet call-out on the lid-front, these Full Patch bullets were cataloged as 295 grains. The Black Powder Lead box from this period is identical to this except for the red "Metal Patched" label. R3+/500-850

From the 1898-1903 period, this box has rounded corners and the lid-top exhibits the "Manufactured by the" line, omitting the "Guaranteed" wording. This style two-piece box and labeling was the last before the full front-sealing label was introduced in this caliber shortly after the turn of the 20th Century. R3/200-400

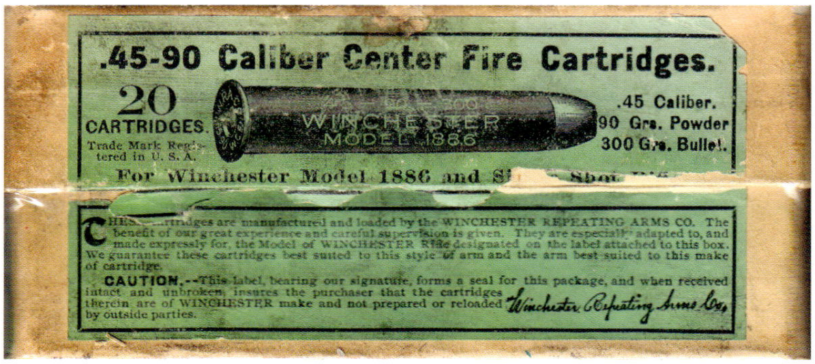

The Black Powder round-corner box, with cartridge cut on the top of a full front sealing-label, is thought to have debuted ca 1904. This style, with minor variations, lasted through 1914. R3-/200-400

The post-1914 box is, like the pre-1900 boxes, square-cornered. The cartridge cut appears on the bottom front. Black Powder was loaded in these boxes, again with minor variations, until 1927. The lid-top label here is dated 3-19 while the front-seal is 5-16. The box remains of taped bottom construction, a typical feature of the larger Black Powder calibers even after 1915. R3-/200-400

Smokeless Powder Boxes

This rare box contains the special-order jacketed Soft Point loading in what is thought to be the earliest Smokeless box, circa 1895-96. Note the difference in type font and layout of this box versus the next. R3+/400-750

Another early label with the "37 Grs. Smokeless Powder" call-out on the front as well as "...and Guaranteed" on the lid top, this square-cornered box believed to be 1897-98. R3+/300-600

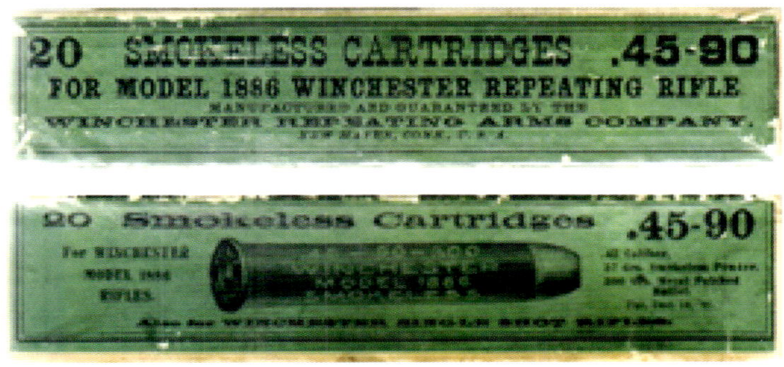

Still another green Smokeless labeling, this with further changes in font and layout. Of particular note in dating this as the third of these boxes is the front ".45-90" call-out: It corresponds exactly to that of the later round-cornered box which carried this loading into the early 20th Century. R3+/300-600

The early-1900s green Smokeless, round-cornered box. What makes this box unusual is the fact that it has a "Sunburst" Soft Point label as well as a 1-7 dated "Red W" end label. Such a combination is rarely encountered. R3/250-500

The fairly common 1925 labels which were over-printed in various ways and forms for the next 15 years with call-outs for Staynless, Non-Mercuric and patent status. An early 1925-dated (but ca 1927-30) Staynless box has been discovered to be of the older folded construction common to pre-1915 boxes. It also has paste-on "Red W" end labels. All other 1925-dated (but later) boxes in the authors' collection are of folded construction with the printed or stamped "Red W". R2/225-425

These 1941 labels (the top is 3-41 and the front, 2-41) exhibit the latest label dates known to the authors. Note the "Western Cartridge Co." call-out on both lid-top and front labels, a practice begun in 1939. The 45-90 was last listed in 1946. Also of interest is the fact that the call-out for Model 1886 and Single Shot Rifles is reversed from the norm. Also the model designation, which at this late date should have read "Model 86" rather than "Model 1886", goes against Company protocol for the period. R3/200-400

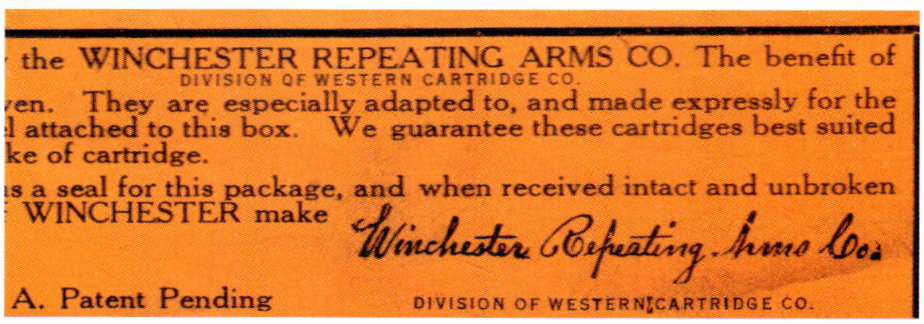

Close-up of the front label with two "Western Cartridge Co" call-outs as well as the 2-41 date.

High Velocity (WHV) Boxes

The first 45-90 WHV box, ca 1903. While the lid-top labels are the same, note the slightly different graphics from the 1904-5 box below. R4-/600-1000

A great sealed box of the colorful WHV Soft Point loading with both "Sunburst" labels, circa 1905. R3/500-900

The rare Full Metal Patch W.H.V. loading in its distinctive lavender label. While the undated labeling is pre-1906 in style and it has 2-10 dated end labels, there is a voided "License to the Trade" label on the back. This box, then, is actually circa 1912-13, further attesting to the fact that this was not a strong selling item. R4-/700-1200

This 5-16 dated box is an example of the last style to be made in the rare WHV loading which was discontinued in 1923. R3+/500-900

"Loaded in France"

An unusually clean example, this "Loaded in France" box is circa 1932-35. The lid-top label (not shown) has the standard domestic labeling for the period, lacking any mention of having been "Loaded in France". R3+/400-750 (Photo courtesy of Scott Soles)

50-110 EX., 50-110 Express, 50-110 W.H.V.

Catalog listings: 1887-1940

Models: 1885, 1886
Bullet types: Ld, SP, SPHP, Ex, FMJ, Shot
Powder types: BP, Smkls
Headstamps: WRACo

By far the more popular of the two M86 50 caliber offerings (the 50-100-450 being the other), the 50-110 was offered in virtually all Winchester's bullet types in both Black and Smokeless Powder. Some of these are rare, however, especially the Soft Point Hollow Point and the Smokeless Express, the latter having been made in only one lot in 1910. All Full Patch (FMJ) boxes are very scarce, the lavender-colored High Velocity (WHV) Full Patch boxes being especially so. While all of Winchester's 50 caliber cartridges are very collectible, the 50-110, relatively speaking, is the most often encountered. Still, all varieties are fairly expensive, reflective of the strong collector demand for them. The 50-110 Smokeless Soft Point was last loaded in 1939 and last cataloged a year later.

Black Powder Boxes

The blue label Black Powder Express box, one of the most collectible of all Winchester boxes. Blue labels are actually more often seen than green labels in the square-cornered Black Powder box. R3/750-1250

The Black Powder Express was the most popular 50-110 loading of its day; however, the much rarer Solid Ball offering was also available and was sold in the same box but with an over-stamped "Solid Ball" call-out. A close-up of the stamped "Solid Ball" is shown here. R4/1000-1500

This is an example of the early-1900s green round-cornered box of the type that was probably still in use when Black Powder was last loaded in 50-110 in 1919. The later (1915) style boxes and labels, while they may exist, are not known to the authors. R3/500-900

Smokeless Powder Boxes

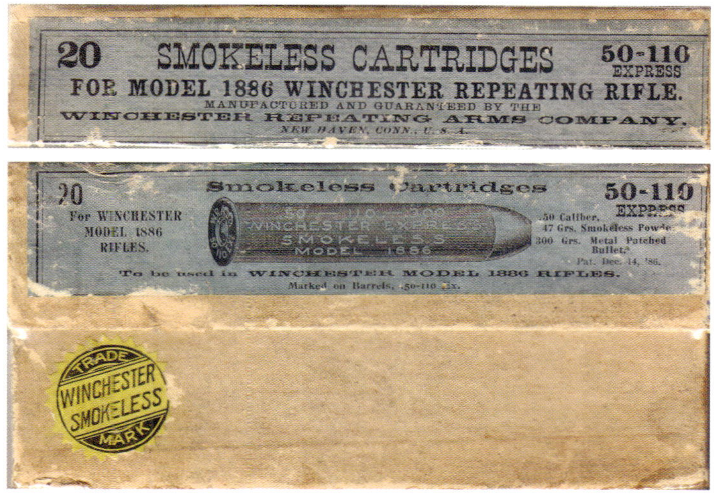

This blue Smokeless "Express" box has the "47 Grs Smokeless Powder" callout, making it the earliest version, circa 1896-98. R3+/750-1250

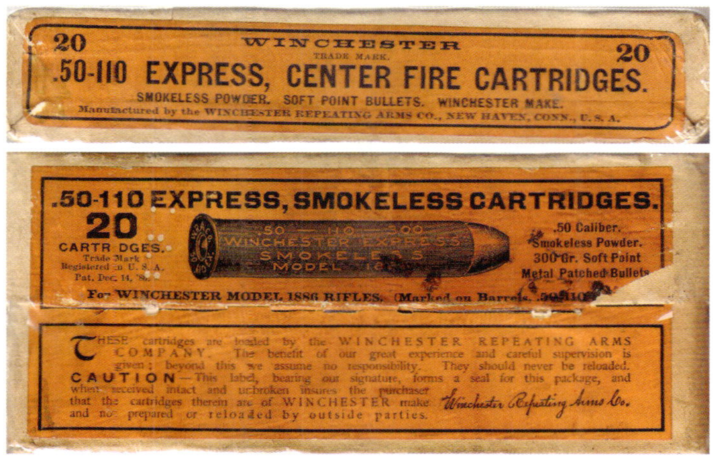

An early undated orange label Soft Point box, circa 1903-06, with "Sunburst" end labels. Except for the end labels, which were pre-1906, these graphics are typical of many of the rifle caliber boxes of the 1902-1914 period. R3+/450-800

While this label is undated, the newly added K-code, next to an undecipherable blackout, marks it as ca 1923. There is a progression of minor label variations throughout the 1916-1939 period. The underlying label dates on these variously over-printed labels are 4-16, 4-19, 11-22, and 3-27. R3/400-700

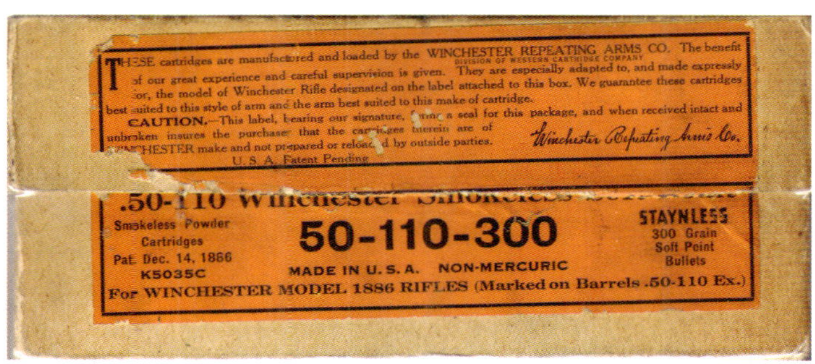

Here is what is thought to be the last style 50-110 box. Note the "Western Cartridge Co" call-out. R3/400-600

High Velocity (WHV) Boxes

Introduced in 1903, these WHV boxes are among the more scarce and collectible boxes in the classic Winchester calibers and loadings. This round-cornered Soft Point box, with both Sunburst end labels, is circa 1903-05. R3+/800-1350

As mentioned earlier, Full Patch (FMJ) boxes, none of which are available to show in this section, are rare. R4/1000-2000

Whether this box or the one following is earlier cannot be determined from the labels. Both are undated and are identical on front, top and ends except for the textual graphics on the lower front. This one appears to be more common, however. R3+/750-1250

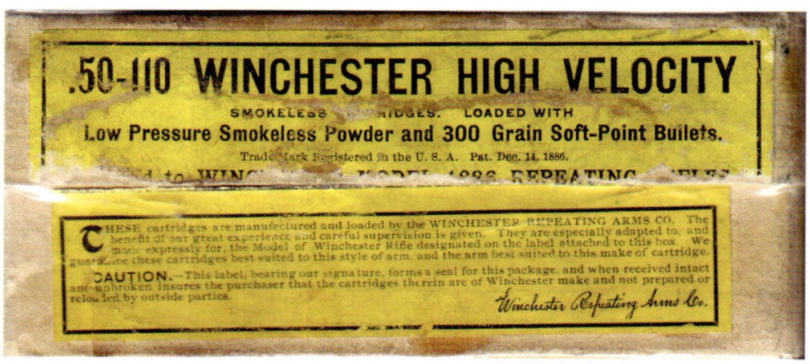

Identical to the above type but apparently the scarcer variety. Both boxes exhibit both Sunburst end labels. Most WHV Soft Point boxes are found to be round-cornered early boxes with 1903-1907 period graphics on undated primary labels. R3++/800-1300

The first box that pictures the WHV cartridge appears to have been this Soft Point box with 11-9 lid-top and end labels but, incredibly, an undated front label. This box has also been found with these same 11-9 front and end labels but paired with the earliest (undated) lid-top label. R3+/600-1000

The WHV loadings were removed from the catalog after 1920 and the last loading date in WHV is 6-19. This square-cornered, 1915-style WHV Soft Point box is label-dated 3-19, making it a late, rare find. The front label is also unusual in that it is small relative to the box size. R3++/650-1150

Shot Boxes

A rare, early Black Powder Shot box. This box was originally labeled "Solid Head Primed Shells" and exhibits an add-on label which calls out "SHOT CARTRIDGES" in red. Two sides of the lower part of the box are stamped the same way, also in red ink. The sentence "These Shells may be reloaded many times" is out of the 1880s. Bearing in mind that this caliber wasn't introduced until 1887, it would appear that this was a very early— probably the first—packaging of Winchester's 50-110 Shot offering. R4+/1000-1500

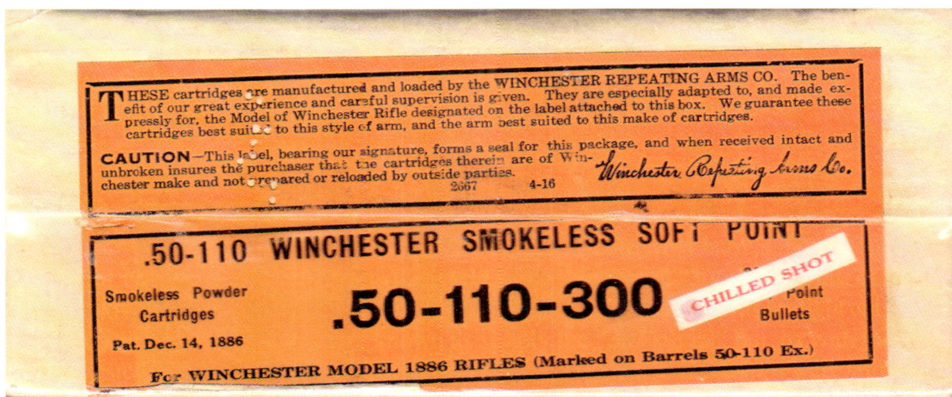

This Smokeless Shot box has top and front add-on labels calling out "Chilled Shot". Many Shot boxes, like this one, are found in clean, sealed condition, but few are found that aren't dated 4-16 as this one is. The Loading Card below shows the date of this last loading as 7-19-22. Note that it's the only loading calling for "Chilled Shot" ("8 ch" on the card below). R3/400-800

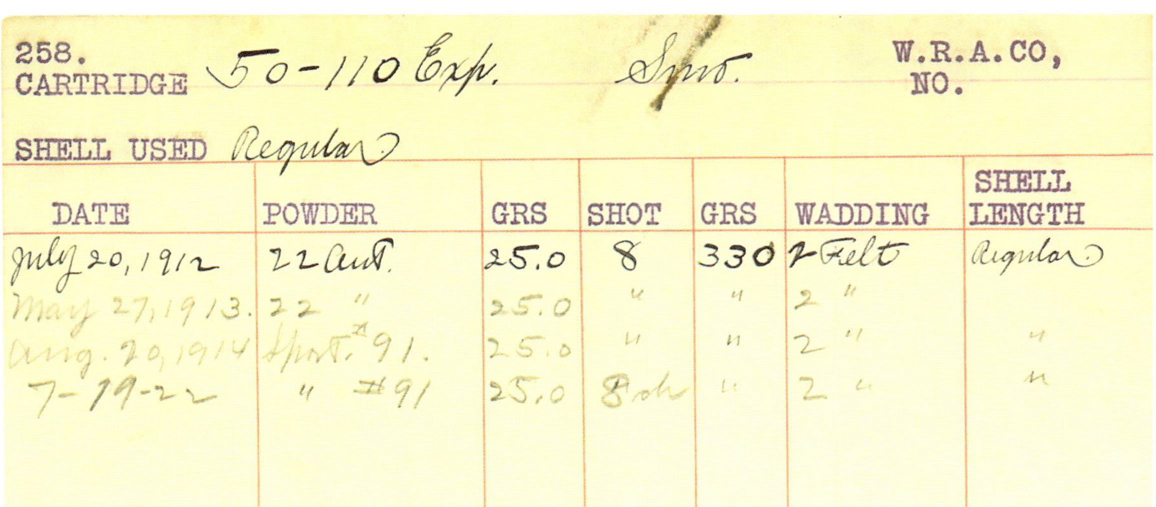

258.
CARTRIDGE 50-110 Exp. Spro. W.R.A.CO, NO.

SHELL USED Regular

DATE	POWDER	GRS	SHOT	GRS	WADDING	SHELL LENGTH
July 20, 1912	22 Aut.	25.0	8	330	2 Felt	Regular
May 27, 1913.	22 "	25.0	"	"	2 "	
Aug. 20, 1914	Sport. #91.	25.0	"	"	2 "	"
7-19-22	" #91	25.0	8 ch	"	2 "	"

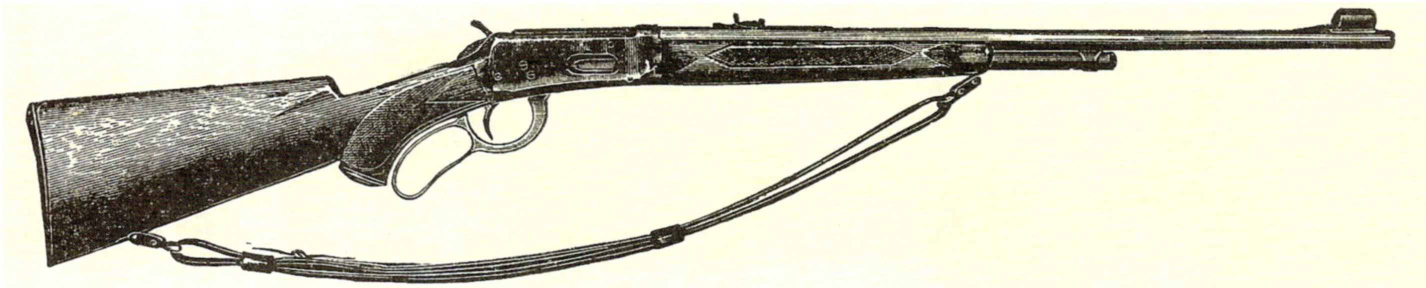

Model 64
In 1933 the Model 64 was added to the line boasting "modern alloy steels" along with a couple more largely aesthetic changes, including a pistol grip stock and semi-beavertail forearm. The 25-35, 30 WCF and 32 Special remained the most popular chamberings; however, the *1938 Winchester Sales Manual* verifies that "...two other cartridges were available in this gun; namely, the .32-40 and the .38-55, both of which have been discontinued." A new Winchester-developed cartridge, the "ultra high" velocity .219 Zipper, was introduced in 1937 only to be dropped, along with the 25-35, in 1941.

219 Winchester Zipper, 219 Zipper

Catalog listings: 1938-1962

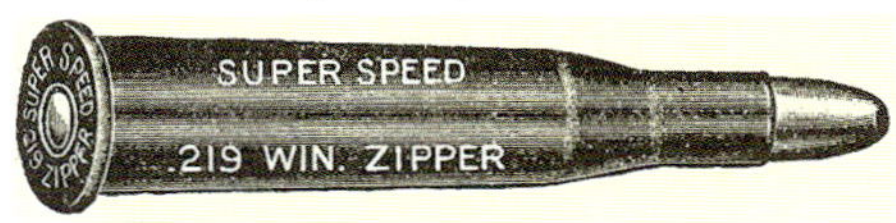

Models: 64
Bullet types: MCHP
Powder types: Smkls
Headstamps: SS

Like all M94, M55 and M64 calibers, the 219 Zipper traces its origins to the old 38-55 casing of the 1880s. In this instance it was derived by necking down the 25-35 and given a name intended to distinguish it from the many wildcat cartridges of the era. Very few varieties exist, the rarest being the 46 grain bullet in the "1935" box. High velocity "varmint" calibers were never very popular in lever action rifles, however, due to the difficulty of adding telescopic sights. The M64 was discontinued in this caliber in 1941 and production of the M64 Zipper then failed to resume after WWII.

The scarce "1935" box of 219 Zipper with the 46 grain bullet. Note the "Winchester Repeating Arms Co." line near the bottom. R3/100-175 [56 grain: R2/75-125

This 56 grain "1939" box exhibits the Western Cartridge Co. affiliation on one side panel. R2-/65-110

An example of the quite common "1946" Zipper box. R1+/50-80

25-35 W.C.F., 25-35 WINCHESTER

Catalog listings: 1895-

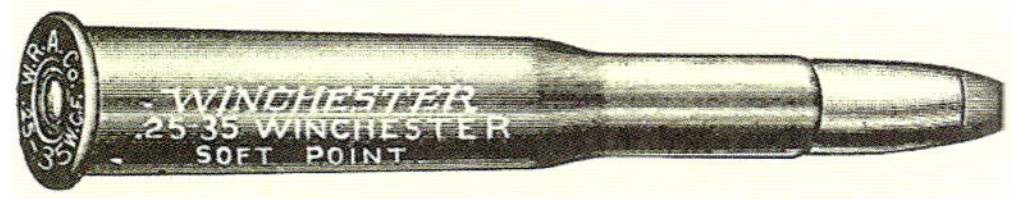

Models: 1885, 1894, 55, 64
Bullet types: Ld SR, MCHP, SP, FMJ

Powder types: Smkls
Headstamps: WRACo, WRA, SS

While their 1894 commercial loading of the 30 Army (30-40 Krag) was Winchester's first smokeless offering, it was 1895 before the company introduced the first of their new "smokeless only" sporting calibers in the Model '94, the 25-35 and 30 WCF (30-30). These three cartridges (the experimental 31-62 W.C.F. might be considered a fourth) are the only ones in which the second number of the caliber was meant to denote grains of smokeless powder rather than black powder. For some reason, however, the 25-35, in spite of its 35-grain powder designation, was loaded with only 26 grains of smokeless. In any event, with the development of new smokeless powders of differing densities and chemical structure being announced with increasing rapidity, this traditional method of naming cartridges was discontinued in 1896. Accordingly, the powder grains call-out was then dropped from the box labels.

The 25-35, like the 30-30, was based on a necked-down 38-55 case. A decent mid-range caliber and very pleasant to shoot, it held a steady market for many years but never approached the popularity of the 30-30. On the other hand, neither did anything else!

The boxes pictured below represent examples of the various major varieties of 25-35 boxes. A study of the following section discussing the 30-30 boxes will set forth many minor variations which, it can be expected, will apply in many instances to the very similar 25-35 boxes.

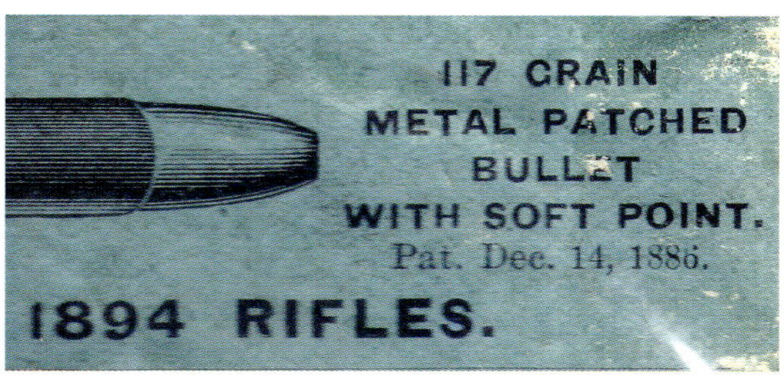

Thought to be the first 25-35 box (ca 1895), this rare blue label has the words "WITH SOFT POINT" under the bullet call-out. The "Dec. 14, 1886" patent call-out refers to the Company's earliest metal jacketed bullet construction. R4-/400-800

Believed to be the 2nd style box, ca. 1896-98, the powder grains call-out remains but the "Soft Point" call-out has been deleted from the front label. R3+/250-500

Top label from the box at left with WINCHESTER in caps and retaining "...and Guaranteed..." in second line.

Identical to the previous top label except that "...and Guaranteed..." has now been omitted from the lid-top label of this third style box, ca.1898-1900.

Also, the "26 Grains" callout of Smokeless Powder has been eliminated on the front label. R3/200-400

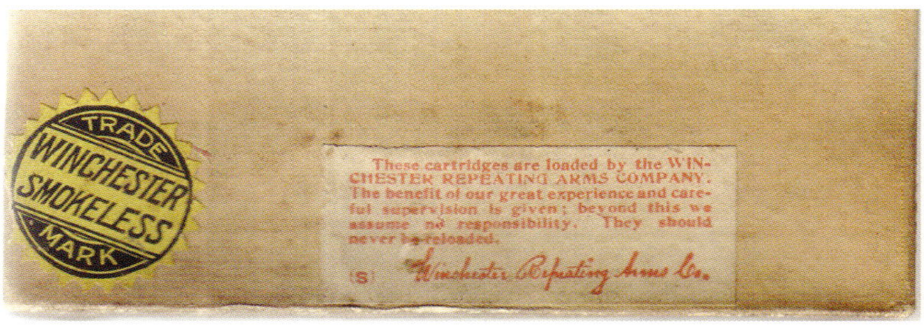

"Sunburst" labels calling out the Smokeless Soft Point loading are found on the back and left end of this box. The labeling remains unusual in its failure to prominently feature the term "Smokeless Cartridges" as is typically found on other green label rifle calibers from the 1895-1902 period.

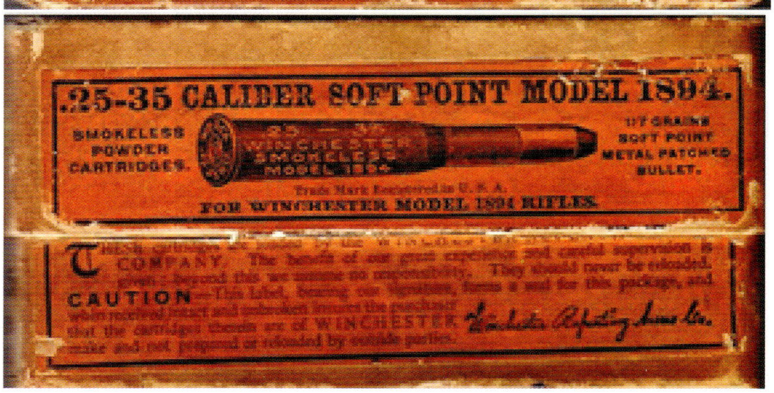

An early, orange label Smokeless example from the 1903-5 period. Both "Sunburst" labels appear on this box, one on each end. R3-/150-250

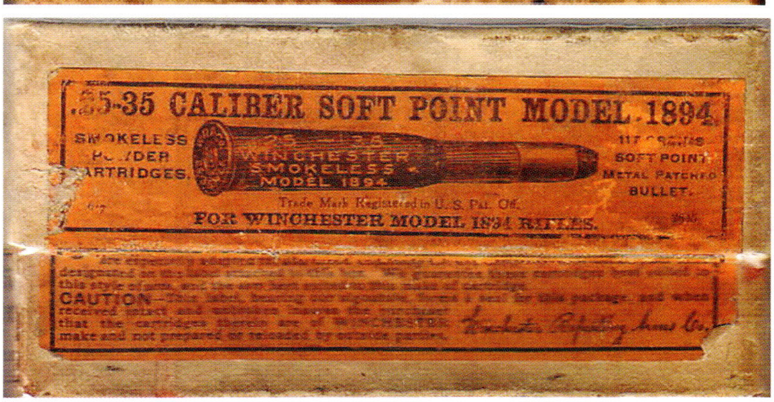

An example of the graphics from a 1906-7 Soft Point box with "Red W" end labels. R3-/125-225

A red label "Metal Patched Bullet" box, circa 1911. R3/175-300

Evolution of the major top label styles, 1906-1925.

In 1915, box construction changed from "taped" to "folded" type. Also, the picture of the cartridge was shifted to the lower half of the front label. R2+/100-200

A "Full Patch" example with a 1919 label date. Note previous "Model 1894" callout exhibits the Company's official change in designation to "Model 94". R3-/150-250

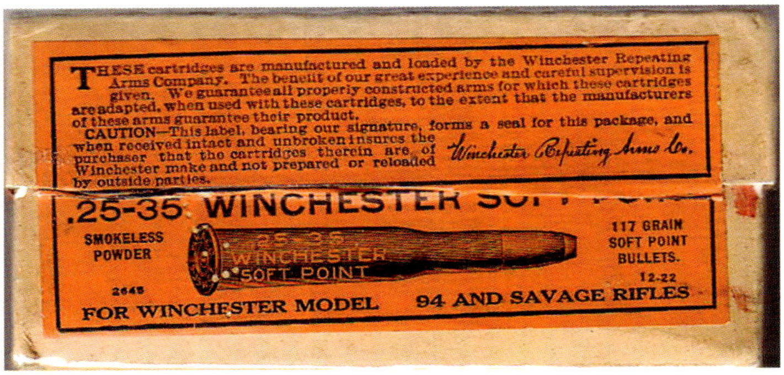

"Soft Point" box circa 1922-4. While nearly identical to the 1919 box above, the gap between "Model" and "94" suggests a minor revision (deleting the "18") was made to an earlier (ca 1915) label design. R2+/100-200

Winchester's first Superspeed box, an 87-grain Hollow Point Mushroom (JHP) offering introduced in 1925. This was the last 2-piece box in 25-35. R3/175-275

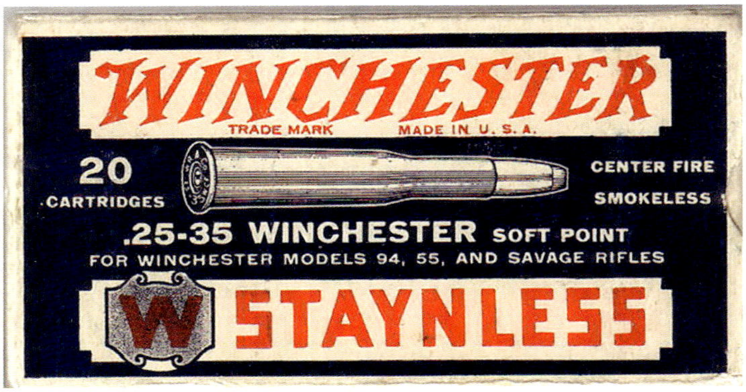

A nice example of the earliest Staynless box, ca. 1928, introducing the Company's new priming compound in a newly designed one-piece box. R2+/100-200

This colorful box first appeared in a limited number of calibers in 1935. Interestingly, the 25-35 boxes are the only ones among the original M94/M55 calibers that call out the M64. This is not only the case with regard to this "1935" box, but holds true for those that follow as well. The "Full Patch" loading pictured here is a fairly scarce variety. R3-/100-200

The "1939" box calls out the Western Cartridge Co. ownership on the side panel and eliminates the Winchester Repeating Arms Co. callout on the lower front. R2/65-130

The "1954" box noting Olin-Mathieson Chemical Corp. ownership on the side panel. R1+/35-65

Short Range Loadings

An early Smokeless Short Range box, ca 1896-97, with "5 Grains" powder call-out. R3+/225-375

Another square-cornered Short Range box, this one with the powder grains call-out deleted. Ca 1898-1900. R3/175-275

The lid-top labels of the three pictured Short Range boxes:

Top, ca 1896-7, with "...and Guaranteed...".

Middle, ca 1898-1900, now reads only "Manufactured by the".

Bottom, post 1905 (in spite of earlier logos and undated labels).

A later box. In spite of the pre-1915 graphics, perhaps the last type issued until discontinuance of the loading in 1919. R3/150-250

30 W.C.F., 30-30 Winchester

Catalog listings: 1895-

Models: 1885, 1894, 54, 55, 64
Bullet types: Ld SR, SP
SS MCHP, FMJ, Blank

Powder types: Smkls, BP*
Headstamps: WRACo, WRA,

It may have been the large bore Black Powder cartridges that "Won the West" and the 30-'06 that won the World Wars, but it was Winchester's 30-30 that led the transition from black to smokeless powder and accounted for the sale of more sporting rifles than any other cartridge in history. As we have mentioned earlier, it used to be said that the "44-40" (44 W.C.F.) put more meat on tables in North America than any other caliber. It must be assumed that the "30-30" has long since overtaken this claim.

Based on a necked-down 38-55 case, the 30 W.C.F. was one of the first of the Company's sporting calibers designed exclusively for smokeless powder. While developments in powders, bullets and primers continue to this day, the period from 1894 through the mid-1930s gave rise to a series of rapid and vast improvements in all areas of cartridge manufacture and performance. What better caliber than the 30-30, then, to illustrate the many varieties of boxes and nomenclatures emanating from these fertile early years of the "modern" rifle cartridge?

The styles and varieties of boxes and labeling used in defining this caliber, while applicable to many other (particularly smokeless) calibers as well, here refer specifically to the lineage of 30-30s. There will be 7 distinct types of box designs as well as over 30 varieties within those basic types, all of which are set forth below in outline form. Please be reminded that the varieties presented here by no means purport to be a complete listing, especially in the 1917-1927 time frame. Far too many minor varieties exist in text, format and typeface to catalog in their entirety while still hoping to retain the reader's interest. Our discussion of the 1915-16 Type 3 labels, both in this caliber and the 32 Special, will suffice to exemplify the difficulties (futility?) of categorizing label variations and the attempt to order them within a definitive time-line. But the sheer numbers of label varieties and loadings, such as the rare Black Powder Blanks or scarce Short Range offerings (covered at the end of this section), make the 30-30 a collector's dream—or nightmare, depending upon your perspective.

*Blanks only

STANDARD LOADINGS

TWO-PIECE BOXES - TYPE 1

- Two-piece box, square corners, taped bottom construction.
- Green label covering lid top and front only.
- Primary call-outs: Lid Top: ".30 Winchester Smokeless."
  Lid Front: ".30 Winchester Smokeless, Model '94."
- Yellow and black "Sunburst" label: "Winchester Smokeless ...".
- Yellow and black "Sunburst" label: "Soft Point Metal Patched Bullets..." on bottom (if applicable).

Variety 1 (Ca. 1895) R3++/250-500

Lid top: a) ".30 Winchester Smokeless" in upper and lower case letters, height of caps and numerals, 5 m/m.
b) *"MANUFACTURED AND GUARANTEED BY THE"* line in italics.

Lid front: a) ".30 Winchester Smokeless, Model '94.", height of caps and numerals, 4 m/m.
b) "30 Grains Smokeless Powder."
c) "Pat. Sept. 9, 1884.", indented.
d) "160 Grains Metal Patched Bullets", aligned left

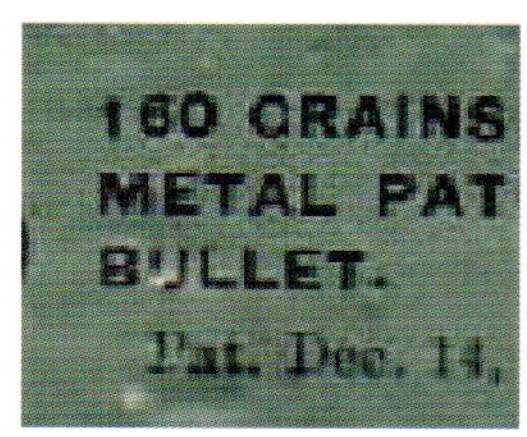

Variety 2 (Ca. 1896) R3+/225-450

Lid top: ".30 Winchester Smokeless", height of caps and numerals: 6 m/m.
"Manufactured and Guaranteed" line more widely spaced than Variety 1.

Lid front: ".30 Winchester Smokeless, Model '94", slightly different type face with height of caps and numerals now 4.5 m/m.

Variety 3 (Ca. 1896-1897) R3+/250-475

Lid top: Same as Variety 2.

Lid front: "Pat. Sept. 9, 1884" no longer indented (relative to "Powder" above it).
Gap between "c" and "h" in "Patched".

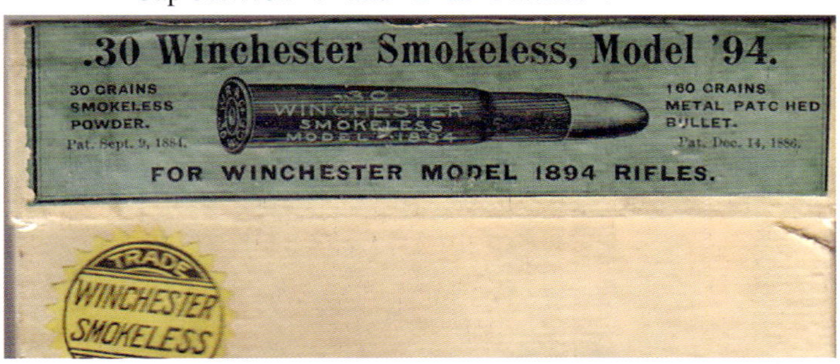

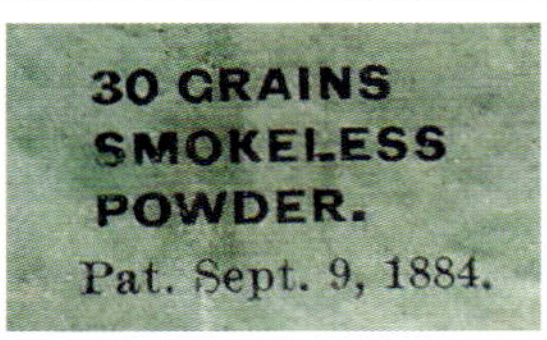

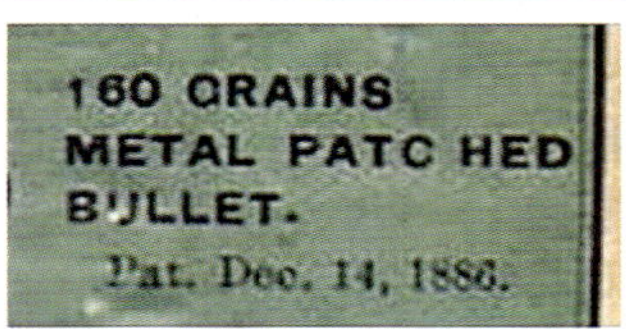

Variety 4 (Ca. 1897) R3/200-400

Lid top: ".30 Winchester Smokeless" now all upper case letters.
"Manufactured and Guaranteed" line no longer italicized

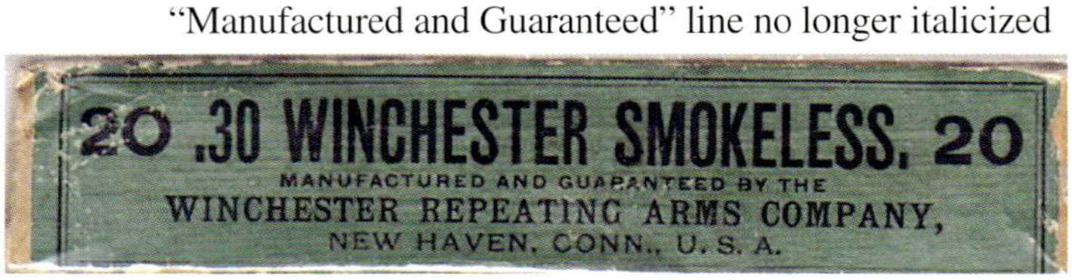

Lid front: Powder grains call-out now omitted.
"160 Grains Metal Patched Bullets" still three lines, now centered.
".30 Winchester Smokeless, Model '94." less bold than Type 1.

Bottom: Both "Sunburst" stickers remain (where applicable.)

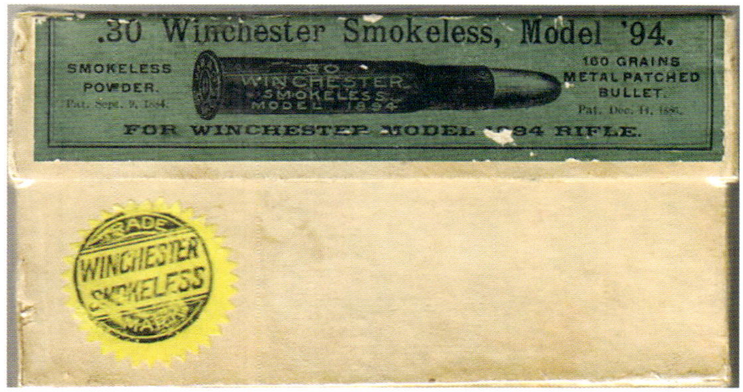

Variety 5 (Ca. 1898) R3/200-350

Lid top: "Manufactured and Guaranteed by the" line now becomes just "Manufactured by the".

Lid front: Same as Variety 4 above.

Bottom back: Label in red cautioning "...should never be reloaded".

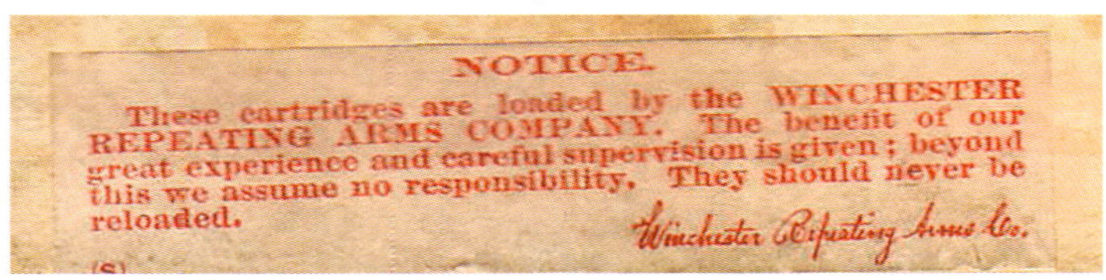

Variety 6 (Ca. 1899-1901) R3/200-400

Lid front: "Trade Mark Registered in the USA" added.
Bottom line now reads "FOR WINCHESTER MARLIN AND SAVAGE RIFLES".

<u>TYPE 1A, Transitional (Ca.1902)</u> R3+/250-450

- Two-piece box, round-cornered taped construction.
- Green label covering lid top and front only, same as Type 1.
- Lid top call-outs same as Type 1.

Lid front: Now " Model 1894" as in Type 2 (below).
Bottom: Reloading caution label retained on bottom but much smaller.

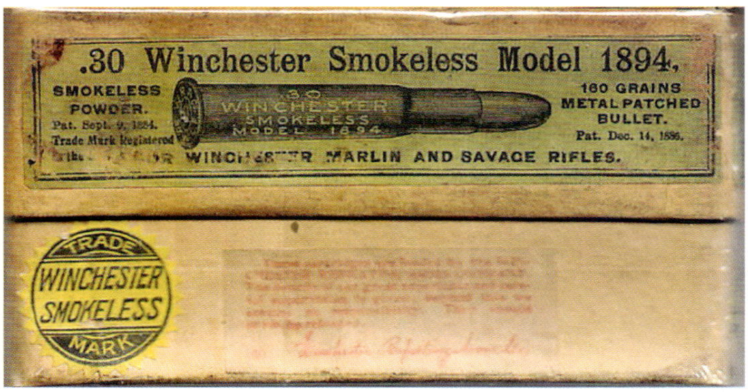

TWO-PIECE BOXES - TYPE 2

- Two-piece box, round-cornered, taped construction.
- Full front-sealing labels, orange denoting Soft Point and Red/Purple denoting Full Patch.
- Primary call-outs: Lid top, ".30 Winchester Caliber Model 1894". Lid front, ".30 Winchester Smokeless Model 1894".
- Separate "Caution" labels replaced by caution verbiage on lower front label.
- Top label the same on all varieties:

Soft Point

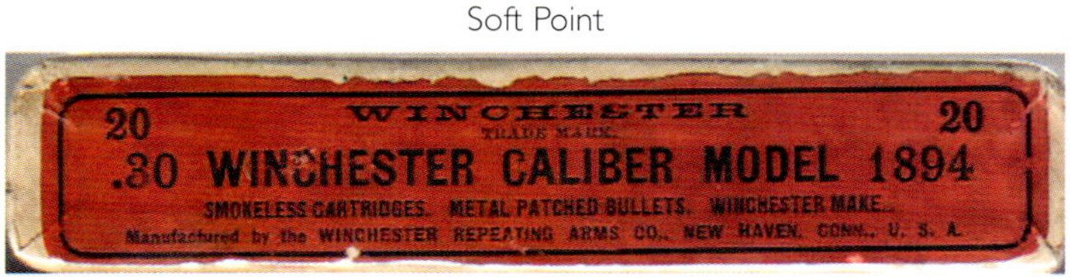

Metal Patched (FMJ)

<u>Variety 1 (Ca. 1902-1903)</u> R3+/225-450
Front: Patent date retained.
"160 Grains....Bullet".
Ends: "Sunburst" labels retained on ends only.

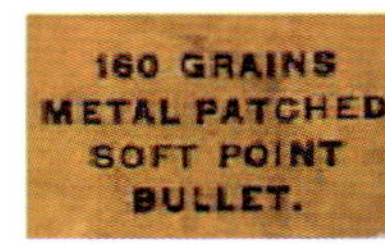

<u>Variety 2 (Ca. 1903)</u> R3+/225-450
Front: Patent date now removed.

<u>Variety 3 (Ca. 1903-05)</u> R3/200-400
Front: Bullet weight now "170 Grains".

A Transitional "Metal Patched" box (Ca. 1903) R3+/250-450
Front: Patent date retained
"170 Grains...Bullet".

Variety 4 (Ca. 1906) R3/175-350
Top: WINCHESTER and TRADE MARK in block capital letters.

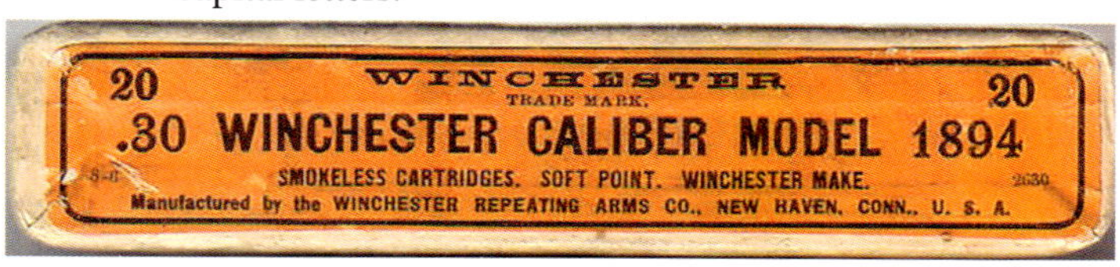

Front: "Trade Mark Registered in the U.S.A." now on three lines.
Minor variations in lower text from Variety 3.
Ends: "Red W" end labels begin; "Sunburst" labels discontinued.

Design dates and codes begin on front, top and end labels.
Both of these are front labels:

Variety 5 (Ca. 1906-1910) R3-/150-300
Lid top: "WINCHESTER" in block letters but now in quotes.

Lid front: "They should never be reloaded" removed from lower text.
Minor format change to lower text.
Trade mark line now: "Trade Mark Registered in U.S. Pat. Off."

Variety 6 (Ca. 1911—1912) R3/150-300
Lid top: "WINCHESTER" in small type and quotes, now italicized.

Lid front: "Trade Mark Reg. In U.S. Pat. Off. & thr'ghout the world".
Bullet call-out includes "Metal Patched".

Variations: with or without overstamp: "Pat. June 28, 1910"

Variety 7 (Ca. 1913) R3/150-300

Lid top: *"WINCHESTER"* in larger type, still in quotes and italicized.

Lid front: Now reads, "Trade Mark Reg. In U.S. Pat. Off. & throughout the world."
Bullet call-out omits "Metal Patched".

Variety 8 (Ca. 1913-1914) R3/150-300

Lid top: Quotes removed from WINCHESTER.
Trade mark data now on top of lid.

Lid front: "Metal Patched" removed.
Trade mark data removed.

TWO-PIECE BOXES - TYPE 3

- Two-piece box, square cornered with folded bottom construction.
- Full front-sealing labels, orange Soft Point and red (or purple) for Full Patch loadings.
- Cartridge now pictured on lower front label.
- Ends now stamped or printed with "Red W"

FULL PATCH

Variety 1, Full Patch (1915-16) R3/125-225

Lid top: 7-15 or 9-16, with full "MODEL 1894" callout.

Front: 7-15, ".30 WINCHESTER MODEL 1894 FULL PATCH".

Lid Top, 9-16

Variety 2, Full Patch, (1915-16) R3-/125-200

Lid top: 9-16, with full "MODEL 1894" callout.

Front label: 7-15 with full "MODEL 1894" callout as in Variety 1 above but type size and font changed.

Variety 3, Full Patch, (1915-16) R3/125-225

Lid top: 7-15, call-out exhibits gapped "MODEL 94" as in Variety 4 below.

Front label: 7-15 with full "MODEL 1894" callout as in Variety 2.

Lid Top, 7-15

Variety 4, Full Patch, (1915-16) R3-/125-250

Front and lid-top labels: Same as Variety 1, including label dates, except "18" removed from "Model 1894" on both labels.

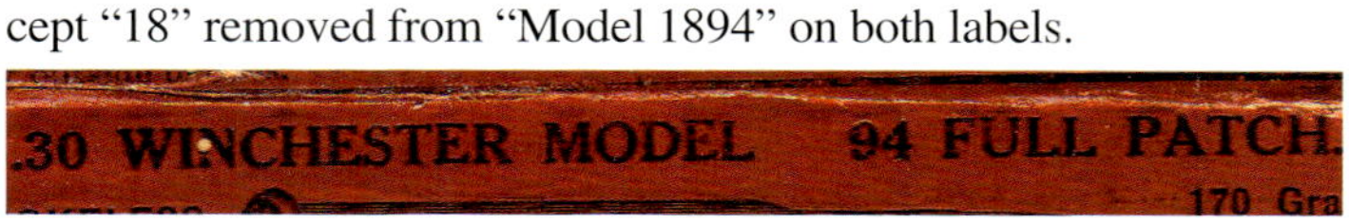

Note: This gapped date front label has also been found in combination with the 9-16 lid label with the full "Model 1894" callout. The mix of top and front labels in this 1915-16 period is almost endless!

Variety 5, Full Patch (1915-16) R3-/125-250

Lid Top: Both 7-15 and 9-16 dates have been noted but both, incredibly, still with the full "Model 1894" callout.

Front: Same as Varieties 1 and 2, except "Model 94" now centered. Still 7-15 label date.

SOFT POINT

Variety 1, Soft Point (1915) R3-/125-250

Lid top: Same as Full Patch varieties above except for color and "Soft Point" wording.

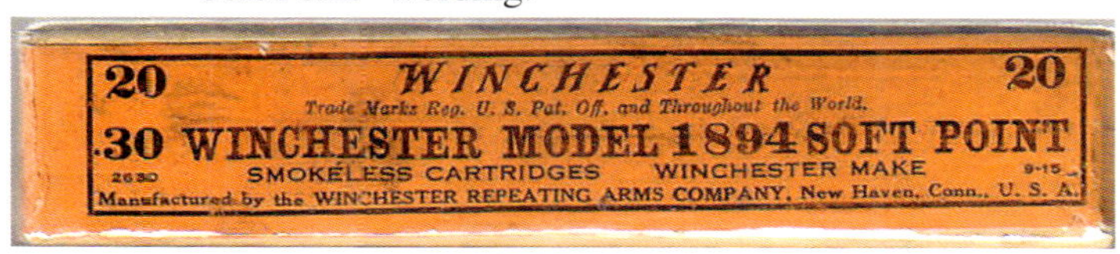

Front: Differs from Full Patch varieties only in ".30 Winchester...Soft Point" line, now upper and lower case.

Variety 2, Soft Point (Ca.1915-1917) R2+/100-200

Lid top: Minor format differences from Variety 1, but still 9-15 label date.

Front: Minor textual differences from Variety 1 (you pick 'em out), but same 8-15 date.

Variety 3, Soft Point (1917-20) R2+/100-200

Lid top: "(Same as .30-30 Smokeless)" added, 9-17 label date.

Front: "(Same as .30-30 Smokeless)" added, 10-17 label date.

Variety 3a (Transitional), Soft Point (1919-20) R3/150-250

Lid top: Still Variety 3 graphics and 9-17 label date but "18" blocked out of "1894"

Front: Still Variety 3 graphics and 10-17 label date, but "18" blocked out of "1894"

Variety 4, Soft Point (Ca. 1920-1924) R2/100-200

Lid top: "Trade Mark" returns to early TYPE 2 style. "Made in U.S.A." added. Centered "Model 94" replaces "Model 1894"

Front: Patent date deleted. Centered "Model 94" replaces "Model 1894".

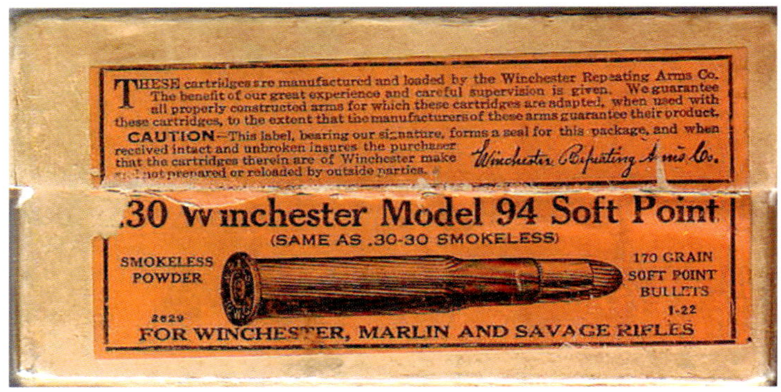

Variety 4, Soft Point (Ca. 1925-1927) R2+/100-200

Lid top: Reference to Model 94 deleted entirely.

Front: Reference to Model 94 deleted. Product Code ("K-code") begins.

TWO-PIECE BOXES - TYPE 4

R3-/150-275

- First SUPERSPEED box, (110 Gr. "Hollow Point Mushroom", 1925)
- Square-cornered two-piece box, folded bottom.
- Green full front-sealing label and top label.
- Last two-piece box style.
- Has K-code.

ONE-PIECE BOXES - TYPE 1

- Box construction: One piece outer box with end flaps, inner tray.
- Identical front and back.
- All lithographed (without labels), blue and white with red *WINCHESTER* and STAYNLESS (or STAYNLESS / NON-MERCURIC).

<u>Variety 1 "1928" Box, (1928-1932)</u> R3-/150-250
[Soft Point: R2+/100-175]

Front/Back: STAYNLESS (only).
Bullet call-out, FULL PATCH (shown) or SOFT POINT.
Ends: STAYNLESS in red.

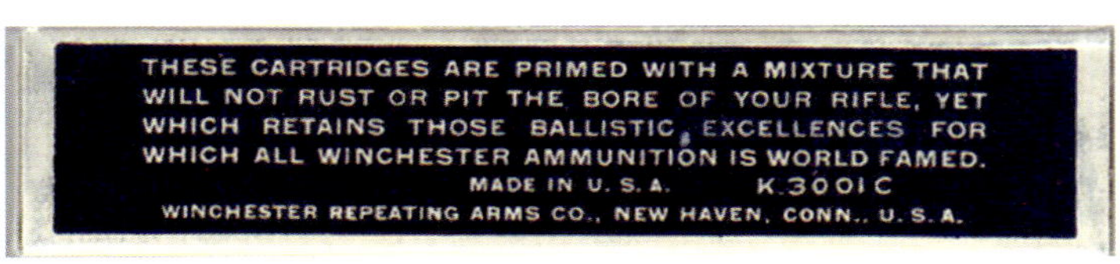

<u>Variety 2 "1932" Box, (Ca. 1932-1935)</u> R2/80-160

Front/Back: STAYNLESS / NON-MERCURIC.
Bullet call-out, SOFT POINT or FULL PATCH.
Ends: Bullet weight replaces STAYNLESS.

Comment: For many calibers in this box type there are transitional boxes with NON-MERCURIC in black over-printed on the red STAYNLESS 1928 box. As this caliber was among the company's fastest-selling, it is possible that no such transitional box was necessary, however, there is also a strong probability that it does, indeed, exist.

<u>Variety 2A "1932 Superspeed" Box, (Ca. 1932-1935)</u>
R3-/125-225
Front: Picture of cartridge has *SUPERSPEED* superimposed on it.
Caliber call-out is ".30 (.30-30) Winchester Superspeed H.P."
Back: "... SIGHT ADJUSTMENTS" add-on label.
Ends: "110 Gr. Bullet".

Comment: It is probable that a Variety 1 Superspeed box also exists, as it does in other calibers, though the authors have none to picture in this caliber.

ONE-PIECE BOXES - TYPE 2

Primary Graphics
- Identical front and back.
- Yellow and blue with red *WINCHESTER* and red and black border lines.
- "SUPER SPEED .30 WIN. (.30-30)" followed by bullet type (S.P., F.P. or H.P.).
- Picture of cartridge in yellow with black.

Variety 1, "1935" Box, (1935-1939) R2/100-200
[Hollow Point or Full Patch: R3-/125-250]
Lower front: "Winchester Repeating Arms Co. New Haven, Conn., U.S.A.", in red, on black line.

"1935" Side

Hollow Point loading graphic.

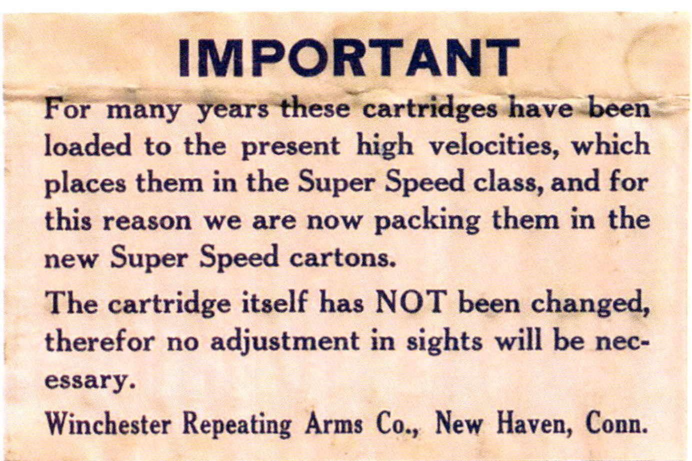

IMPORTANT

For many years these cartridges have been loaded to the present high velocities, which places them in the Super Speed class, and for this reason we are now packing them in the new Super Speed cartons.

The cartridge itself has NOT been changed, therefor no adjustment in sights will be necessary.

Winchester Repeating Arms Co., New Haven, Conn.

Early box insert

Variety 2, "1939" Box, (1939-1946) R2-/85-170
[Full Patch: R2+/100-175]
Lower Front: "Winchester Repeating Arms Co. New Haven, Conn., U.S.A.", omitted.
Side: Western Cartridge Co. ownership called out.

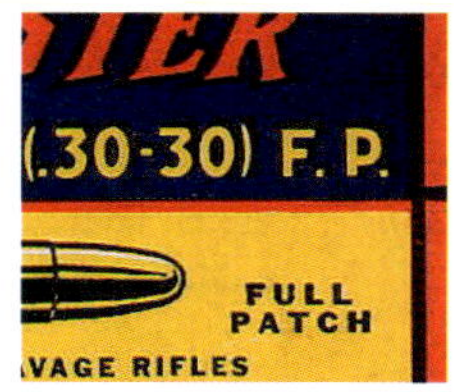

Variety 3, "1945" Box, (1945-1946) R3-?/125-250?
Side: Call-out of Olin Industries ownership.

Comment: Like the "1928/32" transitional box, this one may not exist in 30-30. It has been included here in the expectation of uncovering one among our readers' collections.

ONE-PIECE BOXES - TYPE 3

Primary Graphics:
- Colors similar to Type 2, but graphics dominated by picture of a crouching Grizzly Bear.
- Winchester's new SILVERTIP bullet introduced in this box, described in detail on back.

Varieties, (1940-1946) R3-/150-300

No major varieties, although Silvertip boxes in some calibers mention changes to bullet mixture due to wartime alloy scarcities. All known 30-30 "Grizzly" boxes are "Division of Western Cartridge Co." though a few other calibers in Grizzly boxes are known with the "Olin Industries" call-out. "Bear" boxes in this caliber are surprisingly scarce.

ONE-PIECE BOXES - TYPE 4

Primary Graphics:
- Red and yellow box, red WINCHESTER in white stripe, red "W" outlined in white.
- Picture of cartridge on side.

<u>**Variety 1, "1946" Box, (1946-1954)**</u>
Silvertip: R1/25-50; Hol Pt: R2/40-65; Full Metal Case: R3/75-150

Front: Minor differences due to bullet type call-out.
Back: Silvertip boxes repeat the verbiage from the back of the Type 3 (Grizzly) Box (see "1954" Box for graphics).

Sides/ends: Earlier product code ("K-code") call-outs on side. Later "W-codes" appear on end flaps (and sometimes on side as well)

K-code (1946-52), side only.

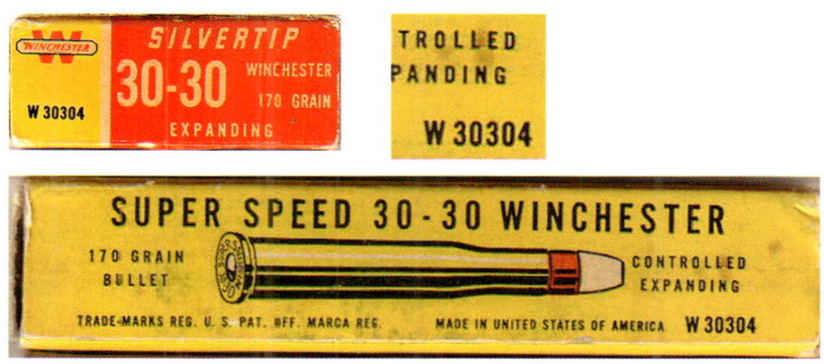

W-code ('52+), both end and side.

W-code, end only.

Variety 2, "1954" Box (1954-1958)
R1/25-50
Front/Back: Unchanged from Variety 1, except thumb-cuts discontinued.
Side: Call-out of "Olin Mathieson Chemical Corporation" ownership.

Back (Silvertip only), "1946" and "1954" Boxes

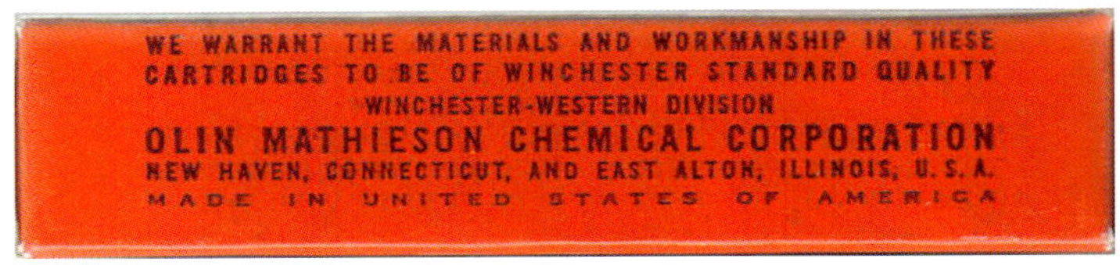

Side: ("1954")

SHORT RANGE BOXES

In Winchester's Catalog #58 of December 1896, we see for the first time a listing for the new cartridge listed as ".30-6-100 Winchester Short Range for Model 1894". This was a 30 WCF case with 6 grains of smokeless powder behind a 100 grain lead bullet and, according to the catalog, was designed "For small game where the more powerful Cartridge is not necessary". A heavier 117 grain bullet was introduced in the June 1904 catalog and continued until the Short Range cartridge was dropped in 1924.

Incredibly, there are 5 varieties which have been identified by the authors as having been produced during the first 10 years of this relatively minor and slow-selling listing. These 5 are pictured below along with the later 1915-style box. All except the 1915 box are of taped box construction and exhibit "Sunburst" labels with the "Winchester Smokeless" callout.

Circa 1896-7

1897-8

1898-9

1899-1903

1904-5 (Transitional)

1915+

Lid top labels of all 6 varieties.

Variety 1, ca. 1896-7

Variety 2, ca. 1897-8

Note the bolder type face of the top lines of both the lid top and front labels on Variety 2 relative to Variety 1. Also the "6 Grains Smokeless Powder" callout is in a larger type size on Variety 2. Both carry the "Manufactured and Guaranteed..." line on lid top. Var 1: R3+/300-550; Var 2: 3+/250-500

Variety 3, ca. 1898-9

The "6 Grains" callout has been eliminated from the front. The words "and Guaranteed" have been removed from the lid top. R3+/225-450

Variety 4, ca. 1899-1903

".30 WINCHESTER SHORT RANGE" on lid top now in caps. "Trade Mark Registered in U.S.A." added to front.

It is possible, even likely, that a 1903-4 round-cornered box exists with graphics similar to this square-cornered box. R3/200-400

Variety 5, ca. 1904-5 (Transitional)

The box now has rounded corners.

The "100" in the bullet weight is blacked out and "117" printed in above "grains". The gap in this lineage suggests other varieties between 1905 and the 1915 box pictured below. We would expect, for instance, to find a red label round-corner box with the "117 grain" callout and a "Red W" end label but lacking the "Smokeless Sunburst" label. R3/200-400

Variety 6, ca. 1915+

This box may have been the only design used until the loading was discontinued in 1924; on the other hand, it is probable one or more varieties exist that we have not yet discovered. R3-/150-250

32 W.S., 32 Winchester Special

Catalog listings: 1902-

Models: 1885, 1894, 55, 64
Bullet types: Ld*, SP, MCHP, ST, FMJ

Powder types: Smkls
Headstamps: WRACo, WRA, SS

Introduced without fanfare in the June 1902 catalog, the 32 Special, as it has come to be known, did little to improve upon the 30 WCF but was said to have been easier to reload with black powder for those "old-timers" inclined to do so. During its first 3 years of production, the 32 Special exhibited 3 box & label styles, 2 bullet weights and 3 primer types. All of these early varieties are scarce and desirable.

*Factory records show a Lead Short Range loading though it was not a catalog item.

The first 32 Winchester Special box. Square-cornered with dark orange label, 1902. R4/300-600 (Courtesy of Lou Behling)

Lid-top label of first box (1902).

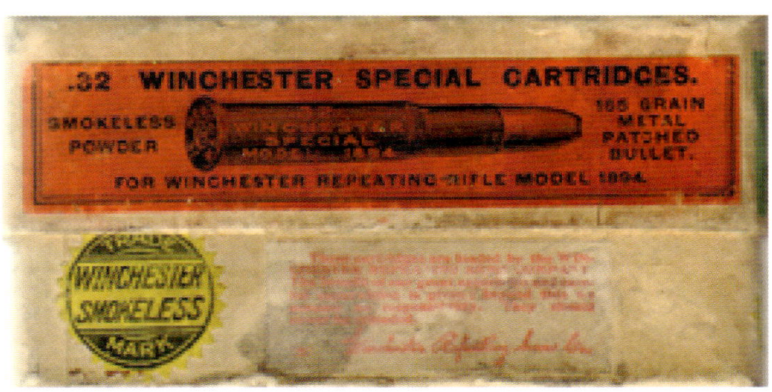

The second 32 WS box, identical to first box except round-cornered (Ca.1902-3). R4-/275-550

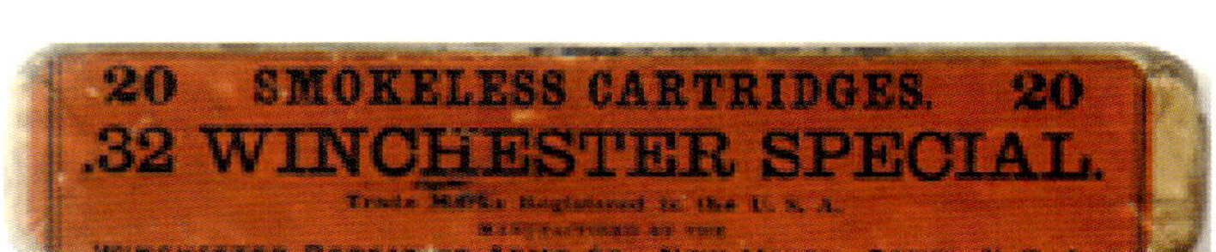

Left: Lid top has the same wording as the first box, but in a different type face. Right: Very unusual green end label on orange second box.

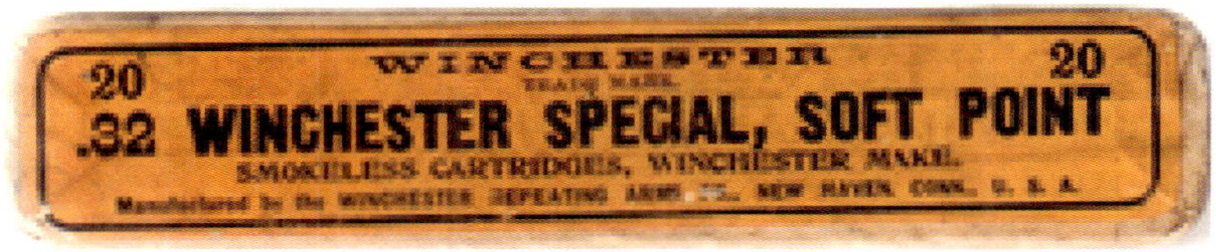

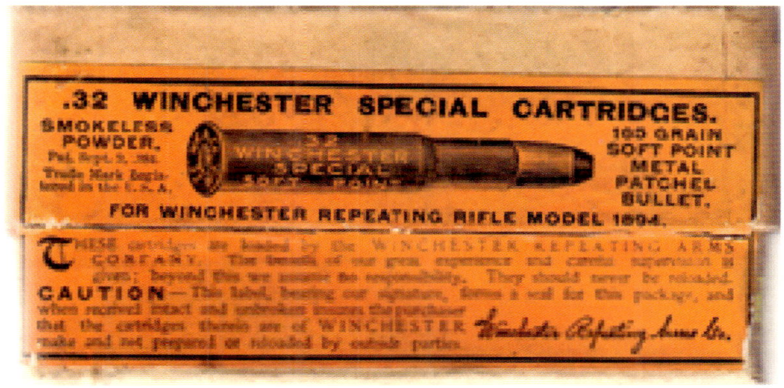

The third 32WS box, ca.1903-4: light orange, 165 grain bullet. R3+/175-275

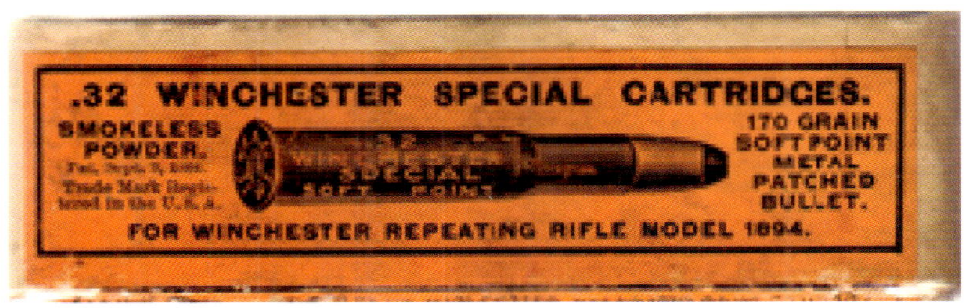

Note bullet weight change to 170 grains on this 1904-1905 lid-front label, a change that took place in 1904. The graphics on the lid-top label of this box are virtually identical to those on the next (1906-1910) box except for the absence of quotation marks around "Winchester". R3/150-250

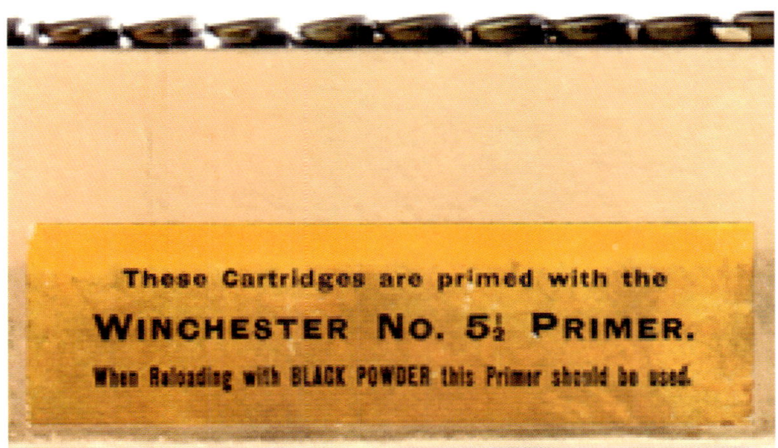

Same box, noting No. 5 1/2 primer which had been introduced during 1903. Interestingly, the 32 WS was developed as an alternative to the 30-30 (30 WCF) for those "old-timers" who wanted to reload with black powder. Ballistics of the two calibers were very similar. The 32 WS rifles, however, in order to account for the lower velocities developed by black powder, utilized a slower twist than was used in 30-30 barrels.

The lid-top labels showing the change in the "Winchester" graphics from block letters (1906-10) to italics (1911-1913).

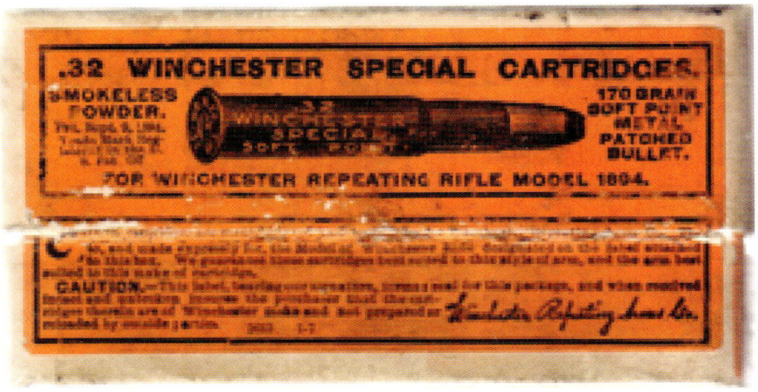

Label-dated 1-7, this box now exhibits the "Red W" end labels as well as a change in patent callout. R3-/125-225

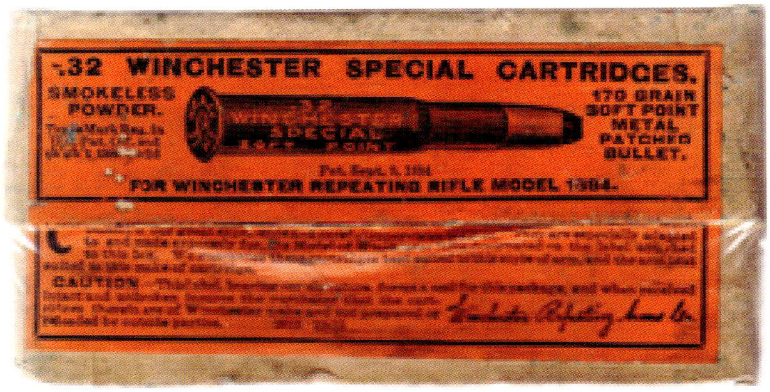

This 10-11 labeled box has a further patent line elaboration as well as a call-out, under the cartridge cut, of the Sept 9, 1884 patent for the protected primer. R3-/125-225

Here are four Soft Point boxes, each with labels dated 8-15. ALL are different! Reader challenge: find the textual and format differences among these four boxes.

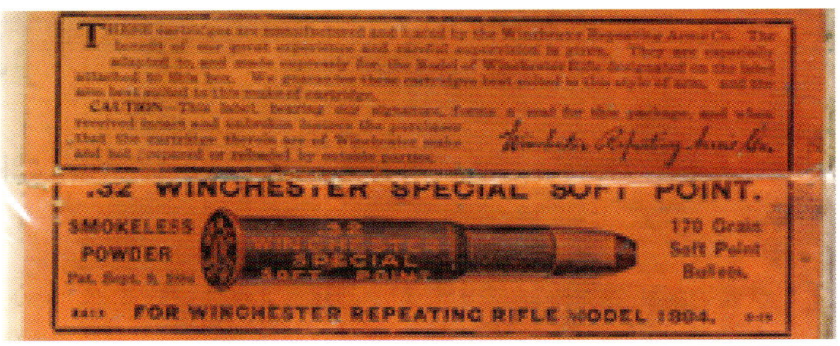

R3-/125-200

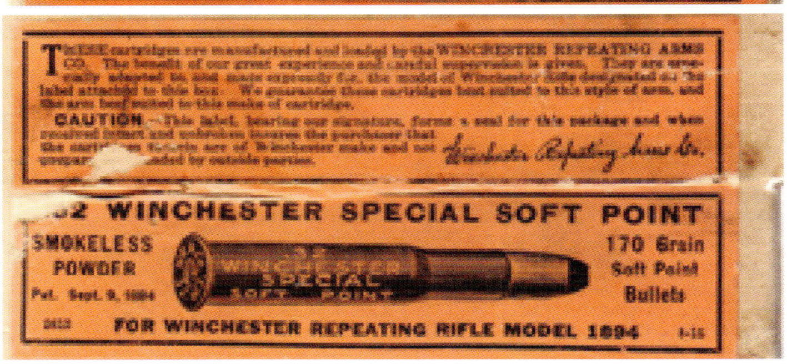

R3-/125-200

R3-/125-200

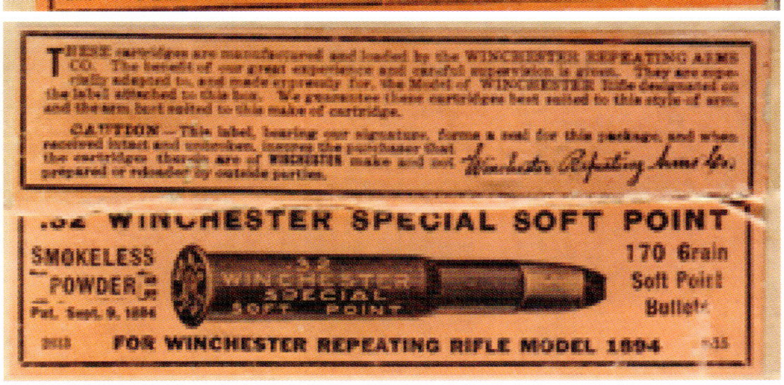

R3-/125-200

The lid tops of the 8-15 Full Patch boxes show little variation from one another, this being a common example. Also shown is a close-up of the 8-15 label date. R3/150-250

If it hadn't been for the typical 1915 graphics on this box one might be deceived by the label date: 8-5! There are no labels dated with a 1905 date, 1906 being the earliest. Still, it is the only such date we have seen, error or not, making it quite an interesting rarity! In all other respects the text matches the 8-15 lid-top label above. R4?/200-400

The front label of the 1915 Full Patch boxes are most often seen with a 6-15 label date and closely resemble the Soft Point versions shown above. As with the Soft Point labels, however, minor variations (usually in the upper text) of these 8-15 Full Patch front labels also exist. The lack of a patent call-out under "Smokeless Powder", on the other hand, differs from all the Soft Point boxes. R3/125-225

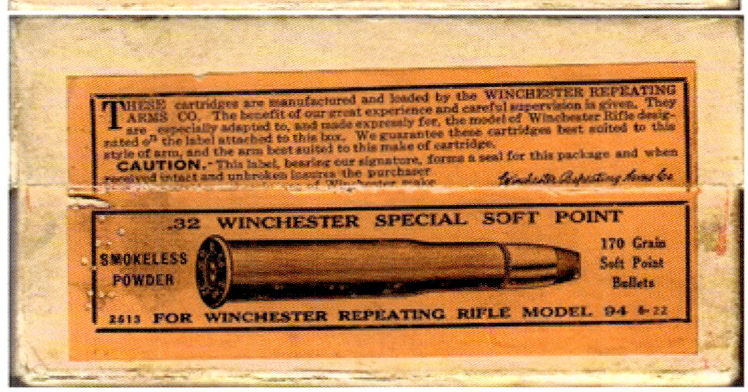

With a lid-top date of 11-21 and a front label date of 8-22, this box predates the establishment of the K-code system. R3-/100-200

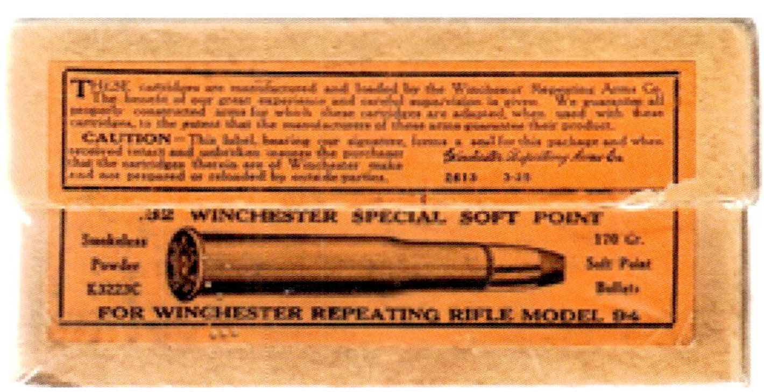

The addition of the K-code and the change in "Smokeless Powder" from all upper-case letters to an upper/lower case presentation represent the only significant differences between this 3-25 label and the previous box. R2+/100-200

"1928" Superspeed, the first one-piece box, 1927-31, with "Superspeed" as one word. It would appear that these "1928" and "1932" Superspeed boxes are found mostly in 32 Special while the 30-30 and 25-35 continued to use the green two-piece box for this light bullet loading for a somewhat longer period. R3/175-275

"1928/1932" transitional box in the Superspeed loading with "Non-Mercuric" over-print, ca.1932. R3/175-275

"1932" Superspeed box, ca.1932-1935. R3-/150-250

Though one would expect this "1932" Soft Point box to be fairly common, it is actually quite scarce as are the similar "1928" boxes which preceded it. Even scarcer is the 32 Special Full Patch loading in these box styles. R2+/85-170

IMPORTANT

For many years these cartridges have been loaded to the present high velocities, which places them in the Super Speed class, and for this reason we are now packing them in the new Super Speed cartons.

The cartridge itself has NOT been changed, therefor no adjustment in sights will be necessary.

Winchester Repeating Arms Co., New Haven, Conn.

Above: Super Speed insert found in "1935" box (Above left).
Above left: "1935" box with WRACo line on lower front. Note "Super Speed" now two words. R2+/85-170

Left: Grizzly box, ca 1940-46. These are far scarcer than one would suppose, especially in top condition. R3-/150-250

32-40, 32-40 Ballard, 32-40 Marlin, 32-40 W.C.F., 32-40 Winchester, 32-40 WHV

Catalog listings: 1885-

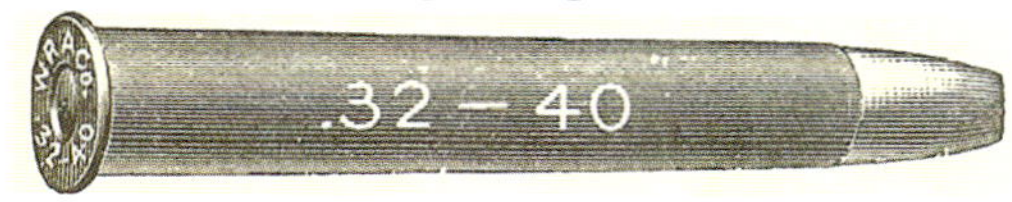

Models: 1885, 1894, 64 (rare*)

Powder types: BP, Smkls, Lsmk**

Bullet types: Ld, Ld SR, Ld PP, SP, FMJ, Shot, Blank

Headstamps: Plain, WRACo, WRA

Originally a Ballard cartridge formed from their 38-55 case, the 32-40 was very popular in the 1880s and 1890s due to its reputed accuracy as both a hunting and target round. Among the many rare and interesting varieties of this caliber are the 100 grain Miniature Full Patch and the 32-40 Ballard boxes, both of which are reported to exist but which the authors have not personally seen. The 32-40 Marlin headstamp is known, but no boxes have as yet been reported. The scarce "32-40 WCF" headstamp is even scarcer than the seldom-seen boxes which picture it. The uncommon Lesmok loadings had the powder callout hand-stamped on the labels. And the black powder, jacketed bullet loadings made just prior to WWI are found in "electric blue" labeled boxes, a very scarce (and usually surprising) discovery for the M1894 collector. It is also interesting to note that no black powder boxes ever specifically mentioned the Model 94.

* Listed in *1938 Winchester Sales Manual.*

** Although not a catalog option for this caliber, boxes stamped "Lesmok" are known to exist.

An early black powder box of 32-40. This style labeling, while it pre-dated the M94, was still used on Black Powder offerings of the 1894-97 period. R3/150-300

Pre-1898 Smokeless box, top label "Central Fire", "...and Guaranteed" (see p 190). R3-/150-275

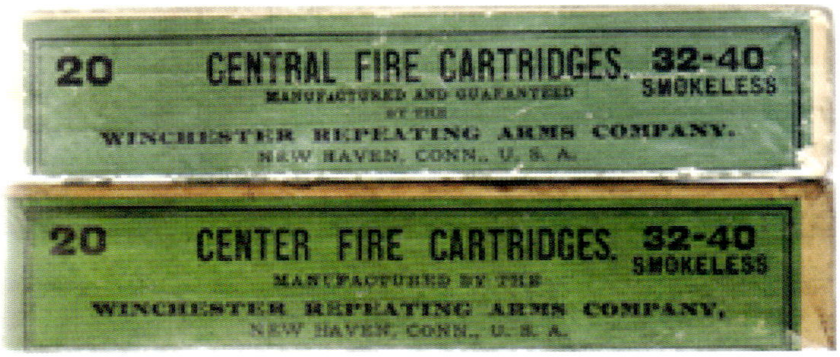

Top labels of pre- and post-1898 types.

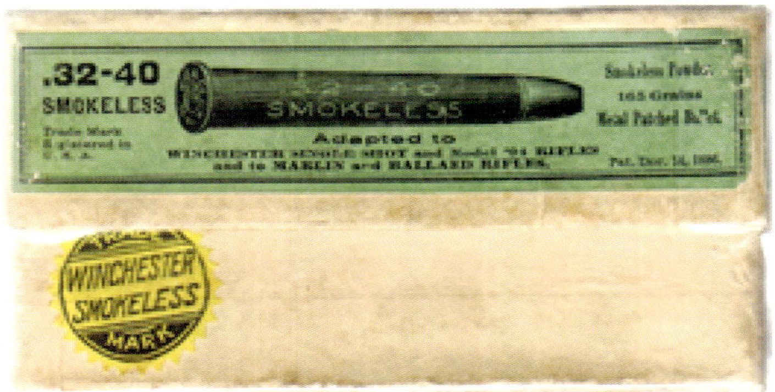

Post-1898 Smokeless box, top label "Center Fire", "Manufactured by the..." (see above). R3-/125-250

Circa 1903-05, this Black Powder box has no label dates or product codes on the primary labels. It is, however, often found with dated "Red W" end labels, attesting to production after 1906. Such mixing of labels from different periods was quite common. R2+/100-200

This green label box, ca. 1906-1907, is one of the more commonly seen Black Powder boxes. Note that a date (6-6) code appears at bottom center but there is no product code. R2+/100-200

Smokeless Soft Point box, ca. 1907. R3/125-225

Here are two variations of the rare blue label Black Powder, Soft Point boxes. No label dates have been found on blue labels. Winchester (without quotes) is pre-1906, however "License to the Trade" labels on back are ca 1910-13 with the later ones over-stamped "Void". This box is the earlier, ca. 1911-12. R3+/275-475

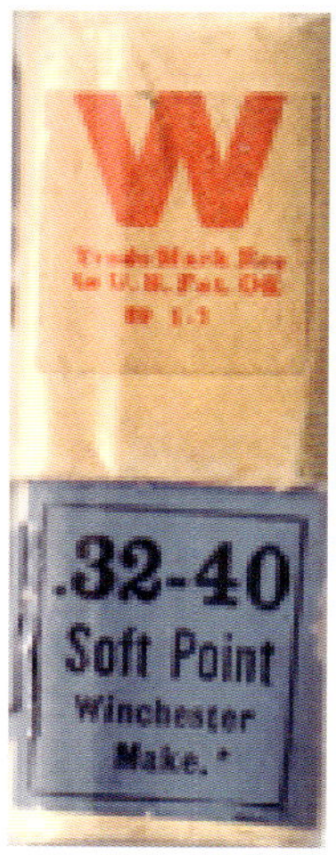

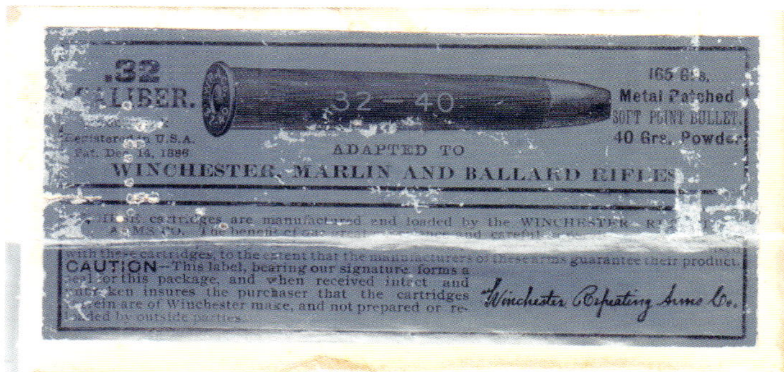

Soft Point Black Powder box, Ca. 1912-13 with voided "License to the Trade" label. R3+/250-450

Front view, 1906-style Full Patch box. Note that the cartridge cut exhibits the very rare "32-40 W.C.F." headstamp. Ironically, this is not the box in which that headstamp is found. R3+/175-325

Top of 1906-style Full Patch lid.

Top of 1915-style Full Patch lid.

Front view, 1915-style Full Patch box. R3/150-300

1915-style Black Powder lid top.

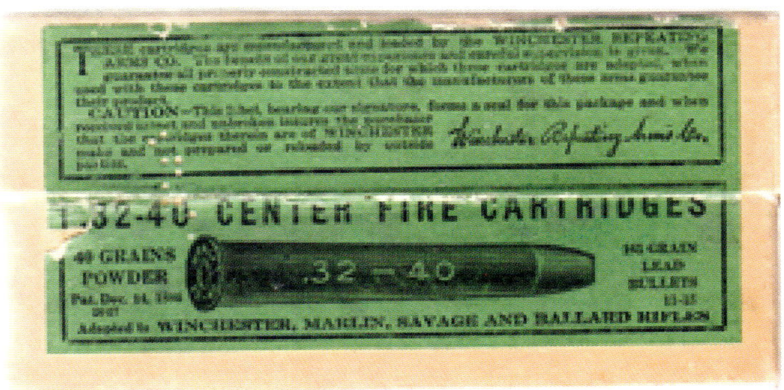

Front label, 1915-style Black Powder box. R2+/100-200

Smokeless Soft Point, 1915-style lid top and front labels. R2+100-200

[For examples of box styles and graphics 1915-1935, please refer to the Caliber 30 WCF (30-30) section, pp 176-180.]

The popular "1939" box. Note that it does not earn the Super Speed designation common to the smaller Model '94 calibers. Very few calibers with black powder origins carried the Super Speed title. R1+/50-100

The "1946" box with "Olin Industries" call-out on side panel. R1+/50-75

High Velocity (WHV) Boxes

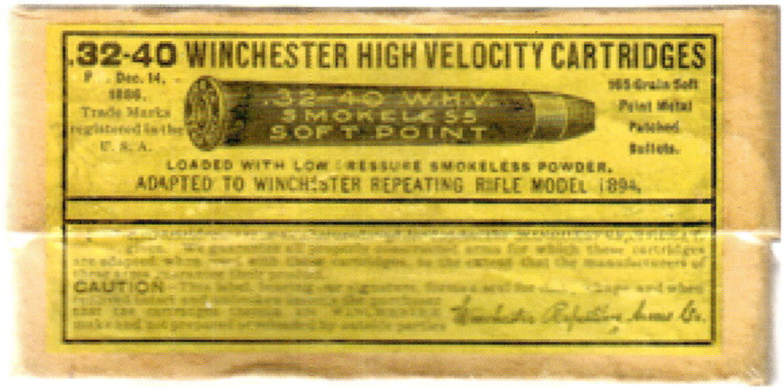

In 1905 the Winchester High Velocity (WHV) loading was offered in 32-40. Here is a nice early, 1905-style WHV Soft Point box without label date or design code yet, incredibly, it is the only WHV box to specifically mention the M1894. R3+/300-500

The 1906-style lid top label from the undated 1905 WHV box pictured above...

...and an undated 1905-style lid top from the 11-15 dated WHV Full Patch box pictured below.

Such anachronisms are fairly common among Winchester boxes especially among the slower selling loadings, a fact which would obviously pertain to this rarely encountered Full Patch WHV box. R3++/300-600

A WHV Staynless box, style of 1928. These 1-piece Soft Point WHV boxes are considerably rarer than the two-piece WHV Soft Point boxes. This, in fact, is the only one known to the authors! R4/400+

Here is a square-corner "Center Fire" Black Powder box, with "...and Guaranteed" deleted. Ca. 1898-1900. R3-/125-250

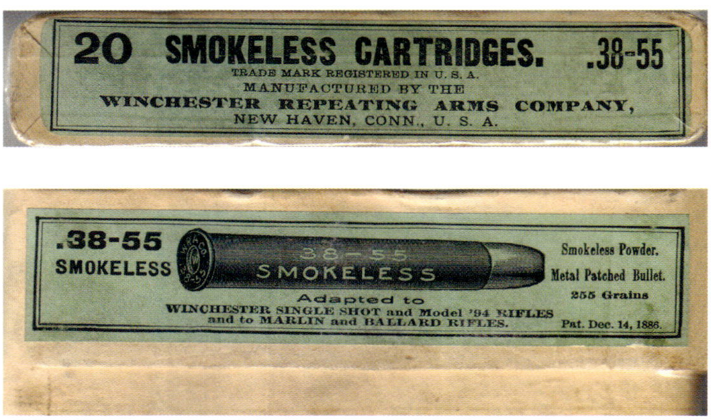

A clean example of the round-corner green Smokeless box with both "Smokeless" and "Soft Point" sunburst end labels. Ca. 1900-02. R3-/125-225

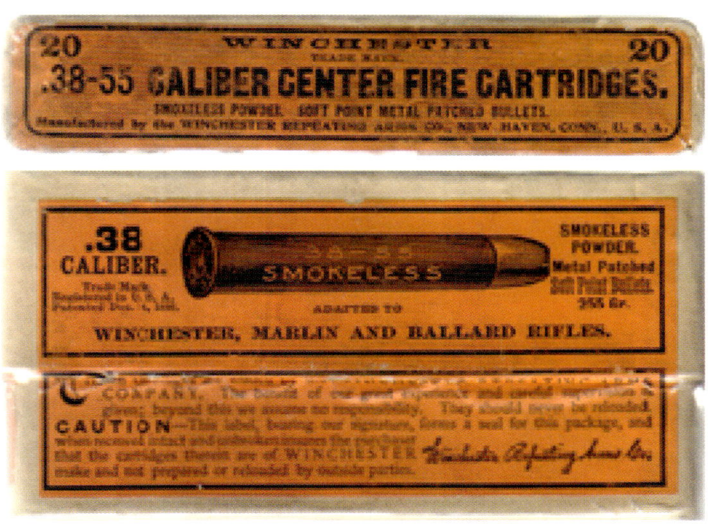

The orange label Smokeless box with both Sunburst end labels, ca. 1903-05. R3-/100-200

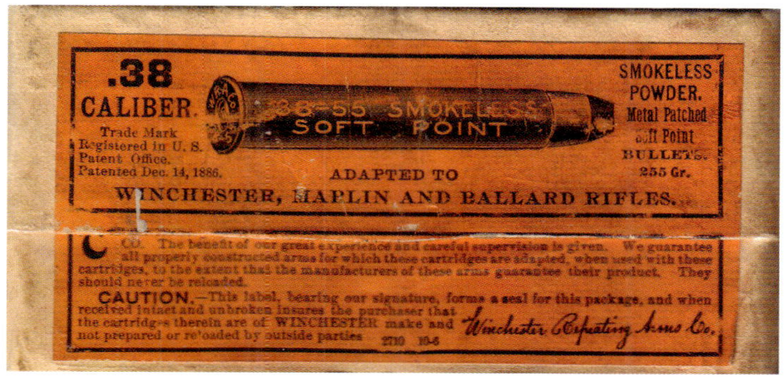

In 1906 the "Red W" end labels begin and "Winchester" on the lid top label is in quotes. This label warns against reloading (see below) an admonition that was removed that same year. Label date is 10-6. R3+/175-275

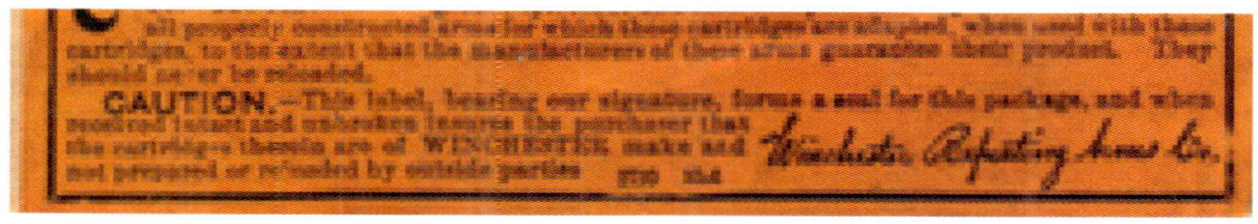

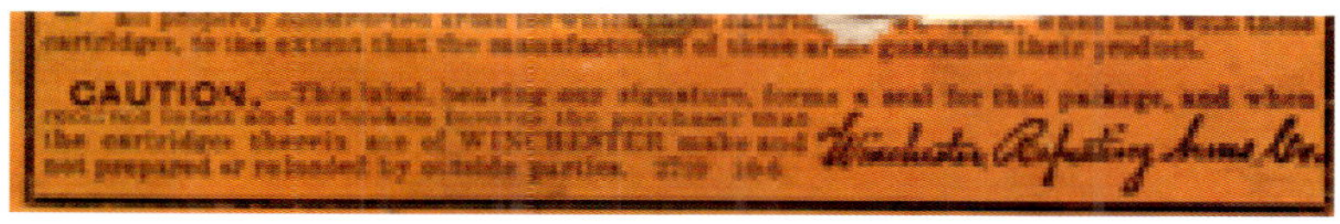

Two 10-6 dated labels, the upper (earlier) stating "They should never be reloaded". [bottom: R3-/100-200]

An example of the rare Black Powder Soft Point loading. The box has the undated label graphics of the pre-1906 variety, but the 2-10 dated "Red W" end labels help us date this box. R3+/250-500

A 1911-12 Soft Point box with "Winchester" now in italics as well as quotes. The trade mark line is now found under the cartridge cut. R3/150-275

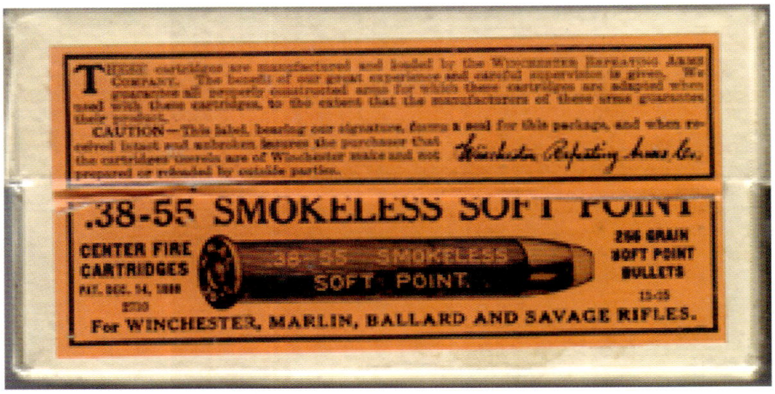

A 1915-style Smokeless Soft Point box with cartridge cut moved to lower front. Box construction now of the folded type. Label date, 11-15. R2+/125-250

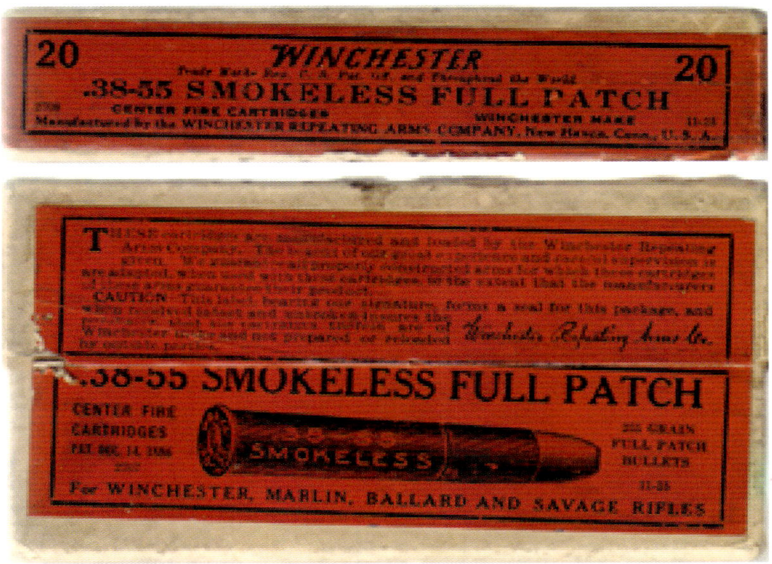

The early Smokeless Full Patch, red label 1915-style box, again with 11-15 label date. "Winchester" remains in italics but quote marks have been removed. R3+/200-350

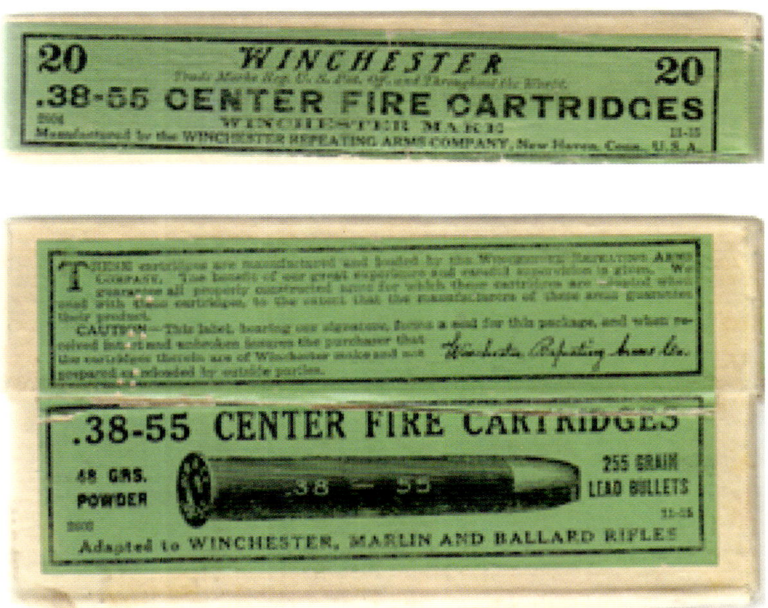

Yet another 11-15 label-dated box, this one with Black Powder, Lead bullet rounds. R2/125-250

Lid top labels, 12-22 showing "Winchester Make" and 3-25 with that callout deleted.

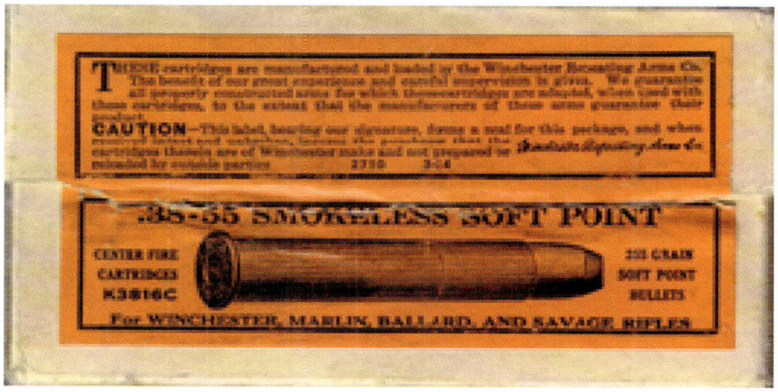

An early K-code box, dated 3-24. K-codes aren't usually seen on boxes until 1925. R2/100-200

[For examples of the earlier one-piece box styles and graphics, ca. 1927-35, please see the 30 WCF (30-30) section.]

An example of the colorful "1939" box in 38-55, calling out "Division of Western cartridge Co." on the side panel. Like 32-40s, 38-55s were never issued in Super Speed. R2-/60-120

The "1946" box, with side panel callout of "Division of Olin Industries". R1+/30-60

High Velocity (WHV) Boxes

An example of what is thought to be the first WHV 38-55 Soft Point box, 1905. Note that there is no picture of the cartridge, unusual for this era. R4-/250-450

Another first year (1905) WHV box, this one in the rare Full Patch loading. R4-/350-650

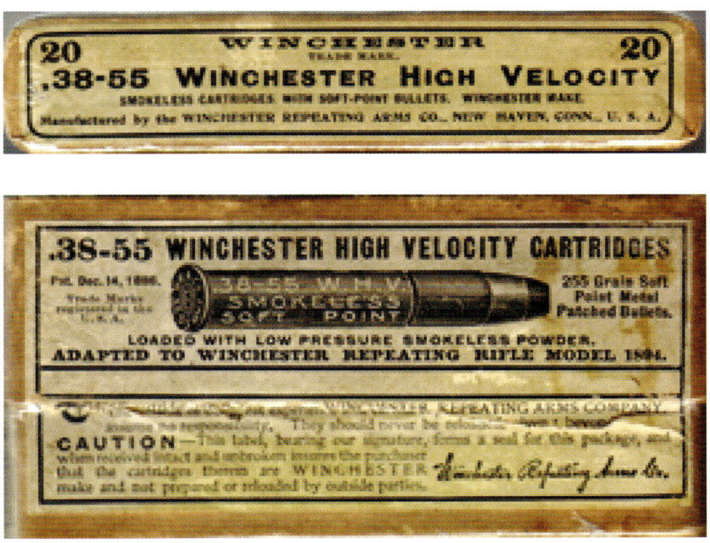

The lack of label dates suggests label design is 1905 or early 1906. The presence of 6-6 dated "Red W" end labels, however, place this box in 1906 but raise the question as to when the cartridge picture was reincorporated into the label design. R3+/200-400

The 12-25 lid-top label with "Winchester Make" again appearing.

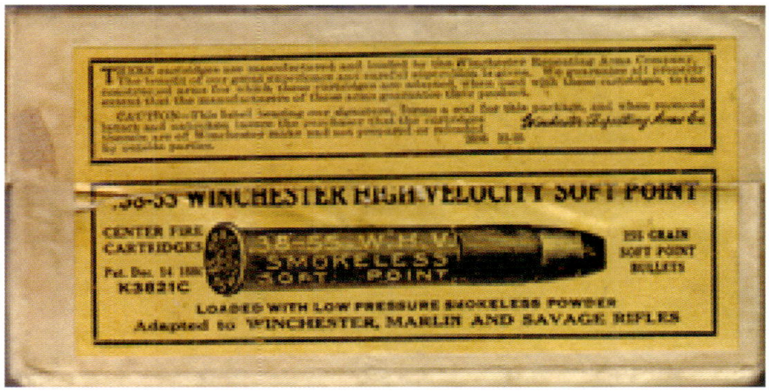

This 12-25 WHV Soft Point box exhibits the K-code. It is also sealed making it an especially nice find for the collector. R3/175-350

A later 12-25 lid-top label with later over-print of "Staynless", "Non-Mercuric", and "USA Patent Pending" callouts all squeezed in. R3/175-350

Shot Boxes

A very unusual blue top label on an 8-6 dated Black Powder Shot Cartridge box.

This is the 8-6 Black Powder Shot box, the lid of which is pictured above. Mixing of label colors (not merely shades of color) was most unusual except in the case of reds and purples, which was common. R3+/200-400

A "Loaded in France" Box

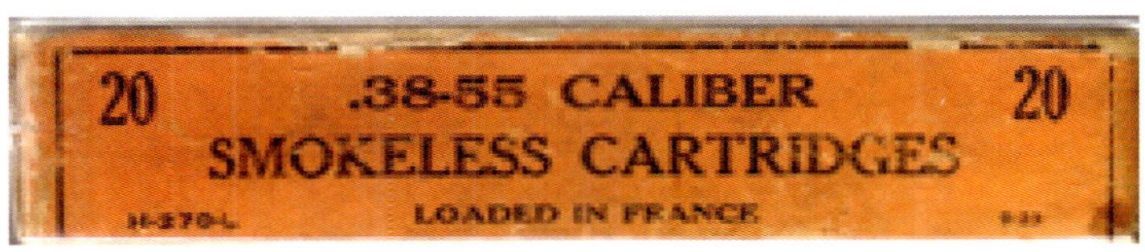

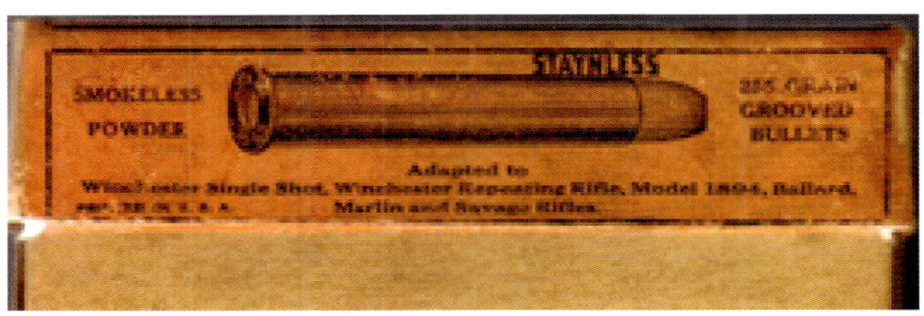

A scarce "Loaded in France" box of primed brass cases loaded with Smokeless Powder and capped off with cork wads. Sometimes mistakenly referred to as "Cork Blanks" these cartridges were not intended as Blanks but, rather, were shipped to France without bullets then loaded in that country in order to comply with French law. The "Staynless" overprint tells us, in spite of the 3-23 label date, that this box is ca. 1927-31. "Loaded in France" boxes are found in several calibers and are most often found empty. R3/200-400

10

Model 1895
Calibers: 236 U.S. Navy, 30-40, 30-'03, 30-'06, 303 British, 7.62 Russian, 35 W.C.F., 38-72, 40-72, 405 W.C.F.

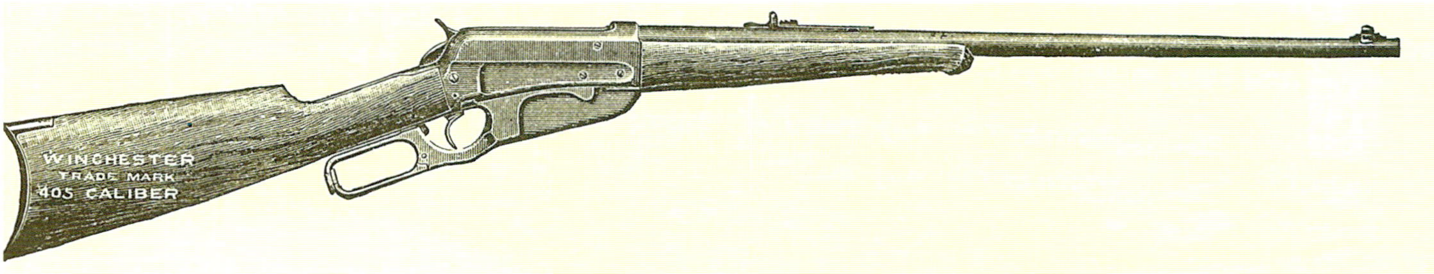

John Browning's achievement in the design of the Model 1894 and its medium-range calibers has already been detailed. His next challenge was to create a lever-action rifle that would handle the new and larger calibers required by big-game hunters as well as the militaries of the world. Such a gun was the Model 1895 ("M95"), which, despite its very different appearance, borrowed heavily from the M94's action. The truly significant difference, however, was the M95's box magazine which allowed use of pointed, jacketed bullets. This eliminated the risk of recoil-caused explosions in the magazine tube where the point-on-primer following of cartridges, one behind the other, posed a real danger.

The June 1896 catalog introducing the new M95 also announced the four calibers in which it was to be offered: 38-72, 40-72, 30-40 and 236 US Navy. In the next catalog, December 1896, the 236 Navy is no longer offered in the M95. We mention it here for completeness (there are at least two M95s known in the caliber) but will cover that cartridge more fully in the next chapter on the Lee Straight Pull Rifle. In same vein, the 7.62 Russian M95 was a contract-only rifle; however, M95 muskets were listed in a 1919 salesman's flyer.

Of the ten calibers chambered in the M95 during its production run from 1895 through the 1930s, only four were created by Winchester while six were of military origin. In their original loadings all the cartridges for the M95, with the exception of the 236 Navy and 7.62 Russian, listed bullets of at least 200 grains and all were over three inches in length. The 30-'06 became, and remains, one of the most successful big-game and military calibers of all time. Teddy Roosevelt said of his M95, "...the Winchester .405 is, at least for me personally, the medicine gun for lions." Perhaps that describes it best: the Model 1895 was Winchester's "Medicine Gun".

30 G. 1903, 30-'03
Catalog listing: 1905-1940

Models: 1895
Bullet types: SP, FMJ
Powder types: Smkls
Headstamps: WRACo, Dated*

Originally a U.S. military round developed for use in the Springfield Model 1903, only one other rifle was ever produced in significant quantities in this caliber: the Winchester M95. Only three years after its 1903 introduction the Government adopted a revised, slightly shorter, version of the 30-'03, the venerable 30-'06. As a result, the popularity of the 30-'03 was never very great although it continued to be a catalog item until 1940.

* Dated rounds will occasionally be found in commercial boxes of both FMJ and Soft Point loadings.

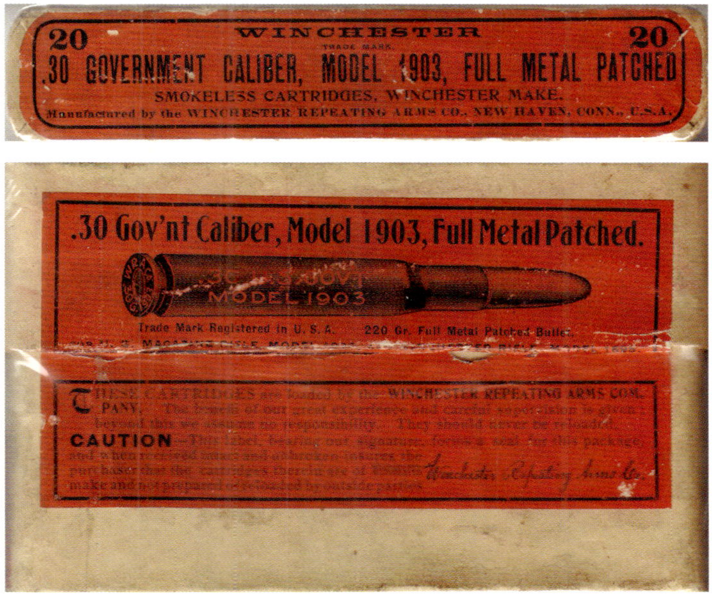

What is thought to be the earliest 30-'03 box, it lacks label dates and has a "Sunburst" Smokeless end label. Also note that the label does not cover the full front of the box. R3+/150-300

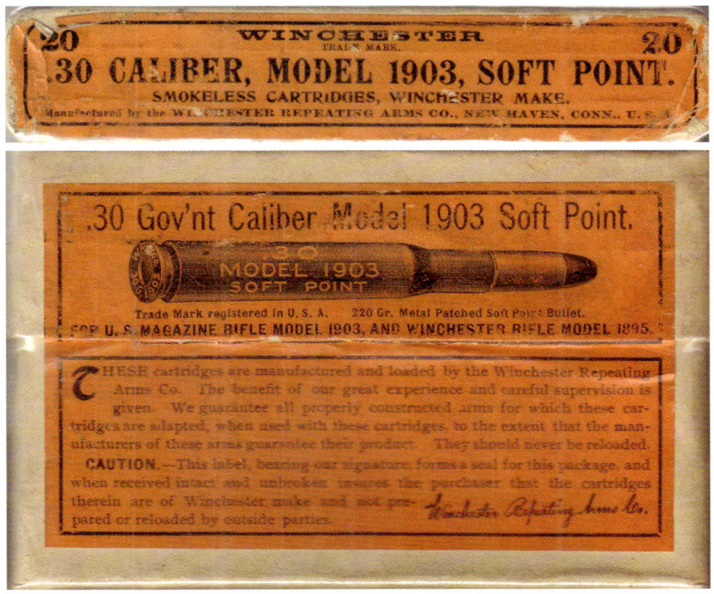

An early Soft Point box with a larger front label than previous photo and without label dates (pre-1906). Contrast with the Full Patch box in the next picture. R3/125-250

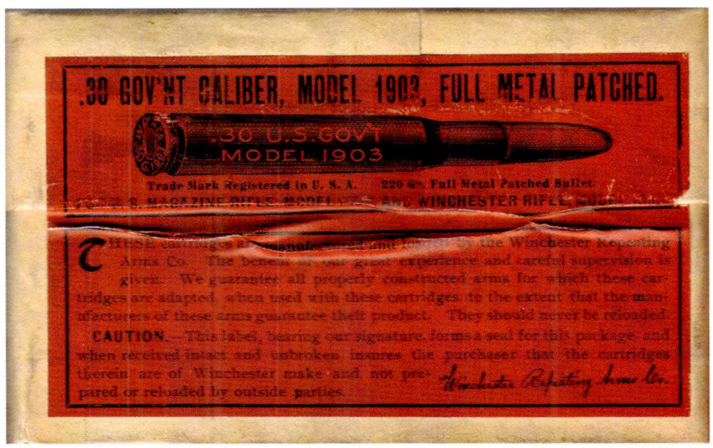

Also without label dates, the lower text exactly follows that of the previous Soft Point box. Note that the type font of the top line differs among all three boxes. R3/125-250

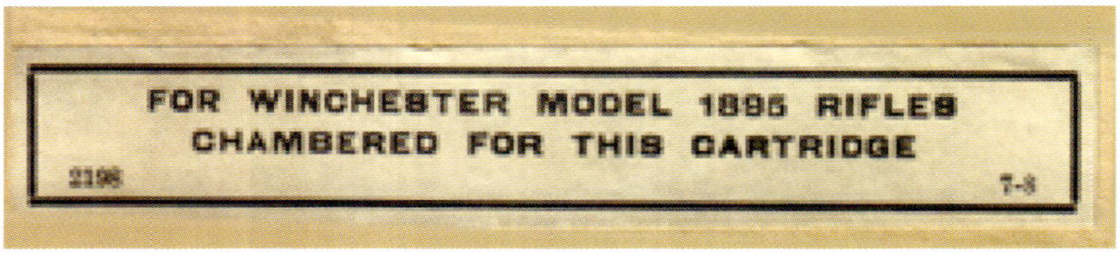

Model 1895 call-out label commonly found on the lower back sides of early boxes.

An 11-6 dated Soft Point box. "Trade Mark registered in U.S. Pat. Off." replaces "...registered in U.S.A." These early boxes are particularly scarce in nice condition. R3-/100-200

A 6-11 Full Patch box. The last line above the "Caution" statement stating "They should never be reloaded" has now been deleted. R3-/100-200

Top labels of the two Soft Point boxes below, both dated 5-16. The lower one exhibits a plethora of overprinted data and is post-1932.

These two Soft Point front labels from 1919-20 are actually the same except for the numerous post-1932 over-prints on the Staynless box (right). R2+/85-175

The Staynless/Non-Mercuric era front label with call-outs which parallel its corresponding lid label (see bottom p 204). R2+/85-175

A Rarity: 30-'03 Winchester box with G.H. Hoxie label

The Hoxie Ammunition Company bought commercial ammo and inserted a steel ball in the nose of the bullet as an aid to expansion. They then re-marketed the ammunition in the original maker's box, adding a label on the back like the one pictured below. As might be expected, the cartridge makers, such as Winchester and UMC, objected to this practice and sued Hoxie, forcing them to repackage the rounds in their own boxes with their own labels but acknowledging the use of cartridges made by others. The box below shows the early "G.H. Hoxie" maker's name on a label applied to a Winchester 30-'03 box, circa 1907. The 10-pack at the bottom of this page is a later Hoxie Ammunition Co. box of 30-'03 calling out the use of Winchester cartridges.

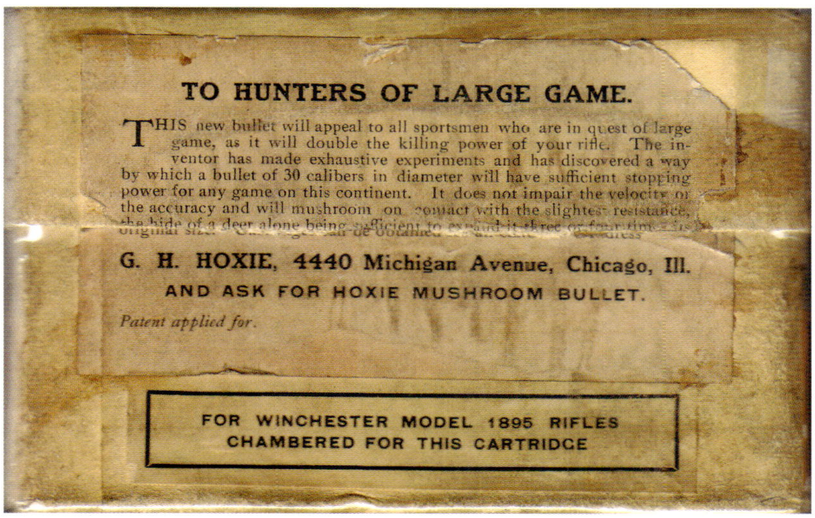

R5/500-1000

R3/175-300

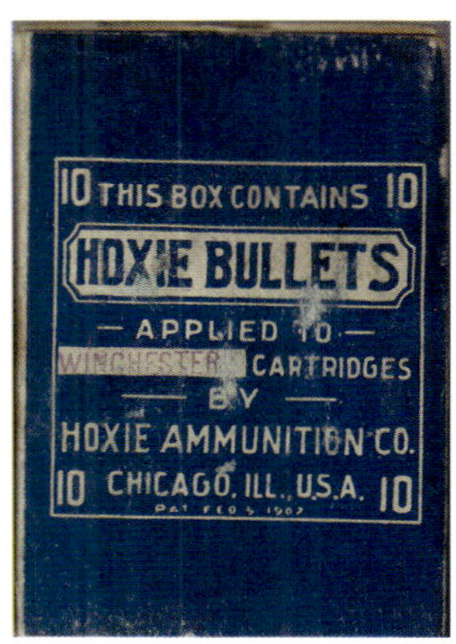

30 G. 1906, 30-'06, 30 Springfield

Catalog listings: 1908-

Models: 1895, 54, 70
Bullet types: SP, MCHP, Ptd Exp, ST, FMJ, Tracer, Match, Blank*
Powder types: Smkls, BP*
Headstamps: WRACo, WRA, SS, Dated**

What remains to be said about one of the oldest and best cartridges of the modern era? A slightly shorter (.07") version of the 30-'03 and loaded with a military 150 grain spitzer bullet, the new cartridge quickly became the world's standard for performance. In March 1908 Winchester added it to their sporting line, continuing with the original full jacket, pointed bullet Government loading. Over the years bullet weights within the industry ranged from 110 grains to 225 grains and were offered in all types of bullet designs, providing what the industry and gun-writers of the first half of the 20th Century considered the best "all-around" rifle cartridge ever devised.

The "30 G. 1906" headstamp was used on commercial runs until 1946 when the "30-06 Sprng" was adopted. Beginning in 1927, match loadings used the "30-06" stamping, as did military exports. As Winchester made the 30-'06 in such vast amounts, both commercially and on military contract, there are few rarities to be encountered in this caliber. There are a few worth mentioning, however, and these include the Black Powder Blanks, Motion Picture Blanks, commercial special-order tracers, and any commercial box with cartridges in clips. On the military side one might hope to find Line Throwing and Grenade Blanks.

* Black powder loads issued only in blanks.
** Dated FMJ (military issue) rounds will occasionally be found in commercial boxes.

What is thought to be the first 30-'06 Soft Point, this 220 grain offering has an undated front label. R3+/200-400

The end label shows the "Long Range" call-out but fails to mention the "180 Grs." deemed so important on the front label. The 3-8 dating represents the first month and year of catalog offerings in this caliber though, interestingly, not in this loading.

Though not cataloged, this 180 grain "Long Range" Full Patch box is label-dated 6-9 on the front label and 3-8 on the top and ends. Given the "180 Gr." call-out on the primary label, it would appear that, for some reason, the Company was especially anxious to ensure that this loading would not be confused with the standard 150 grain catalog offering. That factory records show intermittent loadings from November, 1908 until 1941 should not lead the collector to believe that this is a labeling easily found. It most definitely is not. R3/150-300

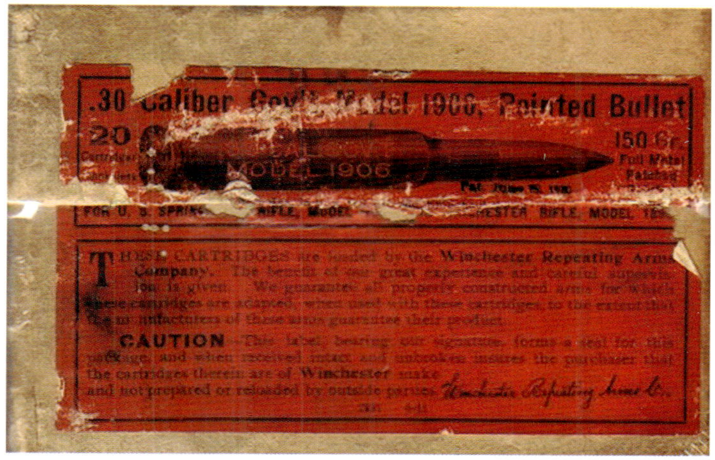

With a primary label-date of 6-11, the Pointed Full Patch offering seen here has the "June 28, 1910" reference to the primer improvement patent of that date. The 3-8 end label, as with the preceding box, is the same date as the initial catalog listing. R2+/100-200.

In 1914 a Winchester 30-'06 target loading won the prestigious Palma Match. For several years thereafter the Company marketed the same loading in a very distinctive box, this one label-dated 7-16. There are three minor variations of this box, the scarcest of which has "Lubricated" hand-stamped on it. R3-/150-250

Purple labels are not uncommon on FMJ boxes in this caliber, especially after 1912. This 150 grain example is dated 5-16 and, as is typical of post-1914 labels, pictures the cartridge cut on the lower front. R2/100-200

Making this 5-16 dated box of more than usual interest is the fact that its 150 grain Soft Point bullet was manufactured under an entirely new patented design. The only clue to this fact is the parenthetic reference to "Pat. Nov. 4, 1913" as seen under the cartridge cut. Referred to by various names including "mushroom" and "umbrella tip", it is a Pointed Soft Point with a protective metal covering over the bullet's lead tip, a design patented that year by Winchester's Henry Starkweather. R3+/200-350

This close-up shows the bullet tip, patent date, and a "For Sporting Purposes Only" line which was evidently inserted on the Soft Point loading of this caliber to warn against its use militarily during WWI.

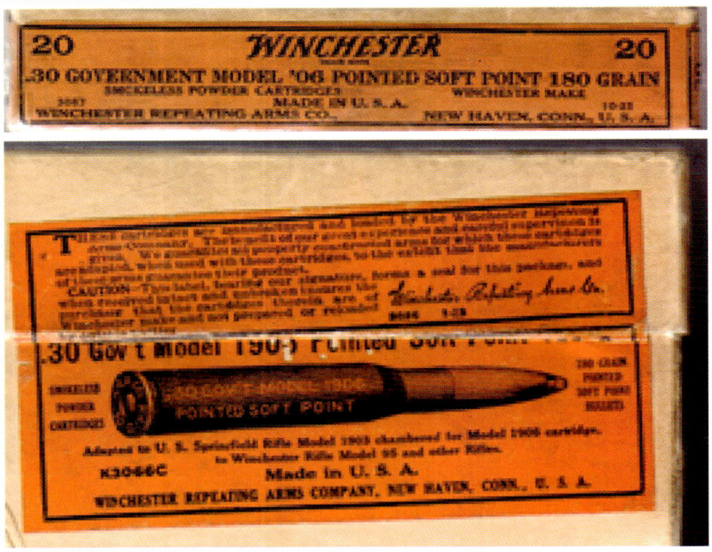

A typical 2-pc box with a 1-23 front label date and K-code. This may be the earliest known K-code label regardless of caliber. R2/100-200

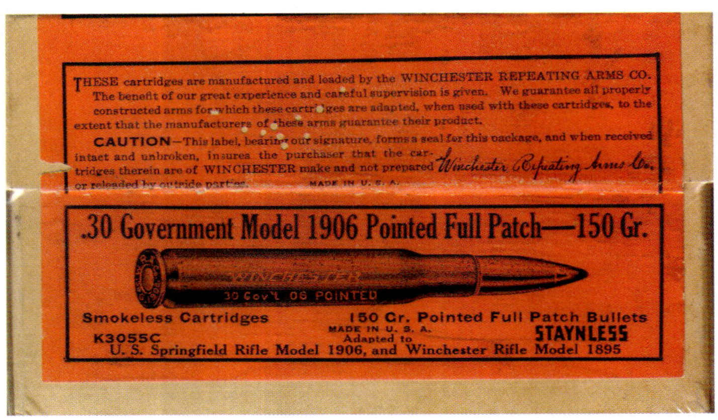

This is the original 150 grain Pointed Full Patch loading of 1906, but at the far end of its rise to popularity, circa 1930. As explained in the 30-40 section, these red two-piece boxes continued to be used in the slow-selling Full Patch loadings near the end of their run. R2-/75-150

30 Army, 30 U.S.G., 30-40 Krag

Catalog listings: 1894-

Models: 1885, 1895
Bullet types: Ld SR, SP, MCHP, Ptd Exp, ST, FMJ, Blank

Powder types: Smkls, BP*
Headstamps: WRACo, WRA, SS, Dated**

The first smokeless caliber ever loaded by Winchester (in 1893, though not cataloged until 1894) was the ".30 U.S.G." Though better known as the 30-40 Krag, that headstamp did not appear on Winchester cartridges until after WWII, probably because the Company always shied away from using a non-Winchester gun in naming their cartridges. The most common headstamp, ".30 Army", was begun in 1910 and lasted until it was replaced by the Krag designation.

As noted in the Model 1894 chapter, the 30-40 designation referred to 30 caliber and 40 grains of Smokeless Powder, one of only three cartridges so denoted (30-30 and 25-35 being the others, see page 167). Until 1898 steel-jacketed bullets were used and should be considered scarce, the soft point version being even rarer as it wasn't introduced until 1896. Short Range loadings were offered in both Smokeless and Black Powder, the latter being extremely rare. Likewise, Blanks were listed in both powders as well as two styles; one, a Blank with a paper bullet and, second, a cannelured-case Blank without a bullet. The former is fairly common, the latter fairly scarce. Pointed Expanding, or "Umbrella Tip" bullets are uncommon and the "Long Range Pointed" and "Hudson" bullet types are very scarce. For consistency, we will refer to this cartridge within these pages as the "30-40".

*Blanks and Short Range loadings only
**Various dated headstamps exist, the earliest being "4-07" and the last being "32".

Lid top of what is thought to be the first commercial box, circa 1894-98.

Same box, front view: Note call-outs of "40 Gr. Smokeless Powder." and "Steel Jacketed" as well as the Smokeless and Soft Point "sunburst" labels, ca. 1896-98. Also note the label is titled "30 U.S. Army" yet the headstamp is "30 U.S.G." R3+/400-600

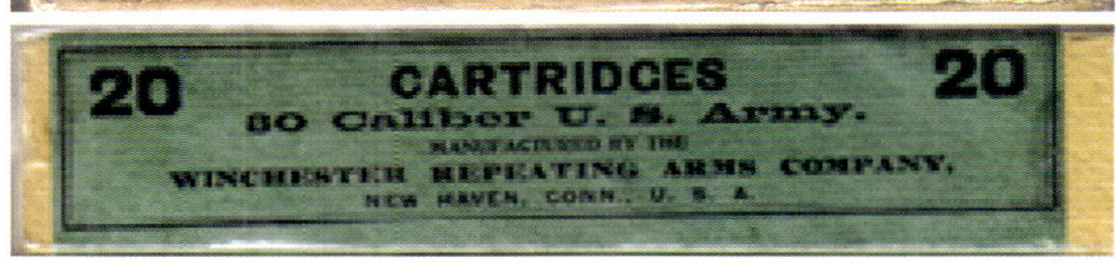

A rare (sealed) "Steel Jacketed" box without "...Guaranteed by" on lid-top label. This appears to be a military contract box with a string-pull double-side label. Thought to be prior to the Spanish-American War contracts of 1898. R3+/300-500

The popular Soft Point offering in Winchester's "new" one-piece box, ca 1927-28. The slower-selling FMJ loadings remained in the red two-piece boxes. R1/50-100

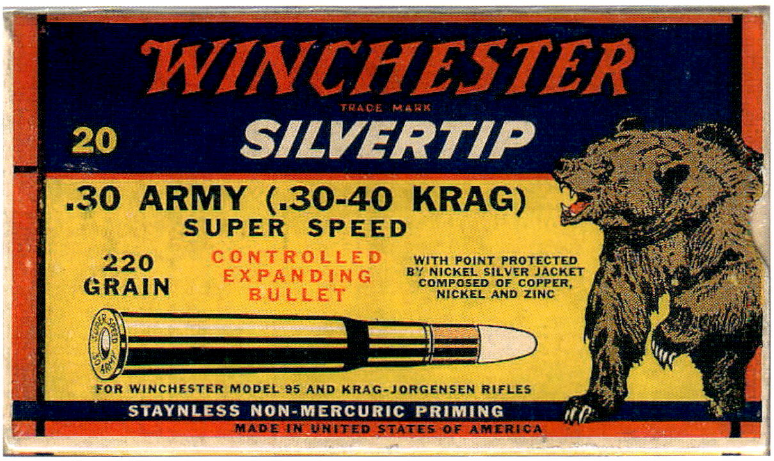

A nice example of one of the scarcest Grizzly boxes, the 220 grain Silvertip. R2/100-200 [180 grain: R1/60-120]

Short Range Boxes

Top and front of an early square-cornered Smokeless Short Range box. Smokeless "sunburst" sticker (on back). Note "7 Grains" call-out on front. Ca. 1897. R3/225-375

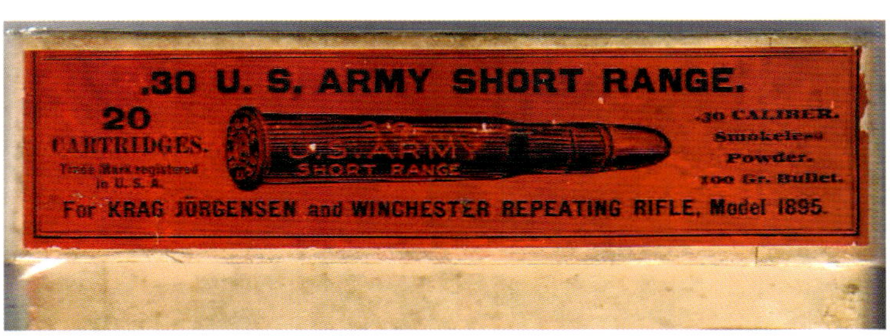

A round-cornered Short Range box, ca 1906, with "Red W" end labels. R3/200-325

A Rarity: The "Wound Test" Box

As with so many other Winchester boxes and labels there is no apparent logic surrounding its evolution. A similar label is shown in Shuey, *Vol. I*, p. 161. The contents of these boxes have long been associated with "wound tests" carried out by the U.S. Army Medical Corps. In examining the contents of the two boxes in Shuey, the 'A' box has traits of pre-1896 ammunition. The 'B' box, which matches the illustrated example here, shows that the cartridges were manufactured post-1910. The reason for the similarities in these two labels, so many years apart, eludes us. R3+/550-800 [Both]

Lid-top

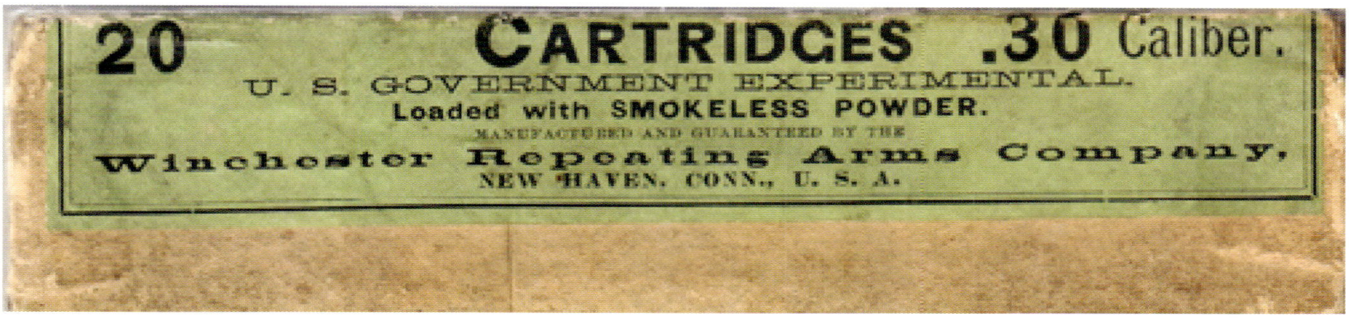

Lid-front

303 English, 303 British

Catalog listings: 1897-

Models: 1885, 1895
Bullet types: SP, FMJ, Blanks
Powder types: BP, Smkls
Headstamps: WRACo, WRA, SS, Dated*

Although this caliber was not cataloged until 1897, the first rounds produced by the Company in 1896 were marked "303 English" and are very rare with no boxes being known. Individual cartridges so headstamped have brought over $2000 at auction! Like the 30-40 Krag, this cartridge was loaded with steel-jacketed bullets in 1897-98 and these early boxes are especially rare; in fact, there is probably no Winchester lever-action rifle caliber that is more elusive in ANY two-piece commercial box than the 303 British.

Hundreds of millions of this standard British military round were turned out during the World Wars. These were the Mark VI (215 grain blunt nose) and the Mark VII (174 grain pointed), both of which, while the individual rounds are very common, remain rare in Winchester two-piece boxes. Small runs of Blanks in both Smokeless and Black Powder were produced on special order and are very rare; however, one lot of Super Speed 215 grain Boat-Tail Soft Points was run in 1948 and would make a super find for any collector.

*Headstamps were dated during WWI, beginning in 1914, and again during WWII.

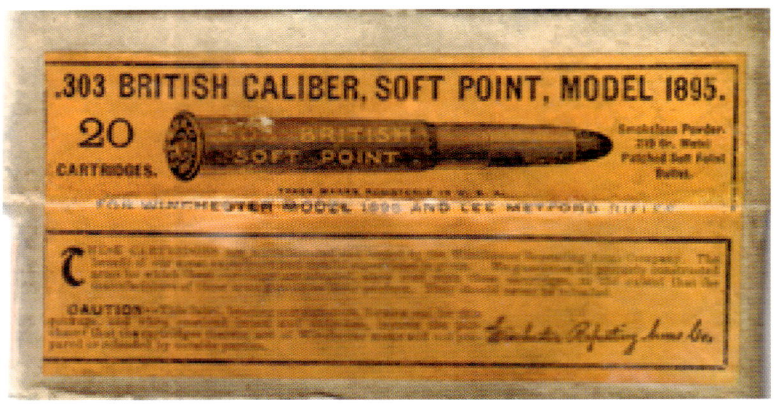

The earliest style box known to the authors in this caliber is this Soft Point box, ca. 1907. The primary labels are both undated although the lid-top shows "Winchester" in quotes. It is most unusual for that logo to be on an undated label; however, the "red W" end labels call out a 1-7 date which is entirely consistent with the logo. R4-/400-800 (Photo courtesy of Cliff Halper)

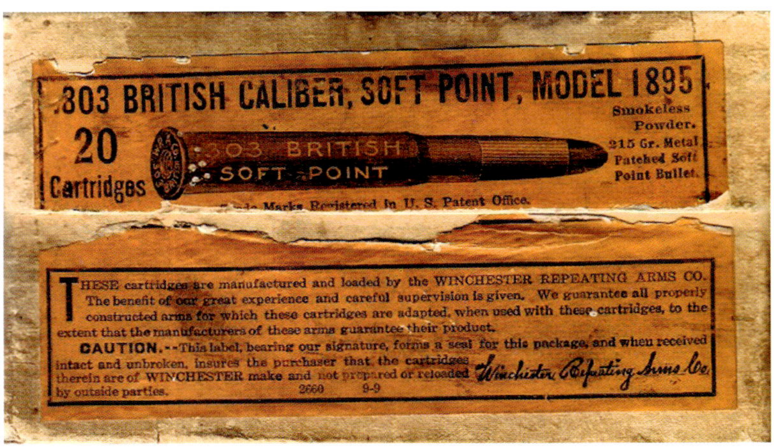

Displaying only minor changes in graphics from the preceding box — the "2" in "20" and the "T" in "These..." being most prominent — this front label is dated 9-9. The lid top is identical to the one on the previous box except it here bears a 10-7 date. R4-/400-800

These next two 11-15 dated Full Patch boxes display identical front labels except for the "Pointed Bullet" over-label. The weight of the two boxes differs by approximately 450 grains, suggesting that the Pointed Bullet rounds exceed the 174 grain Mark VII loading. Unfortunately, the latter box is sealed preventing closer examination of the individual cartridges. R3++/300-600

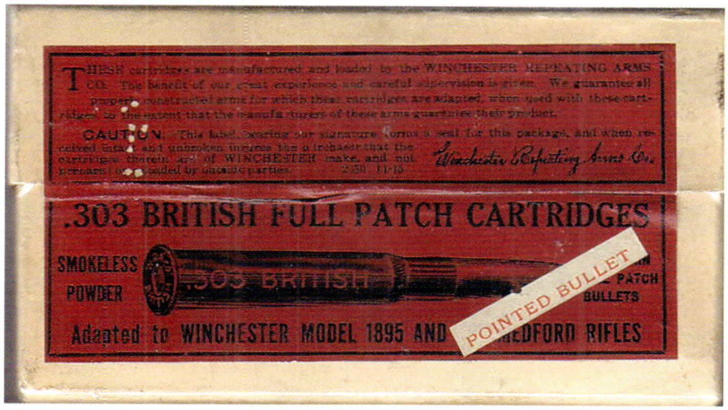

The "Pointed Bullet" over-label box. As the 174 grain pointed Mark VII was first cataloged in 1916, it would be logical that this was the first such box. However the lack of a specific call-out and the weight discrepancy (see above) throw some doubt upon this assumption. R3++/300-600

The respective 11-15 top lid labels for these two boxes. Note that there is a difference in date and code placement layout of the two bottom lines. One wonders how such a minor consideration could prompt a label change.

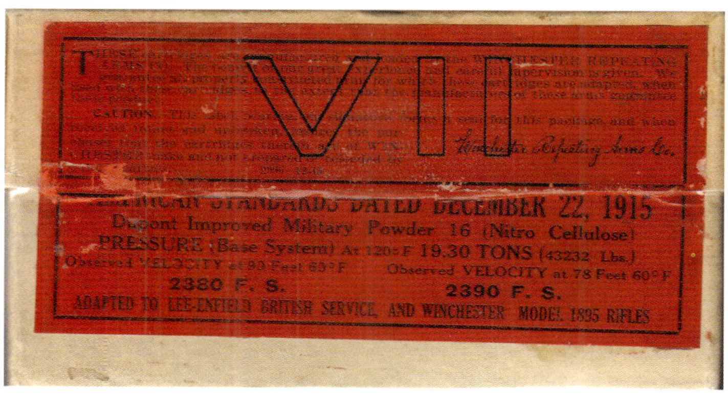

The only WW I era 303 boxes known are the "American Standard" boxes. Early in WWI, Great Britain contracted with several U.S. ammunition manufacturers for significant 303 production. In an effort to keep all loadings within specifications, each lot had to be tested and held to certain standards; hence the existence of the "Standard" cartridges pictured here. These cartridges were usually hand-loaded in lots of 200 to 1000. R3+/300-600

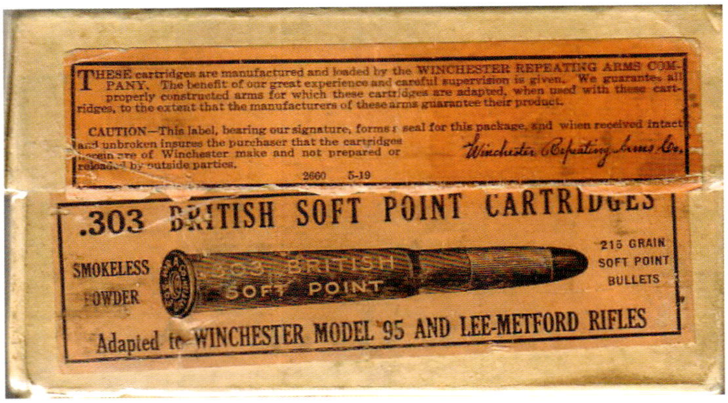

After the 9-9 dated Soft Point box displayed above, the next Soft Point box the authors can show the reader is this 5-19 example. This fact speaks profoundly to the rarity of early Soft Point boxes in this caliber. R3++/350-650

An 11-25 K-code Soft Point box showing both top and front. It can be assumed that whatever variations preceded this, in both bullet types, will closely follow those described and shown in the other Model 95 calibers. Due to the scarcity of boxes in this caliber, however, it is doubtful that many variations will be found to have been issued in either the preceding two-piece, or the following one-piece, boxes. R3++/300-600

In 1938, Winchester listed the Soft Point loading in Super Speed. This "1935" box, then, might be assumed to be quite scarce. It is doubtful that a "1939" style box exists and there is almost certainly no "1945" box, but "1946" red and yellow boxes are not uncommon. [1935 box: R2/75-150; 1946 box: R2-/35-65]

35 W.C.F., 35 Winchester

Catalog listings: 1903-1948

Models: 1885, 1895
Bullet types: SP, FMJ

Powder types: Smkls
Headstamps: WRACo, WRA

Introduced in 1903, the .35 Winchester represents the first smokeless-only cartridge designed specifically for the Model 95. Though an excellent big-game cartridge it was quickly over-shadowed by the .405 in 1904. Still, it remained in the line until 1948. The cartridge box collector will be frustrated to learn, however, that this caliber was never issued in either the "1945" or "1946" Olin Industries marked boxes. The "1939" box, then, represents the end of the line for this fine caliber. Unfortunately its chief claim to fame seems to have been that of "organ donor": the famous 405 Winchester was derived from the casing of this relatively unappreciated round.

A nice sealed example of the 1903-05 box in the scarcer Full Metal Patch loading. R3+/200-400

Another sealed 1903-05 box, this one in Soft Point. Note that the decimal in front of "35 Caliber..." is missing. This and the preceding box are assumed by the authors to represent the earliest label graphics in this caliber. R3+/150-300

An example of the 1915-style box, label dated 7-16. R3/125-250

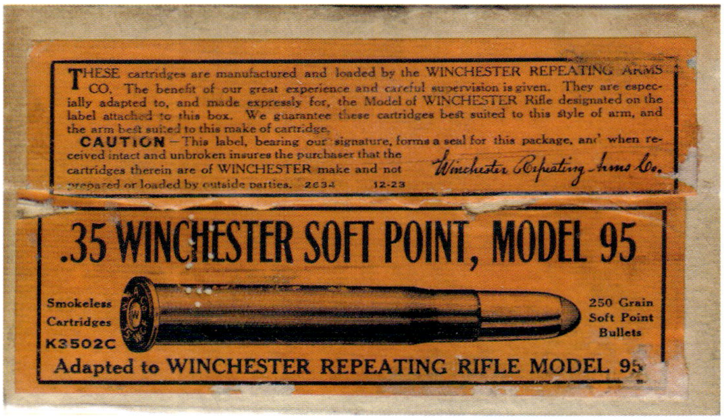

Here's a K-code box dated 12-23. This style, with only the smallest variations, lasted until the 1927 introduction of the one-piece Staynless box. R2+/100-200

Lid top labels, from top to bottom: the undated pre-1906 Full Patch,

1906-dated Soft Point (front label dated 10-9),

1916-dated Soft Point,

1923-dated Soft Point. Note that the "Model 1895" call-out has been dropped.

An Oddity: A Red-labeled Soft Point Box

While common to 50-round Smokeless boxes with either Lead or Soft Point bullets, a red label on a two-piece 20-round Soft Point box is unheard of. The graphics are identical to the 1903-05 orange Soft Point label shown above except for the decimal in front of the ".35 Caliber..." The angled markings which can faintly seen at the top, left center, are the same as the top right of this box label, calling out the Model 1895 and the powder and bullet types. R3+/175-350

38-72 W.C.F.

Catalog listings: 1896-1946

Models: 1885, 1895
Bullet types: Ld, SP, FMJ, Shot
Powder types: BP, Smkls
Headstamps: WRACo

One of the two new cartridges developed by Winchester for the introduction of the M95 (the 40-72 being the other), this one was virtually obsolete at birth. Generally considered today to have been a black powder round, it was actually offered in smokeless as well as black powder from its inception. Never very popular, coming as it did during the early days of smokeless powder and the exciting new high velocity "necked" cartridges, it still found its way into the catalogs until 1946.

Factory records for 1911 and 1912 indicate non-catalog Lesmok loadings in both Soft Point and Full Patch. No labels so marked have ever been found, however, providing us with yet another challenge in the collecting of rare Winchester cartridge boxes.

An early Black Powder, Lead Bullet box in the style that remained much the same until 1915. This one is circa 1899. R3-/175-350

The lid-top label for the Smokeless, Lead Bullet box below, ca 1907, but which is exactly the same as the Black Powder box above.

A typical early Smokeless, Lead Bullet box. These green Smokeless labels, like the Black Powder, Lead Bullet box above, remained in the line until 1915. R3/175-350

This very unusual yellow label is undated, but is very close to the orange label 11-6 box below, the only difference being, besides color, the wording of the trade mark registration call-out. R3/150-300

More interesting differences are to be found in the lid-top labels where the undated "pre-1906" label has "Winchester" in quotes—a post-1906 trait. The lower box is typical of the 1906-1910 labels.

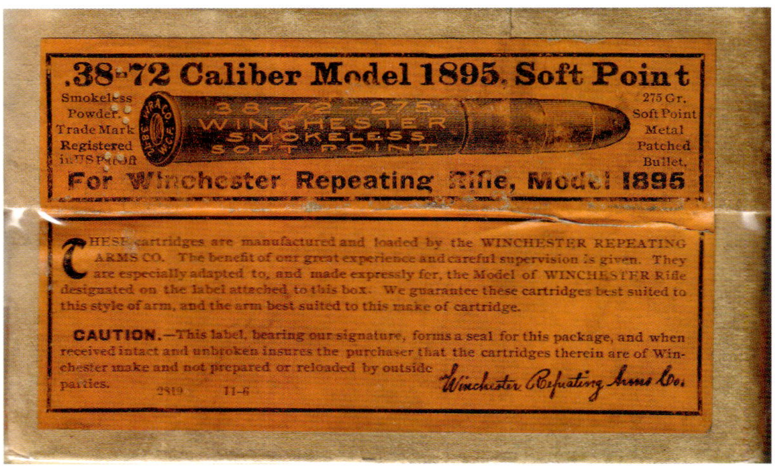

The 11-6 Smokeless, Soft Point box. This basic type, as with so many others in the line, remained in the line with only minor changes until 1914. R2+/125-250

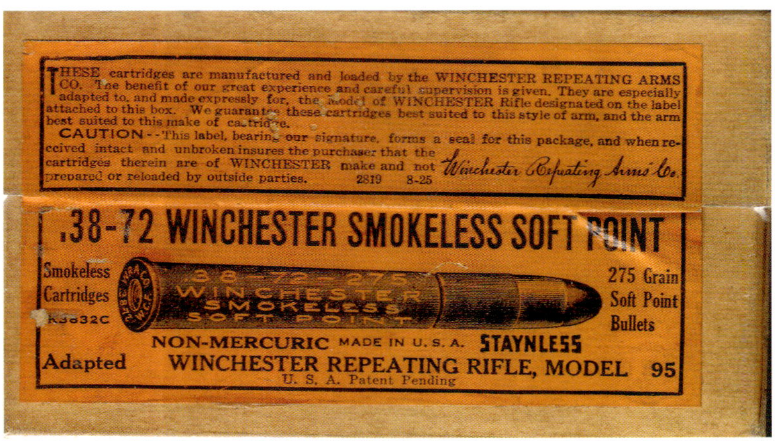

In 1915 the cartridge cut began to be shown on the lower front label. This is a late box; while dated 8-25, it shows the post-1932 call-outs of Staynless and Non-Mercuric. Like the 40-72, this caliber was never issued in a one-piece box. R2/125-200

40-72 W.C.F.

Catalog listings: 1896-1940

Models: 1885, 1895
Bullet types: Ld, SP, FMJ, Shot
Powder types: BP, Smkls
Headstamps: WRACo

Along with the 38-72 discussed earlier, this cartridge was a first-year M95 introduction and designed specifically for that rifle. Also like the 38-72, it was not considered a "modern" cartridge in spite of both its availability in smokeless powder and its having been newly developed and cataloged. One reason for this could have been the fact that both the 38-72 and 40-72 had been named using the old black powder nomenclature: the caliber followed by the grains of black powder call-out. In spite of it all, it lasted as a catalog listing until 1940.

The original 1896 loadings, in both powder types, had a 330 grain bullet, offered in either Full Patch or Lead. By the end of the year, however, the Full Patch bullet had been reduced to 300 grains, thereby creating another rarity for the collector, the 330 grain FMJ.

An early, square-cornered Black Powder box, circa 1897-98. This labeling lasted virtually without change on Black Powder boxes until 1915. R2+/125-250

While this lid-top label is from the Smokeless box below, there is no difference between it and that of the Black Powder box above. Note the early "...and Guaranteed..." call-out.

The "26 Grs. Smokeless Powder" call-out makes this an early box but not the first (1896), which would have been "330 Grs Metal Patched Bullet". The 300 grain bullet call-out on this box, as well as the "Guaranteed" on top, labels it as circa 1897-98. R3/150-300

The next Smokeless box, circa 1899, eliminates the powder grains call-out on the front label as well as the "Guaranteed" call-out on the lid-top label. R2+/125-225

This front-seal label is dated 5-16 and represents the "new look" for Black Powder boxes throughout the line. R2+/125-200

While the early Smokeless boxes with orange labels follow much the same pattern as those of the other calibers, the next three boxes illustrate the evolution of the Staynless boxes of 1927-1940. This 5-24 box is an over-print on top and front and shows no "Made in USA" to the left of the cartridge cut. R2/100-200

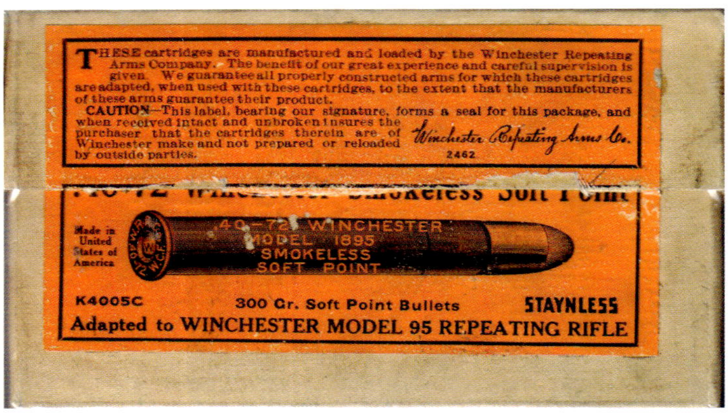

This front label is undated but is most likely ca 1931. "Staynless" is now printed on the label and "Made in United States of America" is to the left of the cartridge cut. R2/100-200

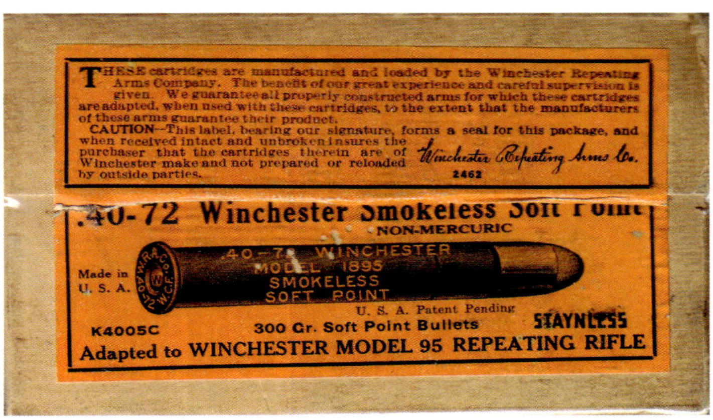

What is probably the last 40-72 box, remaining undated, has the "Non-Mercuric" call-out (above cartridge) along with its related "U.S.A. Patent Pending" (below cartridge). Also, left of cartridge, "Made in U.S.A." is now abbreviated. R2/100-200

405 W.C.F., 405 Winchester

Catalog listings: 1904-1955

Models: 1895, 1885
Bullet types: SP, FMJ
Powder types: Smkls
Headstamps: WRACo, WRA

The most potent caliber ever chambered by a Winchester lever gun, the .405 has earned its way to fame in more ways than one. As mentioned earlier, Winchester ads during the first decade of the 20th Century quoted Teddy Roosevelt's glowing tributes to the Model 95, particularly in 405 caliber, as a result of their success on his African safaris. These ads were not limited to the sporting magazines; they were to be seen in such popular periodicals as *Scribner's* , *McClure's* and *Collier's* as well. As a result, a certain mystique emerged surrounding the .405 and in spite of its discontinuance 50 years ago it remains anything but a forgotten cartridge. On the contrary, recently issued commemorative versions of the M95 as well as newly manufactured ammunition (though not by Winchester) ensure that the legend lives on.

The "African Safari" load immortalized by TR, a first style .405 Full Metal Patch box. Smokeless "Sunburst" label on left end, circa 1904-1905. R3+/200-400

A clean front-sealed, first style Smokeless box, ca. 1904-5. R3/175-300

A 10-9 dated label with "Pat. June 28 1910" over-printed beneath bullet. This Patent refers to a change in primer construction. R3/150-250

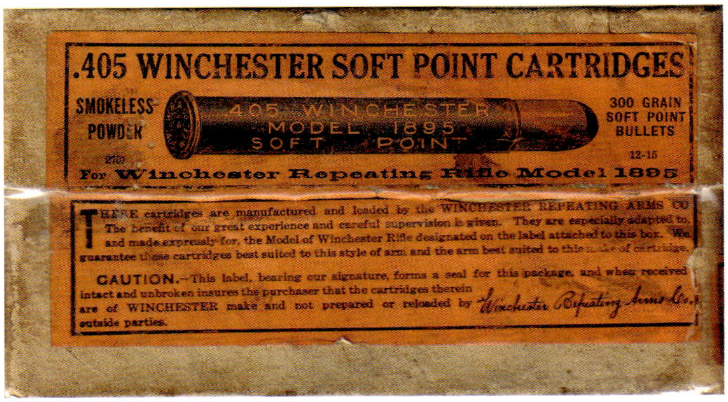

Box construction and label graphics changed between 1914 and 1915. This is one of the very few 1915-dated boxes exhibiting the characteristics of the older style box. This label is 12-15. R3-/150-250

A great example of a 3-19 label-dated box, clean and sealed. R2+/125-225

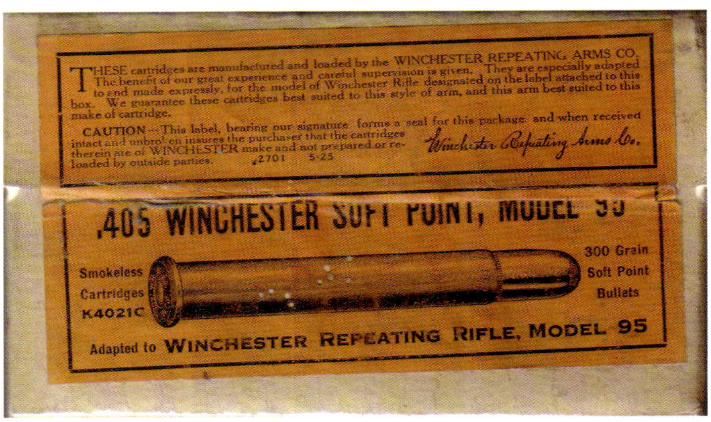

Now K-coded but without "Made in U.S.A." on the front, this box is label-dated 5-25. This 5-25 label without "Made in U.S.A." is quite scarce as most Winchester label designs beginning in late 1923 and throughout 1924 exhibit that call-out. R3+/150-250

The more common 5-25 box with "Made in U.S.A." under the cartridge cut. R2/100-200

Three successive lid top label styles: 5-20, 9-21 and 12-23 dates. Note the unusual change in wording under ".405 Winchester..." from "Smokeless Cartridges" to "Center Fire Cartridges" and back to "Smokeless...", creating a scarce variety in the 1921 label. 1921: R3+/150-250

A not uncommon occurrence: a purple lid top label and a red front label on a Full Patch box, these labels both dated 1-19. R2+/125-250

A yellow/gold "Staynless" over-stamped box of 3-28 design. This type of stamping was common to just a few calibers. They are usually found on Full Patch two-piece boxes or other older and slower-selling loadings where the Company was more inclined to use up old stock boxes and labels rather than ordering the new one-piece "Staynless" boxes. R2+/125-225

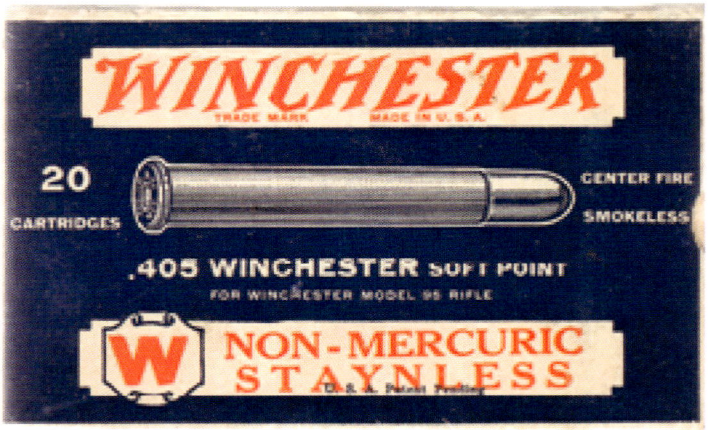

The "1932" box with both "Staynless" and Non-Mercuric" call-outs. R2/100-175

The authors doubt the existence of a "1935" box between this "1939" design calling out Western Cartridge Co and the above "1932" box. Likewise, the existence of a "1945" box in this style, with the Olin Industries call-out, is considered unlikely. R2-/90-150

The last of the .405 boxes, "1946" style with Olin Industries call-out. R1+/75-125

A Rarity: "Loaded in France" box, 10-9 dated.

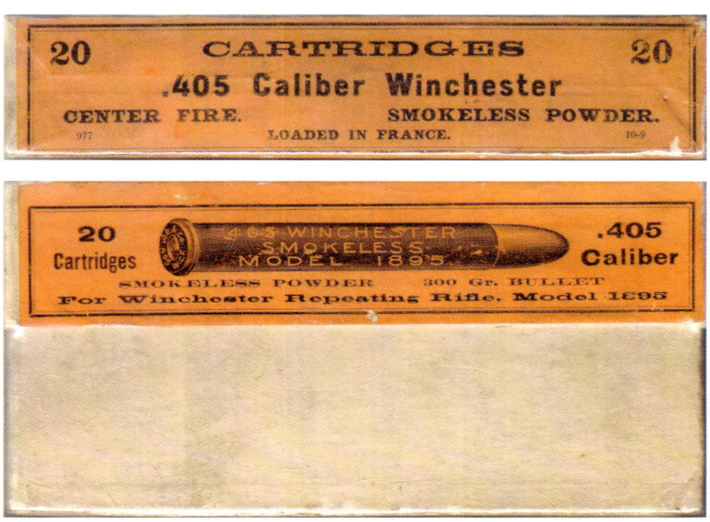

This rare box, unlike many labeled "Loaded in France", is full of its original cartridges and ranks among the earliest of such boxes. R3+/250-450

7.62 m/m Russian

Catalog listings: 1938-1956

Models: 1895
Bullet types: FMJ, MCHP
Powder types: Smkls
Headstamps: WRACo, Dated*

Although more M95s were made in this caliber than all others combined, the cartridge boxes offer the least amount of choices for the collector. The reason for this is simply that the Russian military contract of 1915-16 accounted for over two-thirds of total M95 production but the ammunition was not listed in the Winchester catalog until 1938. As a result only two box styles ever became available to the U.S. commercial market: the "1935" style (possibly including the "1939" variation) and the "1946" style. There are some non-commercial types as well, including the 15-round (3 clips of 5) wedge-shaped export boxes of the dated-headstamp rounds. These were mostly shipped to Russia in 1915-16 but there was also a similar Finnish contract in 1939-40. Two-piece boxes of the late -1920s type but with the 1939 "Western Cartridge Co." call-out and containing "Definitive Proof" rounds also exist (see below). Unfortunately, no such two-piece box containing standard loadings has yet been found.

*Dated headstamps used on military production only.

This rare box has no other labels and "W 15" headstamps. As other American gunmakers were manufacturing guns for Russia in this caliber at this time, these are probably test cartridges. They were not a commercial catalog item. R4/250-450

The "Definitive Proof" box with Western Cartridge Co. call-outs. R3+/200-350

First cataloged in 1938 and displaying "1935" box graphics, this is the earliest 7.62 Russian box cataloged for commercial sale by Winchester. The Hollow Copper Point bullet actually had a grooved break-away tip covering a hollow cavity. R3/100-200

An example of the colorful "1946" box, also a Hollow Copper Point loading. R2/40-80

In spite of the fact that this caliber in commercial loadings is never found with anything except the "WRACo" headstamp, a close-up of the cartridge cut on the side of this "1946" box clearly shows "WRA".

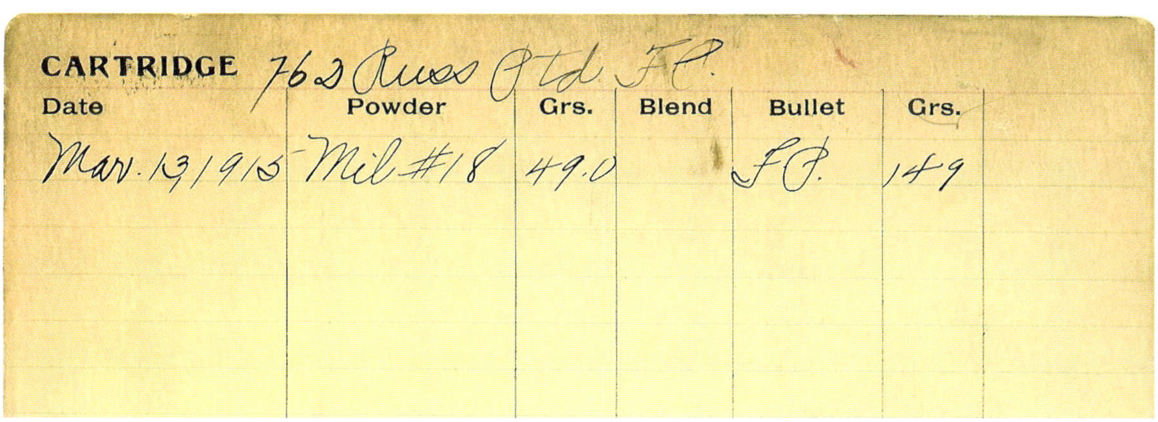

Here is the Loading Card pertaining to the rare 1915 non-commercial loading described earlier in this section.

7.62 m/m Russian

Catalog listings: 1938-1956

Models: 1895
Bullet types: FMJ, MCHP
Powder types: Smkls
Headstamps: WRACo, Dated*

Although more M95s were made in this caliber than all others combined, the cartridge boxes offer the least amount of choices for the collector. The reason for this is simply that the Russian military contract of 1915-16 accounted for over two-thirds of total M95 production but the ammunition was not listed in the Winchester catalog until 1938. As a result only two box styles ever became available to the U.S. commercial market: the "1935" style (possibly including the "1939" variation) and the "1946" style. There are some non-commercial types as well, including the 15-round (3 clips of 5) wedge-shaped export boxes of the dated-headstamp rounds. These were mostly shipped to Russia in 1915-16 but there was also a similar Finnish contract in 1939-40. Two-piece boxes of the late -1920s type but with the 1939 "Western Cartridge Co." call-out and containing "Definitive Proof" rounds also exist (see below). Unfortunately, no such two-piece box containing standard loadings has yet been found.

*Dated headstamps used on military production only.

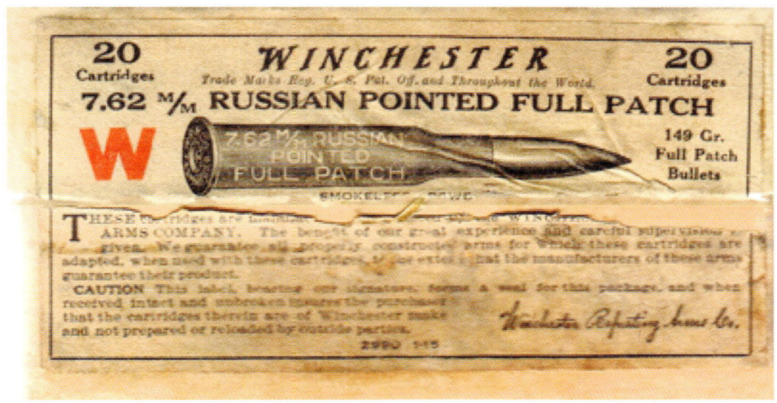

This rare box has no other labels and "W 15" headstamps. As other American gunmakers were manufacturing guns for Russia in this caliber at this time, these are probably test cartridges. They were not a commercial catalog item. R4/250-450

The "Definitive Proof" box with Western Cartridge Co. call-outs. R3+/200-350

First cataloged in 1938 and displaying "1935" box graphics, this is the earliest 7.62 Russian box cataloged for commercial sale by Winchester. The Hollow Copper Point bullet actually had a grooved breakaway tip covering a hollow cavity. R3/100-200

An example of the colorful "1946" box, also a Hollow Copper Point loading. R2/40-80

In spite of the fact that this caliber in commercial loadings is never found with anything except the "WRACo" headstamp, a close-up of the cartridge cut on the side of this "1946" box clearly shows "WRA".

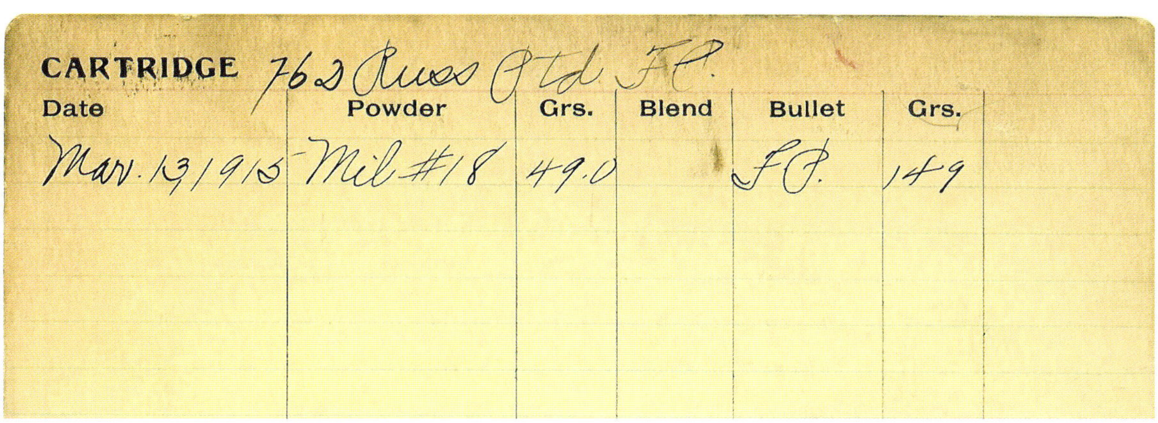

Here is the Loading Card pertaining to the rare 1915 non-commercial loading described earlier in this section.

11

Lee Straight Pull Rifle
Calibers: 236 U.S.N., 6m/m U.S.N.

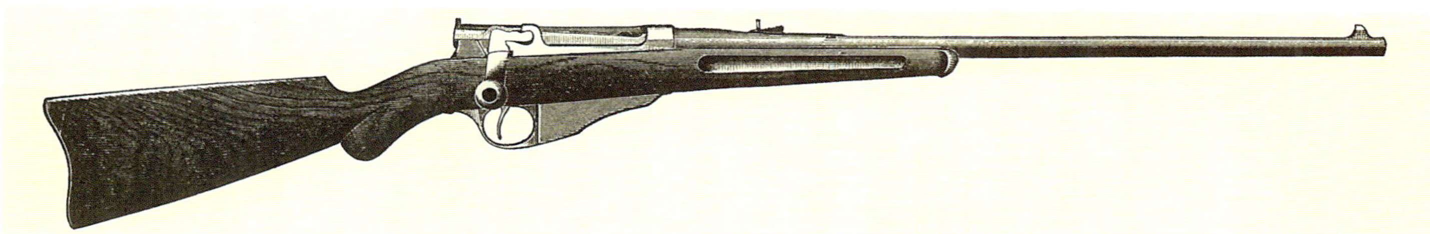

While Winchester's first attempt at marketing a bolt action sporting rifle (the Hotchkiss, see Chapter 6) was not terribly successful, it was obvious that the militaries of the world were headed in that direction whether the sportsmen went along with the idea or not. So, after the Company completed the Navy's order for 15,000 Lee Straight Pull rifles in 1897, Winchester tried once again to interest the public in a bolt-action sporting rifle. This time it was to be based on the Lee Navy musket which the Navy had named their "Model of 1895". It indeed had some new features that the Company had hoped would lead to this model's success. The chambering itself was among the first of the new "modern" small caliber, high velocity Smokeless cartridges. Also, the gun's ability to be reloaded rapidly with five-round stripper clips was seen to be a significant advantage. The main feature, however, was its "straight-pull" design which allowed the bolt to be pulled nearly straight back instead of in the usual "up and back" fashion. While not providing as fast a rate of fire as a lever-action rifle, this system was a definite improvement in that regard over the traditional bolt-actions. And while it became the highest priced standard sporting model in the Winchester line at $32, it was more likely the fact that this was, as the Hotchkiss had been, a gun ahead of its time, at least in the hearts and minds of Winchester's clientele. Only about 1700 of the sporting model rifles were made and the catalog of 1902 was the last to list it.

236 U.S.N., 6 m/m Lee Navy, 6 m/m U.S.N

Catalog Listings: 1896-1939

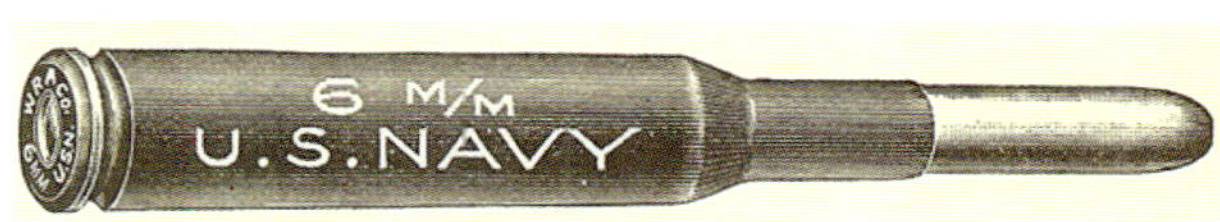

Models: Lee Straight Pull, M95 **Powder types:** Smkls, BP*
Bullet types: SP, FMJ, Blank **Headstamps:** WRACo

A rimmed version of the 236 U.S.N. which, while cataloged 1894-96, was never a cataloged chambering for any Winchester rifle. The rimless 236 U.S.N., first cataloged in 1896 for the M95 lever-action rifle (see previous chapter), was the cartridge in which the Lee Straight Pull sporting rifle was introduced the following year. By the end of 1897, however, the cartridge designation had been officially changed to "6 m/m U.S. Navy". The bullet, which had been 135 grains and steel jacketed from its earliest experimental days, became 112 grains and copper jacketed by the late 1890s. Examples of the earlier type are rare.

Boxes for the commercial market are sometimes found in tall, rectangular 20-round "Copper Jacket Bullet" military style boxes holding 4 clips of five cartridges each. The Soft Point commercial loadings, whether in military or commercial style boxes, simply displayed a Sunburst sticker with that call-out. Even some early commercial style two-piece boxes with "Soft Point" stickers retained a distinct military flavor by including a machine gun call-out!

*Black Powder Blanks were catalogued in 1914 only.

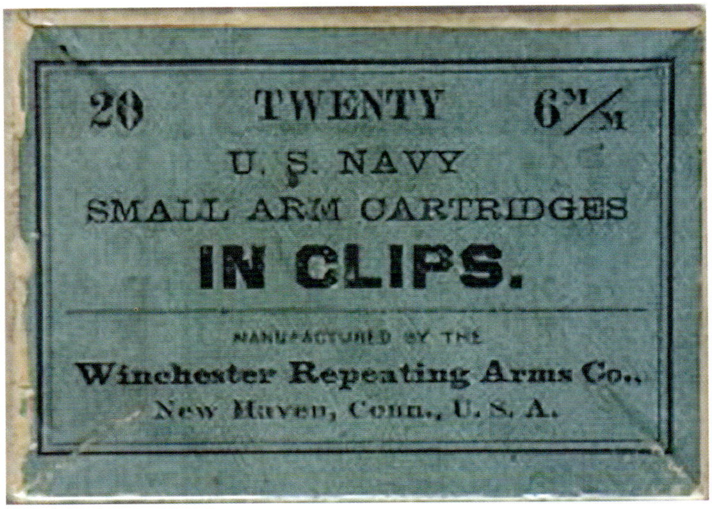

Lid top (enlarged) and Front
Among the most desirable of boxes in this caliber is this 20-round two-piece box containing 4 clips of five rounds each. As issued to the U.S. Navy there are no other labels to be found on this box. Commercial offerings of Soft Point cartridges are also known in this box, however, and will carry a Sunburst "Soft Point" sticker. R3+/500-800

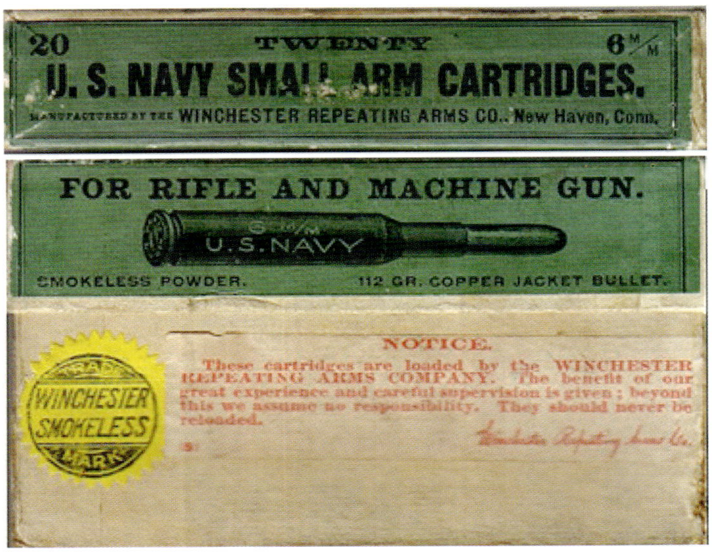

"U.S. Navy Small Arm Cartridges" and "For Rifle and Machine Gun" call-outs leave little doubt that this is a military box. That is until one notices a Sunburst "Soft Point Bullets" sticker on one end, a sure sign of a commercial loading in Winchester offerings of the period. This square-cornered box is ca. 1898-1900. R3/250-450

This round-cornered box, ca. 1900-1902, has no other labels and is therefore an FMJ loading. The "Lot 257" stamp indicates a military contract loading. Since Navy contracts called for the cartridges to be loaded in clips, we can assume that this box was a Marine contract as that branch specified that their lots not be loaded in clips. R3/250-450

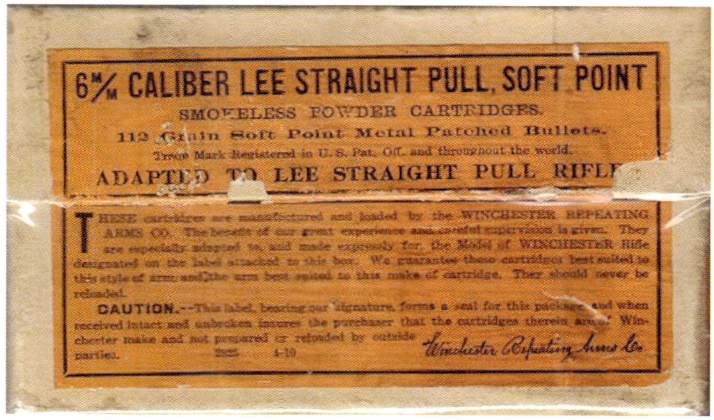

It is unusual for boxes of this period not to show an illustration of the cartridge on the lid-front. Dated 4-10 on the front label, this Soft Point box has earlier (3-8 dated) lid-top and end labels. The prominent "6 m/m Lee Straight Pull" title on this front label is repeated on the lid-top. R3/150-250

While the 11-15 dated front labels on both of these next two boxes are identical, their lid-tops are quite different. The top one, dated 1-19, is typical of the 1915-20 period, while the lower one, dated 5-28 and showing a Staynless over-stamp, dates to the 1928-31 period.

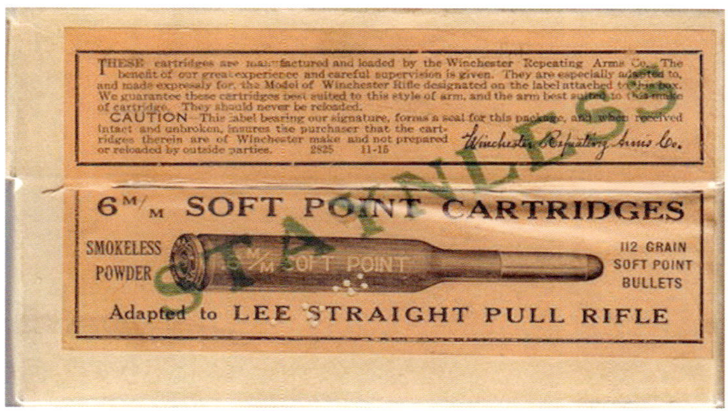

This 11-15 front label is common to both of the above boxes, the only difference being the "Staynless" overstamp. The use of labels of such disparate dates is reflective of the relatively low and declining demand for this caliber during the 1915-1939 period. R2/100-200

A Blanks Box

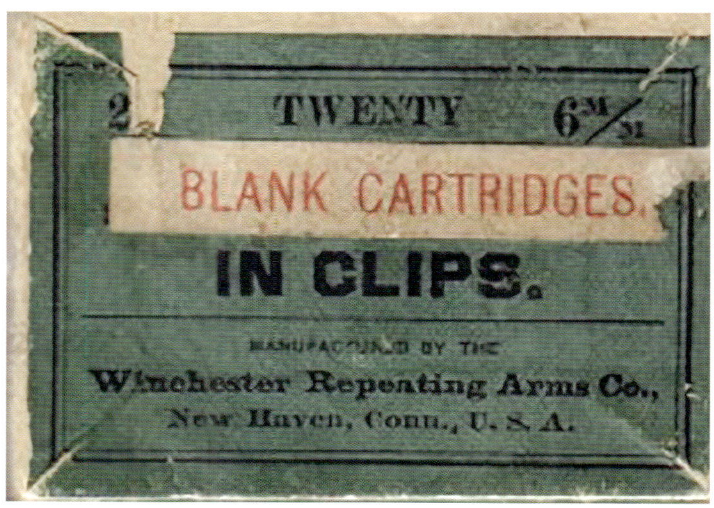

Blanks in clips are not common. This box has no other labels and guessing its date would be futile except to say that 6 m/m Blanks were last loaded in December of 1907 (Shown: lid top, enlarged). R3+/350-550

A Bullets Box

This box of 50 Copper Jacketed Bullets is thought to be circa 1900. R3/ 50-100

And a Rarity: The 236 U.S. Navy "Rimmed"

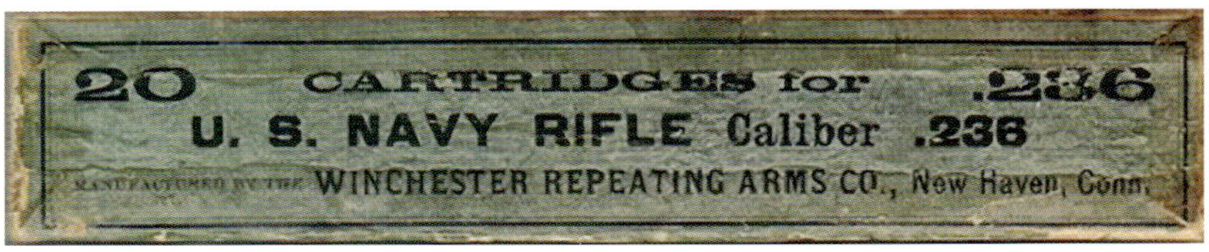

What was essentially an experimental cartridge, this became a catalog item during the 1894-96 period. Except for a M85 test gun, Winchester never chambered a rifle for this cartridge. Note the "Steel Jacketed" call-out on the early 135 grain bullet. These boxes are very rare. R5/500-1000

A close-up of the cartridge cut clearly showing the rimmed case construction and "236 U.S.N." headstamp.

12

Models 1905, 1907, 1910
Calibers: 32 SL, 35 SL, 351 SL, 401 SL

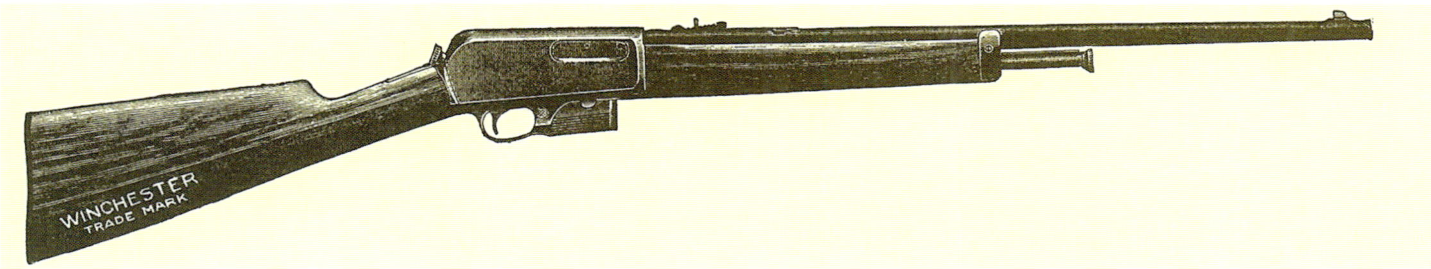

Model 1905 (32 SL, 35 SL)
Once Winchester's association with the Browning brothers had come to an end, it fell upon T.C. Johnson, a long-time Company employee, to lead the new firearm design effort. His M1903 .22 Winchester Automatic utilized a balanced breech, blow-back system which allowed for a slow action cycle yet which was, as termed at the time, self-loading (semi-automatic). Designing and integrating a detachable box magazine into the M1903 system culminated in this series of center-fire rifles. The first was the M1905 which chambered two newly-designed proprietary calibers, the 32 SL and the 35 SL, both of which were woefully underpowered. This model somehow made it to 1920 before it was discontinued with close to 30,000 having been made.

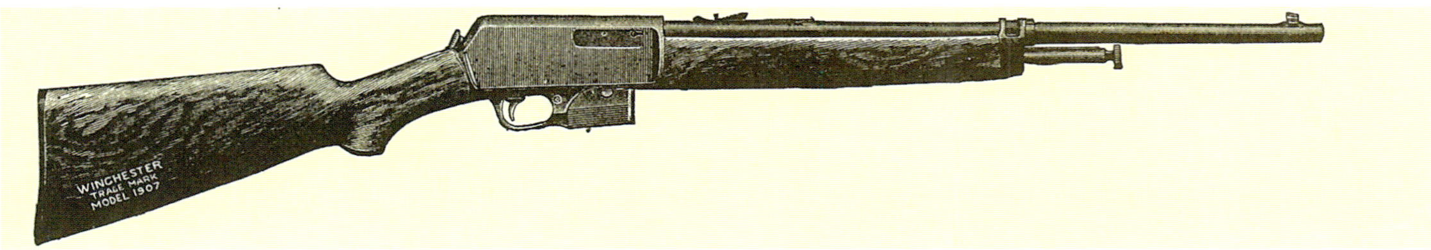

Model 1907 (351 SL)
The shortcomings of the M1905 and its calibers quickly became apparent and shortly thereafter the M1907 was introduced with a new and more powerful cartridge, the 351 SL. Though never very popular as a sporting gun it was promoted to, and widely accepted by, law enforcement agencies. The FBI and many prisons used the M1907 well into the 1960s. The French used these rifles to a limited extent in both WWI and WWII, possibly accounting for their limited success in both wars (pun intended). It was also one of the first guns used to arm aircraft during WWI. Some 58,000 had been sold by 1957 when it was discontinued.

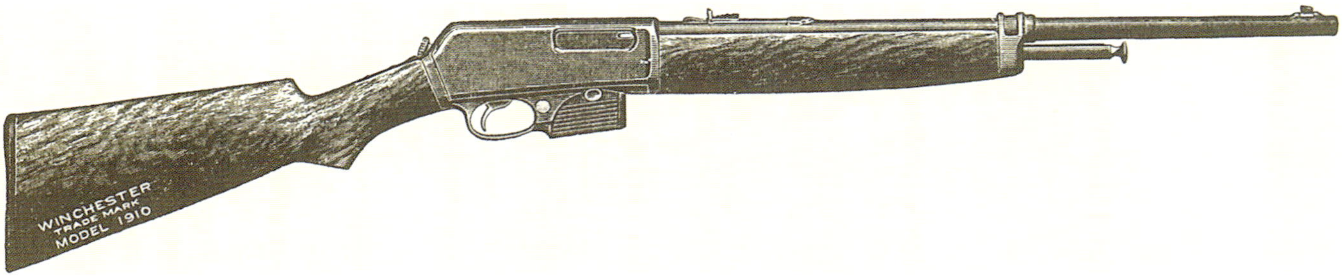

Model 1910 (401 SL)
Using the M1907 action, prototypes of the M1910 were found to require a stronger receiver in order to handle the powerful 401 SL cartridge designed for this new model. Like the M1907, the M1910 saw aircraft action in "The Great War". Also like its predecessor, it found acceptance among law enforcement officials; but, while a great "brush" gun, it met with a lukewarm reception by sportsmen due to its weight and relatively high cost. It was dropped from the line in 1936 after only about 20,000 had been built.

32 S.L.C.F., 32 S.L., 32 Winchester Self Loading*

Catalog Listings: 1905-56

Models: 1905
Bullet types: SP, FMJ
Powder types: Smkls
Headstamps: WRACo, WRA

Introduced in late 1905 along with the M1905 Winchester rifle, this smallest of the Self Loading calibers was never popular due to its poor ballistics and relatively high cost. As Frank Barnes so eloquently stated in his first edition of the very popular *Cartridges of the World* reference work: "[The 32 S.L.] is probably the number one candidate for the title of the world's most useless centerfire rifle cartridge". It might be said that it eventually found at least partial redemption in that it formed the basis for the 30 caliber M-1 Carbine cartridge, an important addition to America's WWII arsenal.

Early cartridges, ca. 1905-1907, are headstamped "32 S.L.C.F." In 1908 the headstamp was changed to "32 S.L." and continued in that form until 1946 when it became "32 Win S.L." Box labels, however, showed a cartridge cut with the "32 S.L.C.F." headstamp for several years beyond the actual use of that designation on cartridge heads. Boxes actually containing "32 S.L.C.F." rounds are rare.

*As the entire series of boxes for the Models 1905 and 1907 are very similar, these sections discussing the 32 SL, 35 SL and 351 SL will show examples of each caliber that, when taken together, will give the reader a very good idea of the graphics and time-line common to all three.

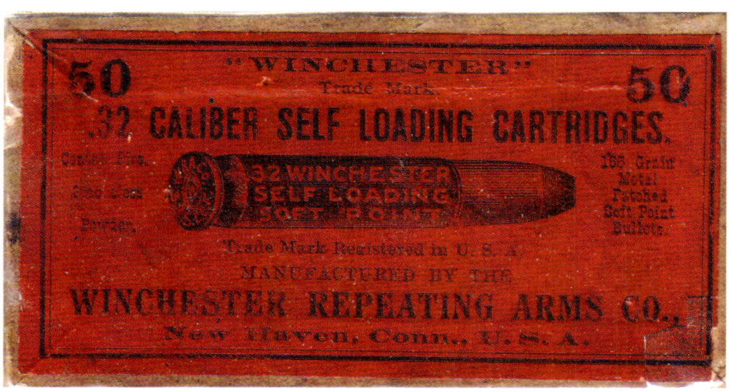

What is assumed to be the first 32 SL box exhibiting the early "Trade Mark Registered in U.S.A." line as well as the "Fancy WRACo" logo on one end. This end label logo was not used after 1905 making this a first year box. R3+/ 125-200

The early Trade Mark call-out.

The "Fancy WRACo" logo, ca.1898-1905.

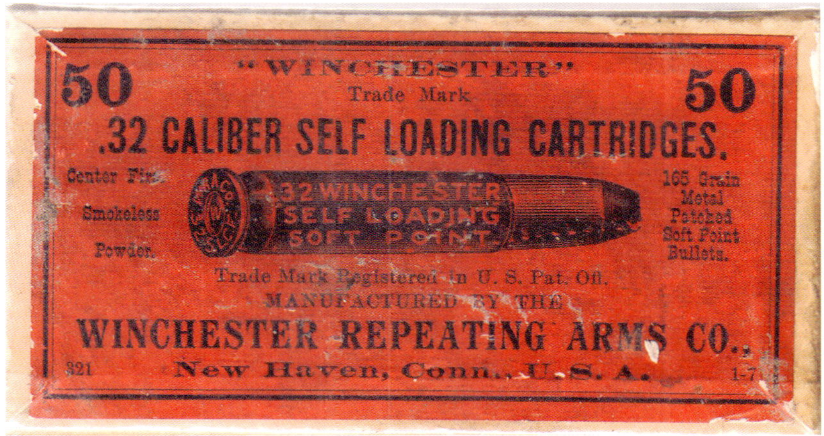

Another early (1-7) Soft Point box, this one with the familiar 1906-10 logo and with "in U.S. Pat. Off." replacing "in U.S.A." in the trade mark line. Note the ".32 SLCF" headstamp. R3-/80-160

The ".32 SLCF" headstamp was used on cartridges for about three years, 1905-07 but it is seen on the label cartridge cut for some years beyond that period.

These K-coded "1946" boxes represent the last style in which the 50-round SL calibers are found. (For other box styles please see the 35 SL and 351 SL sections.) R1+/65-100

35 S.L.C.F., 35 S.L., 35 Winchester Self Loading*
Catalog Listings: 1905-58

Models: 1905
Bullet types: SP, FMJ
Powder types: Smkls
Headstamps: WRACo, WRA

Like its under-powered sister previously discussed, the 35 Self Loading shares the 32 Self Loader's shortcomings as well as its fate as a relatively unsuccessful entry into the Company's product line. In its experimental stage this cartridge was designated "35 Auto" and was so headstamped. The early years of commercial production, however, used the "35 S.L.C.F." headstamp. As with 32 S.L. box labels, the "S.L.C.F" stamp was used on the cartridge cut for several years after its introduction while the contents generally have the "S.L." marking. Cartridges marked "35 Auto" are rare; those with "35 S.L.C.F." are scarce; the "WRACo 35 S.L." is common and the "WRA (or W.R.A.) 35 S.L. is uncommon.

*As the entire series of boxes for the Models 1905 and 1907 are very similar, these sections discussing the 32 SL, 35 SL and 351 SL will show examples of each caliber that, when taken together, will give the reader a very good idea of the graphics and time-line common to all three.

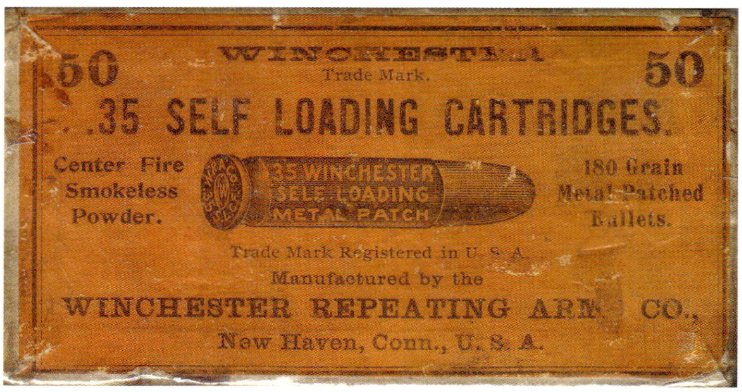

Far left: This undated first-year (1905) "Metal Patched" box is identifiable by its lack of quotation marks around *Winchester* and the trade mark registration "in U.S.A." rather than the 1906-10 "in U.S. Pat. Off.". Orange labels on the 50-round Smokeless boxes were, in contrast to the 20-round boxes, FMJ loadings. R3+/125-200
Left: A close-up of the cartridge cut with the ".35 S.L.C.F." headstamp. Cartridges bearing that headstamp are quite scarce.

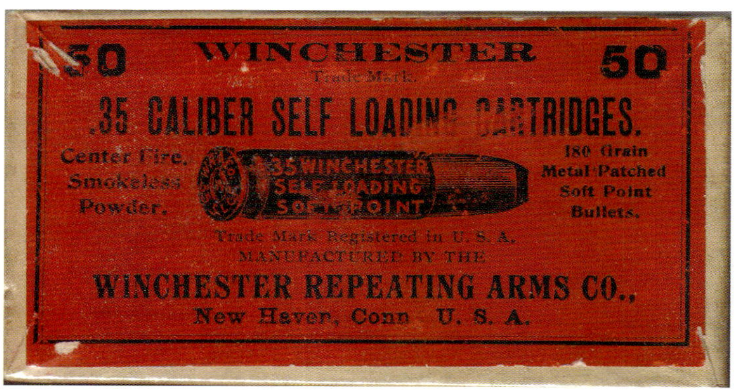

Unlike 20-round Smokeless boxes, red labels on the 50-round boxes denoted the Soft Point loading. Here is an undated, first year (1905) box with the "Metal Patched Soft Point Bullets" call-out. R3+/125-200

Here is the "1939" box, the only one of the "1935/1939/1945" style boxes of which the authors are aware in the four Self Loading calibers. While some variety of the blue and white Staynless boxes of the "1928" and "1932" styles probably do exist (and should by no means be considered rare), the authors have no pictures to show. The less-than-exuberant demand for this caliber accounts for the small number of box styles in 35 SL. R2/65-100

351 S.L., 351 Winchester Self Loading*

Catalog Listings: 1907-

Models: 1907
Bullet types: SP, FMJ
Powder types: Smkls
Headstamps: WRACo, WRA

The ineffectiveness of the 35 SL in the M1905 meant that a revision had to be on the drawing board very quickly. As a result, the Company's new 351 SL cartridge was showcased in the January 1907 catalog, only two years after the M1905 and its 35 SL chambering were first offered. The 351 had a nearly quarter-inch longer case and boasted a muzzle velocity fully one-third greater than its predecessor using identical 180 grain bullets. While a significant improvement, it was still not an acceptable round for any manner of big game and found popularity primarily in the law enforcement arena. It was, however, among the first (if not THE first) caliber to be used in offensive weaponry on U.S. military aircraft in the 1916 punitive expedition against Pancho Villa!

*As the entire series of boxes for the Models 1905 and 1907 are very similar, these sections discussing the 32 SL, 35 SL and 351 SL will show examples of each caliber that, when taken together, will give the reader a very good idea of the graphics and time-line common to all three.

This red Soft Point labeling, dated 8-6, is assumed to represent the earliest 351 box. Neither the caliber, nor the gun for which it was designed, was introduced until 1907. R3+/125-200

Except for the logo and trade mark changes typical of the period, this 10-15 dated box exhibits essentially the same call-outs as its predecessors, albeit in a slightly different arrangement. R2+/75-150

Left: With a 6-16 side-seal label and a 1-20 top label, this Staynless over-printed two-piece box is ca. 1932, a fact revealed by the "Non-Mercuric" call-out. Though found here on a full-cover box, the label itself is for the half-split box. It is a most unusual labeling demonstrating once again that Winchester never destroyed or discarded anything. Above: Nearly hidden and barely visible on the label, the "Non-Mercuric" over-print is shown here in close-up. R2/65-125

By the mid-1930s, as can be seen here, Staynless, Non-Mercuric and Oilproof were well-incorporated into the label design. R2-/65-110

The Soft Point "1928" box was the first of Winchester's one-piece boxes in this caliber and is seldom found in condition much better than this one. R2-/65-125

It wasn't until the introduction of the "1946" box style that the FMJ loading found its way into a one-piece box. This early 1940s box shows the Western Cartridge Co call-out first used ca. 1939. R2-/65-125

Close-up of the Western Cartridge Co. call-out on the above box.

Unlike the FMJ loading pictured above, the Soft Point offering was marketed in this "1939" style box. Like others in the Self Loading series, the "1935" and "1945" boxes do not appear to have been used at all. The "1946" box which followed this one is found in both FMJ and Soft Point (see .32 SL section for picture). R1+/65-125

401 S.L., 401 Self Loading, 401 Winchester Self Loading

Catalog Listings: 1910-55

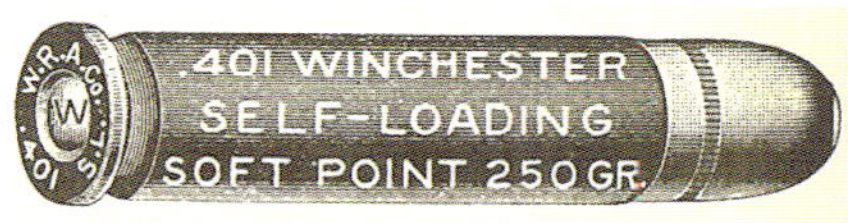

Models: 1910
Bullet types: SP, Tubed SP, FMJ
Powder types: Smkls
Headstamps: WRACo, WRA

In the Company's June, 1910 catalog the last in this series of self-loading rifles was introduced, surprisingly enough, as the M1910. A truly potent round, it is compared favorably with the 30-40 Krag in muzzle velocity and energy in the catalog's introductory write-up. This is the only one of the four Self Loading calibers that offered a choice of bullet weights. Both 200 and 250 grain Soft Point and Full Patch loadings were available during the early years; however, the 250 grain Full Patch offerings were discontinued in 1924 followed by the 200 grain Full Patch in 1926. The 250 grain bullet featured a knurl on the jacket to distinguish it from the 200 grain, a feature which was also portrayed on the cartridge cut on all but the very first 250 grain boxes. All 250 grain loadings command a premium, but the early ones not picturing the bullet knurling are very scarce. In 1913 Soft Point loadings began to use a copper tube insert in the nose of the bullet. Earlier rounds without this feature are scarce.

Unlike the 50-round boxes in which the smaller Self Loading calibers are found, the 401SL came in 20-round boxes. This meant that, following Winchester's label color protocols, the 20-round 401 SL Soft Point offerings are found in orange label boxes while the FMJ loadings were marketed in red label boxes. It will be remembered that the 50-round boxes were labeled in the opposite fashion, with FMJ in orange boxes and Soft Points in red.

The 250-grain loading had a knurl on the bullet jacket to distinguish it from the 200 grain bullet. The cartridge cut on this first 250 grain box (with both labels dated 10-9) shows a plain, unknurled bullet jacket and a broadly exposed soft point. These early boxes were all of round-cornered construction. R3/125-250

Close-ups of the earliest (10-9) label above and a later cut (4-10 250-grain label, see below) showing knurling and a much smaller soft point exposure.

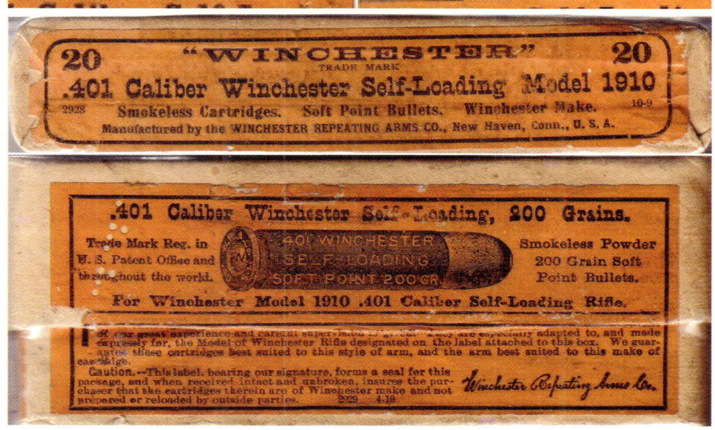

With a 4-10 front label and a 10-9 top label, this is an early 200-grain box. Compare this box to the one below. R2/75-125

The revised 250-grain label on this 4-10 box resembles the 200-grain label above in all respects except for the bullet weight, jacket knurling and the over-printed "Pat. June 3 1913". This labeling endured until the graphics change of 1915 (see below). R2+/85-170

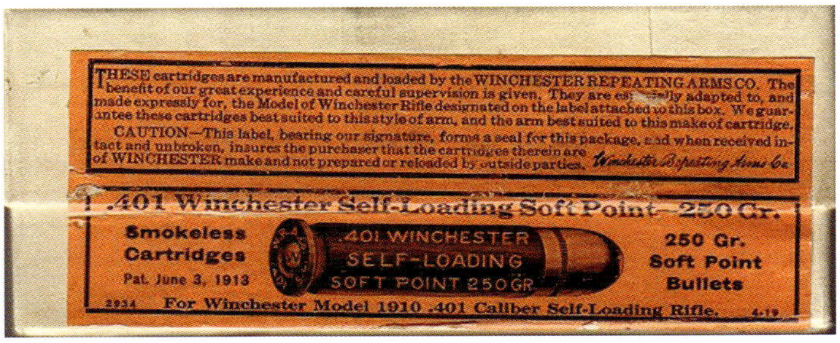

This 250-grain box, now with square corner construction, has 1919 label dates but reflects changes made throughout the Winchester cartridge box line ca. 1915. The cartridge cut has moved to the lower front and the "June 3, 1913" patent date is incorporated into the label design. R2+/85-170

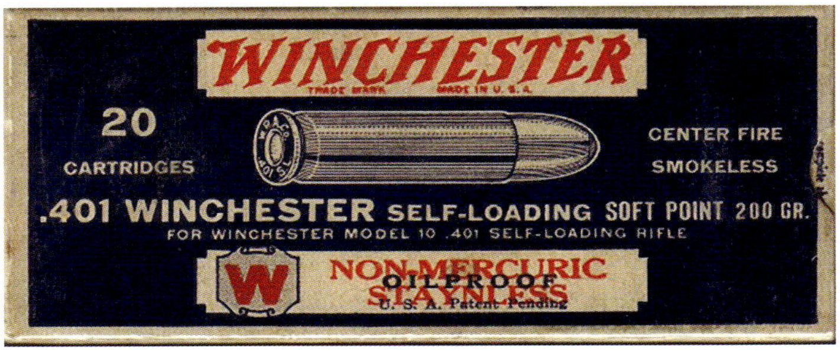

Since the FMJ offering was discontinued in 1925, the Soft Point loading is the only one-piece 401 SL box available to collectors. This one is in the "1932" style. R2/75-125

The "1939" style apparently succeeded the "1932" style pictured above. The authors are not aware of either "1935" or "1945" boxes in this caliber. R2-/75-125

The last box in which the 401 SL was offered before its discontinuance in 1955 was the "1946" style. This one exhibits a K-code, ca. 1946-52. R1/65-100

In spite of the WRA headstamp shown here on the cartridge cut, by far the majority of these late boxes contained cartridges which had the long outdated "WRACo" headstamp. The "WRA" headstamp in this caliber is actually quite scarce.

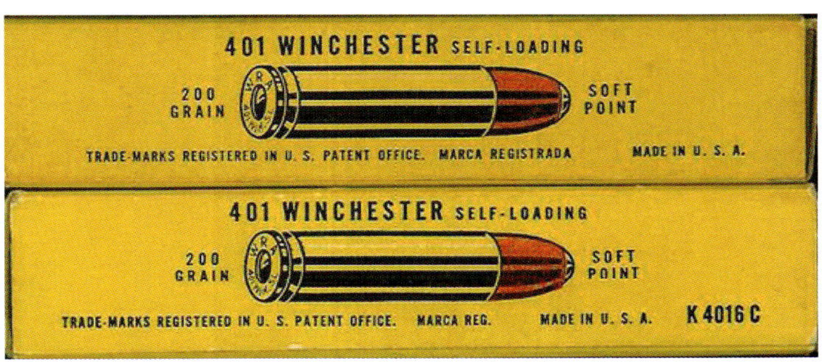

The 1946 style box exhibited two variations as shown here. As has so often been the case with Winchester boxes, no reason is known for these minor changes in graphics.

13

Model 36
Caliber: 9 m/m Rim Fire

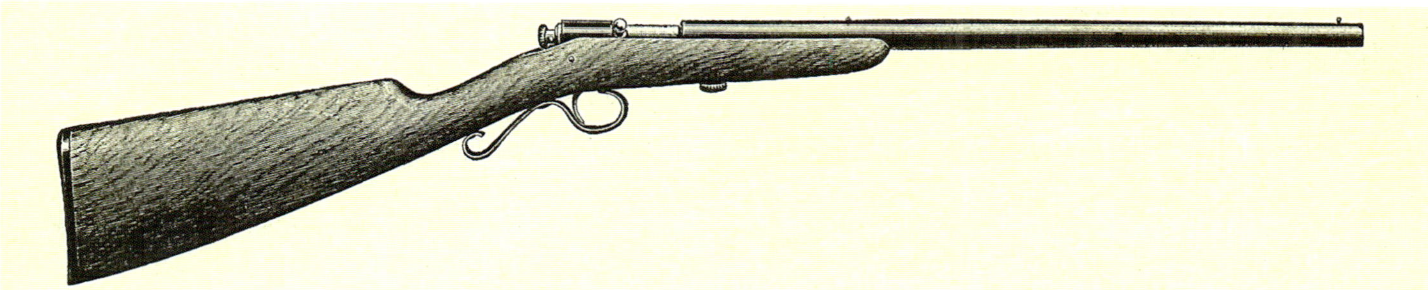

Okay, so it's not a rifle. Technically it's a shotgun and a bit of an oddity at that. Yet this little bolt-action "Garden Gun" has become a favorite of Winchester cartridge and gun aficionados of all types — from collectors of shotguns and Center Fire rifles to 22s — and, as a result, we have opted to cover it here. Introduced in 1920, it was an inexpensive single-shot smooth bore which was chambered for 9m/m Rim Fire Shot in both Long ("double-charge") and Short ("single-charge") loadings as well as the stubby little 9 m/m Ball ("half-charge") lead ball round. Discontinued in 1927, approximately 20,000 were manufactured, many of which were sold in the export market, especially South America.

9 m/m Rim Fire
Catalog listings: 1920-(see below)

9 m/m Ball

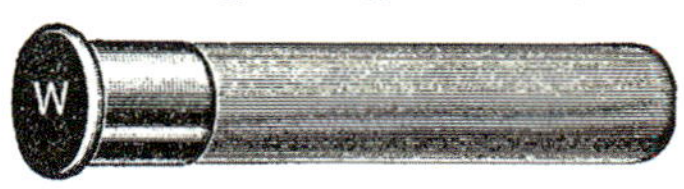

9 m/m Shot (Long)

9 m/m Shot (Short)

Model: 36

Bullet types: Ld ball, Shot

Powder types: BP, Lsmk, Smkls

Headstamps: Impressed "W"

Long popular in Europe and around the world in "Flobert" falling-block-action guns, the 9 m/m Rim Fire came in three case lengths, Long Shot, Short Shot, and Ball (using one 00-Buck as the ball). The single shot M36 would chamber all three lengths and Winchester loaded the Shot versions in all powder types: Black Powder, Lesmok and Smokeless. Constructed with a colored paper case on a copper base like the miniature shot shells that they were, the powder type was denoted by the case color. According to early factory records, blue would denote Black Powder; green, Lesmok; and red, Smokeless. All three colors are known, but domestic price listings for them, unfortunately, are not. In fact no Lesmok boxes, with either domestic or export labels, are known to the authors. Likewise, early export boxes, which have call-outs in Spanish, French and Portuguese as well as English, are known only in Black Powder. To further confuse the issue, the Short Shot does not appear in any of the Company's Domestic Price Lists which we have seen, though boxes with domestic labeling, while quite rare, are known. Export Price Lists show the Short Shot throughout the 1920s, but those boxes are very scarce as well.

Probably as a result of the large export volume of this cartridge, the headstamp used was a "W" rather than the normal "H" (the Company's historical tribute to B. Tyler Henry) that Winchester traditionally used on its Rim Fire line dating back to the 1860s. While there were a couple of early instances in which the Company used a raised "W" headstamp, this is the only Rim Fire caliber within the time frame of this study to ever have used an impressed "W".

The Ball loading, which had been Black Powder only, was last listed in 1927. It is not known when the Short Shot was last listed as that load was mostly for export and our run of Export Price Lists is far from complete. The Smokeless Long Shot loading continued to be cataloged for both domestic and export sales well into the 1950s, being last listed in 1958. A number of European manufacturers have also loaded this caliber, some utilizing full-length cases of copper or brass and others with patterned paper cases, many of which may be found in a variety of interesting and colorful boxes or tins.

9 m/m Ball Boxes

Dated 10-19, this is an early Black Powder box for export. Call-outs are in English, Spanish, French and Portuguese. R2/100-175

This domestic Black Powder label is dated 10-20 and is thought to be the earliest style in this offering. Of particular interest, however, is the fact that that the bottom of this box is covered with a label identical to the one pictured on the preceding box, making this example appropriate for either the domestic or export market! R3+/150-250

Dated only five months after the box above, this domestic Black Powder label shows an expanded "Adapted to..." line which is also now in caps. R3/125-200

9 m/m Short Shot Boxes

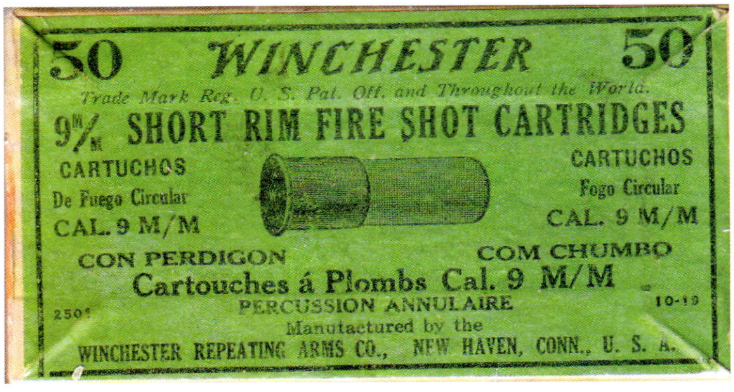

A Black Powder export box of Short Shot cartridges dated 10-19. All Short boxes are scarce. R3++/350-700

Having a picture of the gun on the side label is always a welcome sight for the collector. All these early half-split two-piece Shot boxes, both Short and Long, had the cut of the M36 on the side-seal.

Domestic labeled Short Shot boxes are rare. This 11-20 dated label is an over-label: the black line of the edge of an earlier label, probably for export, can be seen at the lower left corner. As with the foregoing box, this (identical) side-label has the cut of the M36. R4-/400-750

9 m/m Long Shot Boxes

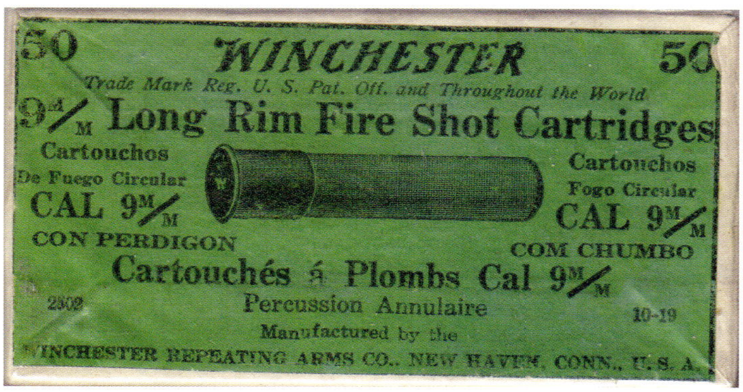

Like both the Short and Ball loadings, the earliest Black Powder export box in Long is of half-split construction and dated 10-19. R3-/200-400

Whether for domestic or export sales, the side-seal label on the green Black Powder boxes was orange and 9-19 dated.

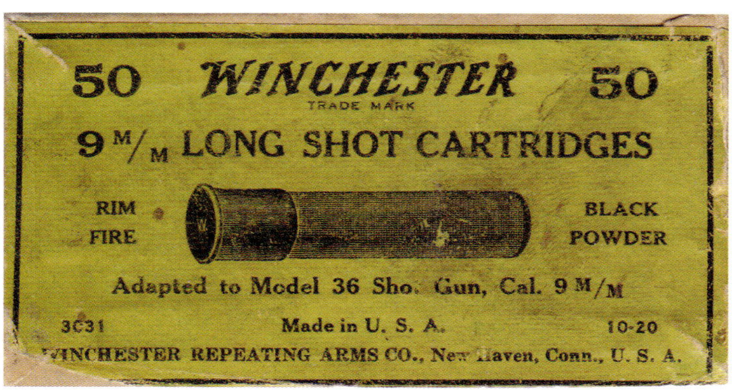

Like other half-split boxes, this domestic Black Powder box also has the orange side-seal label dated 9-19 and picturing the M36. Of interest also is the unusual olive green label which is very seldom encountered. R3/250-500

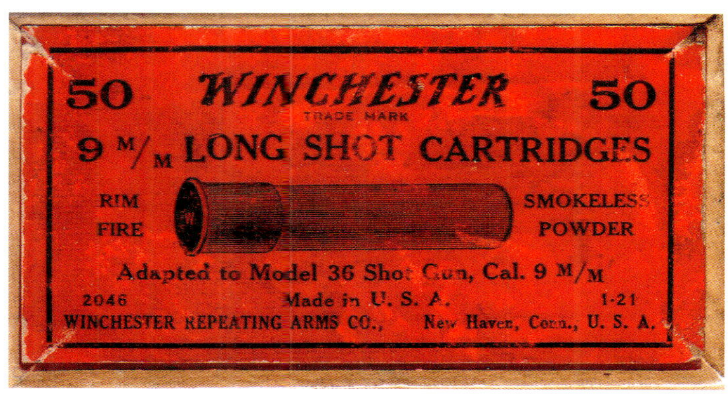

Another early half-split box with the side-seal picturing the M36, this one is Smokeless Powder and the labels are both dated 1-21. All half-split style domestic boxes are scarce. R3/175-350

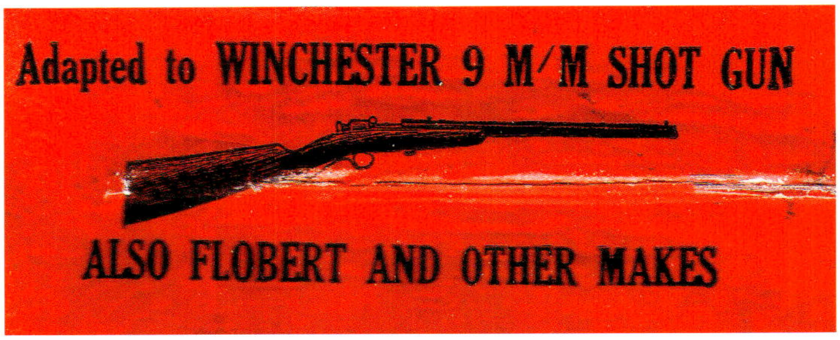

Dated 6-21, this side label from the above box differs only in color and date to the side labels on the two 9-19 Black Powder Long boxes shown above.

Now with a wrap-over label sealing the ends of this full-cover two-piece box, the transition to the basic graphics which would typify the Smokeless loading for the next 30+ years can be seen. This version is found from the mid-1920s till the late-1930s. R2/150-225

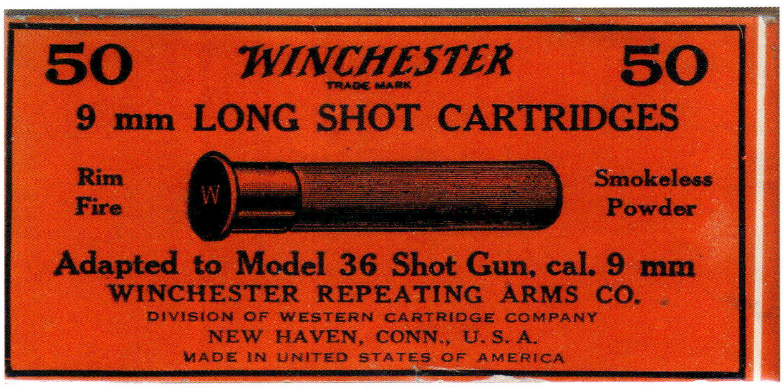

From the period 1939-1945, this version of the Smokeless box has the Western Cartridge Company call-out. R2-/125-200

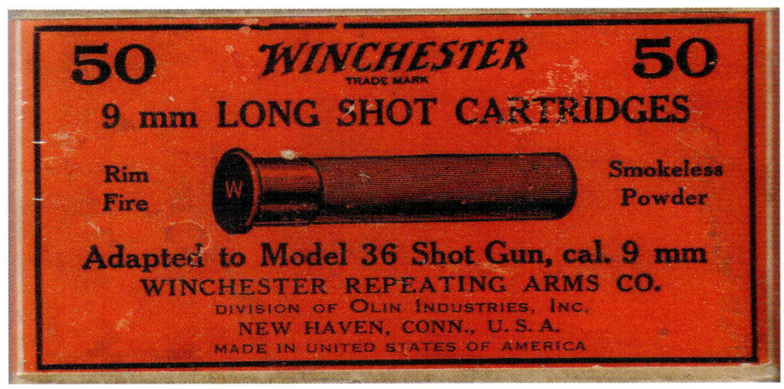

Now with the Olin Industries call-out, this domestic Smokeless labeling dates from 1946 till this caliber was last listed in 1958. The only difference between domestic labels of this period lies in the fact that the K-code was replaced by a W-code, ca. 1952. R1+/100-175

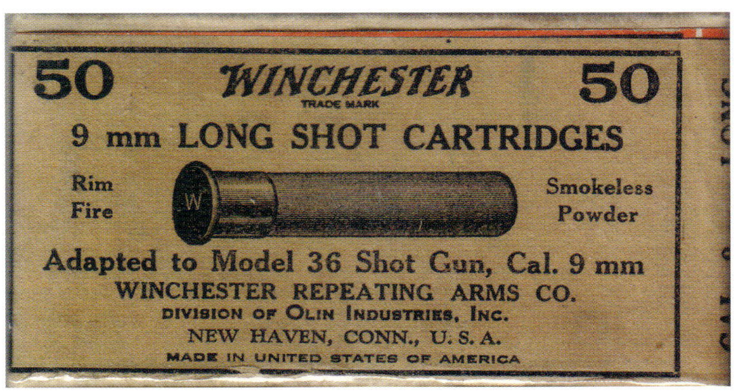

The edge of a red label underneath this tan label can be seen at the upper right margin confirming that this export box differs in nothing more than color. Even the W-code (W9LS) is the same as the domestic offering. R1+/100-175

14

Models 54, 70, 88
Calibers: 22 Hornet, 220 Swift, 243 Winchester, 250-3000 Savage, 257 Roberts, 270 W.C.F, 30 W.C.F.*, 30-'06, 300 H&H, 300 Savage, 308 Winchester, 35 Remington, 358 Winchester, 375 H&H, 458 Winchester, 7m/m Mauser, 7.65 m/m Mauser, 9 m/m Mauser

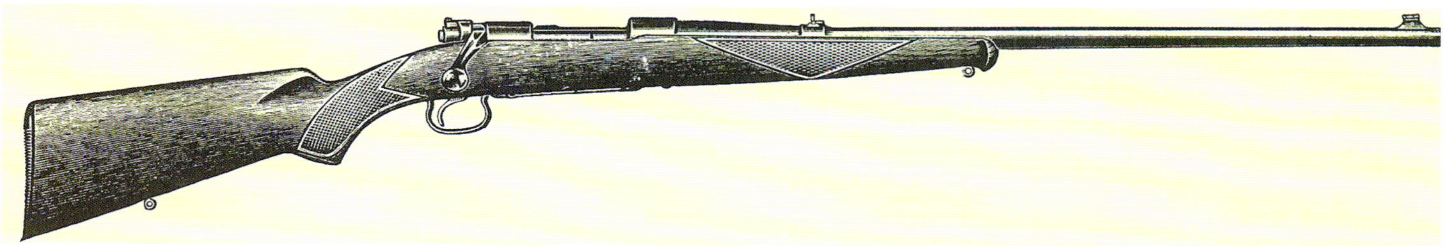

Model 54
Calibers and year of introduction: 1925 - 270 WCF, 30-'06; 1928 - 30 WCF*; 1929 - 7 m/m, 7.65 m/m, 9 m/m; 1932 - 250-3000; 1933 - 22 Hornet; 1935 - 220 Swift, 257 Roberts
As has been seen in earlier chapters, Winchester's attempts to market bolt-action rifles had begun as far back as the late-1870s but had met with little success. After WWI, however, returning servicemen helped popularize the new design which had been gaining world-wide acceptance since the turn of the century. Combining the knowledge and experience gained from the experimental models begun in 1912 and the P-14 and M-1917 military contracts along with production techniques learned from their fine post-war 22 caliber Model 52, Winchester introduced their new high-powered Model 54 in 1925. Along with this marvelous new rifle came a great new high-power cartridge, the 270 W.C.F., which, along with the by-then very popular 30-'06, laid the foundation for a successful 80-year run of building world-class bolt-action sporting rifles. After eleven years and 50,000 guns, the Company's designers, at C.E.O. John M. Olin's behest, had developed and engineered both the M52 and M54 to the point where a new model embodying these improvements was deemed appropriate: the Model 70.

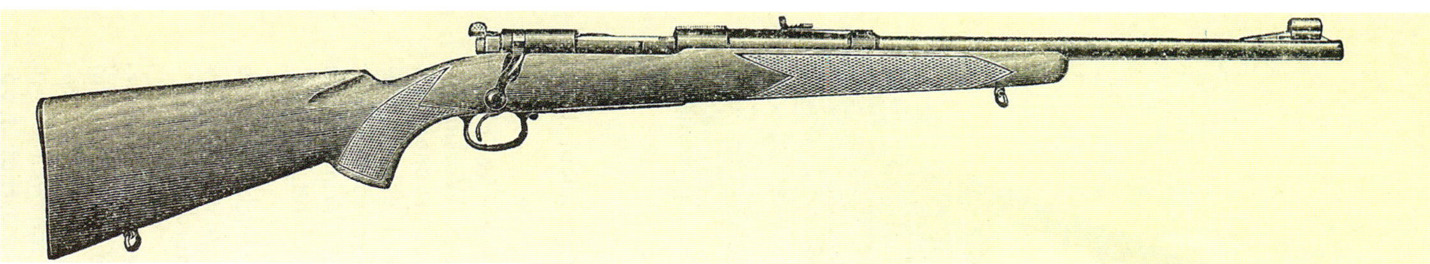

Model 70
Calibers and year of introduction: 1937 - 22 Hornet, 220 Swift, 250-3000, 257 Roberts, 270 W.C.F., 300 H&H, 300 Savage, 30-'06, 375 H&H, 7 m/m, 7.65 m/m, 9 m/m; 1941 - 35 Rem; 1952 - 308; 1955 - 243, 358; 1956 - 458
With production of the first guns taking place throughout 1936, the January 1, 1937 introduction of the M70 was an orchestrated event. Olin's goal was to produce the finest bolt-action rifle on the market and Winchester designers responded by improving the action, trigger mechanism and stock design of the prior models. In the Winchester line until the end, it underwent many changes over the years, not all of them well-accepted or in line with Olin's original desire. But with over 2 million sold in an almost unimaginable number of configurations, the Rifleman's Rifle remains one of the Company's greatest successes.

* This caliber, also referred to as 30-30, is covered in its entirety in Chapter 9.

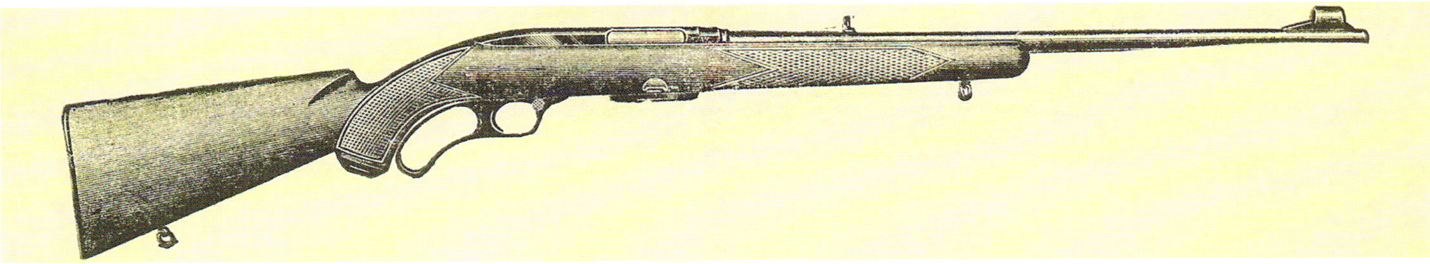

Model 88 (M-88 gunpic.jpg)
Calibers and year of introduction: 1955 - 308; 1956 - 243, 358
With their ballistics research in combination with the U.S. Government nearing fruition and with three new cartridges in the offing, Winchester developed a short-action modern rifle to accommodate them. The Model 88 had a (visibly) hammerless lock system and a detachable box magazine. It was lightweight and a scope sight could be conveniently mounted atop, something never before possible on a Winchester lever-action rifle— all this while requiring only a short throw of the dearly beloved old lever to chamber a thoroughly modern round!

Having been introduced in 1955, the M88 is the last model to find inclusion within the scope of our work, yet it was an important milestone in post-War Winchester history. It was also the last design of a high power lever-action rifle by the Company which had given birth to a generic term that not only had survived, but had been the stuff of legend for over 80 years: the Winchester Repeating Rifle.

Note: There are eighteen calibers discussed in this chapter. Many are non-Winchester calibers of limited interest to the average collector and are presented here in the interest of completeness. Others, indeed most, exist only in the various one-piece boxes which, as has already been shown, exhibit a high degree of similarity among the various calibers. As a result the authors have chosen not to show all the calibers in this chapter in many of their iterations, relying instead on a few examples illustrative of each of the many calibers covered herein. The inclusion or omission of any particular box style should in no way be taken as an indication of its relative rarity or value.

22 Winchester Hornet, 22 Hornet

Catalog Listings: 1932-

Models: 54, 70, 43
Bullet types: SP, MCHP, FMJ
Powder types: Smkls
Headstamps: WRA, SS

Much as the old Black Powder 25-20 Single Shot evolved into the more compact Smokeless 25-20 W.C.F., the modernized 22 W.C.F. became the 22 Hornet. Though listed by the Company as the "Winchester Hornet" in the 1934 catalogs, it had actually evolved throughout the early 1900s, in Europe as well as the U.S., as a successful wildcat cartridge. As with several other attempts by Winchester to add their name to a cartridge not really their own, the "Winchester" part of the labeling was eventually dropped although it was Winchester that, in 1931, had set the Hornet's Industry Standards. The marketplace was quick to accept the Hornet, however, and by 1933 several gun-makers and ammunition manufacturers were committed to it, both at home and abroad.

The first loadings used a W.R.A. headstamp and are much scarcer than the Super Speed designation which replaced it in 1934. The early headstamps, both "W.R.A." and "Super Speed", simply used the word "Hornet" rather than the later ".22 Hornet". A single lot of 48 grain Soft Points (45 grain was standard) was made in 1932 and would make a nice find for the collector.

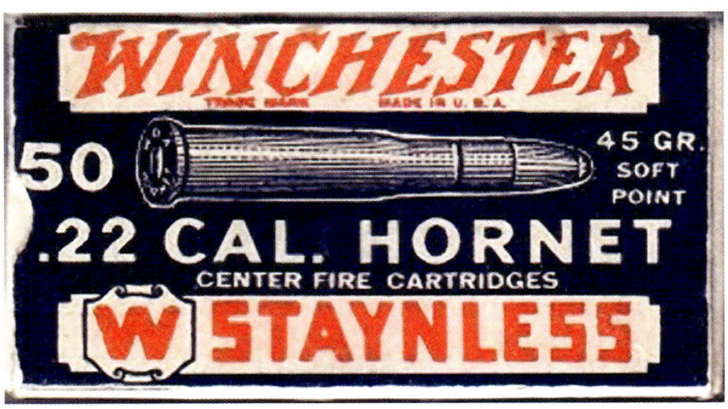

These 45 grain Soft Point boxes, in the "1928" style, were loaded in 1931 and 1932 before issuance of the "1932" style box. The Hornet having been first cataloged in 1932, this first style is rare. R3+/150-300

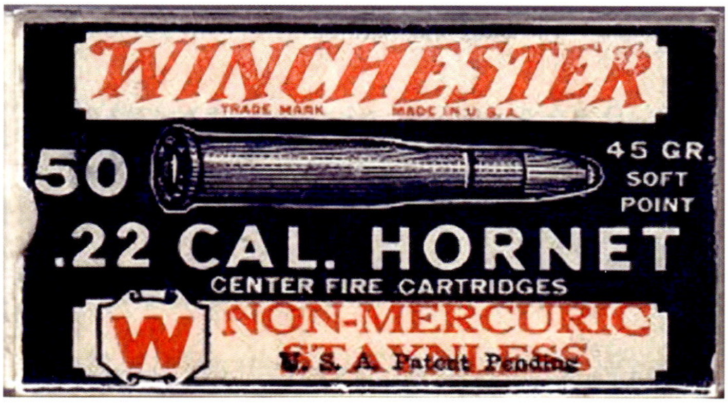

With the "Non-Mercuric" call-out definitive to the "1932" box style, this 45 grain Soft Point offering was also short-lived as the Super Speed offerings appeared in this caliber in 1934 (see below). Hollow Points, to the best of the authors' knowledge, are not found in the "1928" or "1932" box. R3/125-225

The 1934 introduction of Super Speed in this caliber gave rise to these unique, colorful graphics. The 46 grain Hollow Point is the loading most often found in this "1934" box style, but all are collectible. Soft Points are not known to the authors in this box. R3-/125-225

The sides of this "1934" Super Speed Hollow Point box also are interesting as can be seen in this picture and the one to follow.

The cartridge cut has a flat tip and appears in profile as a fully jacketed bullet, as would be appropriate for the Hollow Point loading. Compare this to side view of the Full Patch (FMJ) box below.

On the right is the Hollow Point, K-coded end flap from the box pictured above. On the left, the end flap of the much scarcer Full Patch loading, K-2210T.

The very scarce Full Patch loading in the early ("1934") Super Speed box. R3+/150-250

The Full Patch cartridge cut more resembles a Soft Point profile and tip.

The "1935" Hollow Point box appears to have been introduced in this caliber circa 1938. As such, it can be said to have had a relatively short life. It is thought that FMJ offerings remained in the "1934" box while the Soft Point loading joined the Hollow Points in the new "1935" style. R2+/100-175

Side view of the "1935" box which pre-dates the Western Cartridge Co. call-out. It is thought by the authors that this box was used past 1940 in this caliber.

The "1939" graphics on this Soft Point box, which so closely resemble those of the "1935" box but add the Western Cartridge Co. call-out, were used until at least 1947. R2/80-160

The side view of the "1939" box showing the "Western" call-out.

A casual glance at the cartridge cuts in the Hollow Point and Soft Point "1939" graphics may not reveal any obvious difference between them. These close-ups, however, show that their portrayal is both definitive and accurate. This sort of accuracy and detail was not always found on early (mainly two-piece) boxes.

Sometime in late 1947 or early 1948, the Hornet finally found its way into the new "1946" style box. While all loadings had graphics identical to this Hollow Point box (right), the rarest one is the Full Patch loading as shown below. R1+/40-80

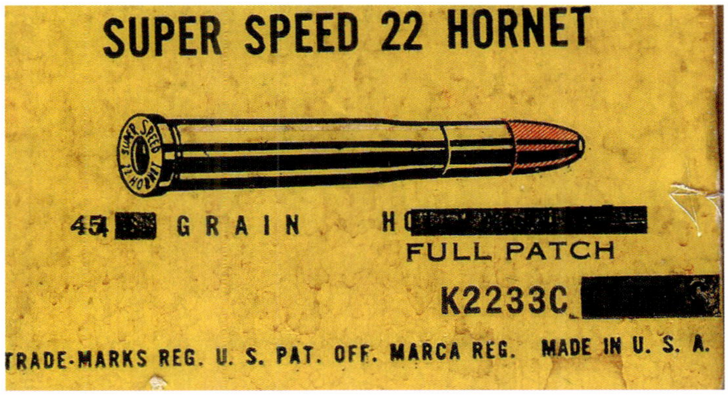

Unknown to the authors before this study, this commercial Full Patch box has a K-code not found in our exam nation of factory records. The K-code suffix was switched from a "T" suffix to a "C" suffix in 1947, narrowing its date range by one year to 1947-1952. While military FMJ loadings are fairly common, this commercial box, with its black-outs and over-stamps, was a great discovery! R4?/150-300

An Interesting and Rare Box

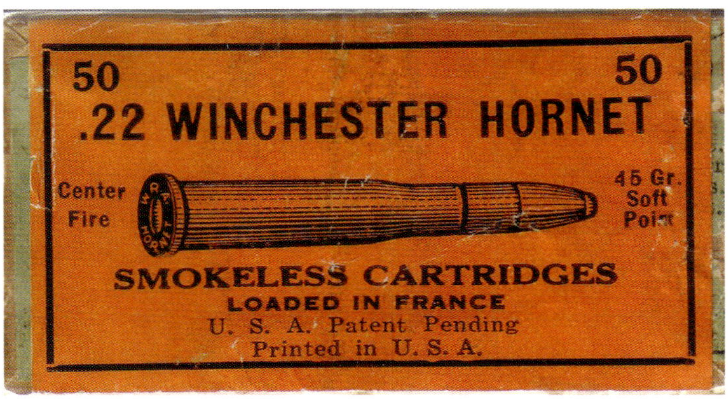

"Loaded in France" labels are found on many calibers of Winchester boxes; however, this is the only one known to the authors in 22 Hornet. The cartridge cut shows a "W.R.A." headstamp indicating production in the 1931-33 period. Also noteworthy is the absence of any mention of "Staynless" or "Non-Mercuric" in spite of the presence of "U.S.A. Patent Pending" which usually accompanies the latter call-out. R4-/150-300

The side-seal label of this rare "Loaded in France" box. No other Winchester boxes in this caliber are known in half-split, two-piece boxes such as this. Further, this is the only box of which the authors are aware that uses an abbreviation (S.P.) for Soft Point.

220 Winchester Swift, 220 Swift

Catalog Listings: 1936-

Models: 54, 70
Bullet types: SP, MCHP, FMJ

Powder types: Smkls
Headstamps: SS

Instant notoriety was assured when this cartridge was presented to the commercial trade as having a muzzle velocity of more than 4,000 feet per second. It shortly became equally famous for the speed with which it wore out rifle barrels. Winchester's ballistic engineering genius, Merton Robinson, had designed the light 46 grain Hollow Point bullet that was so successful in the Hornet and installed it in front of the much larger 6 m/m Lee Navy casing (with a 30-06 head), creating one of the highest velocity loadings in any caliber ever. As they did with the 22 Hornet, Winchester tried to make this a proprietary cartridge by naming it the ".220 Winchester Swift". And, as with the Hornet, the attempt failed.

A 56 grain hollow point was offered until 1940 but is seldom seen. Also, a 55 grain Pointed Soft Point was offered from 1940-1942 and is rare. According to factory records a "W" was to have been stamped on both of these bullet types & weights. That procedure was followed in order to distinguish between similar types of bullets in differing weights in the same caliber. The 56 grain Hollow Point was marked in order to distinguish it from the 46 grain Hollow Point and the 55 grain Soft Point was marked to distinguish it from the 48 grain Soft Point. A picture of the Loading Card calling for the "W' marking is shown below.

Finally, there was a 46 grain Pointed FMJ cataloged in 1937 (only) but no such loading is to be found among factory records nor has it been seen by the authors.

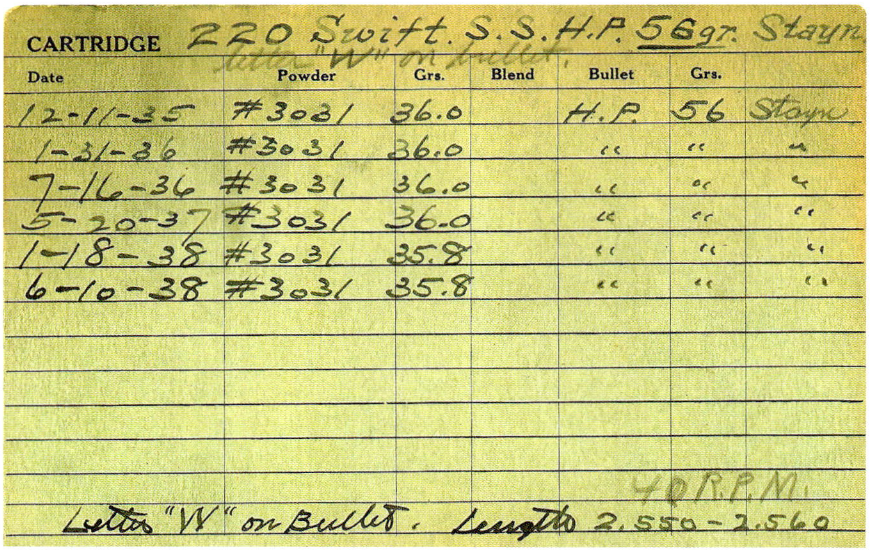

CARTRIDGE 220 Swift. S.S. H.P. 56gr. Stayn
Letter "W" on bullet.

Date	Powder	Grs.	Blend	Bullet	Grs.	
12-11-35	#3031	36.0		H.P.	56	Stayn
1-31-36	#3031	36.0		"	"	"
7-16-36	#3031	36.0		"	"	"
5-20-37	#3031	36.0		"	"	"
1-18-38	#3031	35.8		"	"	"
6-10-38	#3031	35.8		"	"	"

40 R.P.M.
Letter "W" on Bullet. Length 2.550-2.560

Loading Card calling for the "Letter 'W' on bullet" (see both second line and bottom line).

In the "1935" box with the "Winchester Repeating Arms Co..." line, we see here an example of the earliest 220 Swift box as well as Winchester's futile attempt to turn yet another cartridge into a proprietary caliber. R2+/100-175

Comparing the above box with this "1939" box, we find that the only difference is the absence of the "Winchester Repeating Arms Co..." call-out. The primary differences are to be seen below. R2/75-125

The top (or back) edge, the upper photo being the "1935" box with Super Speed logo and the lower being the "1939" box with the "...Western Cartridge Co" call-out.

The lower (or front) edge verbiage containing the Company guarantee. Again, the "1935" box with its Super Speed logo is on top.

On the end flaps the graphics are identical except for the K-code representing the Pointed Soft Point loading. Of interest, however, is the fact that the K-code change from K2221C to K2225C occurred in 1947. This illustrates the fact that certain box styles were occasionally "leap-frogged" in certain calibers. In this case, there were no "1945" 220 Swift boxes. Graphics of this caliber in the "1946" box are virtually identical to those of other calibers and we refer the reader to the following (243 Winchester) section of this work for pictures of that box style.

243 Winchester, 6 m/m Winchester
Catalog Listings: 1955-

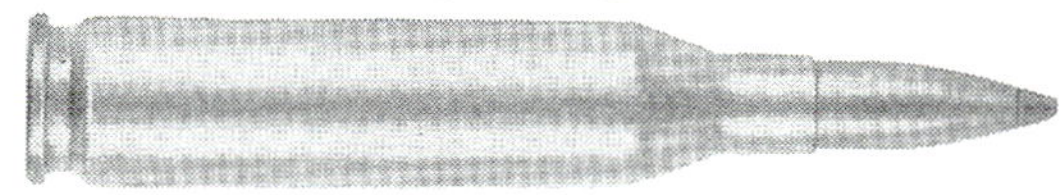

Models: 70, 88
Bullet types: SP
Powder types: Smkls
Headstamps: SS

First announced to the trade in 1953 as the "6 m/m Winchester", this cartridge was the result of the Company's work with the U.S. Government on the development of the 7.62 NATO round (commercially, the .308 Winchester). An early and scarce "Super-X 6 m/m Winchester" headstamp is known on experimental loadings but was apparently not released commercially. The only style box for either the M70 or the M88 that is considered highly collectible is the "1954" box which was parenthetically marked "6 m/m".

The only 243 box within the scope of this book is this "1954" style graphic with the prominent and distinctive "(6 m/m)" call-out. R2/50-100

The "Olin Mathieson Chemical..." call-out distinguishes the "1954" box from previous iterations.

The lower back side of the typical "1954" graphic shows a blurb in fine print outlining the suitability and ballistics of the specific load found in that box.

250-3000, 250 Hi-Power, 250 Savage Hi-Power, 250 Savage

Catalog Listings: 1925*-

Models: 54, 70
Bullet types: SP, MCHP, FMJ, ST
Powder types: Smkls
Headstamps: WRACo, WRA, SS

A Savage Arms introduction of a Charles Newton development, this is one of the greatest of the early high-performance cartridges and remains a very competitive ballistic performer even today. The "3000" figure referred to the muzzle velocity of its 87 grain loading, a statistic so impressive at the time of its announcement in 1914 that it became part of the cartridge's name, a practice unheard of before or since. Early two-piece boxes are very scarce, especially in FMJ. Silvertip loadings, surprisingly, are not at all common, but the 100 grain Hollow Points, first listed in 1936, are quite rare.

*This caliber is found in the Company's price lists in 1923 but wasn't listed in catalogs until 1925.

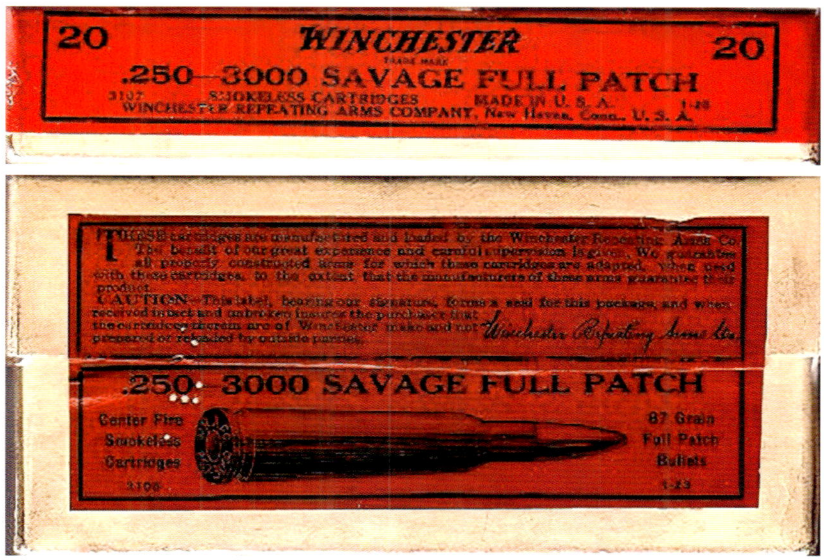

In 1923, nine years before it was chambered in their M54 rifle, Winchester introduced the 250-3000 Savage in their ammunition line. This 1-23 dated two-piece box, pre-K-code, is believed to be the Company's first FMJ offering in this caliber. R3-/100-200

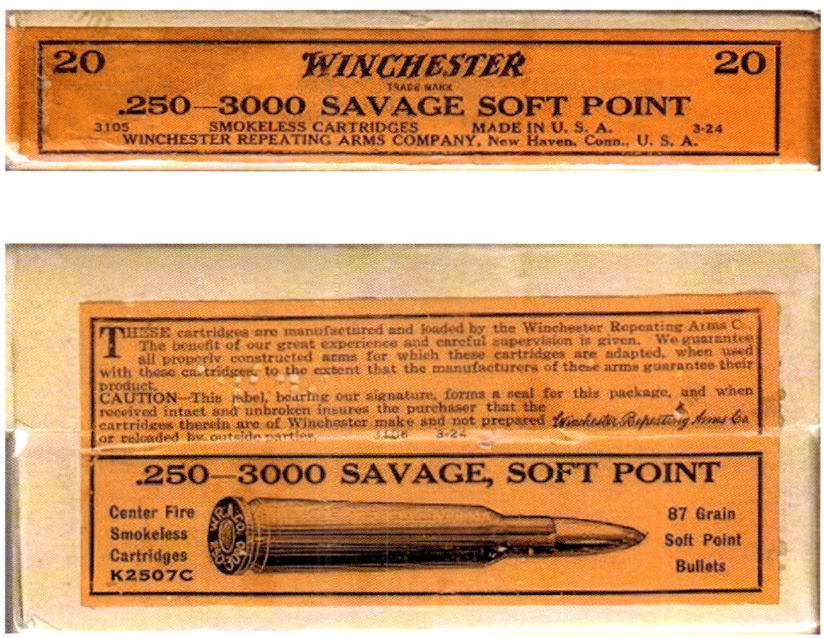

By the time this 3-24 dated two-piece box of 87 grain Soft Points was released it was K-coded. R2/80-160

The "Grizzly" box of 1940 in this caliber contained the 100 grain Silvertip loading. Neither the rare 100 grain MCHP nor any of the 87 grain loadings were offered in this box. R2/80-160

The seldom encountered "1945" box with the "Olin Industries..." call-out is shown here. The authors are uncertain as to which of the 1928/32 and 1935/39 box styles exist, but their characteristics are well-documented in many chapters within these pages. And though we don't have examples to show here, that fact should not be taken as evidence of their non-existence or even scarcity. R3-/75-150

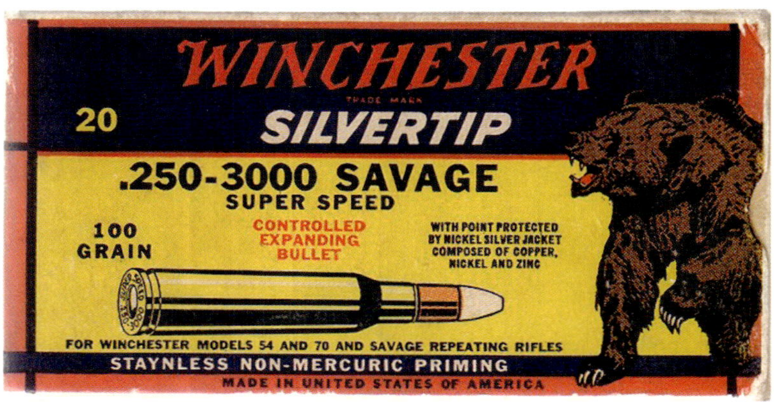

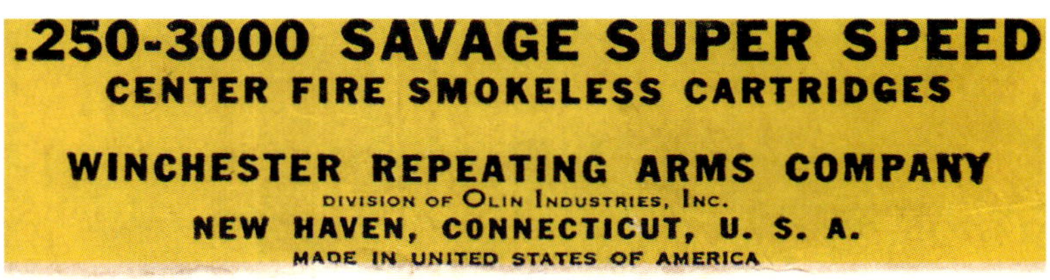

And even less frequently encountered is this "1945" Olin Industries Grizzly box. Very few calibers are known in the "1945" Grizzly box style. R3/125-200

25 Roberts, 257 Winchester Roberts, 257 Roberts

Catalog Listings: 1936-

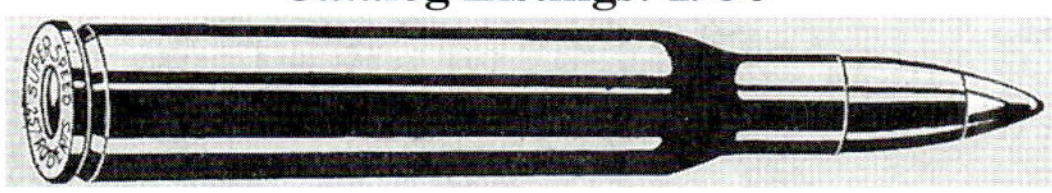

Models: 54, 70 **Powder types:** Smkls
Bullet types: SP, HP, Ptd Exp, ST **Headstamps:** SS

Based on the 7 m/m Mauser case, this great cartridge was drawn from the ranks of wildcat status by Ned Roberts during the 1920s. Remington also had a hand in its design and cataloged it prior to Winchester's 1936 introduction. The first headstamp was "25 Roberts" for both Winchester and Remington with Winchester being by far the rarer of the two. When the caliber was expanded to three digits both companies tried unsuccessfully to co-opt the name; as a result, boxes stacked side-by-side on sport-shop shelves in the mid-1930s could be found labeled "257 Winchester Roberts" and "257 Remington Roberts".

The 87 grain Pointed Soft Point in any pre-WWII box is very scarce. Silvertips are uncommon as are the 117 grain Hollow Points, last listed in 1940. As an additional point of interest, since all 257 bullet weights were loaded to the same over-all length, both Hollow Point weights would appear the same once loaded. Winchester stamped the 100 grain Hollow Point bullet with a "C" and the 117 grain Hollow Points with a "W" to differentiate between them on the loading line. Neither of these loads was listed after 1940, but if the collector ever has occasion to distinguish between these two bullet weights in order to determine the originality of the contents of a box, that ability is now yours. (How's that for a bit of arcana?)

This "1939" box is the second iteration of the ".257 Winchester Roberts" box, following the "1935" box (not shown). It is in the 100 grain Pointed Expanding loading, listed only 1940-42. The soon-to-be-popular Silvertip in the "Grizzly" box (not shown) was also first marketed in this bullet weight beginning in 1940, leaving us to speculate as to the relative rarity of this 100 grain Pointed Expanding offering. R3/100-200

The "1946" 100 grain Silvertip loading. This is the box that succeeded the Grizzly style box in that bullet type. Note that the claim to "Winchester Roberts" has been dropped in favor of simply "257 Roberts". R1+/40-80

A long discourse on the Silvertip bullet is found in the fine print on this lower back side of the "1946" box and mirrors the wording that had appeared on the back of Grizzly boxes.

270 W.C.F., 270 Winchester

Catalog Listings: 1925-

Models: 54, 70
Bullet types: SP, MCHP, Ptd, Exp, FMJ, ST
Powder types: Smkls
Headstamps: WRACo, WRA, SS

One of the most popular cartridges ever developed by Winchester, this caliber has earned its excellent reputation honestly. Accuracy, range, killing power, versatility, light recoil: all have been extolled by sportsmen and sports writers for 80 years. Based on the necked-down 30-'06, the 270 W.C.F. was the first of the Company's proprietary cartridges to exceed the "magic" 3000 fps standard that had been set by Savage's 87 grain 250-3000 eleven years earlier. The 270, however, exceeded that landmark velocity with 130 grain bullets.

In spite of its popularity, pre-war boxes in excellent condition, especially pre-Super Speed, are very difficult to find. All two-piece boxes are very scarce, the FMJ being rarer than Soft Points.

Thought to be the first offering, ca. 1924-25, this 130 grain Pointed Expanding label, though K-coded, has no date on any of the labels, a most unusual phenomenon for this period. Were it not for the fact that the FMJ box below is also undated, we'd say this was the only such box in our experience to exhibit this trait. R3/150-250

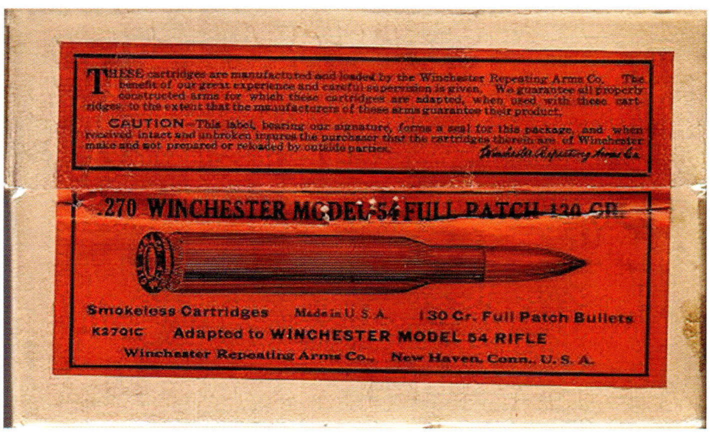

The early 130 grain Full Patch loading in the two-piece red label box, like the box above, is K-coded but undated. There was also a 150 grain Pointed Expanding box cataloged during the early 1930s which the authors have not seen; it would be interesting to note whether those labelings are also undated. R3+/175-275

An example of the scarce 1932 box, this 150 grain Soft Point is made even rarer by the "WRA" headstamps on the rounds within. These are recognized among cartridge collectors as being the most desirable headstamp in the 270 series. During the mid- to late-1930s, headstamps may be found in either the original "WRACo" designation, which had been in use since 1925, or the much scarcer "WRA". The authors believe that the "WRA" stampings appear only on cartridges loaded by the Company's East Alton factory. R3/125-225

Why this caliber was not marketed as a Super Speed offering when it was first loaded in 1936 is a mystery. As a result of that slight, however, it becomes one of the more collectible boxes in the "1935" series since all 270 loadings were dubbed Super Speed in the 1938 catalog just two years later. This one is the 100 grain Pointed Soft Point. R3-/100-175

In 1938, when the 270 was first offered as Super Speed in this "1935" style box, the new "1939" graphics were already close at hand. We will probably never know when the transition was actually made (timing was different from caliber to caliber and even loading to loading), it is safe to assume that the box pictured here is not a common one. R3-/100-175

In January of 1940, Winchester introduced their new Silvertip loadings in a limited number of calibers and bullet weights. Of equal importance was the unveiling of their new "Grizzly" or "Bear" box, a favorite of collectors ever since. It was offered in this caliber with the 130 grain bullet only. R2/80-160

Contrary to the belief of many, the Grizzly box shared the time line of this caliber with the "1939" box as well as those which succeeded it through ca. 1947. Loadings, however, remained separate, the Silvertip being offered only in the Grizzly box with all others being found either in this "1939" style box or the later "1945" style. This particular box contains 130 grain Pointed Expanding rounds. R2-/50-100

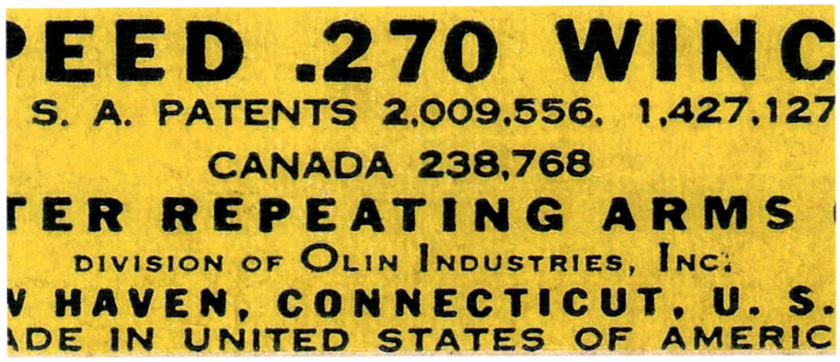

Identical on the front to the above "1939" box except for the bullet call-out, this is actually the scarcer "1945" box. This less common 150 grain Soft Point loading was, like the preceding box, offered concurrently with the Grizzly boxes. Also note use of a Canadian Patent. R2/60-120

In 1948 Winchester changed the 100 grain Pointed Expanding loading (K-code 2704C) to Soft Point. What we see here is an early transition box. What is most interesting is the fact that, rather than throw out the old boxes and use this as an occasion to transition to the newer "1946" style red and yellow box, the Company chose to black-out and over-print the old "1939" boxes. R3/75-150

The distinctive red and yellow style of the "1946" style box is now seen on this Super Speed 100 grain Soft Point offering, which, as we know from the comments and pictures above, did not debut in this loading until sometime after 1948. R1/25-50

After the discontinuance of the Grizzly box, the Silvertip offerings were marketed in the same "1946" style box as the other loads though graphics highlight the Silvertip bullet above the cartridge title. R1/25-50

With K-code, bullet call-out and cartridge cut, the side graphic offers more information than the box front.

As with the previous box, the bullet call-out, K-code and cartridge cut are on the side of the box.

30 G. 1906, 30-'06, 30 Springfield

Catalog listings: 1908-

For our introductory discussion of this great caliber, please refer to the chapter covering the Model 1895. As the early two-piece 30-'06 boxes have been covered in that chapter, we have opted to concentrate here on the later one-piece boxes, several of which are unique to this caliber and which represent some of the most colorful and interesting graphics ever designed by Winchester.

Headstamps remain "WRACo" in this "1932" box containing the 180 grain Pointed Expanding loading. R2/50-100

An example of the "1935" first Super Speed box, with rounds so-headstamped, also in the 180 grain Pointed Expanding loading. R2-/50-100

The "1939" box of Pointed Expanding 180 grain. These are not as common as might be expected because, beginning in 1940, they competed with the "Grizzly" box and its new Silvertip loadings. The 150 grain Pointed Expanding, which is not found in Grizzly boxes, would be expected to be somewhat more common; however, probably due to the greater popularity of the 180 grain, that has not been our experience. R1+/40-80

The more common of the two bullet weights to be found in the Grizzly box is this 180 grain Silvertip. The 220 grain is much scarcer. R2/85-150. [220 grain: R3/125-225]

These 180 grain Soft Points are in the "1945" box which, like the previous box, competed with the Silvertip "Grizzly" offerings, making it quite scarce. R2/50-100

Match Loadings

This very scarce loading is believed to be the first one-piece center fire box made by the Company, circa 1927. There is also an orange Soft Point box which is rare. R3/150-250 [Soft Point: R3+/175-300]

Having lost its distinctive color and graphics after only one year on the market, the Boat Tail Precision was soon to be found in basic "1928" graphics. It is also known in the very similar "1932" box style with the "Non-Mercuric" call-out over-printed in black on the red "Staynless". Like all Precision boxes, it is both scarce and very collectible in high condition. R2+/85-170

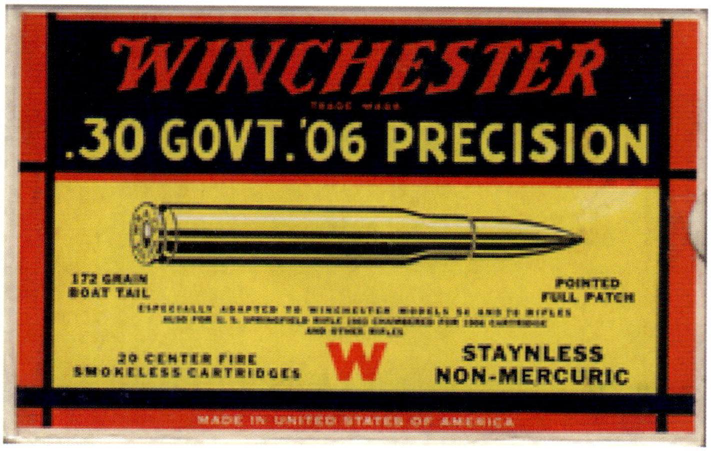

The "1939" Precision box, also scarce and desirable. In 1946, the very year it was discontinued, the Precision loading became 150 grains. Obviously, boxes of the 150 grain Precision loading are rarely encountered. R2+/75-150

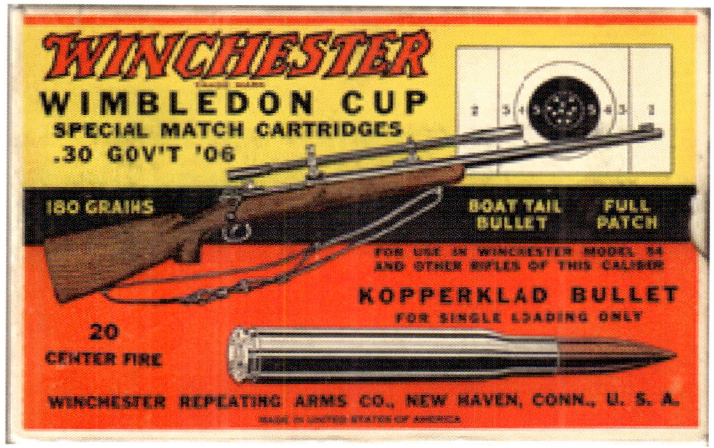

The first iteration of the great Wimbledon Cup box with its striking graphics, ca. 1936. These graphics also are seen with "1939" and "1945" call-outs. R2+/100-200

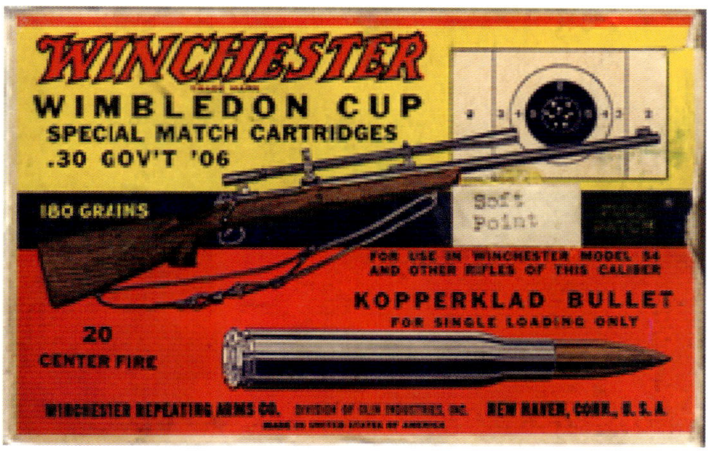

The very scarce Wimbledon Cup "Soft Point" loading with add-on label, circa 1946, with Olin Industries call-out. R3+/150-250

A new Wimbledon Cup Match graphic was introduced in 1947. It remained in the catalogs until after 1956. R2+/80-160

A Rarity: The Commercial Tracer Box

Commercial Tracers were rarely offered in any caliber and would be a salesman's order only, making this a seldom encountered offering. Circa late 1940s. R3+/150-250

300 H&H Magnum, 300 Holland & Holland Magnum

Catalog Listings: 1937-

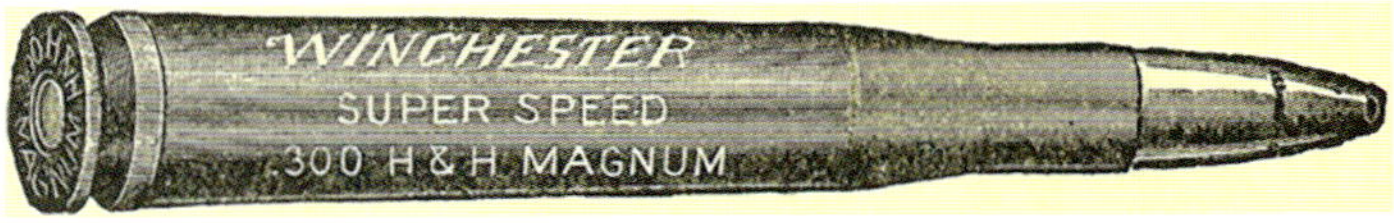

Models: 70
Bullet types: SP, HP, Ptd Exp, FMJ, ST, Match
Powder types: Smkls
Headstamps: WRA, SS

Although this caliber (along with its big brother, the 375 H&H Magnum) had been loaded by the Western Cartridge Company since the mid-1920s, it didn't become a Winchester catalog item until 1937, five years after Western's takeover of Winchester. Key to its rise in popularity was its success in the 1935 Wimbledon Cup Match and subsequent chambering in the new Winchester M70. Also, big game hunters had appreciation for its long-range accuracy and knock-down power, accounting for its success both in the American West and on the African veldt.

Early Match loadings were in two-piece boxes and are scarce. All boxes in which this caliber was issued during its first ten years as a Winchester catalog item are difficult to find in nice condition.

What is believed to be the earliest variety of the "1935" style box in which this caliber was introduced is displayed here. It is in the scarce 220 grain Soft Point loading. R3-/100-200

Here are the sides of the box as pictured above and below. As can be seen, the lower, slightly later, variety shows an additional patent date. Uncommon is the presence of a Canadian patent.

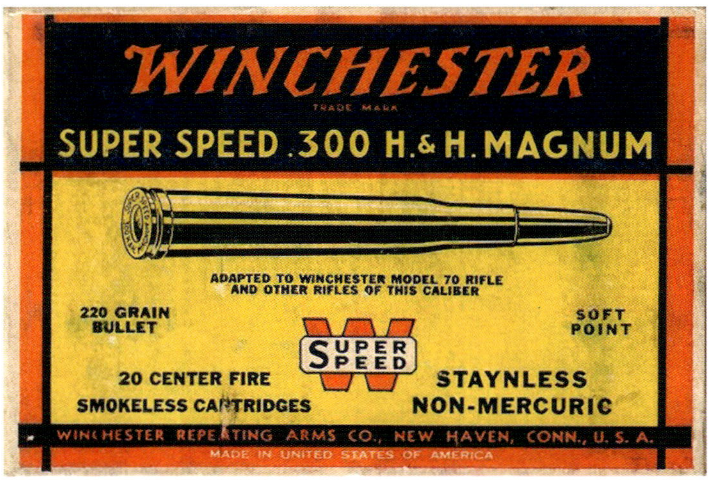

This 180 grain Hollow Point box is the most common of the Pre-war offerings. R2+/75-150

The "1939" box in 180 grain Pointed Expanding. Competing with the popular Silvertip loading, this box is somewhat scarcer than might be assumed. R2+/70-140

Here is the famed Grizzly box in a caliber that could, indeed, be considered worthy of "big game". This is in the lighter 180 grain Silvertip; a 220 grain was also offered and is much scarcer. R2/75-150 [220 grain: R3/100-200]

Also distinguished by the presence or absence of a patent date are these two varieties of the Grizzly box. The top one, displaying a 1935 patent issuance, is the older

Match Loadings

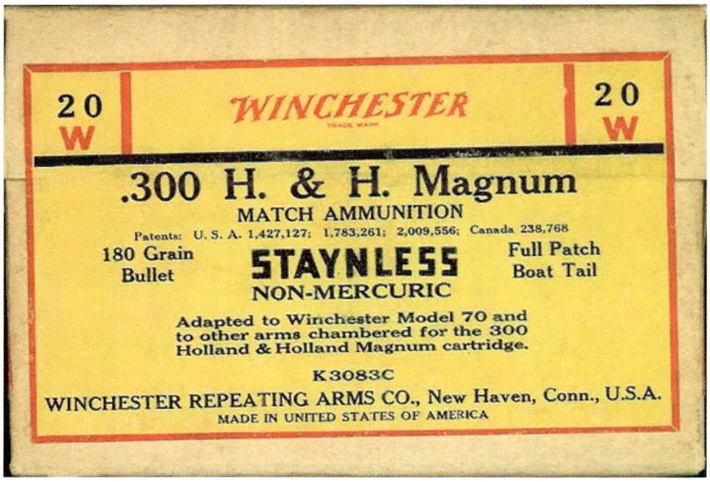

The only Winchester two-piece box to be found in 300 H&H is this Full Patch Boat Tail loading. Even though there is no Western Cartridge Co call-out, this caliber was made only at the East Alton facility and Match loadings continued to use this style label and two-piece box until WWII. R2+/100-200

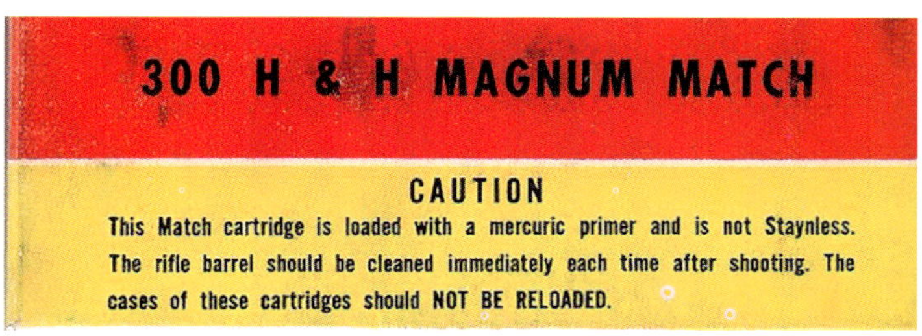

No longer using the Boat Tail bullet, this Post-War loading of 180 grain FMJ Match cartridges exemplifies the box used until the end our study in 1956. Of more interest, however, is the statement on the back of the box cautioning that "This Match cartridge is loaded with a mercuric primer and is not Staynless" then going on to recommend cleaning after each use and advising against reloading the brass. Since Staynless mixtures did not provide 100% ignition, the 300 H&H (as well as 30-06) Match loadings used a corrosive mercuric fulminate primer, essentially the same one as had been used in most Winchester military loadings since WW I. R2+/100-200

300 Savage

Catalog Listings: 1927-

Models: 70
Bullet types: SP, MCHP, ST, FMJ
Powder types: Smkls
Headstamps: WRACo, SS

Another Savage development, the 300 Savage was introduced by that company in 1920 in an attempt to approximate 30-'06 ballistics in a shorter-cased round which would function in their Model 99 rifle. It did garner some success in that attaining that goal and Winchester began offering it in 1927. That year being the introductory year for the phasing-in of the Company's new Staynless priming and one-piece box packaging, it is interesting to note that both one- and two-piece box types were used that year. Even more interesting is the fact that the late-1927 one-piece Staynless boxes did not contain Staynless-primed rounds as the new priming was not compatible with the powder type used in this caliber. This casing formed the basis for the 7.62 NATO which Winchester then managed to adopt as their own proprietary cartridge, the 308 Winchester.

Two-piece Soft Point boxes are rare and two-piece FMJ scarce. All the pre-war offerings are uncommon at best.

In 1927, the year Winchester introduced Staynless priming , the Company also cataloged the 300 Savage for the first time. This is an example of a "1928" one-piece box in Soft Point, the earlier two-piece style being very rare in this caliber. Continuing the older style, it is believed that the FMJ loading was marketed in two-piece, red label boxes during this period. R2/50-100

The "1935" Soft Point box is only slightly more common than its predecessor types, all Pre-war boxes being scarce in this caliber. Interestingly, a lone Super Speed FMJ loading is found on a 1936 Loading Card (see below) leading us to believe a rare "1935 box in FMJ exists out there somewhere! R2/50-100 [FMJ]: R3+/125-250

This "1939/1945" style box front might appear to be quite common, but as this Soft Point loading ran concurrently with the much more popular Grizzly series, it is actually somewhat scarce, especially inasmuch as a "1945" box is also known to exist. The later "1946" and "1954" red and yellow boxes, while not shown here, display essentially the same graphics as other calibers in those styles, differing only in the caliber call-out and bullet weights. ["1939": R2+/40-80; "1945" Olin: R3-/65-125]

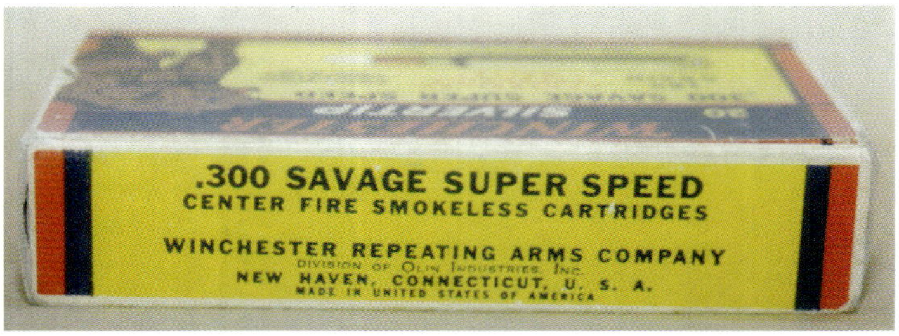

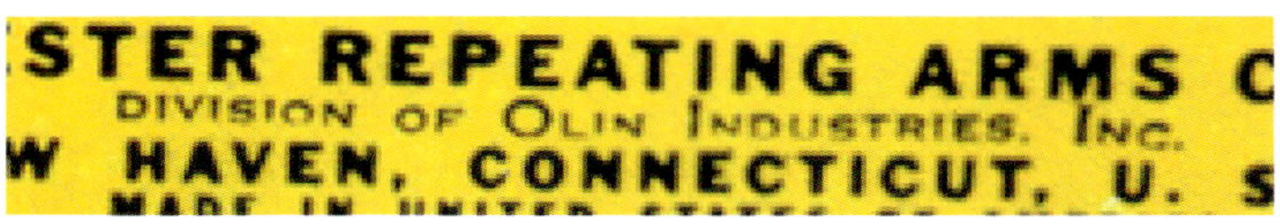

What appears to be an odd view of a 300 Savage Grizzly box is explained by the "1945" Olin Industries call-out, a rarity among Bear boxes. It is not yet known which calibers are to be found in this style. R2+/100-175 (Photos courtesy of Bill Hartman)

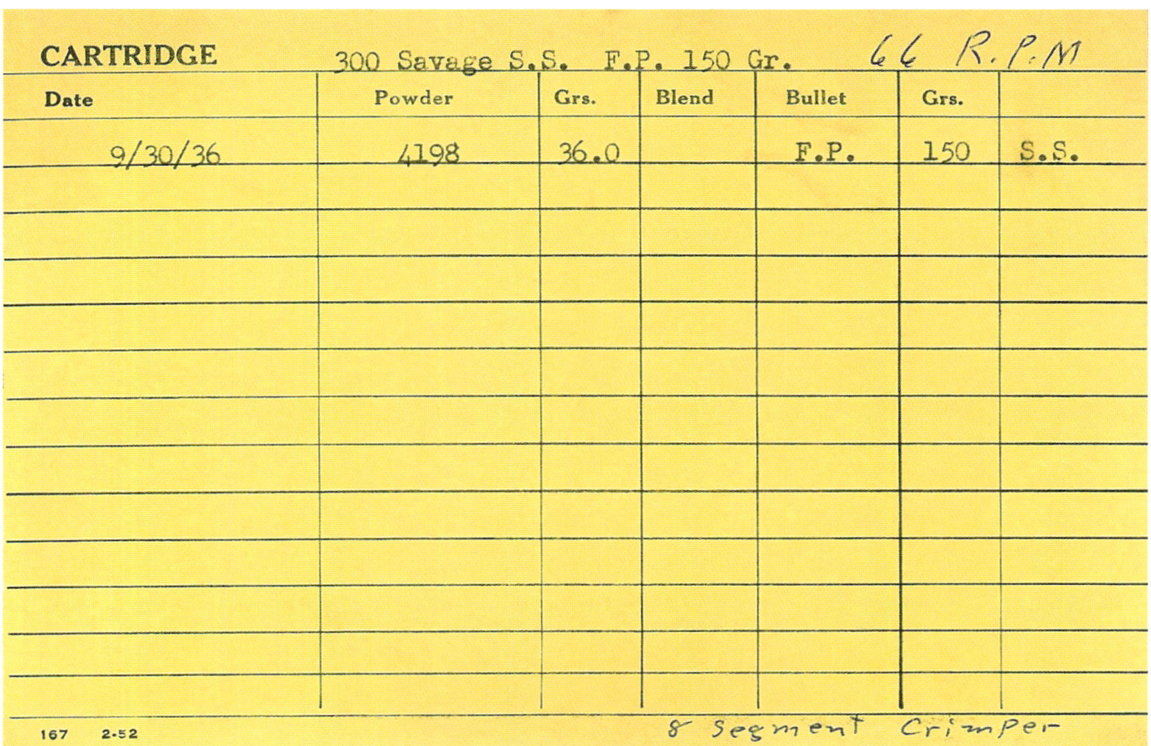

CARTRIDGE 300 Savage S.S. F.P. 150 Gr. 66 R.P.M

Date	Powder	Grs.	Blend	Bullet	Grs.	
9/30/36	4198	36.0		F.P.	150	S.S.

167 2-52 8 Segment Crimper

Loading Card for the rare 1936 Super Speed FMJ loading.

308 Winchester
Catalog Listings: 1952-

Models: 70, 88
Bullet types: SP, ST
Powder types: Smkls
Headstamps: SS

Winchester had worked with the U.S. military in the late-1940s and early-'50s on developing the 7.62 NATO, a round with ballistics similar to the 30-'06 but in a shorter case and capable of being used in a variety of medium-action rifles. This had become possible through the great improvements that had been made in Smokeless powders during and after WWII. Derived from the 300 Savage and 30-'06, the 308 became one in a series of military trial Homologous* calibers. As they were involved with the military in this project, Winchester, in like fashion, went on to develop the 243 and 358 from this basic 308 case. Needless to say, the 308 gained world-wide attention not only because of its compactness and ballistics but because, by the mid- to late-1950s, it had become an international military round.

*The Homologous Series was based on the necking up or down of one basic case size to form (in this case) 18, 22, 25 and 27 caliber experimental cartridges. Headstamps on these were dated as opposed to earlier experimentals which were unheadstamped. None were distributed commercially.

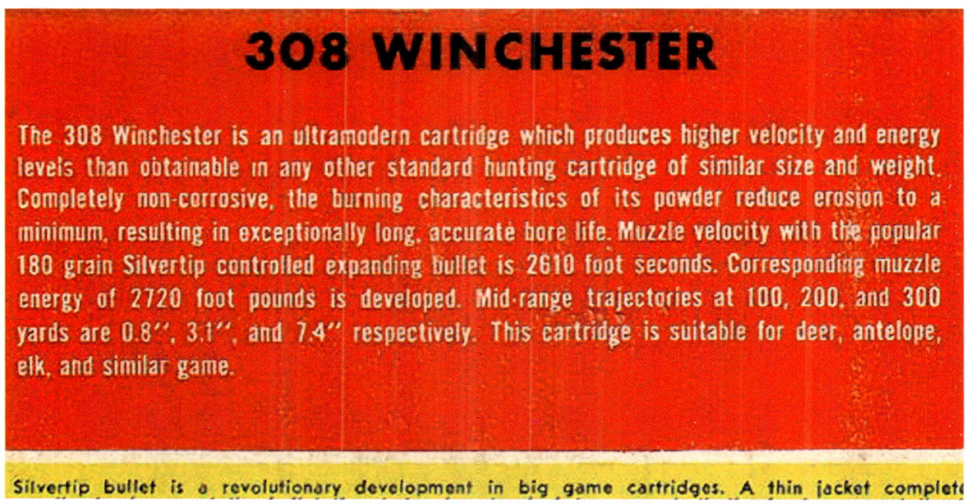

The early 180 grain 308 Silvertip box with its "Olin Industries" call-out on the side is much like the other boxes in the "1946" series. A significant difference, however, is to be found on the back where a full paragraph is devoted to touting the ballistics and suitability for big game of this "...ultramodern cartridge which produces higher velocity and energy levels than obtainable in any other standard hunting cartridge of similar size and weight". Except for a corresponding change in the ballistics, the boxes for other bullet weights in this caliber were the same. R2-/20-40

35 Rimless Remington, 35 Remington Auto Loading, 35 Remington, 35 Rem.

Catalog Listings: 1907-

Models: 70
Bullet types: SP, ST, FMJ
Powder types: Smkls
Headstamps: WRACo, WRA, SS

Remington shortened the then-new 30-'06 case and necked it up to .35 in order to create the most powerful cartridge in the series that introduced their semi-automatic M8. Winchester began loading it almost immediately but didn't offer it in any of their own rifles until 1941 (and then only briefly), yet another example of the Not-Invented-Here Syndrome at work. It is the only one of the four calibers Remington developed in those early years for the M8 and M81, as well as their later pump-action M14 and M141, rifles that is still being produced.

FMJ two-piece boxes are quite scarce, with very early and late examples being even less common than those from the 1910-30 period. Winchester 1940's "Grizzly" boxes are also hard to locate in this caliber.

Though dated 3-12, well before the M70 was introduced, we have deemed it appropriate to include some of the earlier boxes in this caliber in the interest of completeness. Here is a Soft Point box with the basic graphics of the 1907-1914 period. R3-/100-150

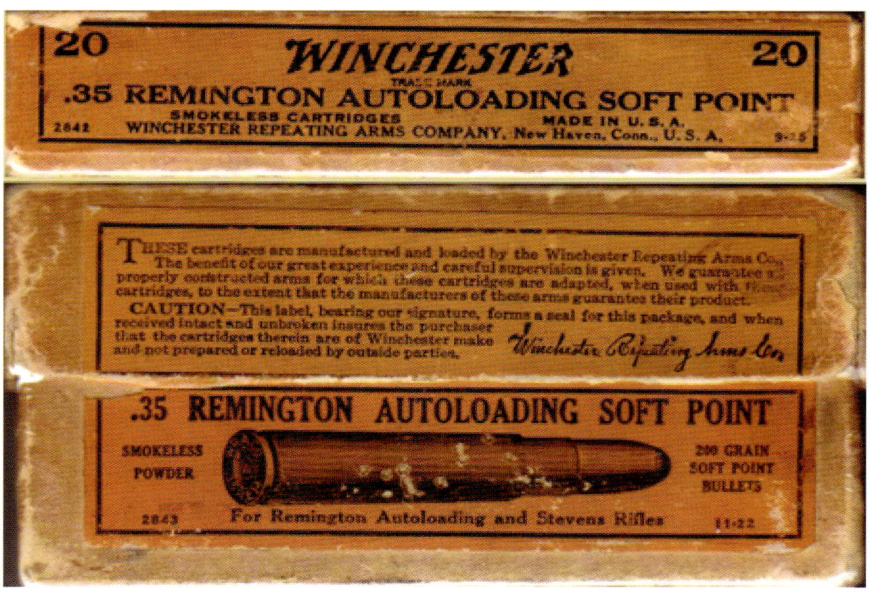

From the early 1920s, this Soft Point front label states "For Remington Autoloading and Stevens Rifles" on the bottom line, the same wording found on the foregoing box under the cartridge cut. It is also K-coded on the end labels. R2/60-120

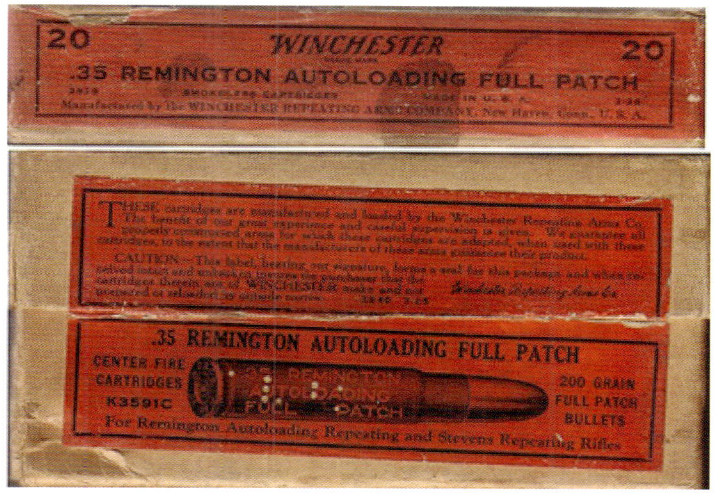

While the front label is dated 7-25 and the lid-top 2-26, this remains in the basic style of the box labeling begun in 1915 with the cartridge cut on the lower front. Note, however that the bottom line callout here reads "For Remington Autoloading Repeating and Stevens Repeating Rifles". This is the box that took the FMJ loading into the Staynless period beginning in 1928 and, it is believed (with over-print callouts for Staynless and Non-Mercuric) to the end of the FMJ listing in 1940. R3-/100-175

Lacking a Non-Mercuric call-out, this FMJ box is circa 1928-32. Both the front (not shown) and lid-top labels are, except for the large "Staynless" over-print, identical to the 7-25 and 2-26 labels on the previous box. R3-/100-175

This "1932" box, calling out Non-Mercuric, is from the 1932-36 period. R2-/40-80

In the basic graphics which are now familiar to the reader also as "1935" and "1939" boxes, this "1945" box with the "Olin Industries" call-out represented the Soft Point offering in this caliber, succeeding the "1932" style. This box is circa 1945-47. R2+/60-120

The Silvertips were introduced in the "Grizzly" box which was initially offered in 1940. Though fairly common in the Western Cartridge Co "Standing Bear" boxes of the same period, this is not a particularly easy caliber to find in the Winchester "Grizzly" box. R2+/75-150

358 Winchester
Catalog Listings: 1955-

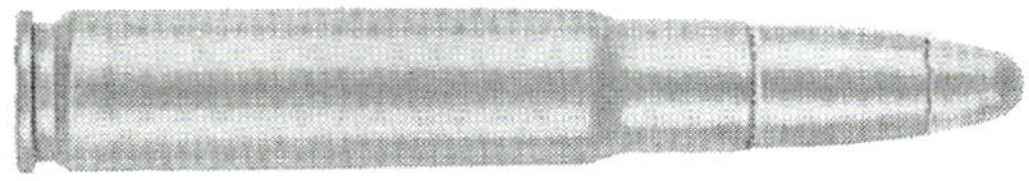

Models: 70, 88
Bullet types: ST

Powder types: Smkls
Headstamps: SS

Based on the necked-up .308 case, the 358 Winchester was one of the Homologous Series* of calibers developed from the 7.62 NATO/ .308 for the Company's new M88 medium-action lever gun. The M70 Featherweight also was introduced in this caliber. Early boxes, in the "1954" style, call out "8.8 m/m Winchester" parenthetically on the title line and are the only really collectible boxes in this caliber, the 250 grain loading being scarcer than the 200 grain.

*See .308 Winchester section for a more complete explanation.

In 1955, the year prior to the end of our study in this book, Winchester debuted the 358 Winchester in the "1954" style box. Most interesting is the prominent "8.8 m/m" call-out, eventually dropped as the cartridge was never referred to in that manner. R2-/25-50 [250 grain: R2+/40-75]

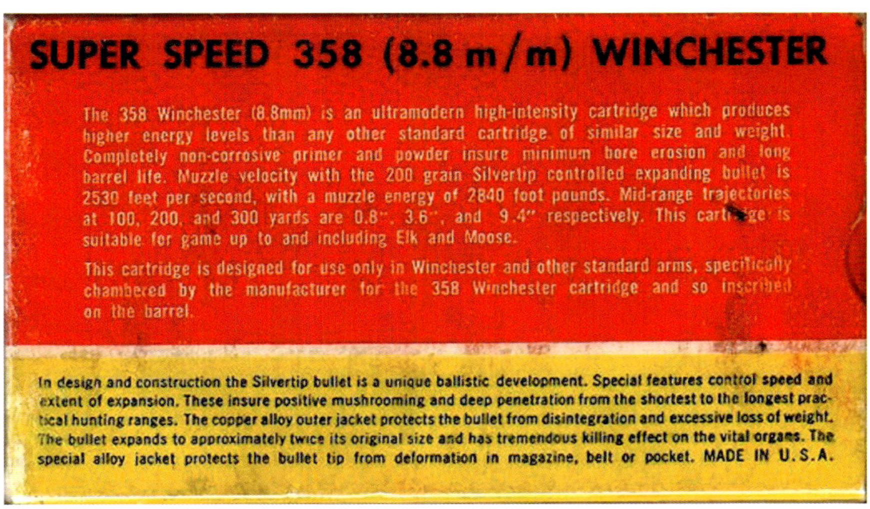

Unlike most of the "1946" and "1954" boxes, which show very similar graphics on both front and back, this earliest 358 box devotes most of the back side (white print on red background) to ballistics and appropriate use of this then-new cartridge offering. The bottom part (in yellow section) is the familiar Silvertip exposition.

375 H&H Magnum, 375 Holland & Holland Magnum
Catalog Listings: 1937-

Models: 70
Bullet types: MCHP, SP, ST, FMJ
Powder types: Smkls
Headstamps: WRA, SS

Long considered a versatile British big game caliber, this is the belted rimless version of the popular Holland & Holland Flanged (rimmed) Magnum for which so many English double rifles were chambered. As with the 300 H&H, Western had loaded the 375 H&H since 1925 and, with the introduction of the M70, Winchester evidently felt that a caliber of African proportions, so to speak, would top off the line.

Some of the earliest Winchester boxes were two-piece and are rare. Like the 300 H&H, early one-piece boxes, including the "Grizzly" box, are also scarce in excellent condition. This is especially true of the seldom-seen 235 grain Open Point Expanding. The 300 grain FMJ box is not known to the authors but is shown by factory records to have been loaded. This would obviously make a great find.

A very early and rare two-piece 375 H&H Magnum box in 270 grain Soft Point. Considering that the "1935" box graphics were well into the marketing system by 1936, especially in new offerings such as the 375 H&H where there was no old stock to use up, it is remarkable to find this caliber in a Winchester box such as this. With no mention of the M70 on the label, it is obvious that this box pre-dates the introduction of the 375 H&H chambering in that rifle. R3-/80-160

The "1935" box was the next Winchester style in which this caliber appeared, though obviously not as early as 1935. As in the two-piece box above, this is the 270 grain Soft Point offering. All of these pre-war boxes are very scarce and collectible. R3-/80-160

In 1936-37 Winchester listed a 235 grain Open Point Expanding under the K3750C product code. Then, in 1939 and 1940, they listed this 235 grain Hollow Point under the same K-code. After 1940 neither ever appeared again. R3-/100-175

The Grizzly boxes were cataloged in both the 270 grain and 300 grain Silvertip bullet weights and, being a true Big Game caliber, are among the most sought-after boxes in the series. They are also among the more difficult to find in high condition. Unlike most Grizzly boxes with two bullet weight offerings, the scarcer in this caliber is the lighter weight (270 grain) bullet. R2+/100-200 [270 grain: R3-/125-225]

Post-war "1946" boxes housed both Silvertip and standard Soft Point loadings. Silvertips, however remained in the Grizzly box until ca.1948. The back side of this box has the "fine print" Silvertip verbiage typical of this series. R1+/40-80

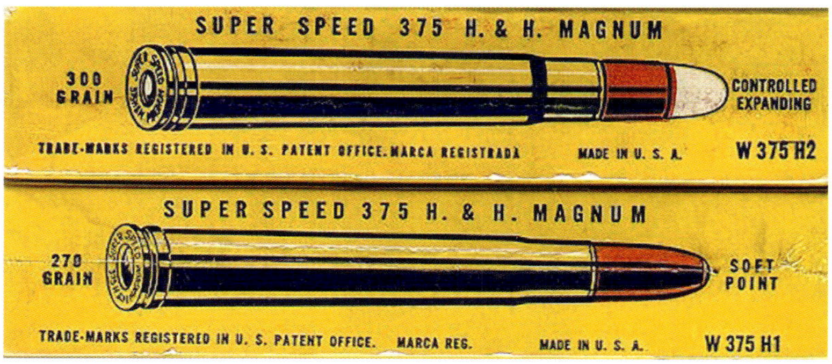

The sides of the 300 grain Silvertip and 270 grain Soft Point boxes, ca.1952-53, with the K-codes having been replaced by the later W-codes.

Front view of the 300 grain "1954" Soft Point box, the last with which our study is concerned. The back side of this box is identical to the front. R1+/35-75

458 Winchester Magnum
Catalog Listings: 1956-

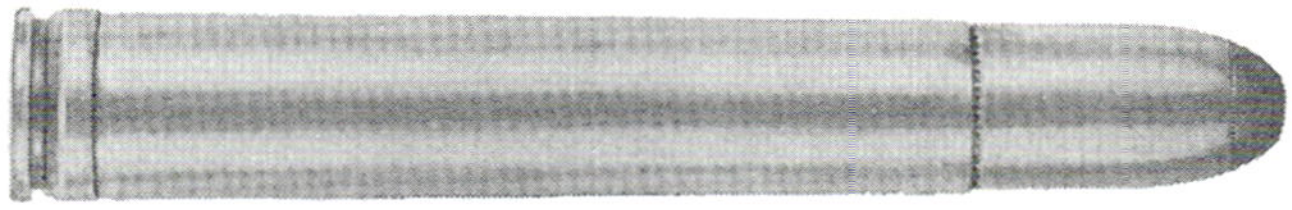

Models: 70
Bullet types: SP, FMJ
Powder types: Smkls
Headstamps: Winchester

Capable of taking the largest game offered on any continent, the 458 became the most potent commercial cartridge ever developed by Winchester. It remains popular for the largest and most dangerous game hunted today in India and Africa. This caliber also represents the Company's first use of the full word "Winchester" in a modern commercial headstamp and it is notable that this head size formed the basis for the belted magnums the Company would develop in the 1960's. Introduced in 1956, the last year of our concentration of study in this work, it presents a fitting climax to Winchester's pioneering, development and marketing in the field of small arms ammunition.

Above: This "Experimental" marked end flap from the above box has been over-printed on a period 30-06 box, the graphics of which can be vaguely discerned beneath the red ink.

Right: The experimental 500 grain Full Patch loading was found in this "1946" style box, both sides of which are identically printed and stamped and which has no print on the side edges. The unheadstamped rounds are typical of prototype or experimental production. R3+/250-400

Both the first 510 grain Soft Point and the 500 grain FMJ loadings were offered in this "1954" style box with the "Olin Mathieson Chemical Co." call-out on one side edge. The other side edge called out bullet type and weight as well as the W-code. Note that the title has changed from "Winchester 458 Magnum" to "458 Winchester Magnum" R1/65-100

As with other 1952-56 cartridge introductions, the "fine print" at the bottom extols the uses, virtues, and ballistics of this new "ultramodern high-intensity cartridge". In this example, the Soft Point loading is recommended for "...dangerous game with medium and thin-skin". The Full Metal Case offering was labeled for "...game with heavy bones and thick skin."

7 m/m Mauser, 7x57m/m, 7m/m, 7m/m Spanish Mauser

Catalog Listings: 1899-

Models: 54, 70
Bullet types: SP, FMJ

Powder types: BP, Smkls
Headstamps: WRACo, WRA, SS

Having been developed by Mauser, it originally gained acceptance as a military cartridge after being adopted by Spain in the early 1890s, a move which was then followed by other Spanish-speaking countries in Central and South America. In fact, the August 1899, Winchester catalog in which this caliber is introduced says, "Adapted to Mauser Rifle used in Cuba". While a very competent sporting cartridge as well, its real popularity in the U.S. was the result of the large influx of surplus (read: cheap) Spanish Mausers into this country early in the 20th Century.

The collectibility of this caliber can be said to include any box except the 175 grain FMJ which is more common than most .22 boxes of recent vintage. Especially rare, however, are those boxes which have the cartridges held "in clips" and were offered from 1899 until 1920. Also of note are the 139 grain Pointed Full Patch loading and Black Powder Blanks (though not a catalog item), both of which should be considered very rare. While only the last three boxes pictured below are relevant to the Models 54 and 70, the unusual earlier and rarer examples of this very collectible caliber are shown in the interest of completeness.

Thought to be the earliest 7 m/m Mauser box, this rare two-piece Soft Point box exhibits both "Sunburst" stickers. The only labels on this box are the ones shown here. There are no back or end labels. Note the "Nickel Covered Bullets" line on the lid-top. The authors are not aware of this call-out on any other Winchester box. The simple call-outs and graphics on the lid front are also unusual. R3+/125-200

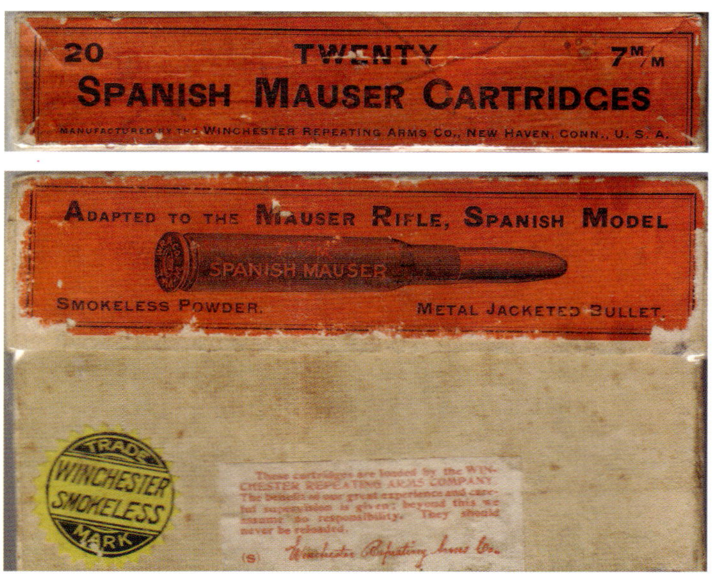

What appears by its labeling and coloring to be ca. 1901-02, this is another rare Soft Point box. With very little to go on, these labels are difficult to date with any degree of certainty. R3+/ 100-200

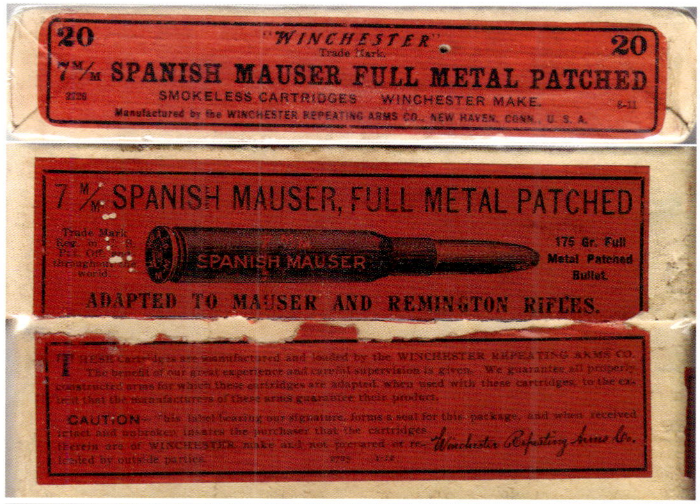

With label dates of 2-10, 8-11 and 1-12, the time period of this box is fairly easy to specify. By 1912 the label graphics and call-outs in this caliber had become "in synch" with the other calibers. R1/20-40

The 1929-1940 FMJ loadings remained in red or purple two-piece boxes and were over-printed with "Staynless" in gold ink. Although label-dated 9-19 this type label with its Staynless over-print was used as the Company's commercial Full Patch offering until its last appearance in the catalogs in 1940. R1+/50-100

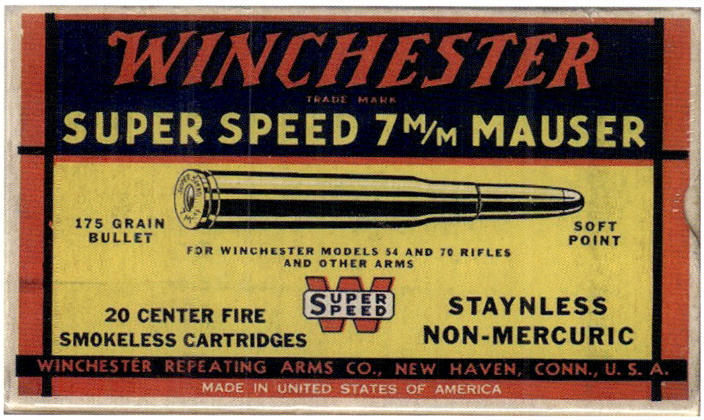

Soft Points, on the other hand, were transitioned into one-piece boxes; the "1935" style is shown here which we know lasted into at least 1940. It is not known whether this variety continued in use until the "1946" style was introduced or whether the "1939" and/or "1945" styles exist as well. R1+/50-80

The "1946" style with W-code dates this box to the 1952-54 period. Only the 175 grain Soft Point offering is found in this style box. R1/25-50

7.65m/m Mauser, 7.65x53m/m, 7.65m/m Belgian Model

Catalog Listings: 1900-1940

Models: 54
Bullet types: SP, FMJ

Powder types: Smkls
Headstamps: WRACo

With very few M54 (or other U.S. rifles for that matter) having been chambered for it and with more of a military than sporting presence, this can be a very difficult caliber to find in Winchester boxes, all of which are two-piece and most of which are found in poor condition. Pointed FMJ boxes are considerably scarcer than the Soft Points. Also difficult are the very early boxes (1900-1909) and the very late ones with the "Staynless" call-out. The many military contract issues were, of course, not catalog items and are not covered here; however, the uniquely headstamped "7.65 Belg." rounds found in boxes with special labels which emanated from a WWI Belgian contract are coveted by cartridge collectors.

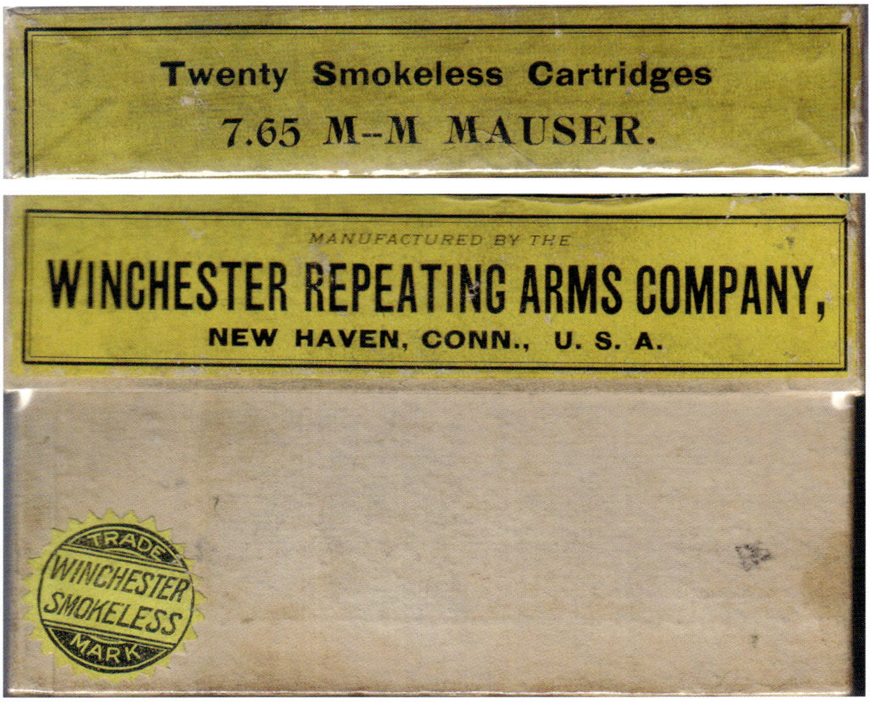

This earliest 7.65 Mauser box takes the prize for the plainest commercial box ever offered by Winchester. Ca. 1900, it reflects the minimum number of possible call-outs. The bold Sunburst "Smokeless" sticker stands out here as a redundancy. Even the bullet weight and type are omitted. Unusual also is the yellow label which, only a couple of years later, would denote the High Velocity Soft Point loading. R3+/150-300

An early red FMJ box with "red W" end labels dated 6-6, we have some help in dating this box. The primary labels shown here, however, are, in the authors' estimation, reflective of a somewhat earlier date. Note the tiny lettering calling out "Winchester Repeating Arms Co..." (bottom line on both top and front of lid). This type size in the Company call-out is found only in metric calibers. R3/100-175

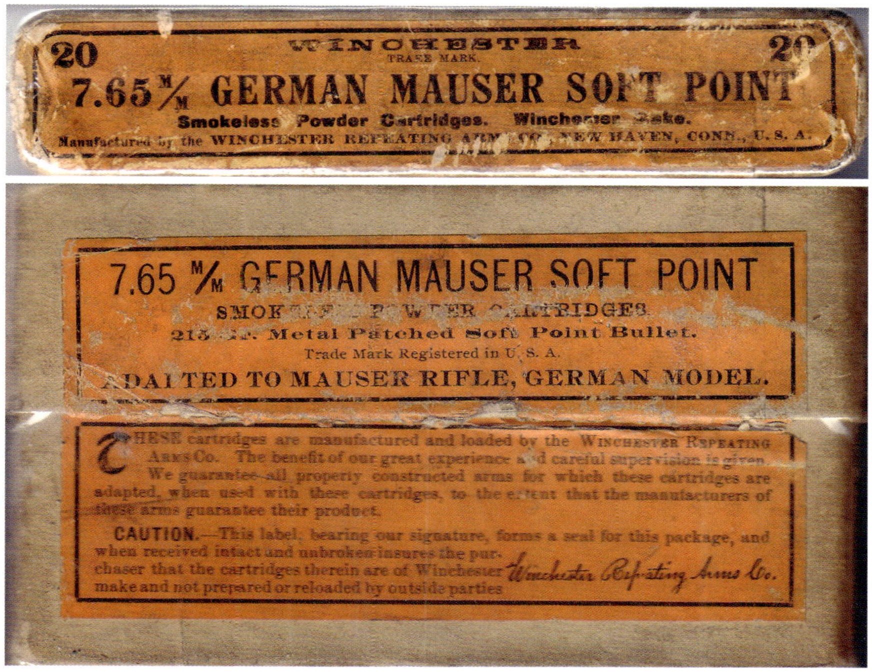

Even though there are dated (though unreadable) "red W" end labels, the undated primary labels on this Soft Point box are ca. 1903-05. This label design, unlike its predecessors in 7.65 Mauser, is much more in keeping with other calibers of the period. R3-/75-150

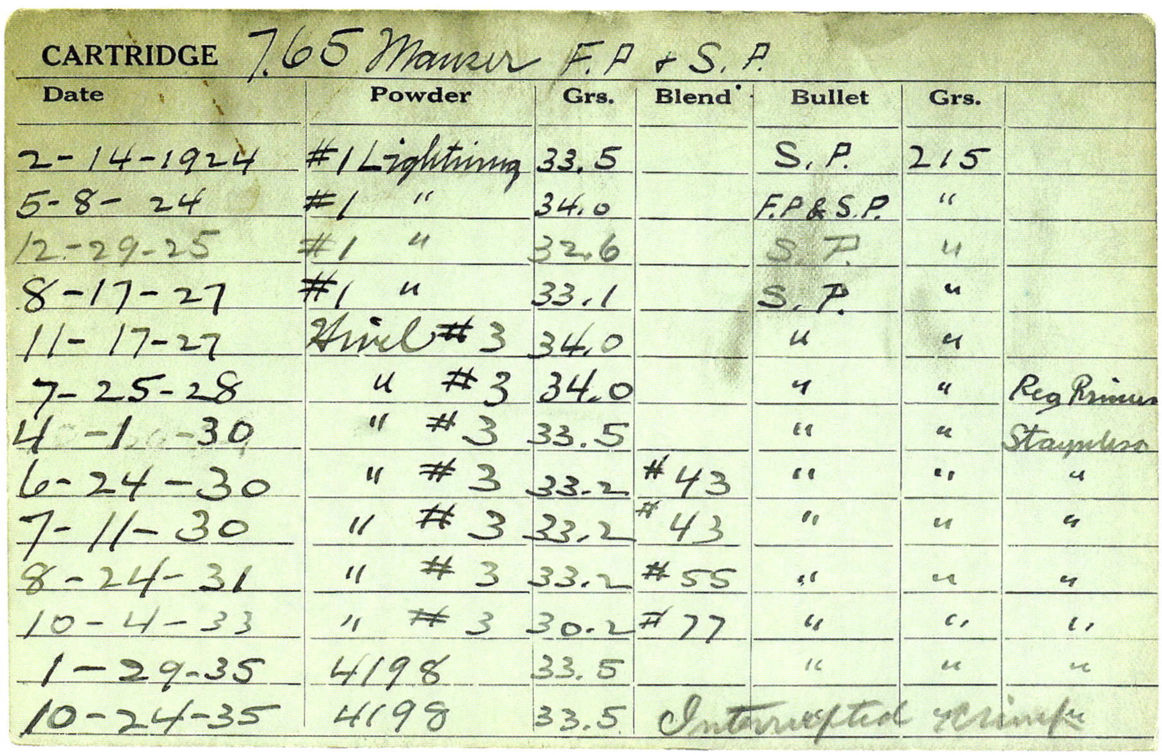

CARTRIDGE 7.65 Mauser F.P & S.P

Date	Powder	Grs.	Blend	Bullet	Grs.	
2-14-1924	#1 Lightning	33.5		S.P.	215	
5-8-24	#1 "	34.0		F.P & S.P	"	
12-29-25	#1 "	32.6		S.P.	"	
8-17-27	#1 "	33.1		S.P.	"	
11-17-27	Hivel #3	34.0		"	"	
7-25-28	" #3	34.0		"	"	Reg Primer
4-1[illegible]-30	" #3	33.5		"	"	Staynless
6-24-30	" #3	33.2	#43	"	"	"
7-11-30	" #3	33.2	#43	"	"	"
8-24-31	" #3	33.2	#55	"	"	"
10-4-33	" #3	30.2	#77	"	"	"
1-29-35	4198	33.5		"	"	"
10-24-35	4198	33.5	Interrupted crimp			

While offered in catalogs until 1940, this Loading Card shows that the last actual factory production run was 10-24-35.

9m/m Mauser

Catalog Listings: 1905-1940

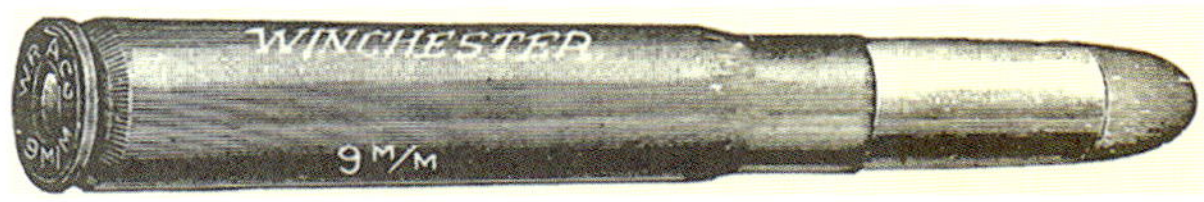

Models: 54
Bullet types: SP, FMJ

Powder types: Smkls
Headstamps: WRACo

The largest caliber of the Mauser "family" which derived from the 8m/m (or 7.9m/m), this one was more of a sporting caliber than the others, all of which had gained their initial acceptance as a result of military contracts. With significant quantities of 9m/m European sporting rifles having been imported and sold by New York jobbers, a demand had been created for the ammunition shortly after the turn of the 20th Century. It was not until some 20 years later, however, that Winchester decided to chamber their M54 rifle for what was, even then, a somewhat obscure caliber. All loadings were in two-piece boxes and are found about equally in FMJ and Soft Point. As with some of the other calibers, very early, undated boxes are quite scarce and late ones with a Staynless call-out are worth a small premium.

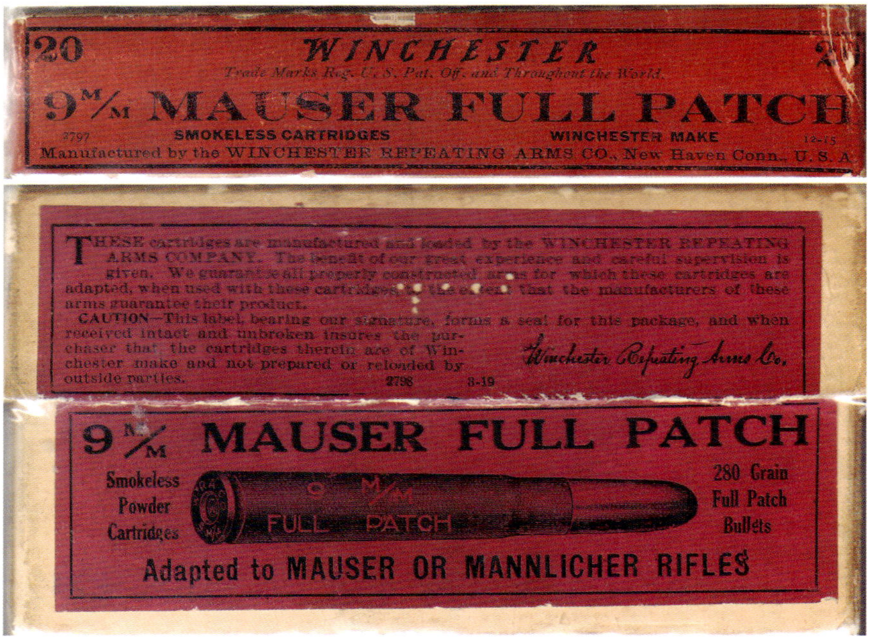

We regret that we don't have any very early boxes to show in this caliber, but we believe it can be safely assumed that the labeling in these boxes closely paralleled other calibers from the 1905-1914 period. Purple labels were common on the Full Patch (FMJ) boxes from the mid-Teens. R2+/75-150

Late for the style, this lid-top is dated 3-20 and exhibits all the details of boxes typical of the 1915-19 period. The front label, however, is dated 1-23 and is typical 1920s graphics (though pre-K-code). Like the earliest style in this caliber, the scarcity of the later Staynless boxes is exemplified by the fact that we don't have an example of one of those to show you either. R2/60-125

15

Winchester Boxes in Non-Winchester Calibers

As has been seen throughout this work, Winchester manufactured a line of cartridges that extended far beyond those chamberings offered by the Company in its own gun lines. And while we have, up till now, limited our study to those boxes and calibers specifically cataloged for Winchester's extensive offerings of rifles (and one little shot gun), we will here show no such constraint. Needless to say, there were a large number of significant and interesting guns — military and sporting, foreign and domestic — during the 1856-1956 period covered herein. We felt, however, that we should share with the reader some of our favorite Winchester cartridge boxes for which Winchester never chambered a gun model. Therefore we will examine here a number of collectible boxes in calibers for which *other* contemporary makers chambered *their* guns.

Rimfire Boxes

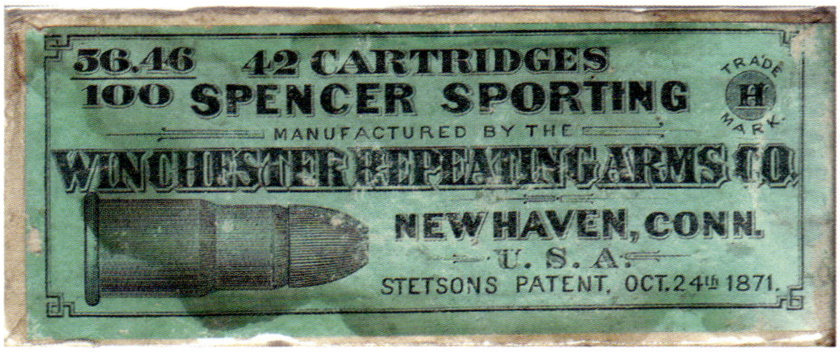

This lid-top label is from an early 1870s 56-.46 Spencer box of 42 rounds. The cartridges were contained in six unmarked flat packets of seven each and stood upright in the box. While this sort of packaging was common and used by various makers for Spencer calibers in the 1860s, it is rare in Winchester. R4/1000-1800

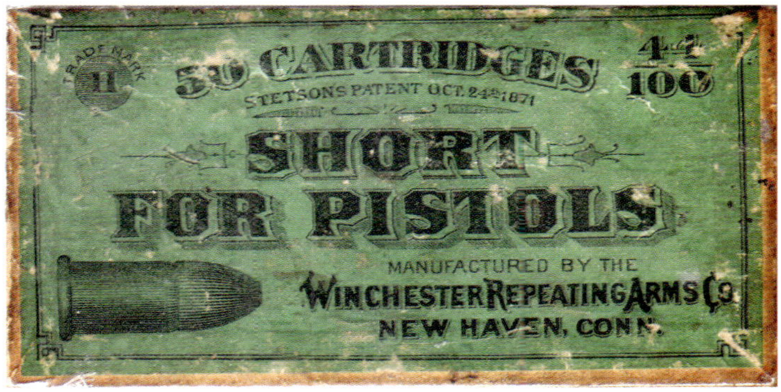

Also from the 1870s is this 44 Rimfire "Short for Pistols" box. The title distinguished this length from the 44 Rimfire Long and Extra Long rifle cartridges as well as the various Henry loadings of the period. R3+/300-600

Loaded in this country because of the large number of obsolete Swiss Vetterli military rifles (dating to the 1870s) that were sold here, the cartridge itself was effectually obsolete before 1900. Of special interest to Winchester cartridge box collectors is the fact that this is the only caliber, rimfire or centerfire, to have been offered in a 10-round two-piece, stand-up box with dividers. While not rare, there are many minor varieties that make for interesting collecting. R2/80-160

Center Fire Boxes (50-round)

This odd looking .25-25 Stevens round came in boxes of 20, 25, and 50, with this 50-round box being by far the rarest. R4-/250-500

A Smith & Wesson 32 S&W Revolving Rifle box is always a great find, no matter if Winchester or UMC. Fewer than 1000 of these rifles were manufactured in the 1879-1887 period and boxes of this caliber (by ANY maker) are rare. R4/750-1500

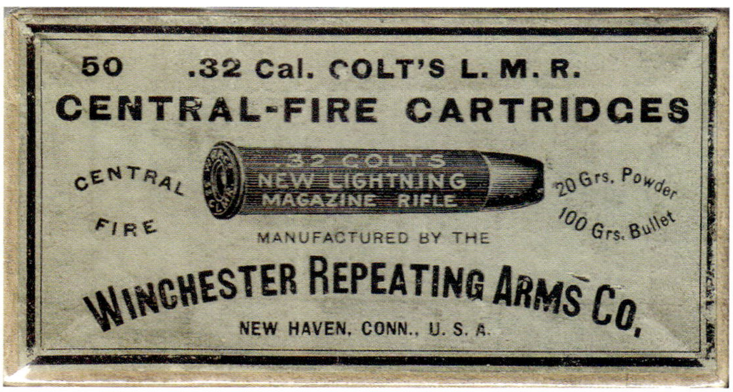

Winchester and Colt competed fiercely when Colt came out with their Burgess lever-action rifle in 1883 followed by their Lightning Magazine Rifle (L.M.R.) in 1884. While Colt quietly laid aside the Burgess in 1885, Lightning rifles were marketed until 1904. This Black Powder 32 CLMR box was for the medium frame gun and dates from the late-1880s or early 1890s. R3+/600-1200

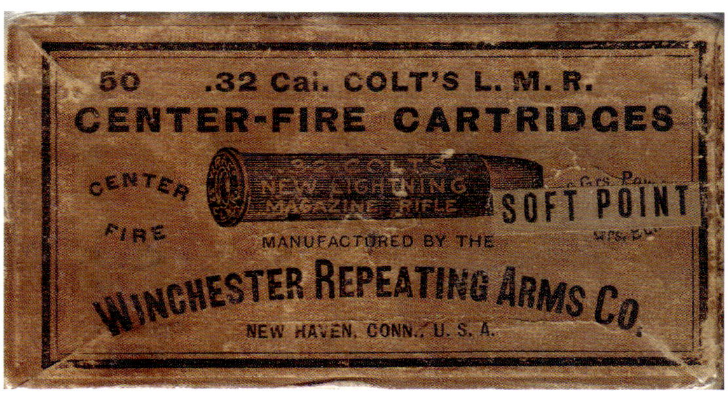

This Smokeless, Soft Point box is marked "Center Fire", dating it as 1898 or later. It was originally a Black Powder, Lead box but now has a "Soft Point" label pasted on top and a Smokeless "Sunburst" label pasted on the side. This is the only such box known to the authors. R5/800-1500

Winchester introduced the 32 Colt New Police caliber in 1896 with a label picturing the Colt revolver. Note the "Central Fire" callout which, as a pistol caliber, should have been "Center Fire" according to protocols adopted in 1885. Both rifle and pistol centerfire calibers were labeled "Center Fire" after 1898. R3/150-250

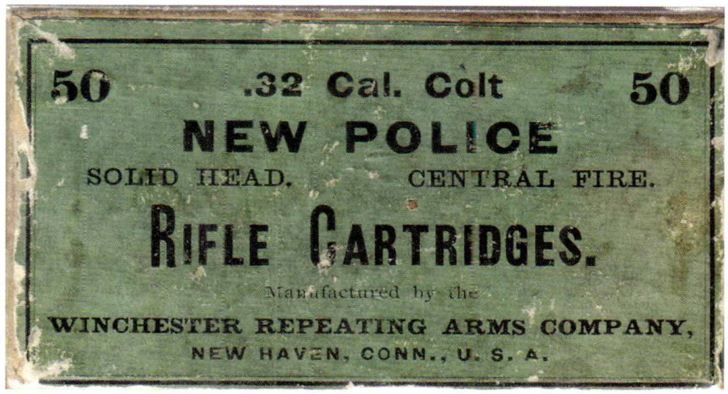

In certain southern states, due to a tax on "pistol" cartridges, this caliber became a "Rifle Cartridge" according to the labeling seen here. The "Central Fire" callout remains, however, telling us this box is most likely contemporary with, rather than a successor to, the foregoing box but destined for sale in Tennessee, South Carolina or some other "Pistol Tax" state. R3/100-175

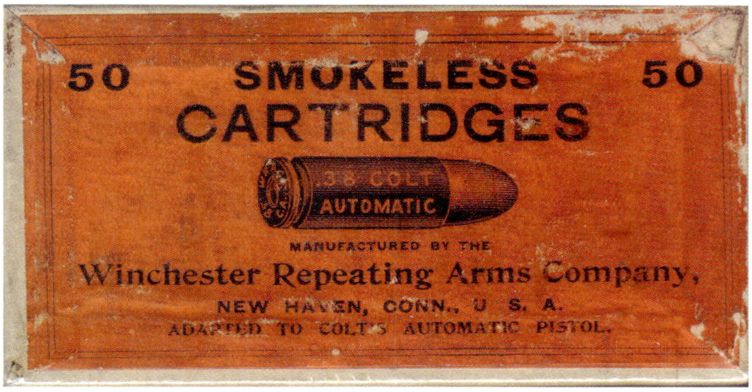

Thought to be the Company's earliest box of 38 Colt Automatic, this box dates to the turn of the 20th Century. Cartridges in this box are headstamped "38 C.A." as opposed to the later and much more common "38 AC". Also, a number of rounds with this headstamp which were made for export have been noted by cartridge collectors. They are discernable by their specially marked export primers. R4-/400-800

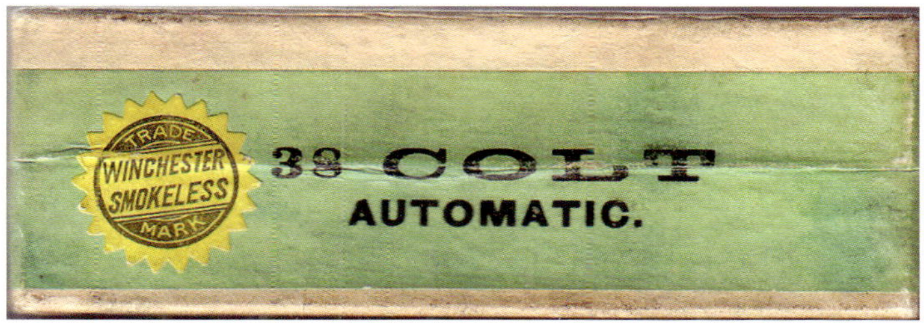

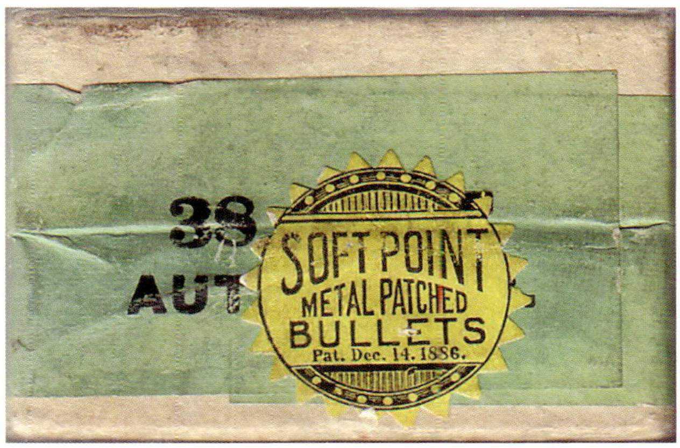

Note the presence of both "Sunburst" labels, Smokeless on the side and Soft Point on the end.

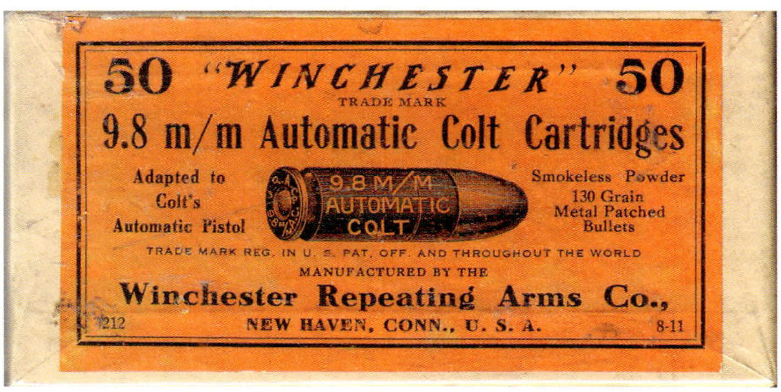

Left: Made only in 1910-11 for a Colt experimental semi-auto pistol (a predecessor to the M1911), which was unsuccessfully marketed to the Rumanian Government, this cartridge became obsolete virtually overnight. Interestingly, these boxes are sometimes found with a mixture of headstamped and unheadstamped rounds. R3+/750-1500

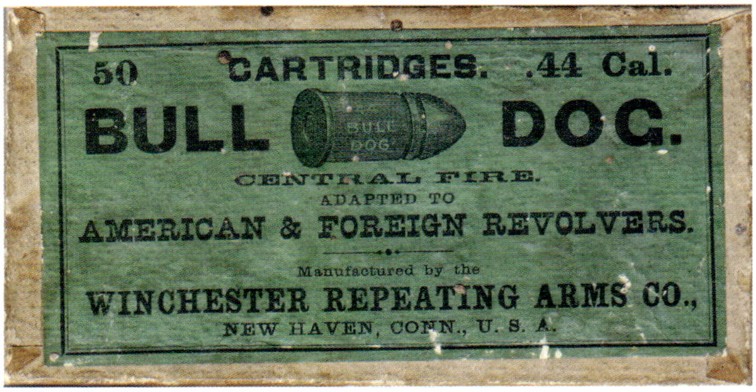

This box contained "dog food" for the Webley Bull Dog, a popular and potent pocket pistol (when the pocket wasn't filled with Peter Piper's pickled peppers) single shot derringer from the late-1860s through the late-1880s. R3/175-350

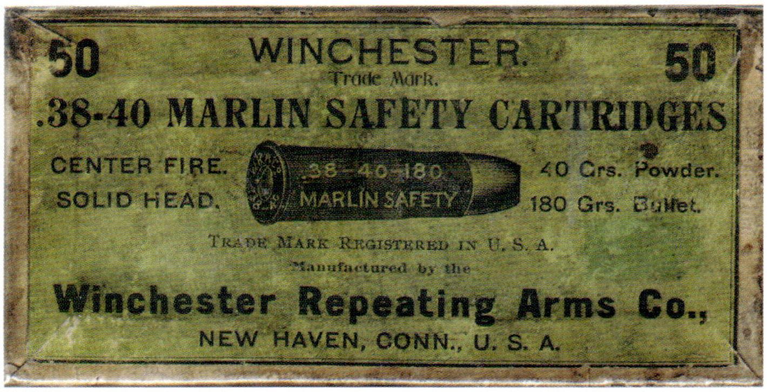

Winchester made ammunition to the specifications of Marlin Firearms. While the word "Safety" had to do with the solid receiver-top construction of Marlin's lever-action rifles, Winchester used it in the title of the cartridge as well. This Black Powder box is ca 1903. R3/600-1000

By 1906, this was the "new look" in Marlin Safety boxes. Here is a Smokeless Soft Point box from that year. All "Marlin Safety" boxes are very scarce. R3+/750-1250 [Smokeless, FMJ: R4-/900-1400]

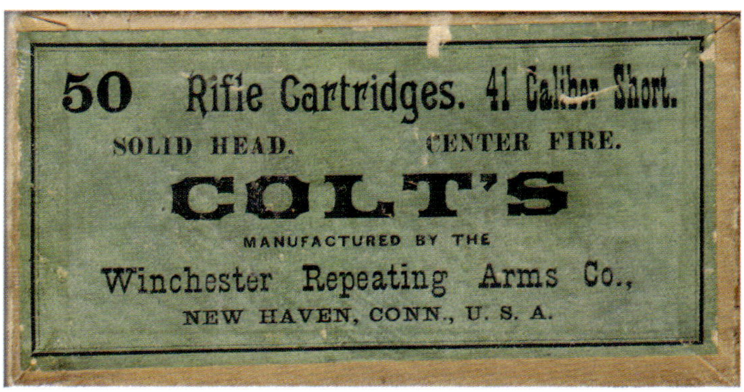

Unusual in the fact that "COLT'S" is featured so prominently, this Black Powder box is thought to be ca 1885. There are few clues with which to date this box but the fact that it exhibits a "Center Fire" call-out tells us it's post-1885. R3/250-450

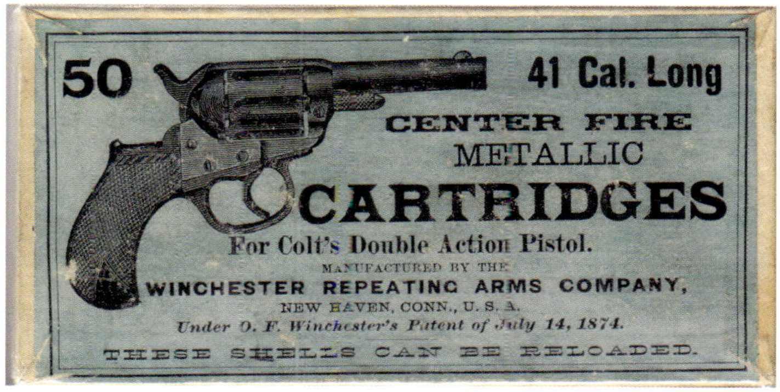

One of Winchester's famous "picture" boxes, this of the Colt 41 Thunderer, Model of 1877. Such boxes are always in great demand. Ca late 1880s (though possibly later) it is a Black Powder loading. R3/550-1000 [38 Colt: R3-/450-800]

Another "picture" box of great popularity is this 45 Colt box showing the Colt M1878 D.A. revolver. A Black Powder label of pre-1885 vintage—note "Central Fire" callout—these boxes are much in demand. As the picture of the Colt M1878 stayed on most Winchester boxes in this caliber for over two decades, however, they cannot be considered rare in spite of their price and popularity. R2+/500-1000

Far rarer than the above 45 Colt "picture" box is this "Rifle Cartridges" box from roughly the same period. It's likely that these boxes were used in those few states which imposed a tax on pistol ammunition. And, as is usually the case, the blue label is much rarer than the green. R4/750-1500 [Green: R3+/500-1000]

The "Colt's Patent Firearms Manufacturing Co." logo appears on the side of this and most other Colt caliber boxes.

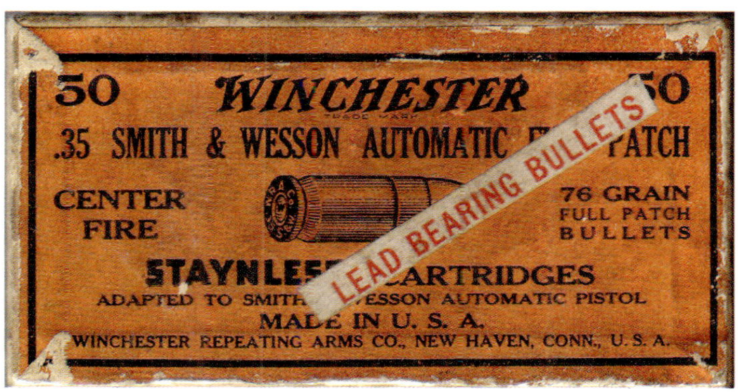

Lead Bearing Bullets (see Glossary) were first offered in 1932 and boxes so labeled are quite scarce. In fact this is the only such box in 35 S&W, for Smith & Wesson's Model 1913 Automatic, that is known to the authors. R5/500-750

This is a great combination of scarce and collectible attributes: Lead Bearing Bullets in an unusual early Super Speed box. This design is found nowhere other than on this 38 S&W Special box, ca 1935. R3/125-225 [Lead Bullets: R3-/80-160]

Thought to be Winchester's first 357 Magnum offering, this rare box was a Winchester-era U.S. Cartridge Co. offering just before that company was closed down as a corporate entity at the end of 1936. R4-/200-400

Center Fire Boxes (Other)

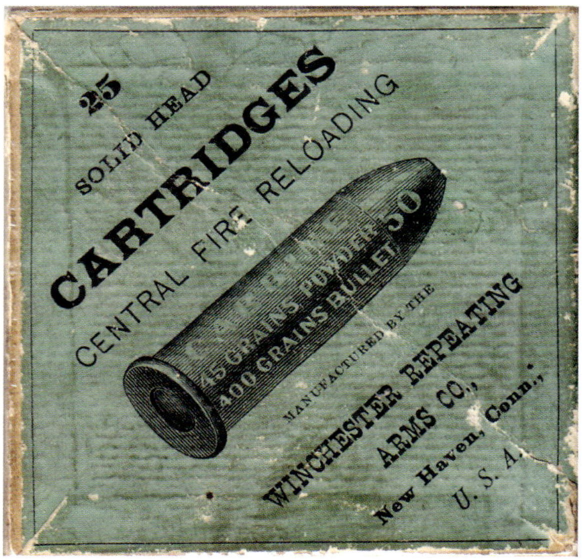

This 50 Carbine box is unusual on three counts: First, it is a 25-round box; second, it has a diagonal label; and, third, the box is square. Though difficult to date, it is thought to be circa 1880. R3+/350-700

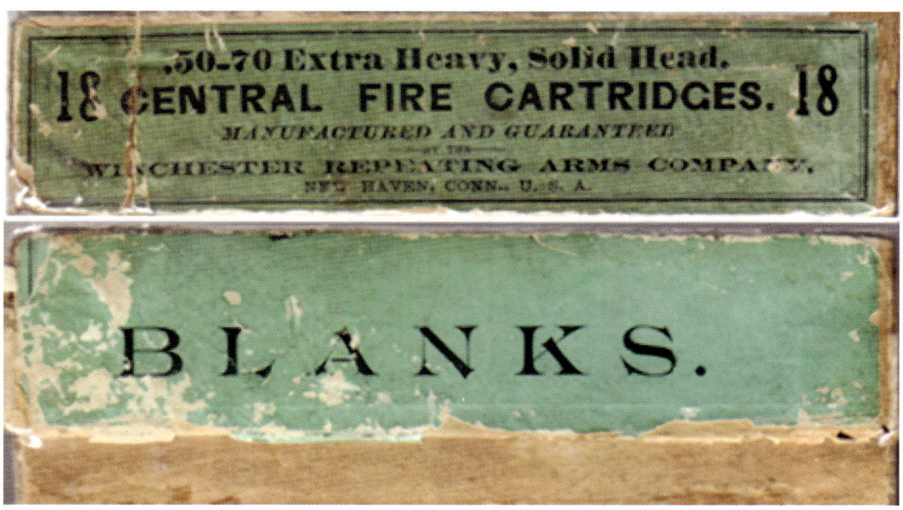

Another oddity in 50 caliber is this 18-count 50-70 Blanks box. A "BLANKS" label has been pasted over the front portion of the original lid label which folds over from top to front, the lined edge of which remains visible in the close-up above. The military style headstamp is "R W 3 89", indicating manufacture by Winchester in March , 1889. While 18-count UMC 45-70 boxes are known, this is one of only two 18-count boxes issued by Winchester of which the authors are aware (the other in 45 Colt). R5?/500-1000

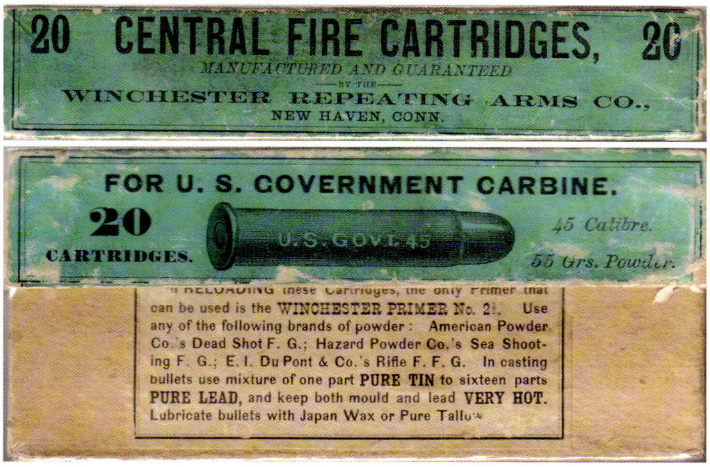

This 45 U.S. Carbine box is very rare. Note the spelling of "Calibre", the unheadstamped cartridge cut and the italicized caliber and powder grains callouts. Such labeling is indicative of late-1870s graphics which continued to appear through the early-1880s. R4/500-1000

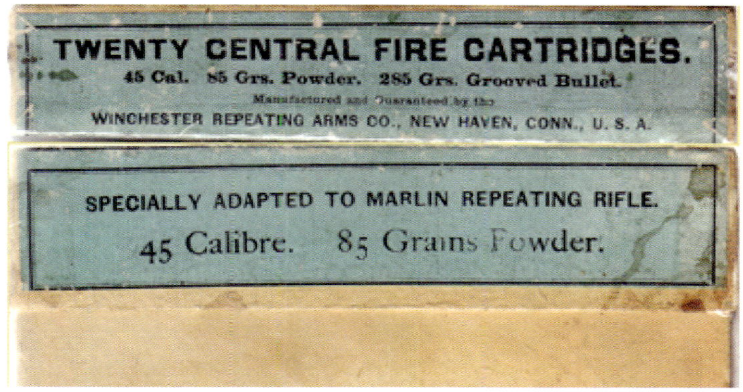

Actually this 45-85 Marlin loading is a "fully-packed" 2.1 inch 45-70 case with 15 grains more powder and a lighter, 285 grain bullet. Colt also used this loading in their large frame Lightning rifles though Winchester's loading of 45-85 Colt, which is a very rare box, used a 290 grain bullet. R4-/1000-1800 [With "45-85 Mar." Headstamp: R4/1250-2000]

Most commonly thought of as a Sharps caliber, the 44-60 was also a Remington chambering. Though there is no such callout, the cartridge cut clearly shows the bullets to be paper-patched. Again judging by the italicized powder and "Calibre" callouts as well as the unheadstamped cartridge cut, this box can be dated to the late-1870s or early 1880s. R3+/500-800

The 42 (42-77) Russian Berdan is one of the rarest of all Winchester boxes in spite of its supposedly having been loaded from 1876 until past 1912. Where have they all gone? This is the only one known to the authors. Without headstamp: R5/1000-2000 [With headstamp: R5/4000-6000]

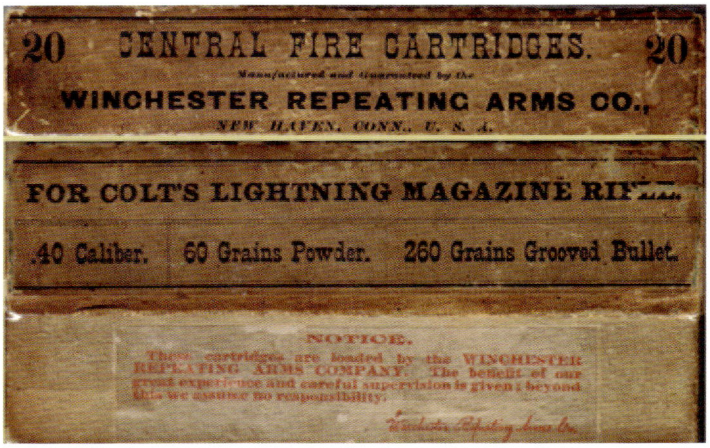

One of the most sought-after Winchester headstamped rounds by cartridge collectors is the 40-60 Colt. Though rare and never officially cataloged by Winchester, it has nonetheless been found in both pre-1898 (square-cornered) and post-1898 (round-cornered) brown label boxes as shown here. Both are Black Powder, Lead labelings. Company records refer to an 1892 loading, likely the box at left, and declared the caliber obsolete in 1919. R5/4500-6500

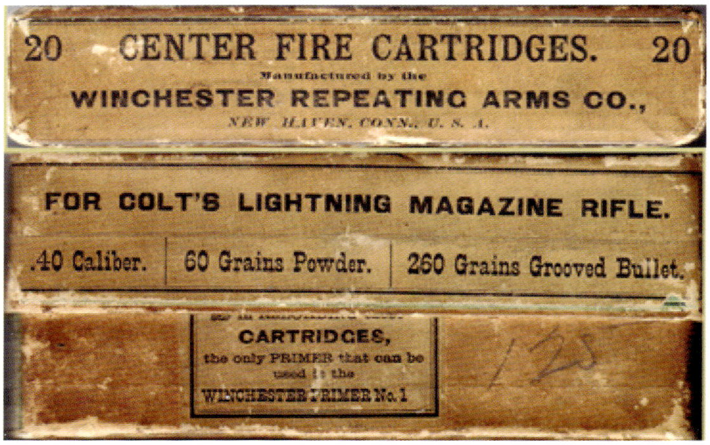

This round-cornered post-1898 box is ca 1906-1907. Dimensionally identical to the 40-65 W.C.F. and 40-60 Marlin, they were used interchangeably. R5/4000-6000

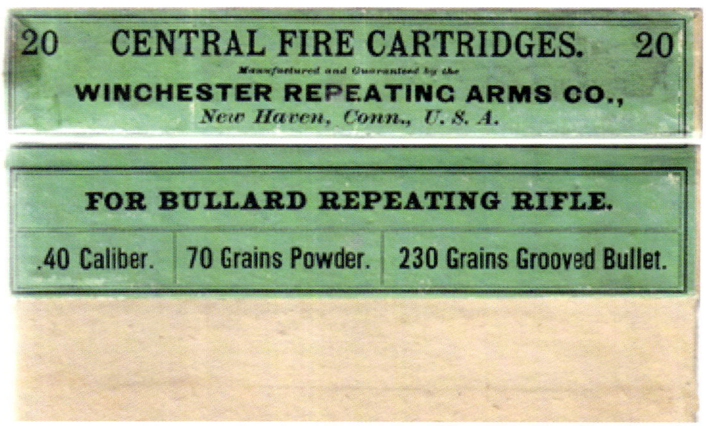

Also of the same dimensions as Winchester's 40-65 WCF as well as the 40-60 Colt/Marlin, all were frequently substituted for one another. This 40-70 Bullard box is circa 1890. Bullard calibers in Winchester boxes are very scarce. R3+/600-1000

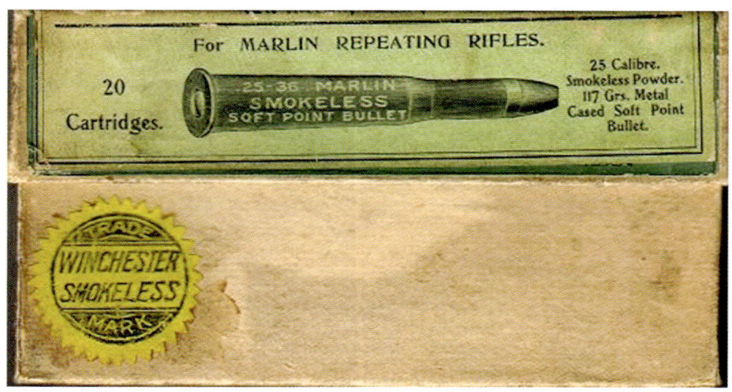

Though rarely seen, both UMC and Winchester made 25-36 Marlin "...for The Marlin Fire Arms Company". On this box there is no sign of Winchester having been the maker except for the Smokeless "Sunburst" sticker. Unlike UMC boxes, there is not even a headstamp on the cartridge cut. The graphic of the end label is, however, purely Winchester. Circa 1895-96. R5/750-1500

16

Winchester Calibers by Other Manufacturers

During the many decades covered by this study a number of different ammunition manufacturers competed with Winchester for a position in the lucrative small arms cartridge market. Though few are still around today many will be recognizable names to those of you who have an interest in American firearms and their history. While we will limit our comments and examples to those companies that competed with Winchester in their proprietary or "mainstream" rifle calibers, this final chapter is not intended as a detailed comparative analysis of the early cartridge-makers. Rather, our goal here is to provide the reader with an idea of what the products of others in the industry looked like, especially in the earlier days of cartridge production.

Domestic Companies

Ethan Allen & Co.

With business origins dating to the 1830s, Ethan Allen was one of several inventive geniuses in firearms and ammunition to come out of the mid-19th Century. Through a number of name changes, Allen and his family and associates, first as partners, then as successors, were innovative contributors to the development of the cartridge business from 1858 to 1874.

Here is an example of the rare 44 Henry box by Ethan Allen & Co., circa late-1860s. The authors are aware of only one other. R5/12,500-22,500

Union Metallic Cartridge & Cap Co.
Union Metallic Cartridge Co.
Remington Arms-Union Metallic Cartridge Co., Inc.
Remington Arms Co., Inc.

During the latter part of the 19th Century, by far the most serious competitor for Winchester in the small arms cartridge marketplace was U.M.C. Formed by the New York City sporting goods firm of Schuyler, Hartley & Graham in early 1866, the new cartridge maker emanated from the buyout of two smaller companies, Crittenden & Tibbals Manufacturing Co. and C.D. Leet, both victims of the shrinkage in demand for ammunition after the Civil War. While the company started in business as Union Metallic Cartridge & Cap Co., the name was changed less than 18 months later, becoming Union Metallic Cartridge Co. in August 1867.

In 1888, UMC's owner, Marcellus Hartley (of the original Schuyler, Hartley & Graham firm), along with Winchester, bought E. Remington & Sons, an old-line but failing rifle and cartridge manufacturer of high repute, re-naming it Remington Arms Company. (See earlier history of that company below). Then, in 1896, Hartley bought Winchester's share in Remington and held both UMC and Remington as separate companies until 1911. At that point it was decided to exploit the Remington name and reputation more fully by combining the marketing aspect of the two companies. By 1916 the combination was "set in concrete" by conjoining both companies into one corporate entity: Remington Arms Company-Union Metallic Cartridge Company, Incorporated. Only four years later the UMC part of the name was dropped and the company became simply Remington Arms Company, Inc.

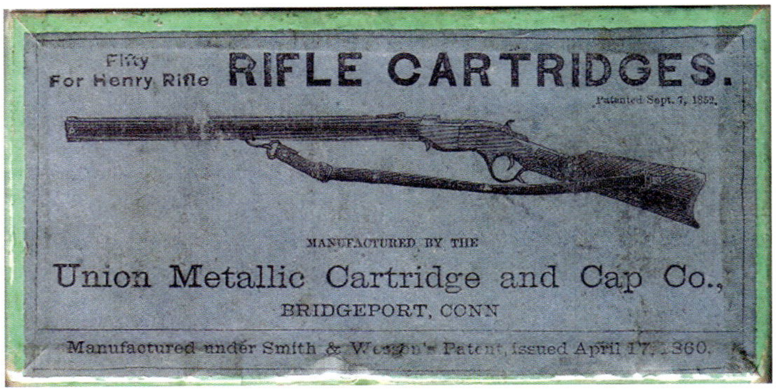

One of the great rarities among collectible cartridge boxes is this "44 Rim Fire Flat" offering which pictures the Henry Rifle on a blue label and green box. Manufactured by Union Metallic Cartridge & Cap Co., predecessor to U.M.C., March 1866 - August 1867. There is no callout for Winchester's new Model of 1866. R5/12,500-20,000

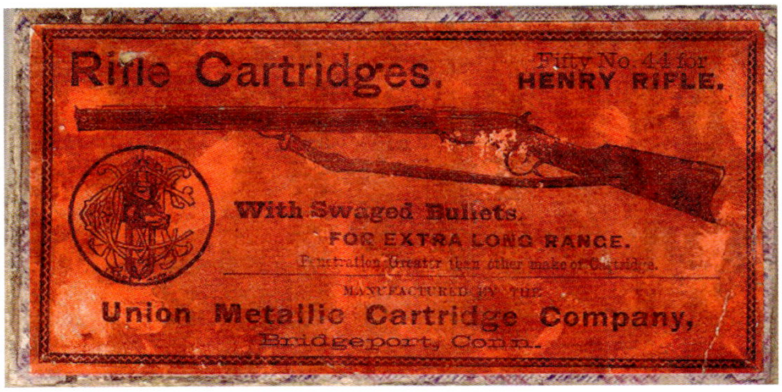

Shortly after the name change, U.M.C. introduced their famous "Dog Logo" seen here on an orange label 44 Henry Rim Fire Flat "picture" box. Note that the underlying box is purple and white plaid, a feature common to U.M.C. 50-round boxes in most calibers until after WWI. Circa 1868-73(?), there is still no callout for the Winchester Model 1866! R4-/8500-12,000

From the 1873-1884 period comes this "Double Dog Logo" U.M.C. 44 Rim Fire Flat box for the "Winchester Repeating Rifle". The cartridge cut identifies that rifle as the Model 1866, the first such mention of that model. R4/ 4000-7500

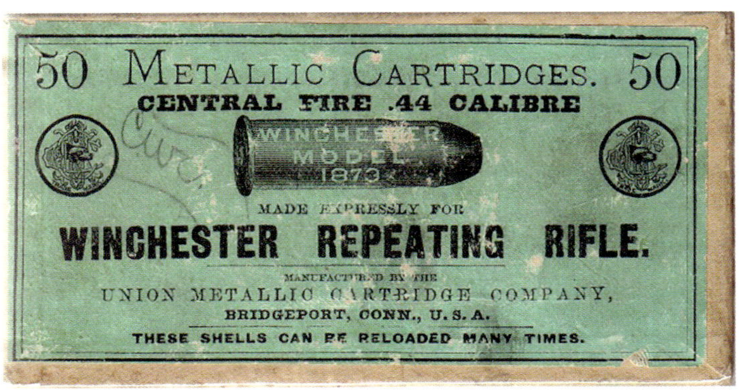

Another U.M.C. box, obviously very similar to, and from roughly the same period as, the one above, is also for the "Winchester Repeating Rifle". Only this cartridge is "Central Fire .44 Calibre" (44-40) and calls out the Model 1873 on the cartridge cut... R4-/750-1250

...as well as on the side label.

Unfortunately, the label on the opposite side pictures the Marlin Model 1881, a gun that was never chambered in 44-40!

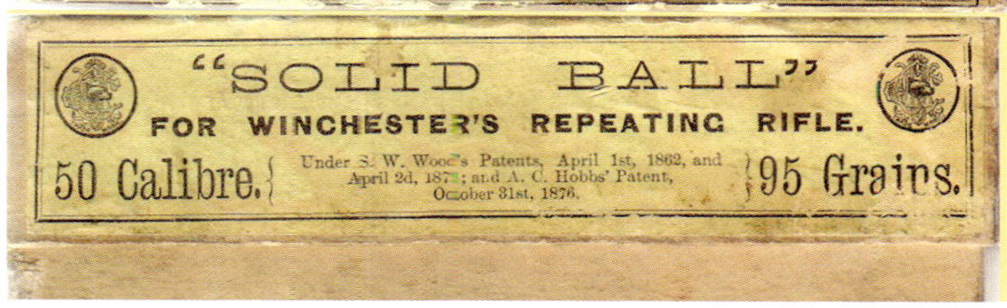

Yet another "Double Dog Logo" box, this one in the very scarce 50-95 caliber introduced by Winchester in 1879 as a new chambering for their Model 1876. The "Solid Ball" bullet loading is quite rare and far less commonly found than the copper-tubed Express bullet. Though it should be pointed out that this tan/yellow box is seldom encountered in ANY loading. R4/1500-2500

In an attempt to coat-tail the great success of Winchester's new Model 1886, UMC briefly but boldly offered their Black Powder, 405 grain Lead Bullet loading as being "...adapted to Winchester Model 1886 Rifles". R3+/250-500

When Winchester introduced their new "Express" calibers for the Model 1885 High Wall in 1886, U.M.C. soon followed suit. This late-1880s box exhibits the Company's elongated oval logo with black print rather than its negative (see following entry below) in which the letters were outlined in black. R3/350-600

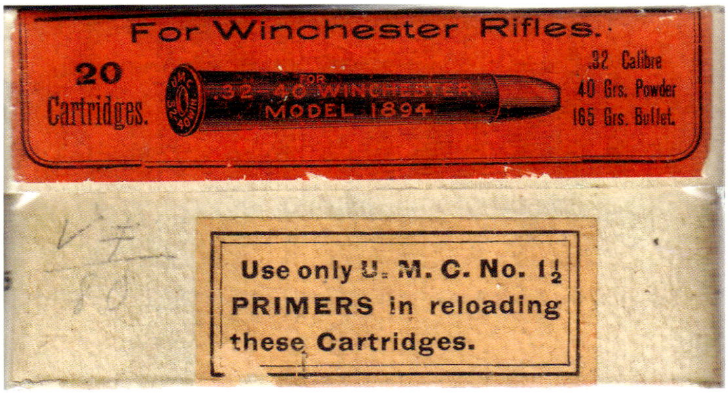

".32-40-165 Winchester"? This titling is highly unusual in that the 32-40 is a cartridge even Winchester didn't really try to claim as one of their own, yet this U.M.C. labeling suggests it to be a Winchester proprietary caliber. The scarce "UMC 32-40 Win" headstamp is collectible in its own right; however, a similar (".32-40 W.C.F.") headstamp on a Winchester cartridge is a real rarity, often bringing over $500 per cartridge among collectors. Most headstamps in this caliber by either maker will be simply ".32-40" with no further reference to "Win." or "W.C.F." R3+/200-400

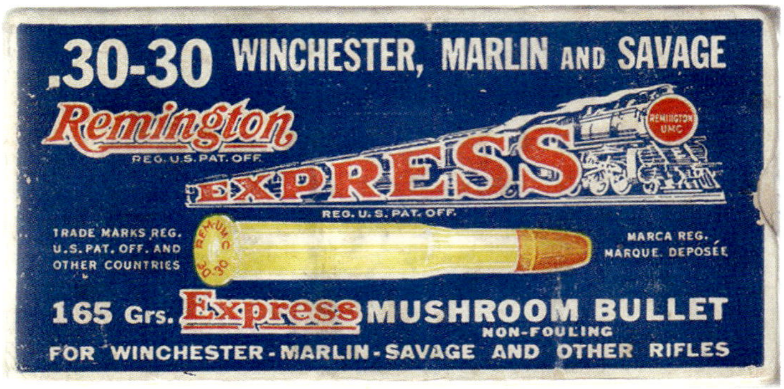

While Remington Arms Co. had dropped "U.M.C." out of the corporate name in 1920, it did remain on the cartridge headstamps. This is one of the earliest and most collectible of Remington's one-piece boxes. R2+/125-250

Hall & Hubbard

In 1869 Hall & Hubbard purchased the cartridge-making assets of its predecessor, Smith, Hall & Buckland, itself a descendent of Smith and Wesson. A short-lived enterprise, Hall & Hubbard produced a limited line of rimfire cartridges until about 1874. One rimfire caliber, however, is significant to us in this book: the 44 Henry Flat.

An nice example of the very rare box of Hall & Hubbard 44 Henry, circa 1870. R5/ 12,500-20000 (Courtesy of Charlie Busch)

United States Cartridge Company

Formed by Samuel F. Butler, a former Union Army Major-General and Congressman of great notoriety and dubious reputation (though that's another story), the U.S. Cartridge Co began operations in 1869, operating under the same name and Butler family ownership for over fifty years. In 1920 Butler heirs sold the company to National Lead Corp., who in turn sold it to Winchester in 1926. While USCCo.'s equipment was moved to New Haven and ran on the same factory floor as Winchester's, production and even marketing remained separate until, as agreed, Winchester shut down the company ten years later, closing the doors at the end of 1936.

USCCo.'s "wood-cut" box label exhibits some of the most detailed graphics of the 1870s. The "44 Henry Pointed C. & W." callout was their designation for the pointed bullet "Colt & Winchester" offering. Other makers, including Winchester and UMC, also cataloged this loading. By any maker, however, the pointed bullet is significantly harder to find than the relatively common flat bullet loading which was usually titled, simply, "44 Flat". R3+/2500-4500

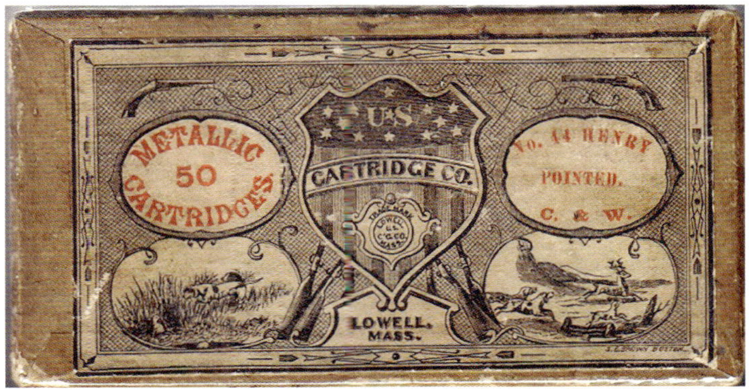

Orange labels were fairly common in the 1870s (both UMC and USCCo used them) but this very early 45-75 box, ca 1876-77, is especially unusual in its emphasis of "Bottle Neck". Prior to the introduction of this caliber in Winchester's lever-action M1876, only single shot rifles of the period were chambered for cartridges that displayed a significantly bottle-necked profile. R4+/1000-1500

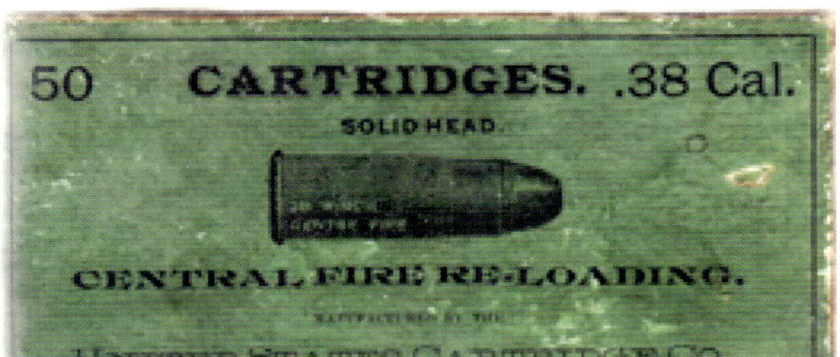

Circa early-1880s, this Black Powder box of 38-40 box is typical of USCCo.'s 1880s style label for Winchester (and other) calibers in 50-round boxes. R4-/400-800

Unknown to many, this is probably Winchester's last Henry offering. Winchester combined facilities with U.S. Cartridge Co. in late 1926 with an agreement to maintain the line for ten years. The New York address is the primary clue in dating this within the Winchester era. R3/1250-2000

E. Remington & Sons

While Remington had been making firearms for decades and had had agreements with Johnston & Dow for the manufacture of pistol ammunition during the Civil War, their entry into the cartridge business did not take place until 1871. Naturally enough most of their early production was directed toward military calibers of the period as well as those calibers for which their own guns were chambered. Even as late as 1882 only three Winchester calibers are to be found in Remington catalogs: 44 WCF (44-40), 45-75 WCF and 50 Express (50-95 WCF). As the Company's ammunition factory was destroyed by fire in 1885 and not rebuilt, the probability of finding E. Remington & Sons boxes in Winchester calibers is, to say the least, extremely limited.

E. Remington & Sons was the first ammunition manufacturer to offer the stronger solid head (as opposed to folded head) cartridge construction. This 44-40 box for the "Model Winchester 1873" is from the early 1880s and displays graphics that are about as simple as can be found from that period (for contrast see American Metallic Cartridge Co. 44-40 box below). R5/1800-2500 (Courtesty of Vic Engel)

Phoenix Metallic Cartridge Company
American Metallic Cartridge Company

The Phoenix Cartridge Co. began production in 1874 and is known largely as a producer of Rimfire cartridges; consequently, very few calibers are Winchester related. Still, Phoenix, as one of the founders of the Ammunition Manufacturers Association, was a major competitor in the small arms cartridge business in the 1870s and 1880s. Its founders were the well-known revolver makers of Merwin, Hulbert & Co., Joseph Merwin and the Hulbert brothers, Henry and Milan. For reasons unknown, the Hulberts, after Merwin's death in 1879, formed an unincorporated entity named American Metallic Cartridge Company to market the Phoenix line of ammunition. This curious arrangement continued until 1891 when the assets of Phoenix were purchased by UMC and Winchester, the two controlling members of what was then left of the Ammunition Manufacturers Association. The Phoenix/American operation was evidently wound down by its new owners before 1900 as American Metallic Cartridge Co finally disappeared from the records circa 1898.

Displaying a September 1879 patent date, this rare Phoenix Metallic Cartridge Co. box of 44-40 "Multi-Ball Cartridges, for Winchester Rifle, Model 1873" is thought to date very close to that time, probably 1880-81. Phoenix boxes calling out ANY Winchester caliber are seldom found. R4/1500-2500

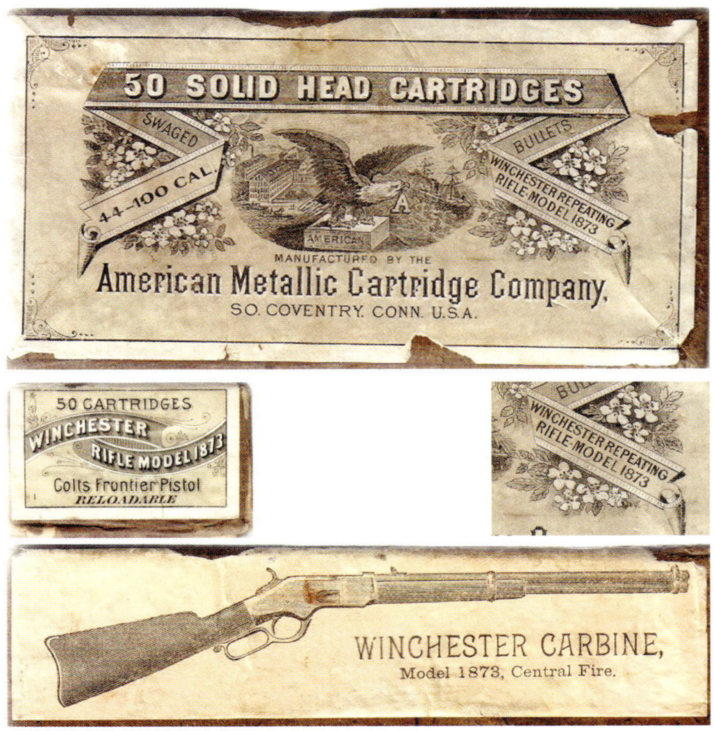

Right: Obviously when American Metallic Cartridge Company began marketing cartridges in the 1880s, the importance of graphics were recognized and exploited to the utmost: consider these views of the top, one end and one side of this 44-40 box highlighting the Winchester '73 on all three labels, including a picture of the carbine on one side. Not missing a beat, the end label also calls out "Colt's Frontier Pistol". And all that's before mentioning engraved scenes featuring guns, flowers and eagles. It just doesn't get any better than this! R3+/750-1500

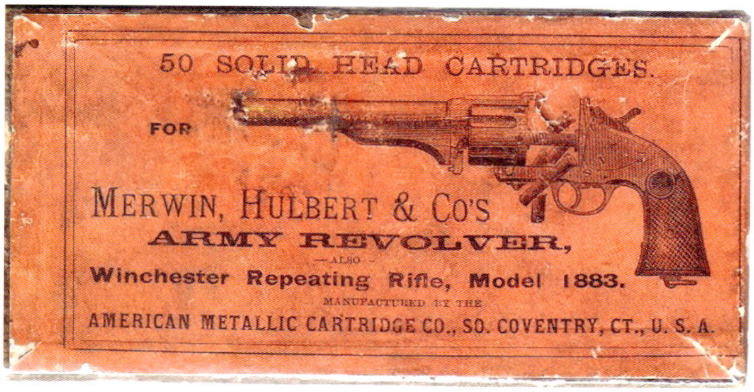

Here's a rare one: boxes by any maker picturing Merwin, Hulbert & Co's large frame revolver are very rare. This one is in 44-40, rather than 44 M&H, and therefore justifies inclusion here. Note, however, that the callout is for the "Winchester Repeating Rifle, Model *1883*" (rather than 1873). Hey, nobody's perfect. R5/4000-6000

Creedmoor Cartridge Company

Creedmoor began operation in Barberton, Ohio, in late 1890. While the only Winchester calibers the Company produced were 32-20, 38-40 and 44-40, Creedmoor is interesting mainly because of its very short corporate life and the rarity of its output. It has been said that the members of the Ammunition Manufacturers Association refused Creedmoor the components and materials they needed to continue business and effectively drove them to sell out to the Association in 1892. Production continued through 1893 but was brought to an end with the sale of the Company's assets the following year.

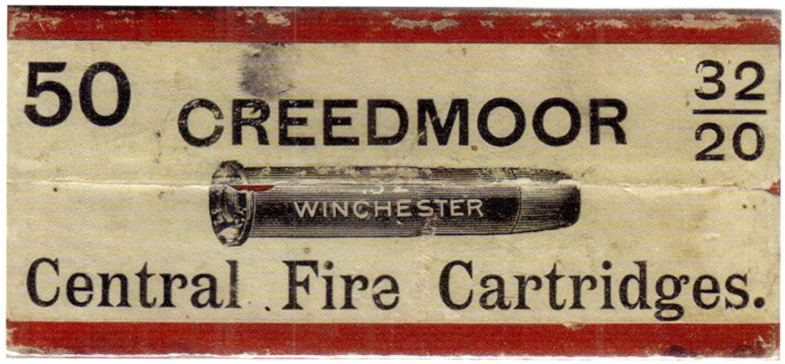

This may be the only Creedmoor Cartridge Co. centerfire box you'll ever see as they are, indeed, that rare, especially full of their original cartridges as is this one. R4/1000-1500

Peters Cartridge Company

While the Company started in business in 1887, Peters didn't begin loading Winchester rifle calibers until the late-1890s. Early on, Peters purchased virtually all their components except for their own King Powder Company's powder. The Ammunition Manufacturers Association, however, through prohibitive pricing, forced Peters into a position whereby they either had to produce their own components, close their doors, or sell out to the Association as had Creedmoor and Phoenix. Peters was evidently made of "stronger stuff" than their non-Association contemporaries and survived independently until merging into the Remington Arms/DuPont Chemical group in 1934.

The earliest Smokeless loadings by Peters, like Winchester, called out "30 Grains Smokeless Powder" on the label. Also like Winchester, the early Peters boxes show a "Manufactured and Guaranteed..." line on the lid top which is believed to be pre-1898. R3+/150-300

This Black Powder box with the big, bold ".40-82" lid-top callout is the only caliber known to the authors to exhibit these graphics in a Peters offering. Two varieties are known: this one with the "Winchester Repeating Rifle, Model 1886" top line and another version which, instead, states merely "40-82-260" in bold type above the cartridge. Note the shortened, "Manufactured By" line on the lid top, thought, as with Winchester, to be post-1898. R3+/300-600

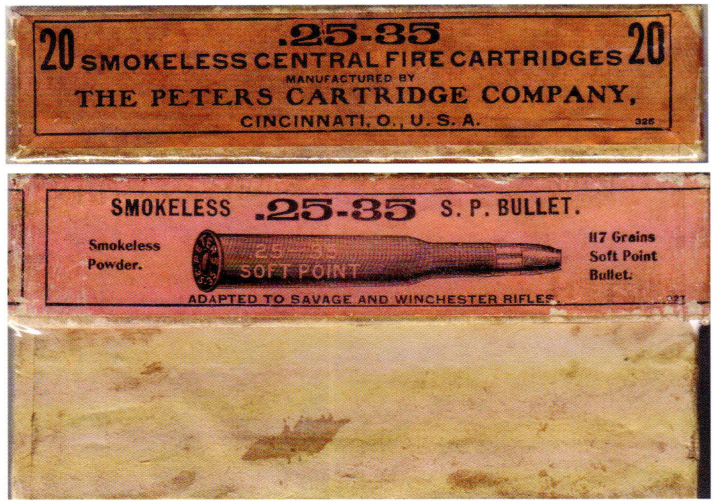

Also like Winchester, Peters changed to a color coding of their labels as seen here on what collectors refer to as the salmon-colored label. This color denoted Smokeless Soft Points. Variations in color as evidenced by the difference in these top and front labels was common among most cartridge makers in the 1900-1920 period. R3/150-300

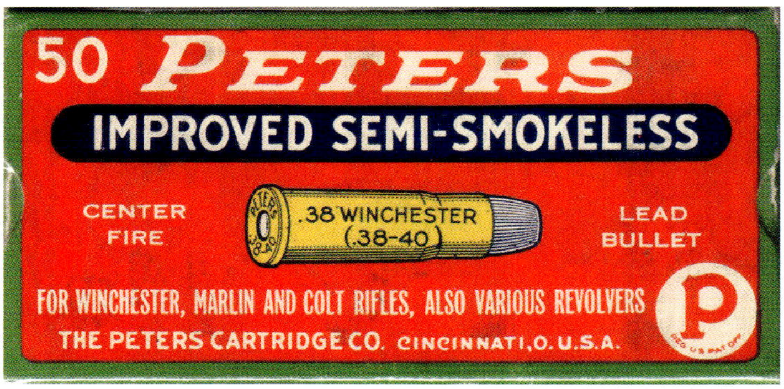

Peters has always been known for its very colorful boxes. This earliest of their one-piece boxes highlights their "Improved Semi-Smokeless" powder offering. Within only two or three years, however, in 1927, their new Rustless priming became the big news at Peters just as Staynless priming did at Winchester that same year. R3/200-400

High Velocity loadings like this one from the mid-1930s are always desirable and very collectible boxes. Note the white paste-on labels calling out "High Velocity" and cautioning "Not to be used in Pistols or Revolvers". R3+/200-400

Robin Hood Company
Robin Hood Ammunition Company

A subsidiary of the Robin Hood Powder Company of Swanton, Vermont, Robin Hood Company was formed to manufacture a line of Shotshells in 1900. The Ammunition Manufacturers Association, however, was just as determined to put the new company out of business as they had been with others in the previous decade. Forced to reorganize in 1906 in order to finance the capital equipment needed to produce its own components, the Company was then renamed Robin Hood Ammunition Company. Robin Hood then used their expanded production capabilities to broaden their Shotshell product line to include Rimfire and Centerfire cartridges. While the Company produced a broad line of Shotshells and 22 Rimfires, the metallic Centerfire and larger Rimfire line was quite limited and listed very few Winchester calibers. Only nine years later, in1915, Robin Hood was sold to Remington Arms Company.

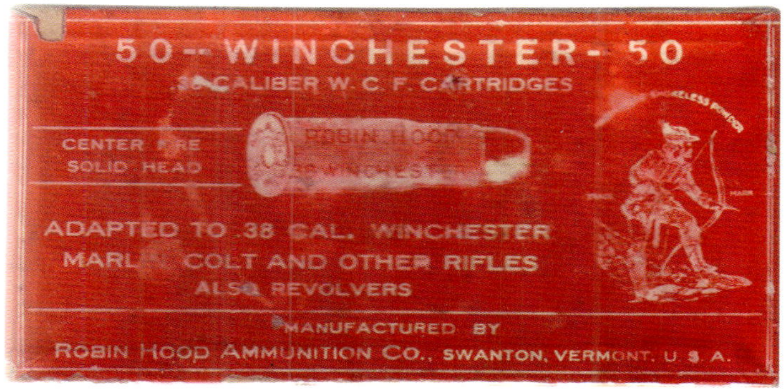

The Winchester calibers to be found in these great Robin Hood boxes are few and limited to the 50-round variety. This 38-40 box exhibits the typical Smokeless, Lead labeling of the 1906-1915 period, the entirety of this very popular Company's brief existence. ALL Robin Hood boxes are collectible. R4/1000-1500

Savage Arms Company
Savage Arms Corporation

The Savage Arms Company was incorporated in 1897 as successor to the Savage Repeating Arms Company of Utica, NY, which had begun operations in 1893. Ammunition production, however, was not initiated until around 1900 when that ever-present "big bully" cartel, the Ammunition Manufacturers Association, stopped supplying Savage with sub-contracted ammunition under the Savage name. As with Peters and Robin Hood, however, the entrepreneurial spirit reigned supreme and Savage set up facilities to manufacture their own cartridges though primers were purchased from other vendors. The Company loaded a number of Winchester calibers as well as a number of their own pace-setting numbers, specifically the 22 Savage High Power and the 250-3000 Savage developed by the legendary Charles Newton. By 1928 Savage had turned over the cartridge-making aspect of its business to Remington on a contract basis, an arrangement which lasted until 1963 when the brand was discontinued.

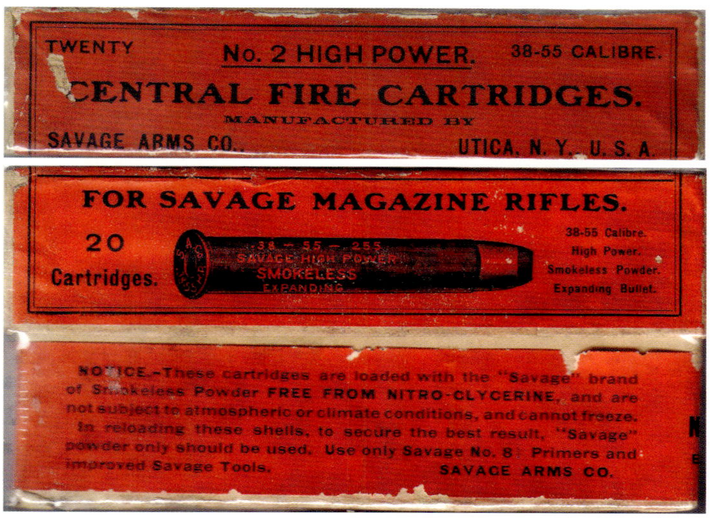

Thought to be the earliest style box made by the Savage Arms Co., 38-55 also happens to be one of the rarest calibers in that brand. A Winchester as well as a Savage rifle caliber, though not proprietary to either, it was introduced in the Savage line in 1905. The bottom front label advises using Savage brand reloading components, an aspect of the business that was discontinued in 1907. R4-/300-600

This low-key ad for repeat business was soon replaced by the Company's colorful "Moose-horn Logo" back-seal label shown below.

This "Moose-horn Logo" adorns a later (ca 1912) non-Winchester caliber box in 22 Savage High Power. The front and top labels, however, are much the same as the 38-55 box above. This great label is shown here not only for its graphics, but also because it exists in several Winchester caliber boxes by Savage Arms.

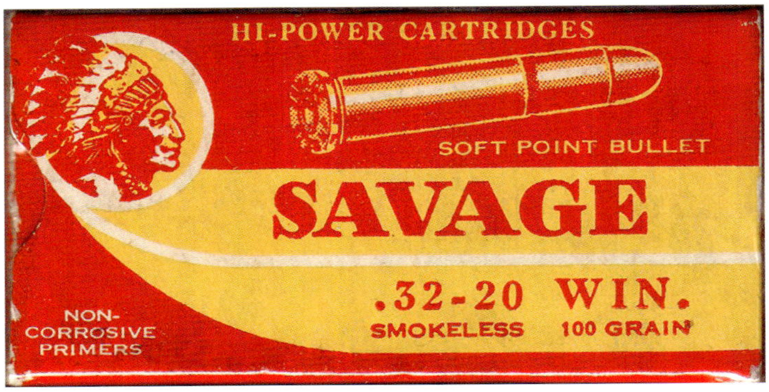

Here is an example of a post-WWII "Indian Head" box . This popular and collectible box was available in a number of rifle and pistol calibers, including at least ten Winchester calibers, and was discontinued in 1963. R1+/50-100

Western Cartridge Company

Western began making shotshells in 1898-99, but, like so many cartridge companies of the period, was forced to produce its own components as the Ammunition Manufacturers Association cut off supplies to the Company around the turn of the Century. With the help of Austin Cartridge Co., a Cleveland shotshell maker, Western set up a plant to produce primers and caps and named the operation Union Cap & Chemical Company (UC&CCo). From 1905 until 1908, UC&CCo also produced a line of rimfire ammunition, concentrating on the popular 22, 32 and 38 calibers. Then, in 1908, Western bought out Austin Cartridge Co. and converted the UC&CCo line to Western Cartridge Co. products. It was also at this time that a centerfire line was added and Winchester calibers began to be produced by Western.

This 44-40 "Maltese Cross" box of 1908-10 was the direct descendent of UC&CCo's rimfire labeling. As these graphics were only around for two or three years and in a limited number of calibers (all of them in 50-round boxes), they are all extremely collectible. R3+/600-1200

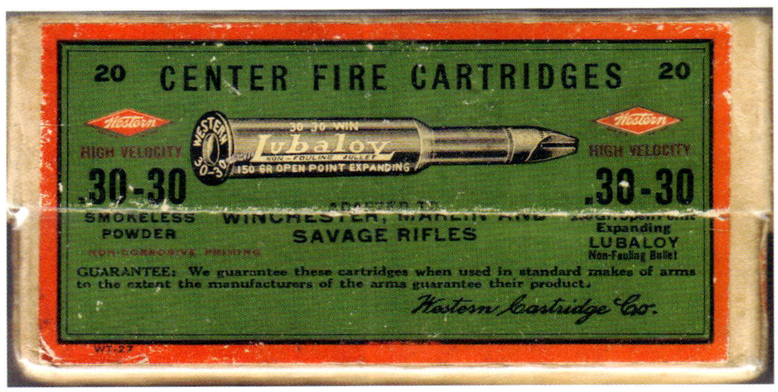

While the "Red Diamond" logo came into being in 1910, this is one of the later iterations as evidenced by the "Lubaloy" callout on the cartridge cut. Combining Lubaloy with the two-piece box construction creates a scarce and interesting combination: the last of the old style boxes containing the newest in bullet technology, circa 1927. R3-/80-175

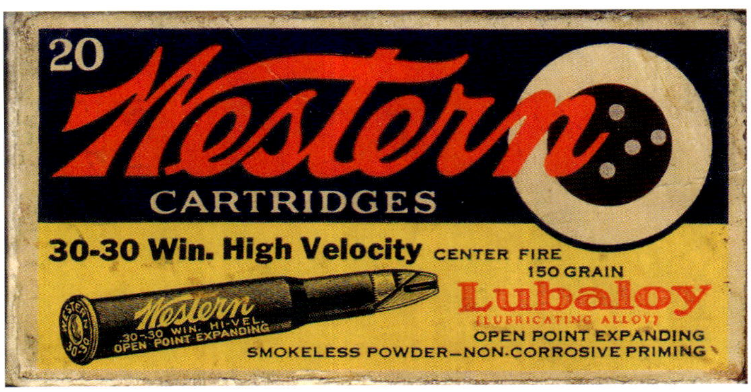

Introduced by Western in 1927, the "Bullseye" graphic on their new one-piece box was destined to be around for over 30 years in many calibers. This 150 grain Open Point Expanding loading named "30-30 Win. High Velocity" has, for many years, had cartridge collectors chasing after a cartridge with a headstamp reflecting that title. You can relax, guys: there aren't any. R3-/100-200

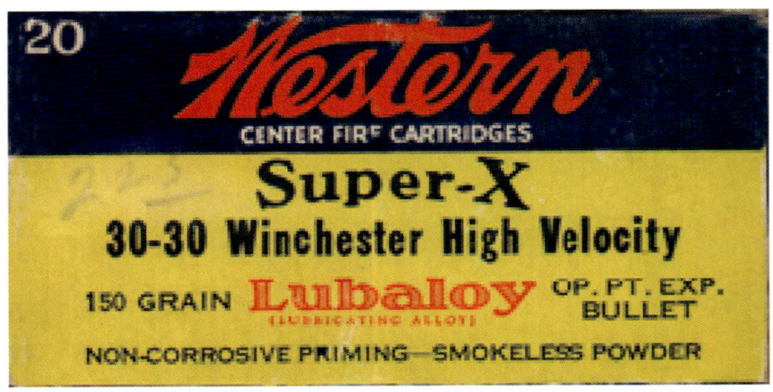

Here is the same "30-30 Winchester High Velocity" loading in the Super-X box, circa late-1930s. (But still no "30-30 WHV" headstamp!). R2+/80-175

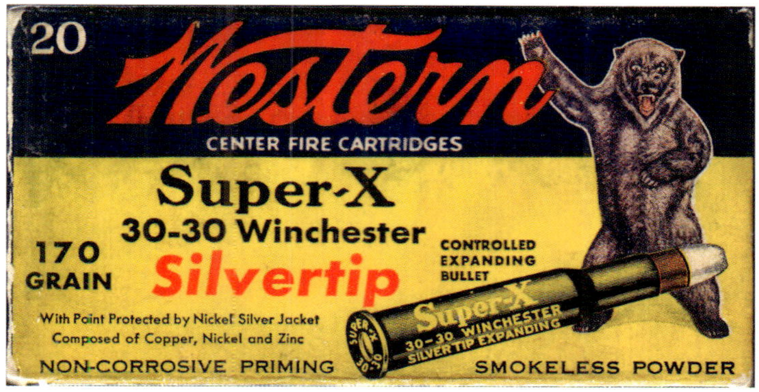

As with Winchester, Western introduced its Silvertip line in a "Grizzly" box in early 1940, albeit with a different bear picture. Although it varies by caliber, Western's Grizzly boxes apparently had a slightly longer life in the marketplace than did Winchester's. Before 1950, however, all the "bears" had disappeared. R1+/75-165

Retail Chain Store Brands

Very little research has been expended on the centerfire cartridge lines offered by some of the old-line major retailers under their own label, but it is an interesting area that deserves exploration. Just not right here, right now, by us.

What makes this Gamble Stores 32 Winchester Special box especially unusual is the fact that it is a private label brand in a two-piece box, a combination seldom seen in the 20-round rifle calibers. All Gamble's ammunition was made under contract with Federal Cartridge Co. R3+/150-250

Sears, Roebuck & Co marketed centerfire cartridges, such as this box of 30-30s, under the Sportload name. Apparently from the 1930s, it was undoubtedly produced by Western which had for many years contracted with Sears to produce their line of 22 Rimfire cartridges. Note the Sta-Klean trademark and see the next entry below. R3-/80-175

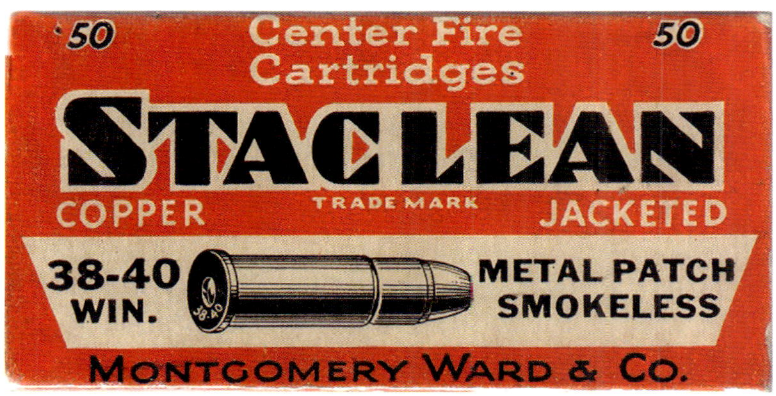

Contemporary with the Sears box above, Montgomery Ward & Co. also had a line of centerfire cartridges with the trade name "Staclean". The rivalry of the catalog mail-order giants, Wards vs. Sears, seems to have found common ground in their desire for those of us who can't spell to at least stay clear. R3/150-300

Foreign Companies

The several companies represented here will be presented by country of origin with no attempt to provide detailed company histories. All, however, are (or were) major factors in the cartridge manufacturing business both here and abroad. It is likely, therefore, that within the historical context of the small arms of the world, the reader will have heard of most, if not all, of these major contributors and competitors in the cartridge industry.

Canada
Dominion Cartridge Co., Ltd.

The graphics on this two-piece Black Powder 38-40 box point to manufacture in the earliest years of the Company's existence, ca late 1880s. Especially notable is the double "Beaver Logo" featuring the detailed beaver pictures as opposed to later versions which were more of an outline. R4/450-800

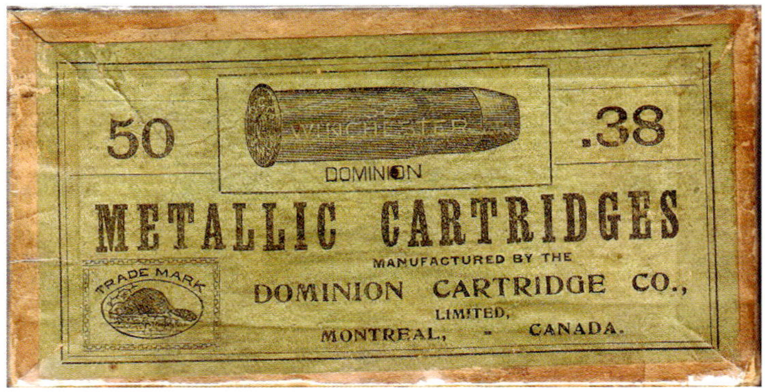

Thought to be the next style 38-40 two-piece Black Powder box, ca 1890s, this graphic retains the detailed "Beaver Logo". It's interesting that the word "Metallic" is emphasized here: that word as a major callout was obsolete on American boxes before, or around, 1880. R3+/400-750

In 1899 and 1900 Dominion Cartridge Co made runs of 45-75 cartridges for the Royal Canadian Mounted Police, some of whom still evidently carried Winchester M1876 carbines in that (by then obsolete) caliber. The headstamps on those cartridges included the last two digits of the year of production, "99" and "00", and are considered of the highest collectibility by gun, cartridge and "Mountie" collectors. This box is full of the "00" headstamped rounds. R3+/1000-1500

France
Societe Francaise des Munitions (SFM)

Soft packs made of paper rather than cardboard were seldom seen after 1870 in the U.S., but this 10-round packet of 50-110 "Winchester Express" is of just that sort of construction. While this caliber is always very collectible, finding it in a soft pack is a particularly nice bonus. R4/500-1000

While manufactured by SFM, this colorful 44-40 two-piece box (above) was offered by Gevelot & Guapillat, a major French sporting goods retailer located in Paris. The firm was very similar to our Schuyler Hartley & Graham in New York or, later, Abercrombie & Fitch. R2+/200-400

Germany
Rheinisch-Westphalische Sprengstoff (RWS)
H. Utendoerffer

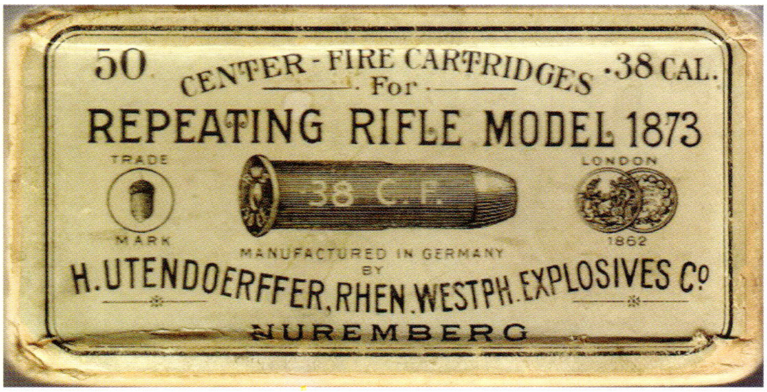

A great Black Powder two-piece box, circa 1900, by the Henry Utendoerffer firm of Nuremburg shortly after its acquisition by RWS. Note that for some reason "Winchester" is not mentioned on this label. However we doubt that there was any real ambiguity or confusion, then as now, regarding the gun for which it was intended. R3+/175-350

"J.L. Galef, New York, D stributor" is the callout on the bottom line of this 32-20 Black Powder box manufactured by RWS at the former Utendoerffer factory in Nuremburg. Thought to be early 1900s. R3/80-175

Great Britain
Eley Bros., Limited

Thought to be circa 1870, this two-piece box of 44 Henry Rimfire "Made Expressly For Henry's Winchester (U.S.) Repeating Rifles" is a great find given both its age and condition. Interestingly, it's "Henry's Winchester" rather than "Winchester's Model 1866" or similar wording naming Winchester as manufacturer. Still, both names are found on the label, a fact which cannot be said about Winchester labels of the period! R4/4000-6000

The "Winchester Repeating Rifle, Model 'Centennial' 1876" was introduced in this caliber only. This would appear to be among the earliest boxes in 45-75, whether domestic or foreign. R4/600-1200

Thought to be from the late-1890s, this Black Powder box of 45-70 calls out a "350 gr. flat-nosed bullet" for the "Winchester (Model 1886) & Marlin Repeating Rifles". R3+/250-500

(Right) This "Ghost Logo" 10-round soft-pack of 45-125-300 (45 Winchester Express) for the M1885 High Wall is found here with a hand-written date of 20-5-14 (May 20, 1914). A scarce caliber by any maker, it appeared as an Eley offering only once, in their 1914 Export catalog. Found in India, this is the only full, sealed packet known to exist. R5/2000-3000

Kynoch Limited

This Kynoch Black Powder two-piece export box of 45-70s was "Made Specially for The Hudson's Bay Co." as the sticker on the back says. A great piece of British-Canadian history, thought to be circa 1900. R4?/400-800

Mexico
Paulsen Cartridge Co.

In spite of the early two-piece, half-split, staple-corner box construction, as well as a product code and label dating in the Winchester style pointing to a "3-9" box, don't be fooled. We are assured by one of the best cartridge researchers in the business, George Kass, that this box is as late as the 1950s! R4-/250-450

Abbreviations and Glossary

Abbreviations

AP –	Armor Piercing
BN –	bottle neck
BP –	Black Powder
C&T –	Crittenden & Tibbals
C&W –	Colt and Winchester
CF –	centerfire
DA –	double action (pistol)
Ex –	Express (bullet)
FMJ –	Full Metal Jacket (bullet)
FP –	Full Patch (bullet)
Gov't –	government
HP –	Hollow Point (bullet)
Ld –	Lead (bullet)
Lsmk –	Lesmok (powder)
MCHP –	Metal Cased Hollow Point (bullet)
Mfg –	manufacture(ing)
NHS –	no headstamp
NPE –	new primed empty (case)
PP –	Paper Patch
Ptd Exp –	Pointed Expanding (bullet)
RMF –	rimfire
RWS –	Rheinisch-Westphälische Sprengstoff
S&W –	Smith & Wesson
Smkls –	Smokeless Powder
SFM –	Société Francaise des Munition
SP –	Soft Point (bullet)
SR –	Short Range
SS –	Super Speed
ST –	Silvertip (bullet)
Str –	straight
UMC, U.M.C. –	Union Metallic Cartridge Co.
USN, U.S.N. –	United States Navy
WCF, W.C.F. –	Winchester Center Fire
WHV, W.H.V. –	Winchester High Velocity
WRF –	Winchester Rim Fire

Glossary

Add-on: a small paper label, denoting a loading or change thereof, added over a portion of the existing main label.
Armory Practice: a low velocity loading used for indoor target practice; most common to the 45-70 USG caliber.
Ball: a common term for a bullet, no matter the shape or type; especially military applications.
Blank cartridge: a cartridge loaded without a bullet; just with powder and wad.
Bottle Neck: a cartridge case necked or reduced for a smaller diameter bullet.
call-out: any term specifically stated on a box label referencing caliber, gun model, loading specifications or other facts of interest; e.g., patent data.
cannelure: a groove made perpendicular on a cartridge case used to seat a bullet or wad.
cartridge cut: the illustration of a cartridge as on a box label or catalog page, made using a woodcut or metal printing block.
centerfire: the contemporary term for a cartridge casing containing a primer centered in the case head.
Central Fire: an accepted 19th Century term for centerfire.
conical: a bullet, usually of lead, with a rounded body and a semi-pointed nose.
dated headstamp: a cartridge headstamp with the date of manufacture included; associated mostly with military use.
export: special sized boxes and/or labels used only for overseas orders.
Express: usually considered a lighter-than-normal bullet weight; also for those Lead bullets with a copper tube insert.
folded head: a casing made by folding a piece of brass tubing thus creating a folded, weak head.
Grizzly box: the term denoting the Silvertip loadings as originally offered in 1940 with a bear illustrated on the box.
impressed headstamp: a headstamp made on the casing by pressing a male die into the head.
K-code: a product code system begun in 1921 by Winchester; suffix T for pistol calibers, C for rifle calibers.
label colors: a system of coding labels by their color to denote a specific loading.
Lead Bearing: a Lead bullet with a metal cap covering the nose, leaving exposed lead to bear on the barrel's rifling.
Lee-Navy: a common term for the Lee Straight Pull rifle as made by Winchester.
Mercuric: a priming mixture with a modified mercury-based ingredient which caused pitting in gun barrels.
Non-Mercuric: a later Staynless priming mixture which did not use mercury as an ingredient.

Oilproof: a process of sealing the primer pocket with shellac to prevent oil from ruining the primer. In common use by 1938.
one-piece: a box, die cut and glued together to form a one-piece enclosure; cartridges in a slide out tray.
over-labeled: a complete label, usually the top, placed over an existing complete label.
over-printed: factory added or struck-out printing as with a correction or addition to the existing label.
Plain headstamp: a cartridge made without a headstamp.
Primary labels: on 20-round boxes, the top and front labels; on 50-round boxes, the top and side labels.
Political Correctness: While seldom correct (though thoroughly political), this euphemistic term is used by hyper-sensitive, guilt-ridden, intellectually barren elitists to justify the imposition of their ideological tripe on the vulgar masses. Espoused by hypocrites hiding behind "freedom of speech" while proscribing limits on the freedom of others' speech, it is an extraordinarily offensive attempt to make societal intercourse inoffensive.
Proof cartridge: a specific loading of a cartridge to use in the Definitive Proving process of a firearm. Usually with a tin plated casing.
raised headstamp: a headstamp made on the casing the by pressing a female die into the head.
rimfire: a cartridge type in which the priming mixture is contained within the rim where it is struck for ignition.
Rocket Ball: patented by W. Hunt, it was a self-contained bullet having the powder held within. It was ignited by a percussion cap.
rubber stamped: a stamp placed by hand noting a change or addition to the existing label.
Short Range: a low-velocity loading, using a Lead bullet, for standard rifle calibers.
Shot cartridge: a cartridge loaded with bird shot rather than a standard bullet.
Solid Head: the process of making a cartridge case by stamping and drawing from a solid piece of brass, thus making a solid head.
Standard cartridge: a cartridge made specifically to test fire and calibrate firearms in a ballistics lab.
Staynless: the trade name for Winchester's patented priming mixture that was advertised as non-corrosive.
Sunburst: a small paper add-on label that denotes smokeless powder or soft point bullets on a box not so-marked.
Super Speed: originally offered in 1925 as a high-velocity MCHP loading. By 1932 it was the term for premium loadings.
Tubed bullet: in modern usage only for the 401 SL soft point. In earlier times for any Lead Hollow Point bullet with a copper tube insert.
two-piece: a box with a removable lid which covers a portion of the box.
Umbrella Point: a Pointed Soft Point bullet with a metal cap placed over the exposed lead portion; for protection in box magazine rifles. Also called Pointed Expanding and Protected Point.
W-code: a product code adopted in 1952 by Olin as a simplified revision of the previous K-code.

Bibliography

anon. *Winchester Ammunition*, Historical Notes And Tests, Date Codes And Other Neat Info.
anon. *Winchester Factory Drawings*, A Collection of Winchester Factory Drawings.
Barber, John L. *The Rimfire Cartridge In The United States & Canada*. Armory Publications, Tacoma, WA, 1987.
Barnes, Frank C. *Cartridges of the World*. Third Edition. Chicago, IL, 1972. (Edited by John T. Amber)
Barnes, Frank C. *Cartridges of the World*. Fourth Edition. DBI Boooks, Inc. Northfield, IL, 1980 (Edited by Ken Warner).
Brophy, William S. *Marlin Firearms*. Stackpole Books, Harrisburg, PA, 1989.
Dunn, Tony. *A Catalog Of The .22 Boxes Of The U.S.A.*. Sturgis, MI, 1983. First Update 1992.
Flayderman, Norm. *Flayderman's Guide To American Firearms ...and their values*. Sixth Edition. DBI Books, Inc. Northbrook, IL, 1994.
Hackley, Woodin & Scranton. *History of Modern U.S. Military Small Arms Ammunition*. Volume I. The Gun Room Press, 1967.
Hackley, Woodin & Scranton. *History Of Modern U.S. Military Small Arms Ammunition* , Volume II. The Gun Room Press, 1978.
Henshaw, Thomas. *The History of Winchester Firearms 1966-1992*. Sixth Edition, Winchester Press, 1993.
Hoovestal, Howard. *E. Remington & Sons Cartridges*. Bismarck, ND, 2000.
Hoovestal, Howard. *Savage Cartridges*. Bismarck, ND. 2001
Houze, Herbert G. *Winchester Bolt Action Military & Sporting Rifles 1877 to 1937*. Andrew Mowbray Inc., 1998.
Houze, Herbert G. *Winchester Repeating Arms Co.* Iola, WI, 1994.
Jamieson, Scott G. *Bullard Arms*. The Boston Mills Press, Erin, Ontario, Canada, 1988.
Kimmel, Jay. *Savage & Stevens Arms, Collector's History*. Fourth Edition. Cory Stevens Publishing, Inc. Portland, OR, 1997.
Kowalski, David D., editor. *The Standard Catalog of Winchester*. Krause Publications, Iola, WI, 2000.
Labbett, Peter. *British Small Arms Ammunition 1864-1938*. Ann Arbor, Mi, 1993.
Madis, George, *The Winchester Book*, published by the Author, Dallas, TX, 1961.
Madis, George, *The Winchester Book*, Art and Reference House, Brownsboro, TX, 1979. Lithographed by Edwards Brothers, Inc. Ann Arbor, MI.
Madis, George. *The Winchester Handbook*, Edwards Brothers, Ann Arbor, MI, 1981.
Malloy, John J.; Thomas, Dean S.; White, Terry A.; *Percussion Ammunition Packets, 1845-1888*. Thomas Publications, Gettysburg, PA. 2003.
Murray, Douglas P. *The Ninety-Nine, A History of the Savage Model 99 Rifle*. Third Edition. Published by the author, Westbury, Long Island, NY. 1985.
Parsons, John E. *The First Winchester, The story of the 1866 Repeating Rifle*, William Morrow and Company, New York, NY, 1955.
Shuey, Daniel L., *W.R.A. Co. Headstamped Cartridges and their Variations, Vol 1*. WCF Publications, Inc., Rockford, IL, 1999.
Shuey, Daniel L., *W.R.A. Co. Headstamped Cartridges and their Variations, Vol 2*. WCF Publications, Inc., Rockford, IL, 2003.
Sones, James K. *United States Small Arms Ammunition Patents 1937-1990*, Denver, Co, 1991.
Sones, James K. *United States Registered Trademarks For Ammunition And Gun Powders*. Denver, CO, 1992.
Thomas, Dean S. *Round Ball to Rimfire, A History of Civil War Small Arms Ammunition, Part Two, Federal Breechloading Carbines & Rifles*. Thomas Publications, Gettysburg, PA, 2002.
West, Bill. *Winchester Handbook*, Volume Two Stockton Trade Press, Commerce, CA, 1981.
Williamson, Clyde "Snooky". *The Winchester Lever Legacy*. Buffalo Press, Zachary , LA, 1988.
Williamson, Harold F. Winchester - *The Gun That Won The West*, Washington, DC, 1952.
Yearout, Lewis E. *Winchester's North West Mounted Police Carbines*. Great Falls, MT, 1998.
Zimmerman, Peter L. *Savage Ammunition, Cartridges and Boxes from 1895 to 1963*. Published by the author. Traverse City, MI 2002.

Reprinted Material

Catalogs of New Haven Arms Co. and Winchester Repeating Arms Co.1865-1918, 12 Volumes. Reprinted by George Hoyem, Armory Publications, Tacoma, WA 1991.

Original Material
Bellemore, Walter M. - Personal files, memos and data.

Non-Published Material
Haven, Charles T. *History of The Winchester Repeating Arms Company.*

Watrous, George. *Winchester Metallic Ammunition - Brass and Paper Shotshells; The History of Winchester Primers; Winchester Rifles and Shotguns.*

[All of the above are in-house publications by the Winchester Repeating Arms Co.]

Paul, Jim and Adams, Tom. *Winchester Model 1886 Caliber 50/100/450.*

Periodicals
Lewis, Ed, M.D. *The Gun Report.* "Volcanic Firearms." Volume 51, #4, September 2005, pp 34-45.

I.A.A. Journal - and various publications of The International Cartridge Collectors Association and International Ammunition Association.

R.T.B. Limited - Cartridge Auctions Catalogs, various issues.

Index